JOURNAL FOR THE STUDY OF THE HISTORICAL JESUS
SUPPLEMENT SERIES

Editor
Robert L. Webb

Published under
JOURNAL FOR THE STUDY OF THE NEW TESTAMENT
SUPPLEMENT SERIES
262

Executive Editor
Stanley E. Porter

Editorial Board
Craig Blomberg, Elizabeth A. Castelli, David Catchpole,
Kathleen E. Corley, R. Alan Culpepper, James D.G. Dunn,
Craig A. Evans, Stephen Fowl, Robert Fowler, George H.
Guthrie, Robert Jewett, Robert W. Wall

Historiography and Hermeneutics
in Jesus Studies

An Examination of the Work of
John Dominic Crossan and Ben F. Meyer

Donald L. Denton, Jr

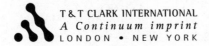

T & T CLARK INTERNATIONAL
A Continuum imprint
LONDON • NEW YORK

To Diane

Copyright © 2004 T&T Clark International
A Continuum imprint

Published by T&T Clark International
The Tower Building, 11 York Road, London SE1 7NX
15 East 26th Street, Suite 1703, New York, NY 10010

www.tandtclark.com

British Library Cataloguing-in-Publication Data
A catalogue record for this book is available from the British Library

Library of Congress Cataloging-in-Publication Data
A catalogue record for this book is available from the Library of Congress

Typeset by CA Typesetting, Sheffield
Printed on acid-free paper in Great Britain by The Bath Press, Bath

ISBN 0-567-08203-2

CONTENTS

INTRODUCTION   1
  1. Jesus Studies Today: The New Quest, the Third Quest, and Method   3
  2. Statement of Purpose and Method   8
  3. The Contributions of Crossan and Meyer   9
  4. Issues in Historiography and Hermeneutics   14

Part I
JOHN DOMINIC CROSSAN AND TRADITION CRITICISM

Chapter 1

THE EARLY CROSSAN: POST-HISTORIOGRAPHIC STRUCTURALISM   18
  1. *In Parables*   19
  2. *The Dark Interval*   25
  3. *Raid on the Articulate* and *Finding Is the First Act*   29
  4. *Cliffs of Fall*   37
  5. Evaluation   39

Chapter 2

THE LATER CROSSAN: THE INTERDISCIPLINARY APPROACH   43
  1. Transition   43
  2. Mature Method   48

Chapter 3

THE METHOD CONSIDERED   57
  1. The Existence of Parallels   60
  2. Data and Interpretation   67
  3. Interactivism   74

Part II
BEN MEYER AND CRITICAL REALISM

Chapter 4

EPISTEMOLOGY AND HERMENEUTICS   80
  1. Critical Realism   81
  2. Hermeneutics   92

Chapter 5
HISTORIOGRAPHY   102
   1. Telling Presuppositions   102
   2. Inference and Hypothesis   106
   3. Historiography and the Metacritical Moment   124

Chapter 6
MEYER'S METHOD IN PRACTICE   130
   1. The Portrait   130
   2. Hypotheses, Indices and the Handling of Data   136
   3. Summary and Evaluation   143

Part III
HISTORIOGRAPHIC PROPOSALS:
FROM HOLISM TO NARRATIVE INTELLIGIBILITY

Chapter 7
HOLISM AND ITS IMPLICATIONS   154
   1. Holism   155
   2. Data-as-Evidence   160
   3. Reciprocity   162
   4. An Objection   163

Chapter 8
NARRATIVE INTELLIGIBILITY   168
   1. Narrative in Historiography   168
   2. Narrative Realism   171
   3. The Context of the Sources   176
   4. Narrativity and Historiography: Outline of a Proposal   181
   5. Narrativity and Hermeneutics   186

Appendix 1
THE CRITERIA OF AUTHENTICITY: CRITICISMS AND NEW DIRECTIONS   193

Appendix 2
VARIETIES OF CRITICAL REALISM   210

Bibliography   226
Index of References   237
Index of Authors   238

INTRODUCTION

There is a situation in historical Jesus studies today that requires attention. The situation is not an especially recent development; it has been around for at least two or three decades, quite a while in the rapidly developing world of contemporary Jesus studies. But the situation warrants greater attention than it has received. I am referring to the emergence of distinct approaches to historical Jesus studies, based on distinct conceptions of the historiographic enterprise and how it relates to basic hermeneutical concerns. Trends have developed in Jesus studies that can be categorized in terms of these historiographic and hermeneutical issues. An understanding of these trends will help the observer of, and participant in, historical Jesus studies to sort through the surplus of current options on the basis of informed decisions about root issues that guide historical investigation.

What I am proposing here is an examination of issues in historiography and hermeneutics in contemporary Jesus studies. But it should be pointed out, first of all, that I am not identifying the present diversity of historical Jesus portraits as itself the occasion for this study. This diversity is widely recognized, and does seem to be unprecedented in the field.[1] But to take the differences among the results of Jesus portraits as the point of departure would imply that I am providing explanations or proposing resolutions for that diversity in the present investigation. That type of resolution is not my immediate concern. I am not undertaking anything as ambitious as demonstrating a necessary connection between particular results and chosen methods; if there is such a connection, it is not in our purview here. Now it may be that a clarification of historiographic and hermeneutical issues will have the effect of supporting certain portraits of Jesus and weakening others. But if it does that, it will only be indirectly, on the basis of supporting or calling into question the approaches that underlie the portraits, for I will indeed be making decisions and taking stands on what are legitimate historiographic manoeuvres. What I intend here is to compare formulations of and approaches to historiography and hermeneutics in the area of historical Jesus studies. Nor am I primarily comparing portraits themselves. To evaluate a historiography on the basis of its results

---

1. See Colin Brown, 'Historical Jesus, Quest of', in Joel Green, Scot McKnight and I. Howard Marshall (eds.), *Dictionary of Jesus and the Gospels* (Downers Grove, IL: InterVarsity Press, 1992), p. 337; John Dominic Crossan, *The Historical Jesus: Life of a Mediterranean Jewish Peasant* (San Francisco: HarperSanFrancisco, 1991), pp. xxvii-xxviii; William Telford, 'Major Trends and Interpretive Issues in the Study of Jesus', in Bruce Chilton and Craig Evans (eds.), *Studying the Historical Jesus: Evaluations of the State of Current Research* (Leiden: E.J. Brill, 1994), pp. 49-51; N.T. Wright, 'Jesus, Quest for the Historical', *Anchor Bible Dictionary* (ed. David Noel Freedman; New York: Doubleday, 1992), p. 800.

in a particular case would of course be to operate first of all with an undeclared criterion for acceptance or rejection of the results, and the results would in turn serve as the basis for acceptance or rejection of the historiography. Rather than operate with such an undeclared criterion, I will attempt to examine approaches to historical investigation of Jesus on their own merits, based on their own claims and in light of general historiographic and hermeneutical issues.

At least two other investigations of issues in historiography and hermeneutics in Jesus studies have appeared recently.[2] Among these there are similarities with the approach I am taking here, which I will address below. But the present study is warranted in addition to these others for two reasons. First, while one of the subjects of the present study, John Dominic Crossan, is examined in some detail by both of the other studies, the other subject, the late Ben F. Meyer, is not. The work of Meyer is the main occasion for contrast with the historiography reflected in Crossan, and as such will serve as the foil against which Crossan is ultimately viewed. This will allow an observation of both Crossan and the wider historiographic issues in a unique light. Second, while both of the other studies focus on the impact of hermeneutics, my conclusions in this area contrast with theirs. It will remain for the reader to determine which conclusions are most warranted. Additionally, while the other studies are concerned with the field of historical Jesus work, neither reaches the findings of our study in the area of critical historiography. Childs treats of a group of philosophers of history that can be called the 'narrative anti-realists'. I will demonstrate that there are other options in current historiography, some of which I believe offer more constructive proposals for historical Jesus studies.

The need for this study, and its rationale, will be further highlighted if it is set within the wider context of contemporary Jesus studies. Important issues in historiography and hermeneutics have been brewing in the cauldron of the Quests for some time.[3]

    2.   Hal Childs, *The Myth of the Historical Jesus and the Evolution of Consciousness* (SBLDS, 179; Atlanta: Society of Biblical Literature, 2000); and Robert Byron Stewart, 'The Impact of Contemporary Hermeneutics on Historical Jesus Research: An Analysis of John Dominic Crossan and Nicholas Thomas Wright' (PhD dissertation, Southwestern Baptist Theological Seminary, 2000).
    3.   Surveys of the history of Jesus studies that have been published since the New Quest are legion. The survey by William Telford documents many of the most important of these up to 1994, 'Major Trends'. Also important are the *Forschungsberichte* of W.G. Kümmel, 'Jesusforschung seit 1981', *Theologische Rundschau* 53 (1988), pp. 229-49; 54 (1989), pp. 1-53; 55 (1990), pp. 21-45; 56 (1991), pp. 27-53, 391-420; as well as the annotated bibliographies of Craig Evans, *Life of Jesus Research: An Annotated Bibliography* (Leiden: E.J. Brill, 1990); *Jesus* (Grand Rapids: Baker Book House, 1992, 1996). Since 1994, some of the treatments of recent research to have appeared include: Marcus Borg, *Jesus in Contemporary Scholarship* (Valley Forge, PA: Trinity Press International, 1994); Colin Brown, 'Historical Jesus, Quest of'; Charlesworth and Weaver, *Images of Jesus Today*; Donald A. Hagner, 'An Analysis of Recent "Historical Jesus" Studies', in Dan Cohn-Sherbok and John M. Court (eds.), *Religious Diversity in the Greco-Roman World: A Survey of Recent Scholarship* (The Biblical Seminar, 79; Sheffield: Sheffield Academic Press, 2001); a survey that is entirely unsympathetic with historical Jesus studies is Luke Timothy Johnson, *The Real Jesus: The Misguided Quest for the Historical Jesus and the Truth of the Traditional Gospels*

1. *Jesus Studies Today: The New Quest, the Third Quest, and Method*

The standard grand narrative of the history of Jesus studies divides it into phases, traditionally named the Old Quest, the New Quest and the Third Quest. The first phase is the most widely recognized by name and by contour. The Old Quest was first identified, and presumably brought to an end, by Albert Schweitzer. It had begun with the work of Samuel Reimarus in the late eighteenth century,[4] continued through the nineteenth century with the liberal lives of Jesus, and rounded off at the beginning of the twentieth century with the options of the 'thoroughgoing eschatology' of Johannes Weiss and Albert Schweitzer versus the 'thoroughgoing skepticism' of William Wrede.[5] That is, either the Jesus of history is conceived along thoroughly apocalyptic lines, taking account of the presentation of Jesus in eschatological terms in the Gospels, or else one regards the Gospel portraits, beginning with Mark's 'messianic secret', as essentially unreliable because of their theological nature and so the Jesus of history remains mostly unknowable. Such is the standard account of the first century of historical Jesus studies, and it remains intact for the present.

After this, consensus on the progress of Jesus studies begins to weaken. The received version has it that the Old Quest was followed by a period of 'no quest', in which historical investigation of Jesus was neglected because it was considered historically impossible and theologically illegitimate. Historical Jesus studies were not resumed until the inauguration of the New Quest among the students of Rudolf Bultmann.[6] But this account has not gone unchallenged. Dale Allison has recently

(San Francisco: HarperSanFrancisco, 1995); Ben Witherington, III, *The Jesus Quest: The Third Search for the Jew of Nazareth* (Downers Grove, IL: InterVarsity Press, 1995); N.T. Wright, 'Jesus, Quest for the Historical', and *Jesus and the Victory of God* (Minneapolis: Fortress Press, 1996), pp. 1-124; W. Barnes Tatum, *In Quest of Jesus: A Guidebook* (Nashville: Abingdon Press, rev. edn, 1999); Mark Allan Powell, *Jesus as Figure in History: How Modern Historians View the Man from Galilee* (Louisville, KY: Westminster/John Knox Press, 1998); the most thorough treatment of issues is probably that of Gerd Theissen and Annette Merz, *The Historical Jesus: A Comprehensive Guide* (trans. John Bowden; Minneapolis: Fortress Press, 1998); a popular-level but incisive treatment is C.J. den Heyer, *Jesus Matters: 150 Years of Jesus Research* (trans. John Bowden; Valley Forge, PA: Trinity Press International, 1997). Also important is the three-volume work-in-progress, *The Historical Jesus in the Twentieth Century*, vol. 1 of which has been completed by Walter P. Weaver, covering 1900–1950 (Harrisburg, PA: Trinity Press International, 1999).

4.   But see Colin Brown's account of the genesis of historical Jesus studies, where he points to its origins in the decades preceding Reimarus, with Reimarus' own ideas derived from English Deism. See Brown, *Jesus in European Protestant Thought, 1778–1860* (Grand Rapids: Baker Book House, 1985), pp. 2ff.

5.   Albert Schweitzer, *The Quest of the Historical Jesus: A Critical Study of Its Progress from Reimarus to Wrede* (Baltimore: The Johns Hopkins University Press, 1998), p. 330.

6.   The inauguration is identified with the programmatic address delivered by Ernst Käsemann in 1953, 'The Problem of the Historical Jesus', published in *Essays on New Testament Themes* (Studies in Biblical Theology, 41; trans. W.J. Montague; London: SCM Press, 1964). Historical Jesus study was now thought to be theologically necessary to avoid the dangers of a docetic Christology. It was historically possible because of a new conception of history that allowed access

argued at length that the description of the first half of the twentieth century as void
of serious study of Jesus is wholly inaccurate.[7] While it was the case that, at that
time, in certain German-speaking circles interest in the historical Jesus waned,
there was actual activity that continued undiminished among English and French-
speaking scholars. The habit of viewing the time from 1906 to 1953 as a 'no quest'
period is largely the result, as Allison says, of seeing the past through Bultmannian
eyes.[8] There were many contributions to Jesus studies at this time outside those of
Bultmann and the post-Bultmannians, enough that it is in fact most appropriate to
view Jesus studies as a continuous and ongoing venture since its inception. It is
hard to contest Allison's point, especially in view of the recent survey by Walter
Weaver. Weaver has spent some 400 pages documenting serious studies of the
historical Jesus that were published at the time when there was supposedly no such
study undertaken.[9] It would appear that rumours of the silence in Jesus studies have
been, to say the least, greatly exaggerated.

Allison uses the misconception of this period as his point of departure for criti-
cizing attempts to delineate periods of both New Quest and the most recent Third
Quest. He points to the fact that the period between 1950 and 1980, when the New
Quest was supposedly underway, saw much activity outside the work of the students of Bultmann, with whom the New Quest is by all accounts most closely
associated.[10] So the New Quest, in view of the continuous activity preceding it, was
not truly 'new', and neither was it the exclusive locus of Jesus studies in its day.
Allison further contends that the Third Quest is not really set apart from its predecessors by any trait other than its diversity.[11] Concerning contemporary Jesus studies he concludes

> Although there is indeed a contemporary quest for Jesus, it is not manifest that
> there is really much new or distinctive about it. Certainly the current search is not
> a thing easily fenced off from its predecessors. It has no characteristic method. It
> has no body of shared conclusions. It has no common set of historiographical or
> theological presuppositions. And trying to locate its beginning is like trying to find

to historical agents by means of encounter with their existential selfhood, the very thing that the
kerygmatic Gospels communicated about Jesus. On the latter, see the work by the greatest
apologist for the New Quest, James M. Robinson, *A New Quest of the Historical Jesus* (Studies in
Biblical Theology, 25; London: SCM Press, 1959).

7.   Dale C. Allison, Jr, 'The Secularizing of the Historical Jesus', *Perspectives in Religious
Studies* 27 (2000), pp. 135-51.

8.   Allison, 'Secularizing', p. 137.

9.   Walter Weaver, *The Historical Jesus in the Twentieth Century*. Weaver remarks: 'The
impression that remains with me after completing this work is that our usual views of the "Quests"
of the historical Jesus do not do justice to the actual history. We have grown accustomed to
appealing to the "Old Quest–No Quest–New Quest–Third Quest", but we may have to reconsider,
for the common language represents a distinctively German perspective for the most part', pp. xi-
xii.

10.   Such luminaries as Oscar Cullmann, Ferdinand Hahn, Werner Kümmel, Leonard Goppelt
and Joachim Jeremias were publishing works on Jesus with historical interest, which deserve
recognition for their contribution to historical Jesus studies.

11.   Allison, 'Secularizing', pp. 141-43.

the origins of modern science: the ever-present continuity with and debt to the past make convenient divisions into neat periods suspect.[12]

On the one hand, Allison may be going too far to make a point. It would seem that, at the least, the New Quest designation continues to be useful as a tag for the study pursued among the post-Bultmannians and described by James Robinson and formulated methodologically by Norman Perrin.[13] Similarly, 'Third Quest' is helpful, if for no other reason than to distinguish current Jesus studies from what was undertaken in the uniquely existentialist New Quest. But on the other hand, Allison's point about Jesus studies proceeding more or less continuously over the last two centuries is well taken. So too is his observation of the complexity of current studies and their debt to and relationship with previous studies, making boundaries between 'quests' very difficult to draw. But the latter would be the same difficulty suffered by almost any periodization in history: when one begins marking off historical epochs, one is working on the highest level of historical abstraction. The higher the level of abstraction in describing historical particularities, the more the historian will need to hold labels loosely and apply them gingerly.[14] We can take from Allison the advice to use the 'quest' designations, particularly Old Quest and Third Quest, as the broadest of chronological markers for the course that Jesus studies has taken. In fact, it seems that most Jesus historians are using 'Third Quest' in this very way.[15] Among those who are not comfortable identifying current Jesus studies as a 'quest' at all, the rationale of a loose designation may be useful as a way of accommodating the current diversity.[16]

12. Allison, 'Secularizing', p. 143.

13. Norman Perrin, *Rediscovering the Teaching of Jesus* (New York: Harper & Row, 1967).

14. So Allison's recommendation that we 'lay aside the diachronic in favor of the synchronic' when we discuss the course of Jesus studies is not necessarily warranted, any more than it is warranted in historical interpretations generally. See Allison, 'Secularizing', p. 145.

15. See for example Colin Brown, 'Historical Jesus, Quest of', p. 337; Mark Allen Powell, *Jesus as a Figure in History*, p. 23; Witherington, *The Jesus Quest, passim*; Gladstone Hudson Stevens, III, 'Towards a Theological Assessment of the Third Quest for the Historical Jesus' (PhD dissertation, Marquette University, 1997), assumes 'Third Quest' as an overall designation for current Jesus studies.

16. William Telford, despite identifying seven distinctive traits of current Jesus studies, recommends that we not identify a 'Third Quest', but rather identify continuity between previous studies and present studies, 'Major Trends and Interpretive Issues', p. 61. James Charlesworth questions the notion that what historians are doing in Jesus research is anything like a 'quest' at all, *Jesus Within Judaism: New Light from Exciting Archeological Discoveries* (New York: Doubleday, 1988), pp. 6, 9; the term does not appear in Charlesworth's survey of the contemporary scene in 'Jesus Research Expands with Chaotic Creativity', in James H. Charlesworth and Walter P. Weaver (eds.), *Images of Jesus Today* (Valley Forge, PA: Trinity Press International, 1994), pp. 1-41. No distinction is made between New Quest and Third Quest (the terms are not used) in twentieth-century Jesus studies in Joachim Gnilka, *Jesus of Nazareth* (trans. Siegfried S. Schatzmann; Peabody, MA: Hendrickson, 1997), pp. 7-11; Gnilka seems to be assuming the kind of continuity Allison emphasizes, though Gnilka does follow the usual 'no quest' designation for the early twentieth century. For a position similar to Allison's, see Stanley E. Porter, *The Criteria for Authenticity in Historical-Jesus Research: Previous Discussion and New Proposals* (Sheffield: Sheffield Academic Press, 2000), pp. 52-53.

Of course, using 'Third Quest' as a loose chronological designation is not the intention of the term's originator, N.T. Wright. Wright coined the term in the early 1980s to identify a movement in Jesus studies distinct from the New Quest.[17] This movement Wright sees as beginning as early as 1965, emerging during the New Quest period.[18] Both quests in fact continue to the present, running concurrently. He has defended the Third Quest as distinct from the New Quest partly on the basis of what the former sees as the key issues to address in historical investigation of Jesus. Generally, Wright classifies the New Quest as continuing the 'thoroughgoing skepticism' of Wrede, as pointed out by Schweitzer: it denies the veracity of the synoptics' general portrayal of an apocalyptic Jesus. This approach is seen most fully in the work of the Jesus Seminar. The Third Quest, on the other hand, is more in line with Schweitzer himself in accepting the synoptics' basic outline of Jesus in eschatological terms.[19] But more fundamentally, Third Quest historians are addressing issues such as pluriform first-century Judaism, including Qumran and apocalyptic writings, and questions which emerge such as the meaning of Jesus' message in this context and the reason for his crucifixion. So Wright's distinction between New Quest and Third Quest is based at least partly on the results of his-torical investigation (even the concern for first-century Judaism as the most signifi-cant context for understanding Jesus is results-oriented, in that such a context will dictate that results also be thoroughly Jewish).

But one should note that Wright's distinction is based only *partly* on results. Just as important for Wright are more basic methodological issues that warrant a dis-tinction.[20] He sees the New Quest's method as characterized primarily by applica-tion of tools such as form and tradition-criticism and criteria of authenticity applied to individual bits of material in the sources, in an effort to verify what in the sources is historical and what they can tell us about the historical Jesus.[21] These tools the New Quest inherited from Bultmann, as it did its 'thoroughgoing skepticism' (the latter actually *through* Bultmann, from Wrede). But the Third Quest goes a differ-ent way methodologically: it proceeds by means of hypothesis and verification, by

---

17. Stephen Neill and Tom Wright, *The Interpretation of the New Testament* (New York: Oxford University Press, 2nd edn, 1988), p. 379. At one point Wright states that he coined the term as early as 1982, 'Doing Justice to Jesus: A Response to J.D. Crossan, "What Victory? What God?"', *Scottish Journal of Theology* 50 (1997), p. 345.

18. Wright, *Jesus and the Victory of God*, p. 84.

19. Wright, *Jesus and the Victory of God*, pp. 28-29, 83ff.

20. This point seems to be lost on some commentators, such as Clive Marsh, 'Quests of the Historical Jesus in New Historicist Perspective', *Biblical Interpretation* 5 (1997), p. 403; and Stanley Porter, who lists four features of the Third Quest as described by Wright, and method is not among them, *The Criteria for Authenticity*, p. 53.

21. Similarly, Powell says the New Quest was 'evaluating each individual tradition on its own merits rather than considering the whole corpus of material in light of some grand hypothesis', *Jesus as a Figure in History*, p. 22. W. Barnes Tatum sees as one characteristic of the New Quest that history writing is understood more in terms of 'event' than 'sequence of facts'. A 'life' of Jesus cannot be written, but each individual Gospel event *may* go back to Jesus, *In Quest of Jesus*, p. 102. This seems to be a description of the 'atomism' depicted by Wright and Powell, only in terms that are more sympathetic with it.

'the advancement of serious historical hypotheses – that is, the telling of large-scale narratives – about Jesus himself, and the examination of the *prima facie* relevant data to see how they fit'.[22] Wright highlights not only the variety of results among portraits of Jesus, but more importantly, the contrast of methods. If one cannot exactly adopt Wright's specific use of the New Quest / Third Quest distinction, one can appreciate his effort to identify root methodological issues that must be addressed if discussion among competing portraits of the historical Jesus is to advance.

Wright is not alone in recognizing the need to address methodological issues in Jesus studies. Crossan, with whom Wright has had the most vigorous exchanges,[23] has made the same point just as forcefully. Crossan says his study *The Historical Jesus* was written partly to inaugurate a full-blown debate on methodology among Jesus historians, but 'there is still no serious discussion of methodology in historical Jesus research'. Yet the need for discussion is great because without method and methodology, one portrait of Jesus is as good as any other.[24] It will not do for us to compare contemporary portraits of Jesus if fundamentally different means were used to arrive at those portraits. Comparisons and contrasts on the former level will result in the portraits talking past one another, for one portrait can criticize another as historically illegitimate only on the basis of some criteria of historical legitimacy. Such criteria are found, in critical history, in the means by which the historian claims to investigate the historical object.

So the milieu in which we find ourselves is that of the Third Quest of the historical Jesus, whose contents are variegated and whose perimeters are vague. But what is promising amidst this variety and obscurity is the presence of methodological discussion, a discussion which took root in the specific methodological efforts of the New Quest (form and tradition criticism) and has continued to the present. There has been no lack of methodological deliberation in Jesus studies since the New Quest, but it has centred primarily on issues such as the specific criteria for determining authentic data on Jesus.[25] Other methodological issues commonly

---

22. Wright, *Jesus and the Victory of God*, p. 88.

23. As in their discussion in the *Scottish Journal of Theology* 50 (1997), Crossan 'What Victory? What God?', pp. 345-58; Wright 'Doing Justice to Jesus: A Response to J.D. Crossan, "What Victory? What God?"', pp. 359-79.

24. Crossan, *The Birth of Christianity: Discovering What Happened in the Years Immediately after the Execution of Jesus* (San Francisco: HarperSanFrancisco, 1998), p. 139.

25. Among the more recent: John Dominic Crossan, 'Materials and Methods in Historical Jesus Research', *Foundations and Facets Forum* 4 (1988), pp. 3-24; and 'Divine Immediacy and Human Immediacy: Towards a New First Principle in Historical Jesus Research', *Semeia* 41 (1988), pp. 121-39; Gerd Theissen, 'Historical Scepticism and the Criteria of Jesus Research', *Scottish Journal of Theology* 49 (1996), pp. 147-76; Craig Evans, 'Authenticity Criteria in Life of Jesus Research', *Christian Scholar's Review* 19 (1989), pp. 6-31; Gerald Downing, 'Towards a Fully Systematic Scepticism: In the Service of Faith', *Theology* 89 (1986), pp. 355-61; Dennis Polkow, 'Methods and Criteria for Historical Jesus Research', *SBL 1987 Seminar Papers* (ed. K.H. Richards; Atlanta: Scholars Press, 1987), pp. 336-56; Eugene Boring, 'The Historical-Critical Method's "Criteria of Authenticity": The Beatitudes in Q and Thomas as a Test Case' (*Semeia*, 44; ed. Charles W. Hedrick; Atlanta: Scholars Press, 1988), pp. 9-44; Gerd Theissen and Dagmar Winter, *Die Kriterienfrage in der Jesusforschung: Vom Differenzkriterium zum Plausibilitätskriterium* (Göt-

explored are the relative value of different sources on Jesus and the use of the social sciences.[26] I intend to exploit the environment inclined to methodological discussion, but to advance the front specifically on historiographic and hermeneutical lines. There have been distinct historiographic approaches that have arisen in the context of the Third Quest.[27] I will examine these approaches, setting them within wider issues in historiography to illumine the methodological discussion.

This placing of the discussion in a wider context is necessary because most of the discussion of method in Jesus studies in the past has been guided by its particular object. Matters like the criteria of authenticity, the nature of the sources on Jesus, and the dynamics of oral tradition are all issues that are dictated by the character of the materials the historian has to work with in the case of Jesus of Nazareth. It is only fitting that these types of things receive the attention that they do; it reflects the detailed and highly specialized work that must be done. Such specificity helps assure that the methodological discussion and development will be relevant to its object. But it is also the case that extreme specificity runs the risk of lapsing into special pleading. If we fail to situate the discussion in the context of larger issues in historiography, we are in danger of claiming a set of procedures and standards for the investigation of our object that are utterly unique, thereby making the object unintelligible in the larger historiographic world. Our object is intelligible only for those who share our means of observing the object. If historians of Jesus claim to be presenting a portrait of Jesus of Nazareth that is truly historically understandable, they must reckon with general canons of historical intelligibility, ones that are applicable to any historical object. This is not to say that the world of historiographic discourse itself is uniform – far from it, as we shall see. But willingness to participate in the discourse is part of doing history.

2. *Statement of Purpose and Method*

I intend in this study to examine the work of two historical Jesus scholars who stand out in the field for their rigorous attention to method. These scholars are John Dominic Crossan and Ben F. Meyer. I will analyse and compare their contributions to historical Jesus studies, and will do that with a view to framing what I believe are contrasting methodological options that have solidified in the field, options bearing on larger issues of both historiography and hermeneutics. I will frame these options for the ultimate purpose of formulating a rationale for a historiographic

tingen: Vandenhoeck & Ruprecht, 1997); Stanley Porter, *The Criteria for Authenticity*. See the discussion in appendix 1, 'The Criteria of Authenticity: Criticisms and New Directions'.

26.   On the latter see the work of Gerd Theissen, *Sociology of Early Palestinian Christianity* (trans. John Bowden; Philadelphia: Fortress Press, 1978); Richard A. Horsley, *Sociology and the Jesus Movement* (New York: Continuum, 2nd edn, 1994); and the work of the Context Group, a consortium of scholars committed to using the social sciences in biblical interpretation. The group includes such scholars as Jerome Neyrey, Bruce Malina and Vernon K. Robbins, and meets annually for presentation of papers and collaboration on group projects. See the group's website at www.serv.net/~oakmande/index.html

27.   Contra Porter, who sees consistency among quests, criteria and methods since the nineteenth century, *The Criteria for Authenticity*, p. 55.

contribution to Jesus studies in the form of what I call 'narrative intelligibility'. So this study, as I have pointed out, moves principally on the level of the most fundamental issues of historiography, hermeneutics and epistemology, concerned with such questions as the nature of historical data and of historical knowledge, and the various dimensions of the historian's resources for construing data in pursuit of the historical object.

I will investigate the chosen subjects by reviewing their major published works, especially those in historical Jesus studies. I will discuss in detail their explicit formulations in historiography and hermeneutics, as well as assumptions in these areas that are implicit in their proposals and investigations. Their respective portraits of Jesus will be viewed in outline, but specifically for the purpose of observing how their methods operate in practice. I will consider how their methodological offerings reflect the distinct options that have emerged in Jesus studies, and will make a case for Meyer's method as presenting advances over that of Crossan, while Crossan's method has strengths of its own. Finally, I will distil these advances into a formulation of a methodological 'holism', and survey some of its current advocates in Jesus studies. I will make a case for the historiographic importance of beginning with the context of the sources for understanding discrete historical data, based on the notion of the narrative intelligibility of historical actions and events. A consideration of some hermeneutic resources implicit in narrative intelligibility will round out the presentation.

3. *The Contributions of Crossan and Meyer*

3.1. *Crossan*

Crossan was born in Ireland and began his academic career as a Servite priest in the Roman Catholic Church, taking degrees at Maynooth College in Kildare, Ireland, and at the Pontifical Biblical Institute in Rome.[28] He left the priesthood and the order in 1969, because he felt his integrity as a scholar demanded it.[29] Soon after leaving the priesthood he began teaching at DePaul University in Chicago, and spent his entire teaching career there. He took early retirement in 1995.

Crossan began work on the historical Jesus with the publication in 1973 of *In Parables: The Challenge of the Historical Jesus*. Through the 1970s he published several works on Jesus' parables, eventually employing structuralist and post-structuralist theory in the task of interpretation, but always with an eye to recovery of the words and message of the historical Jesus. In the early 1980s he expanded

---

28. See Crossan's memoirs, *A Long Way from Tipperary* (San Francisco: HarperSanFrancisco, 2000).

29. Crossan, *Tipperary*, pp. 80, 86. 'The only integrity that scholars have is to say honestly what they have learned and to say clearly what they have discovered. They should not trim their reports to what a leader expects or a people want. That is the conflict of interest I found in being a priest-scholar and a seminary professor. Others do not find it so, and maybe it is not always inevitable, but it was unacceptable for me then, and it still is. It is one thing to be a strategic consultant, another to be a defensive scholar; one thing to find an answer as you proceed, another to know the answer before you begin; one thing to do research, another to do apologetics. It is also necessary, I think, to declare which you are doing', p. 96.

his work to an investigation of other of Jesus' sayings materials, beginning with *In Fragments: The Aphorisms of Jesus*. This period saw development of Crossan's historiography, more extensive exploration of non-canonical sources for their value as sources on Jesus, and his adoption of anthropology as an interpretive tool in the formulation of his interdisciplinary method. In 1985 Crossan, along with New Testament scholar Robert Funk, founded the Jesus Seminar, the now well-known group of scholars that has met biennially for discussion of the various data on Jesus, to collaborate on determining their authenticity, and for the express purpose of publishing their findings to a broad, non-academic audience. It was during the early years of the Jesus Seminar that Crossan began expanding his investigation of Jesus into a wider emphasis not only on Jesus' words, but also on his life.[30]

In 1991 Crossan published his best-selling work *The Historical Jesus: Life of a Mediterranean Jewish Peasant*. This work established Crossan as one of the most visible historical Jesus scholars of the present day. His work on Jesus has been widely read, even more widely discussed, praised, hailed, assailed, derided, but not in any wise ignored. It has found an audience not only among scholars, but also among the educated general public.[31] As a result it has generated a considerable secondary literature.[32] The reason for this attention is partly that Crossan (like the Jesus Seminar), by his own admission saw his historical Jesus work as 'not just a study of the past but, as [Jesus] himself had been, a critique of the present. It was, indeed, a way of doing necessary open-heart surgery on Christianity itself.'[33] Crossan's work undoubtedly has appealed in one way or another to contemporary spiritual sensibilities, to many people who have felt religiously disenfranchised and sought religious or spiritual truth and experience outside the bounds of any particular religious tradition.[34] It is in fact on this basis, that is, on the basis of its

30. See *Tipperary*, pp. 173-74.

31. Crossan says he followed up *The Historical Jesus* (San Francisco: HarperSanFrancisco, 1991) with *Jesus: A Revolutionary Biography* (San Francisco: HarperSanFrancisco, 1994) for the purpose of making his findings more accessible to a wider audience; though *The Historical Jesus* was a best-seller, he 'had a strong suspicion that more people bought it than finished it', *Tipperary*, p. 175.

32. In addition to the numerous reviews of his works, the several articles, and his inclusion in various surveys of historical Jesus studies, dedicated volumes include Jeffrey Carlson and Robert A. Ludwig (eds.), *Jesus and Faith: A Conversation on the Work of John Dominic Crossan* (Maryknoll, NY: Orbis Books, 1994); Gregory A. Boyd, *Cynic Sage or Son of God? Recovering the Real Jesus in an Age of Revisionist Replies* (Wheaton, IL: Victor Books, 1995) [critique of Crossan along with Burton Mack]; Paul Copan (ed.), *Will the Real Jesus Please Stand Up? A Debate Between William Lane Craig and John Dominic Crossan* (Grand Rapids: Baker Book House, 1998); Hal Childs, *The Myth of the Historical Jesus and the Evolution of Consciousness*; Robert Byron Stewart, 'The Impact of Contemporary Hermeneutics on Historical Jesus Research' [a comparison of Crossan and N.T. Wright].

33. Crossan, *Tipperary*, p. 175.

34. Crossan says that when he left the priesthood and began teaching comparative religion courses, he developed two convictions: (1) religion is a fundamental, universal necessity of the human spirit, and (2) the one Holy is manifested differently in different religions. For Crossan, 'because it is a mystery to be faced, not a question to be answered or a problem to be solved, the Holy receives multiple responses...none of which is absolute (although each may claim it), and all of which together are truer than any one alone', *Tipperary*, p. 101.

contemporary relevancy and appeal, that Crossan's historical Jesus work has often been criticized.[35] Because Crossan's Jesus has this kind of relevancy, it is frequently suspected that in his portrait of Jesus Crossan is (as Harnack and the nineteenth-century liberals were so accused by George Tyrell) actually seeing his own face at the bottom of a deep well.

One is inclined to think there may be something to this criticism, if for no other reason than that it is so often repeated, and not only by those who would make such an accusation of historical Jesus studies in general. But whatever truth there may be there, the present analysis of Crossan will take another approach. I have said that I am not evaluating my two subjects primarily on the basis of their results, but on their methods. Crossan's work is distinctly suited to this analysis, because he stands out among Jesus historians as one who has recognized that it is issues in method that must be addressed if there is to be any real progress in our comparisons of competing portraits of Jesus. We can endlessly compare and argue the merits of various versions of the historical Jesus, but if the historians who have constructed those versions are operating with different assumptions of how to go about their task, we can never hope to approach anything resembling a true conversation on the propriety of one portrait over another. Crossan knows this, and has devised and outlined his method carefully and publicly. He has laid out his tools and his assumptions plainly, making them accessible for scrutiny, and he has followed his chosen procedure judiciously, making it formidable. Formidable, but not invincible. As we shall see, Crossan is the apotheosis of a methodological tradition that is itself subject to fundamental criticisms. So if Crossan's Jesus portrait is an easy target, his method is not, and it is largely for that reason that I have selected him as one of our subjects for an examination of historiography.

3.2. *Meyer*

There are interesting parallels between Crossan's life and career and that of Ben Meyer. Crossan spent most of his career in Chicago, and Meyer was born in Chicago. Like Crossan, Meyer began his career as a Catholic priest, but Meyer was a Jesuit. Meyer was also educated at the Pontifical Biblical Institute, and at the Gregorian University in Rome.[36] While at the Gregorian, Meyer came under the tutelage of Jesuit philosopher and theologian Bernard Lonergan, whose influence on Meyer was pervasive and life-long.[37] Also like Crossan, Meyer left the priest-

---

35. See for example, Howard Clark Kee, 'A Century of Quests for a Culturally Compatible Jesus', *Theology Today* 52 (1995), pp. 22-23; Leander Keck, 'The Second Coming of the Liberal Jesus?', *Christian Century*, 24 August 1994, pp. 784-87; Franz Josef van Beeck, SJ, 'The Quest of the Historical Jesus: Origins, Achievements, and the Specter of Diminishing Returns', in *Jesus and Faith*, p. 97.

36. B.F. Meyer, Curriculum Vitae, 1975, obtained from the Lonergan Research Institute, Regis College, Toronto, Ontario.

37. It is not known whether Meyer studied with Lonergan, but Lonergan is known to have been teaching at the Gregorian while Meyer was preparing his doctorate. Meyer resided in Rome during his studies in the years 1959–61 and 1962–63. Lonergan taught at the Gregorian from 1953 through the 1960s. See Frederick E. Crowe, SJ, *Lonergan* (Collegeville, MN: Liturgical Press, 1992).

hood in the late 1960s. He began teaching at McMaster University in Hamilton, Ontario in 1969 (the same year Crossan began at DePaul) and remained there until his death in 1995 (the same year Crossan retired). The parallels between Crossan and Meyer are interesting, but incidental. There is little similarity in their work on the historical Jesus.

Meyer's first work related to the historical Jesus was his early *The Man for Others* (1970), a short book in the *Faith and Life* series for adult religious education. This work is a brief and small-scale discussion of issues surrounding the Jesus of history, intended for the educated non-specialist in an ecclesial context. A year later his attention turned to the historical grounds of an ecclesiology in *The Church in Three Tenses*, an exploration of the development of the church's self-understanding from the first century to the present.[38] This was followed in 1979 by *The Aims of Jesus*, Meyer's major Jesus work and his initial exploration of the hermeneutical and epistemological context for doing historical work in general and on Jesus in particular. Throughout the 1980s Meyer continued to expound on his hermeneutics and its application in historical Jesus and New Testament studies in articles and papers, several of which are collected in *Critical Realism and the New Testament* (1989), and in *Christus Faber: The Master Builder and the House of God* (1992). Meyer most deliberately and systematically laid out his New Testament hermeneutics in his final published monograph, *Reality and Illusion in New Testament Scholarship: A Primer in Critical Realist Hermeneutics* (1994).

If Crossan stands out among Jesus historians for his recognition of the need to address issues in historical method, Meyer is distinguished by his fundamental orientation to the root issues that drive not only historical study of Jesus, but New Testament interpretation generally. Meyer was first of all a New Testament exegete, convinced of the propriety of a historical-critical approach to the texts; but the defining moment of his exegetical work was the desire to get at the bases of the interpretation and understanding of any text. So in this sense, he was as interested in the largest questions of hermeneutics as in the most practical matters of exegesis. This placed Meyer in a very specialized group, for few of the most skilled historians are inclined to devote the necessary attention to study of the fundamental rationale for their historical and interpretive enquiries. Meyer gave his attention to both areas, with equal success. He was as occupied with the epistemology and cognitional theory of Bernard Lonergan, the hermeneutics of Hans-Georg Gadamer and the historiography of R.G. Collingwood as he was with the study of the historical Jesus and Christian origins.

Meyer's work did not attract the attention of the wider public in the way Crossan's has, but there have been several scholars in the New Testament guild who have acknowledged a debt to Meyer's pioneering work in historiography in Jesus studies. Meyer helped to rehabilitate the focus on human intentionality in history, rescuing the concern for Jesus' 'aims' from the psychologizing and existentialist

---

38. The concern for early Christian identity Meyer would take up again later in *The Early Christians: Their World Mission and Self-Discovery* (Good News Studies, 16; Wilmington, DE: Michael Glazier, 1986).

portraits of the Old Quest and the New Quest.[39] William Farmer commended Meyer for his concern to account for Jesus' aims, which are commonly thought to be off limits to critical scholarship.[40] E.P. Sanders cites Meyer's as 'the richest and best nuanced' description of Jesus' aims and intentions.[41] Sanders also identifies with Meyer's understanding of history as taking place through hypothesis and verification, and with the concern reflected in Meyer's work to relate Jesus to the history of Israel and to early Christianity.[42] The orientation to historiography as 'hypothesis and verification' reflects some of Meyer's groundwork in the area of historical method. His hermeneutical achievements have influenced Bruce Chilton's formulation of 'generative exegesis' as an approach to historical study of the sources on Jesus.[43] Chilton says his approach 'owes more to Meyer than to any other single scholar'.[44] The scholar most visibly influenced by Meyer is N.T. Wright. Wright's critical realism resembles Meyer's epistemology of the same name, and in my analysis of Meyer I will examine the relation between them. But some comments of Wright aptly describe the significance of Meyer's work for historical Jesus studies, and the importance of further discussing and carrying on the seminal work Meyer began in historiography and hermeneutics. In talking about Collingwood and the importance of intentionality in history, Wright notes: '[I]f we are to talk about historical method, this is the discussion we need to have. It has not yet taken place, to my knowledge, in the main guild of New Testament scholarship. To engage in it would be to honour the memory of its greatest exponent in our field, the late Ben F. Meyer.'[45]

39. See the discussion below, on Meyer and intentionality in history, pp. 107-113.

40. William R. Farmer, 'Reflections upon "The Historical Perimeters for Understanding the Aims of Jesus"', in Bruce Chilton and Craig A. Evans (eds.), *Authenticating the Activities of Jesus* (New Testament Tools and Studies, 28.2; Leiden: E.J. Brill, 1999), p. 59. This volume and its companion (*Authenticating the Words of Jesus* [ed. Bruce Chilton and Craig Evans, New Testament Tools and Studies, 28.1; Leiden: E.J. Brill, 1999]), are both dedicated to the memory of Ben Meyer.

41. E.P. Sanders, *Jesus and Judaism* (Philadelphia: Fortress Press, 1985), p. 47.

42. N.T. Wright cites Sanders and Meyer as examples of 'convergence on the question of appropriate method', 'Jesus, Quest for the Historical', p. 801. Meyer and Sanders collaborated on an earlier study in Christian origins, *Self-Definition in the Greco-Roman World* (London: SCM Press, 1982). Together they were early proponents of an accurate representation of Second Temple Judaism, and of situating Jesus within that context. James Charlesworth echoes Sanders's comments when he says he shares Meyer's and Sanders's concern to understand Jesus' intentionality. Charlesworth lists other points of similarity among them: 'most important, each of us uses the historical critical method, attempts to be self-critical, shuns with great disdain the distortions of Early Judaism and Jesus' place within it caused by New Testament scholars' antipathy to early Jewish phenomena, affirms the necessity of checking hypotheses as the research proceeds through induction, struggles to place Jesus within what can be known of pre-70 Palestinian Judaism, and tries to understand Jesus' intentionality', *Jesus within Judaism: New Light from Exciting Archeological Discoveries* (New York: Doubleday, 1988), p. 163 n. 61.

43. On generative exegesis, see below, pp. 166-67, 177.

44. Bruce Chilton, 'Assessing Progress in the Third Quest', in *Authenticating the Words of Jesus*, p. 24.

45. N.T. Wright, 'In Grateful Dialogue: A Response' in Carey C. Newman (ed.), *Jesus and the*

4. *Issues in Historiography and Hermeneutics*

So our two subjects have been chosen for their attention to the historiographic issues that ground any investigation of the historical Jesus. Each represents a methodological option, Crossan the zenith of a long tradition in Jesus studies, and Meyer a pioneer in many respects. I have said that the situation in Jesus studies that demands our attention is not a new situation, but is rather two or three decades old, at the least. I am identifying its beginning with the publication of Meyer's *The Aims of Jesus*. Since that time the options we will analyse have surfaced in different forms and in different treatments of Jesus, affecting the course of those investigations mostly as unstated historiographic and hermeneutical assumptions. Our chosen subjects help us to compare these options because they have been most successful in identifying and formulating them, making them explicit and open for inspection.

Though I am treating the topic of 'Historiography and Hermeneutics in Jesus Studies' as found in the work of two major scholars, I should further clarify the nature of the issues that will arise. I am not identifying two contrasting sets of procedures for Jesus studies, or anything like two complete and self-contained historiographic packages. Each of the two scholars indeed has a high level of consistency in his approach, but the issues I am treating are better conceived as root assumptions that ground any historical investigation. Lonergan said that method is best thought of not as a recipe or a set of directions, but as a means of asking and answering questions.[46] Ultimately, we are dealing with matters that help the historian define historical questions and thereby direct the search for answers.

One of the historiographic areas where questions will arise in this study is that of historical data. What is the nature of historical data? How are they to be evaluated for their usefulness in an investigation? How are they to be understood and interpreted? What is the relation between the evaluation of the data and their interpretation? This leads to questions in the area of historical knowledge. How is historical knowledge obtained? How does it relate to knowledge in general? What justifies historical knowledge? What makes it true? What are the historian's resources for obtaining historical knowledge?

In the area of the nature of historical explanation, questions include: What is the proper role of such tools as the social sciences for historical explanation? To what extent do historians generalize in their explanations and interpretations of data? What kind of attention should be given to human intentions when explaining historical events?

In all this the hermeneutical question will always be in the background, with the consideration of how hermeneutics relates to historiography. In our study, 'herme-

Restoration of Israel: A Critical Assessment of N.T. Wright's Jesus and the Victory of God (Downers Grove, IL: InterVarsity Press, 1999), p. 250. At one point Wright cites Meyer as proleptically providing a methodology for the Third Quest in his *The Aims of Jesus*; see *Jesus and the Victory of God*, p. 83 n. 2.

46. Bernard Lonergan, 'A Post-Hegelian Philosophy of Religion', in Frederick E. Crowe (ed.), *A Third Collection: Papers of Bernard J.F. Lonergan* (New York: Paulist Press, 1985), p. 204.

neutics' is used in its broadest sense, as the understanding of understanding, rather than rules for interpretation of texts or the means of contemporary application of an ancient text. Using hermeneutics in this generalized sense, how do one's assumptions in hermeneutics affect one's historiography? How should the notion of the historian's hermeneutic involvement with history (a notion shared by both Crossan and Meyer) be factored into historical method? Or, more broadly, what is the relation between such involvement and the doing of history?

With these kinds of questions we will be occupied in this study. There are ample resources for deliberating them in the work of Crossan and Meyer. It is my hope that, if answers are not forthcoming, at least the questions will have been sharpened and the discussion focused, and progress in Jesus studies furthered as a result.

Part I

JOHN DOMINIC CROSSAN AND TRADITION CRITICISM

Chapter 1

THE EARLY CROSSAN:
POST-HISTORIOGRAPHIC STRUCTURALISM

Crossan once wrote that his historical Jesus work has always been characterized by a dialectic of diachrony and synchrony, that is, by an interplay between two types of analysis: (1) an analysis of the Jesus traditions chronologically, as they underwent change and development, and (2) an analysis of the traditions as they function as a system, or within a system, sharing particular, more or less atemporal and constant, features.[1] He made these comments in response to an examination of his work by Bernard Brandon Scott, who sought to relate the method seen in Crossan's work in *The Historical Jesus* to Crossan's earlier work on Jesus' parables.[2] Crossan said Scott's examination of his work seemed to reflect such a dialectic, and this dialectic was appropriate since Crossan's own work is itself dialectical in this way.

I will eventually give some attention to the 'dialectical' part in this treatment of Crossan, but what I am most interested in now is the 'diachronic' dimension. A measure of development is probably characteristic of the work of most scholars, but Crossan's work seems especially to lend itself to this type of examination, one that identifies distinct stages along with the evolution of concepts and tools throughout those stages. The present approach to Crossan is organized in two parts: the early Crossan, consisting of his work on Jesus' parables in the 1970s (up to and including *Cliffs of Fall*); and the later Crossan, beginning with *The Historical Jesus* and continuing to the present. The works in between will be treated as a sort of transition phase, the nature of which will hopefully become clear as the study proceeds.

Consistent with the stated purpose of appreciating the interplay of hermeneutics and historiography in Jesus studies, I will examine the stages in Crossan's work along these lines, considering his expressed or assumed hermeneutic and the historical methods he employs along the way. With these I will also review details of his understanding of the historical Jesus at each stage, and observe how it reflects his hermeneutic and historical method.

The tortured diction of the title of this chapter reflects an attempt to bring together distinct tendencies in Crossan's early work on Jesus' parables. On the one

---

1. John Dominic Crossan, 'Responses and Reflections', in Jeffrey Carlson and Robert A. Ludwig (eds.), *Jesus and Faith: A Conversation on the Work of John Dominic Crossan* (Maryknoll, NY: Orbis Books, 1994), p. 146.

2. Bernard Brandon Scott, 'to impose is not / To Discover: Methodology in John Dominic Crossan's *The Historical Jesus*', in *Jesus and Faith*, pp. 22-30.

hand, Crossan's fundamental interest has always been in recovery of the historical Jesus. This will be evident in the historiographic element in our observations. But Crossan's other, consciously hermeneutical hand holds some surprises. The relation between the two hands has been variously evaluated,[3] and I will offer my own assessment. But in spite of any estimation of consistency or otherwise at this stage of Crossan's work, what arises here is seminal in the course of development of tools and orientations in this always-engaging interpreter of Jesus.

1. In Parables

Crossan opens his first work on the historical Jesus, *In Parables*, with interesting comments on the nature of parables and of all reality. First, parables are understood only from inside their own world. They speak their revelation to those who have learned to live 'in parables'. Second, and following from this, reality itself is parabolic, it is 'images projected on the white screen of chaos'.[4] At this point Crossan elaborates little on these cryptic observations. He quotes Roland Barthes on von Ranke's history; Barthes says that narrative is waning in historiography, being replaced by 'structures', because history is seen to be no longer about reality but about intelligibility; narrative is concerned with 'reality' while 'structures' are concerned with intelligibility. Crossan also quotes Heisenberg, whose Uncertainty Principle in physics implies that even in science, method and object (more properly, observation and object) cannot be easily separated. It will remain for Crossan's interpretation of Jesus' parables to flesh out the significance of all these comments. But it appears that Crossan opens his study of the parables of the historical Jesus with the general observation that 'reality' is at least partly fashioned by its observers, and is not simply 'out there'.

Exploration of these musings is deferred by historiographic first things. After the Preface in which he comments on the parabolic nature of reality, Crossan begins the first chapter by situating his study squarely within what he describes as the twenty-year-old new quest of the historical Jesus. He outlines the five-step method of the new quest,[5] which we can summarize as follows:

1.   comparison of synoptic materials with one another, revealing dissimilarities between versions of a tradition that demand discovery of the earliest form of the tradition.
2.   a temporary bracketing of the historicity question of these various extant forms.
3.   uncovering a history of the transmission of the piece of tradition.
4.   invoking the criterion of dissimilarity to determine the historicity of the earliest form of the tradition.

---

3.   Most recently by Bernard Brandon Scott, 'to impose is not / To Discover'; and by Robert Byron Stewart, 'The Impact of Contemporary Hermeneutics on Historical Jesus Research', both of whom see continuity; and by Hal Childs, *The Myth of the Historical Jesus*, who sees discontinuity.

4.   *In Parables: The Challenge of the Historical Jesus* (New York: Harper & Row, 1973), p. xv.

5.   Crossan, *In Parables*, pp. 4-5.

5.   invoking the criterion of dissimilarity with respect to style and form, not just subject and content.

This outline constitutes the bulk of Crossan's discussion of historiography in this work, and I would call attention to three items, corresponding to the first, third and fifth steps. First, comparison of the synoptic materials, revealing differences in accounts of the same tradition, forms the point of departure for historical method in relation to Jesus. These differences constitute a historical problem that calls for a method to deal with them. This is a consistent theme that we will encounter again in Crossan's later works: similarities and differences among accounts cry out for an explanation, and it is of the essence of a historical approach to the data on Jesus that the explanation of these be given priority. The full significance of this point will emerge when Crossan responds to challenges to his method with the insistence that source relationships are the necessary presupposition of any study of the historical Jesus.

Second, the uncovering of the history of the transmission of the piece of tradition, followed by application of a 'criterion of authenticity', is what Crossan would eventually call the 'classic methodological model' for Jesus research.[6] The history of the transmission of the tradition is traced by comparing the extant versions with one another, determining which among the versions was earlier and which later development. Once the earliest form of the tradition is determined, the criteria are applied to verify that this form derives from Jesus and not from some unidentifiable moment in the development of the tradition. This basic method, of tradition criticism followed by application of criteria, Crossan employs consistently throughout his historical Jesus works, culminating in his most sophisticated formulation of method in *The Historical Jesus*. What is at this point the primary criterion, dissimilarity, Crossan later rejects as inadequate, to be replaced with, first, a criterion of 'adequacy', and eventually with multiple attestation. But the basic method centred on *tradition criticism followed by application of some criterion* remains consistent and constitutive of a historical approach to the data for Crossan.

Third, Crossan points out that the criterion of dissimilarity is to be applied with respect to style and form, not just to subject and content. Crossan is in fact most concerned here with this final step in his method, considering the uniqueness of the *form* of Jesus' words. Specifically, Crossan is interested in Jesus' use of metaphor in sustained parabolic fashion and how this use is different from that of the early church and contemporary Judaism.[7] He points out that this uniqueness will involve consideration of philosophy and poetry in examination of fundamental hermeneutical problems. This observation is his point of departure for extended discussion of the hermeneutics of metaphor.

So Crossan launches a career of exploration of the historical Jesus with a straightforward articulation of historical method, combined with intimations of a

6.   Dominic Crossan, 'Divine Immediacy and Human Immediacy: Toward a New First Principle in Historical Jesus Research', *Semeia* 41 (1988), p. 123. Norman Perrin gave the classic formulation of this model. See the discussion of tradition criticism and criteria of authenticity in appendix 1, 'The Criteria of Authenticity: Criticisms and New Directions'.

7.   Crossan, *In Parables*, p. 7.

hermeneutic with far-reaching ontological implications. The methodological presentation is brief, but seminal. The hermeneutical suggestions are pregnant, and it is these that are the focus of Crossan's study here. It is significant that historical method is briefly discussed but the hermeneutic is treated at length. We are set on a course here that will lead to interesting literary-critical territory in the 'early Crossan'.

The form of Jesus' parables is metaphorical. This is in contrast to parables that are allegorical. Metaphorical parables create participation in their referents; allegorical parables illustrate information on their referents. Metaphors seek to express what is inexpressible, or what can be expressed in no other way than by inviting participation in the referent. Metaphors are thus aptly suited to religious expression; they are fit for expressing the permanently inexpressible Wholly Other. 'The Wholly Other must always be radically new and one can experience it only within its metaphors.'[8] The metaphor is the incarnation of the poetic experience, and poetic experience is analogous to religious experience, so the language of religion is the language of poetic metaphor. Both poetic and religious experience can be said to be incarnate in metaphor.

Jesus' use of parable as poetic metaphor is in contrast to the rabbinic use of parable as didactic figure. In the rabbinic use, parable functions as illustration of an independent dogmatic point, one which could just as easily be expressed without the parable. But Jesus' parables are different; they are not linked to specific biblical texts requiring interpretation, as commentary or exposition of them; nor are they exemplifications of specific moral situations. The rabbis' parables serve the teaching situation, while Jesus' parables serve to articulate the revelation that exists through them.[9] Jesus' parables, as metaphorical, express his experience and invite participation in that experience. Crossan notes that the fact that Jesus expressed his experience in metaphor says something about that experience. There is an intrinsic unity between religious experience and its expression in metaphors or symbols. Religious experience involves both the moment of perception of the experience and the embodiment of the experience in symbolic form. 'The fact that Jesus' experience is articulated in metaphorical parables, and not in some other linguistic type, means that these expressions are part of that experience itself... There is an intrinsic

---

8. Crossan, *In Parables*, p. 13.

9. For more recent studies of Jesus' parables compared to the rabbis', see Geza Vermes, *The Religion of Jesus the Jew* (Minneapolis: Fortress Press, 1993), pp. 90-119. Vermes concludes that Jesus' parables are unlike those of the rabbis in that the former are not exegetical by nature, not interpreting a passage from the Bible; and the point of Jesus' parables is not explained. These two features make Jesus' parables relatively autonomous, and their significance was meant to be immediately discernible. In these conclusions Vermes is similar to Crossan. But Vermes contrasts with Crossan in insisting that each of Jesus' parables urges a single religious/ethical message. 'The aim of the parable is...to impress on the listener, in a lively and colourful manner, the obligation to adopt an attitude, or perform an act, of fundamental importance', p. 117. See also Craig A. Evans, 'Jesus and Rabbinic Parables, Proverbs, and Prayers', in *Jesus and His Contemporaries: Comparative Studies* (Arbeiten zur Geschichte des antiken Judentums und des Urchristentums; Leiden: E.J. Brill, 1995), pp. 251-97; and Arland J. Hultgren, *The Parables of Jesus: A Commentary* (Grand Rapids: Eerdmans, 2000).

and inalienable bond between Jesus' experience and Jesus' parables. A sensitivity to the metaphorical language of religious and poetic experience and an empathy with the profound and mysterious linkage of such experience and such expression may help us to understand what is most important about Jesus: his experience of God.'[10]

The function of Jesus' parables has long been recognized to be the proclamation of the Kingdom of God. Crossan treats the function of the parables in these terms, distinguishing Jesus' proclamation of the Kingdom as characterized by a prophetic eschatology as opposed to apocalyptic, and a 'permanent' eschatology, as opposed to futurist (Schweitzer), realized (Dodd), or 'in process of realization' (Jeremias). Apocalyptic eschatology is concerned with *the* end to *this* world (the only world), and looks forward to an afterlife after the end. But prophetic eschatology, the more ancient of the two, is concerned with an end to world (in the sense of 'one's world', the world within which one lives, or possibly an era or epoch) and has no concept of an afterlife. Permanent eschatology is of a piece with the prophetic view, seeing the presence of God as 'the permanent presence of the one who challenges world and shatters its complacency repeatedly'.[11] 'Jesus was not proclaiming that God was about to end *this* world, but, seeing this as one view of world, he was announcing God as the One who shatters world, this one and any other before or after it...God, in Kingdom, is the One who poses permanent and unceasing challenge to man's ultimate concern and thereby keeps world free from idolatry and open in its uncertainty.'[12]

Jesus' alternative understanding of temporality is key to his kingdom proclamation in the parables. Crossan criticizes a linear view of time and history as inconsistent with Jesus' proclamation. The linear view sees history as a sort of structure abstracted from actual events; in von Rad's words, time in this view is like 'the blanks of a questionnaire, only needing to be filled up with data which will give it content'.[13] Crossan suggests as an alternative God's presence which, in calling us to a response, *creates* our history and our time, rather than acting in history or intervening in time. Thus history is like the spokes coming out of a wheel rather than a line or a circle. 'Time is...the present of God.'[14] Crossan says this understanding of time is based on Heidegger's notion of the advent of Being in *Ereignis*. Authentic human time and history arise from a human response to Being as it comes out of the unexpected. The advent of Being destroys one's projections of future and even the supposedly objectively given past. These are often reversed in the advent of Being, as the present is constituted by action. The succession of past-present-future in time is replaced by the ontological simultaneity of three modes in advent-reversal-action.[15]

In this light, Jesus' parables are seen to express the ontological ground of his life. They contain the temporality of Jesus' experience of God and proclaim and

10. Crossan, *In Parables*, p. 22.
11. Crossan, *In Parables*, p. 26.
12. Crossan, *In Parables*, p. 27.
13. Crossan, *In Parables*, p. 28.
14. Crossan, *In Parables*, p. 31.
15. Crossan, *In Parables*, pp. 31-32.

establish the historicity of Jesus' response to the Kingdom.[16] They are not illustrations of a separate message, but are constitutive of both Jesus' experience of God and his historicity. By his parables Jesus attacked the 'idolatry of time' which was characteristic of the religious groups of Judaism in Jesus' day (and of early Christian groups, to the degree that they were apocalyptic in their eschatology). Against the view of time as humanity's future Jesus presented time as God's present, not an eternity beyond us but an advent within us. Against the planning and projection of the future is God's sovereign freedom to create one's time and establish one's historicity. The parables proclaim the Kingdom's alternative temporality and the three modes of its presence: *advent* as God's gift; *reversal* of the recipient's world; and the empowering to *action*.

Crossan invokes comments of the structuralist Claude Lévi-Strauss to insist that the parables of Jesus as a whole are the context in which individual parables must be heard, in order to be heard fully. There may also be identified an axis along which key parables may be identified. There are three parables in particular 'which show most clearly the deep structures of the Kingdom's temporality and which contain in themselves the entire parabolic melody'.[17] Those parables are the Treasure (Mt. 13.44); the Pearl (Mt. 13.45-46) and the Great Fish (*Gos. Thom.* 8).

The remainder of the book is devoted to treatment of various parables in three groups, based upon their reflection of one of the three modes of the Kingdom's temporality. In each section, Crossan begins his treatment of the relevant parables with tradition-critical analysis, followed by interpretation of the resulting historically authentic parabolic material.[18] I would note two features of his interpretations here that will become significant when we look at his later works.

The parables of reversal feature a 'polar' reversal, one in which opposites are exchanged (good is bad, bad is good), in contrast to a single reversal in which only one pole is reversed. A polar reversal has the effect of overturning one's world and creating utter uncertainty. The Kingdom does this in its advent; it challenges 'the complacent normalcy of one's accepted world'.[19] Later tradition tended to turn the historical Jesus' parables of reversal into 'example stories', such as the Good Samaritan (Luke was especially bad about this); such stories teach by giving an

---

16. Crossan presents this understanding of Jesus' parables specifically against Jeremias. Whereas Jeremias saw the parables as Jesus' defence against criticisms of his proclamation and ministry (particularly his association with outcasts and sinners; see Jeremias, *The Parables of Jesus* [London: SCM Press, rev. edn, 1972], pp. 145-46), Crossan here sees the parables as the *cause* of Jesus' conflicts with religious authorities, in that they embody his experience of God and constitute the historicity of that experience (*In Parables*, pp. 32, 74). For Crossan, Jesus' parables are not 'to be located *in* Jesus' own historical experience as visual aids to defend a proclamation delivered before them and without them. Jesus' parables are radically constitutive of his own distinctive historicity and all else is located in them. Parable is the house of God', pp. 32-33.

17. Crossan, *In Parables*, p. 33.

18. He draws the reader's attention to this procedure early on: 'For each parable we shall have to write a history of the sequential stages of its transmission, tracing the history of the tradition back to the earliest form of the story. When this is done for each one, some general conclusions on both can be drawn within the understanding of the parabolic intentionality of Jesus', p. 39.

19. Crossan, *In Parables*, p. 75.

example of ethically good or bad behaviour. But the point of the parables of reversal, as can also be seen in Jesus' aphorisms, was not to teach an ethical point by example, but to speak in the language of paradox, and thereby to shatter the listener's expectations and thus the listener's world, upsetting the idolatry of time and making room for permanent eschatology. In this way, 'Paradox is the form of eschaton'.[20] This theme of paradox is to become very important for the early Crossan.

Concerning the parables of action, Crossan decries the tendency among many interpreters of Jesus' parables and aphorisms to moralize them, that is, to see in them a moral lesson or ethical example. An instance of moralization would be to see in 'turn the other cheek' a moral admonition or an exhortation to non-violence. Against this Crossan insists, along with Käsemann, that both Jesus and Paul resisted such teachings as efforts at self-sanctification, seeking a righteousness not from God. Alternatively, Crossan cites Heidegger's idea of dwelling with Being as the ground of ethics. Similarly, Jesus' parables overthrow both world and ethics, in favour of the experience of God that grounds ethics. Jesus' parables call us to dwell with God in Kingdom and to act and live from the gift we experience there. The shattering of world that characterizes Jesus' parables includes a shattering of all absolutes, including ethical ones. 'Turn the other cheek' is not an exhortation to non-violence, but a shattering of one's sense of justice and equity.[21] Only in the face of such shattering and the utter uncertainty that it brings can the 'action' mode of the Kingdom arise out of one's experience of God. This relativizing of the ethical is another feature that we will see again in the early Crossan and will become an interesting point of comparison with the later Crossan.

I have a final observation on *In Parables*. It is difficult to overlook the New Quest orientation of this work. Two aspects are telling: (1) Crossan treats the historical Jesus exclusively in terms of his teachings. He states explicitly in the Preface that 'The term "historical Jesus" really means the language of Jesus and most especially the parables themselves... One might almost consider the term "Jesus" as a cipher for the reconstructed parabolic complex itself... An expression such as, for example, "Jesus' experience of God", will mean within the context of this book no more and no less than the experience of God which is articulated within the parabolic system under study.'[22] An advance over the exclusive orientation to Jesus' words characterizes recent historical Jesus studies, even the recent work of Crossan himself, as we shall see. But at this early stage, Crossan has taken up his scholarly milieu in seeing Jesus' *teachings* as exhaustively constituting the data on the historical Jesus. (2) The existentialist flavour of Crossan's interpretations of Jesus' parables is evident, and on this Crossan out-Heideggers the post-Bultmannians.[23]

---

20. Crossan, *In Parables*, p. 76.

21. Contrast the interpretation of Walter Wink, who sees the 'turn the other cheek' saying as an exhortation to creative but non-violent resistance, in which the oppressed places himself on a par with the oppressor. Walter Wink, 'Neither Passivity Nor Violence: Jesus' Third Way', in *SBL 1988 Seminar Papers* (ed. Kent H. Richards; Atlanta: Scholars Press, 1988), pp. 210-24.

22. Crossan, *In Parables*, p. xiii.

23. In an earlier book on the theology of the Johannine corpus, Crossan had considered the

But alongside these New Quest influences (which are not unique to Crossan in this study; we will see some New Quest echoes in Meyer as well) are intimations of innovations that will be more characteristic of the early Crossan. I am referring here to the beginnings of a structuralist orientation in Crossan's historical Jesus work. I noted that Crossan cites Lévi-Strauss in making the point that any of the parables have to be understood in the context of all the parables as a whole, as a system. In his discussion of the parables of action, Crossan comments on the over-all structure of the two groups of Servant parables he is examining, and on how the reversal of expectations that is the theme of the parables is reflected in that structure. References like this reflect an orientation that moves Crossan beyond his New Quest roots, at least in terms of his explicit hermeneutic. A structuralist orientation also helps bring together his comments in the Preface on the parabolic nature of reality, with his interpretation of Jesus' parables as shattering and relativizing world.

2. The Dark Interval

In Parables evinced harbingers of structuralism. In *The Dark Interval* structuralism is in full flower. Indeed, Crossan offers this work as an indirect introduction to structuralist analysis.[24] The subtitle, *Towards a Theology of Story*, witnesses to the importance of structure and story. If Crossan suggested in the previous work that reality is 'parabolic', here he states plainly that reality is exhausted by the structure of language and story. Story *creates* world, rather than telling of a world that exists apart from story. Structure, specifically linguistic structure, constitutes reality. For Crossan, this is the meaning of structuralism, and he is now advocating a thoroughly structuralist hermeneutic.

It would be helpful at this point to identify some major elements of structuralism. The linguistic theories of Ferdinand de Saussure are most often identified as the precursor of what would become a paradigm for much wider application in the social sciences. In the early part of the twentieth century, Saussure insisted that a linguistic *sign* is not a link between a thing and a name, but between a concept and

relation between the historical Jesus and the Christ of the Gospels. He described a new approach to history that has made recovery of the historical Jesus possible, after the positivism of von Ranke and the scepticism of form criticism in the early twentieth century. In the new approach, the historian does not just relate 'what happened' in history, on an external level; rather, he 'must find a relation between himself and the past events whose personal protagonists he faces. Only within the historical ordeal and existential problems of his own time and place can he understand the dead past as a living reality and so appreciate it adequately. The past and present must meet within his awareness of common existential challenge', *The Gospel of Eternal Life: Reflections on the Theology of St. John* (Milwaukee: Bruce Publishing Company, 1967), p. 36. This new approach echoes the new understanding of history expounded by James Robinson as the very possibility of the New Quest. History is about the historian's encountering the existential selfhood expressed in the intentionality of historical agents. See Robinson, *A New Quest of the Historical Jesus* (London: SCM Press, 1959), pp. 66ff.

24. Crossan, *The Dark Interval: Towards a Theology of Story* (Niles, IL: Argus Communications, 1975), p. 10.

a sound pattern, or between a *signified* and a *signifier*. (The existence of the extra-linguistic referent is bracketed, because it is not part of the internal structure of language. And the structure of language is also the structure of thought. There is no structured thought without language. So thought and language are coextensive.) Saussure also noted that the link between signifier and signified is arbitrary; there is no *necessary* link between the sound used to signify a particular concept and the concept itself. Now this fact is not disputed by anyone, but its consequences had not previously been recognized. What this arbitrariness implies is that signifiers are distinguished only by their *difference* from all other signifiers in the linguistic system. A signifier has meaning only by virtue of what it is not, i.e., it is not any other signifier. So, 'in language, there are only differences. Even more important: a difference generally implies positive terms between which the difference is set up; but in language there are only differences *without positive terms*.'[25] The most important implication of all this for Saussure was that language is radically systemic or interrelational. Words only have meaning in relation to other words, in the total system of a given language.

As noted above, 'structuralism' took this concept of the necessity of system for meaning in language and gave it broader application, mostly in the social sciences, in the 1960s and 70s. This need to view a given subject (whether a language, a text, or a culture) systemically usually called for examination of the system as closed, from the 'inside', without reference to external categories of meaning. Significantly, for biblical studies this often involves the 'bracketing' of the historical or extra-textual referent. The text has meaning only as a self-referential system, and not by virtue of any historical events or persons to which the text purportedly refers.

So Crossan now situates himself within this structuralist hermeneutic. Such is one of the hermeneutical surprises in Crossan to which I referred earlier. What is most surprising is that, unlike most structuralists, Crossan does not bracket the historical referent as a significant dimension of meaning in the text. At least this is true of his exegetical method, if it is not articulated in his hermeneutic. In discussing the parables of Jesus in this work, Crossan makes determinations as to what form of the parables belonged to the earliest strata of tradition, or what actions attributed to Jesus are probably historically authentic, and thus what we may determine of the historical Jesus' own words or deeds, i.e., Crossan continues to employ the methodology of the Quest as outlined in *In Parables*. Not insignificant is his treatment of the parable of the Great Feast (Mt. 22.1-14 pars.). He sees the *Gospel of Thomas* version as the earliest, and the Matthew version as the latest.[26] But his historical approach to the parables is reflected more generally in his stated concern to distinguish between the stories of Jesus in their original intentionality and in their present interpretations within the Gospel texts.[27] As he pointed out in *In*

---

25. Ferdinand de Saussure, *Course in General Linguistics* (ed. Charles Bally and Albert Sechehaye; trans. Wade Baskin; New York: Philosophical Library, 1959), p. 120. Most of the preceding summary is gleaned from Stephen Moore's helpful introduction in *Post-structuralism and the New Testament: Derrida and Foucault at the Foot of the Cross* (Minneapolis: Fortress Press, 1994), pp. 14-17.

26. Crossan, *Dark Interval*, pp. 108-119.

27. Crossan, *Dark Interval*, p. 98.

Parables, the later tradition tends to allegorize or moralize Jesus' parables, and such reinterpretation must necessarily be removed if one is to recover the authentic words of Jesus. If Crossan's hermeneutic is informed by structuralist literary criticism, which for him means that reality is exhausted by language, his historiography continues to operate on the assumption that the historical referent is essential for understanding Jesus' parables.

To return to structuralism, we may note that Crossan is concerned with story as limit. He comments on the limit that is our mortality and the limits imposed by our language itself. Story constitutes the limit of language: 'Our intentions, our theories, our visions are always confined within both language and story. A theology of limit seeks above all to explore this limitation, which is posed by the inevitability of life within story, or existence in this story or that but always in some story.'[28] We can use this observation as entrance to Crossan's theological concerns that motivate his structuralist theory. Recall that in *In Parables* Jesus' experience of the Wholly Other was contained in his parables. Crossan is equally concerned to articulate the experience of the transcendent in the present work, but no longer sees parables as containing or communicating such experience. The transcendent is beyond expression in language, so exploration of the *limits* of language is key to the experience of the transcendent. Crossan articulates this as he considers our (structuralist) limitations within our own stories, and the implications of this for our talk and knowledge of God. He anticipates the objection that because our reality is limited to language, such limitation implies that either God is simply inside our language, which would amount to idolatry, or that He is outside language, which would mean that He is not knowable. Crossan's answer is that there is the transcendent, but it is experienced only at the 'edges' of language: 'My suggestion is that the excitement of transcendental experience is found only at the edge of language and the limit of story and that the only way to find that excitement is to test those edges and those limits. And that…is what parable is all about.'[29] Crossan's theological concern remains with the Wholly Other, the ineffably transcendent, but how this is experienced is subject to revision in *The Dark Interval*. This leads us to consideration of the parables in this work, and their subversive nature.

In Parables had argued the point that Jesus' parables contain his experience of the Wholly Other through the shattering of temporal world, mediating the advent of Being, or the Kingdom. Parable continues its subversive role in *The Dark Interval*, but the mediation of Being is abandoned in view of a structuralist orientation. The concept of Being represents an absolute that is no longer possible since reality is constituted by story or the linguistic system. Brown and Malbon effectively summarize Crossan's change in course. Since all language is self-referential, a closed system, constituting all of reality, 'master stories that try to establish a world in relation to some knowable Being or Truth' are rejected.[30] Rather than parable

28. Crossan, *Dark Interval*, p. 14.

29. Crossan, *Dark Interval*, p. 46.

30. Frank Burch Brown and Elizabeth Struthers Malbon, 'Parabling as a *Via Negativa*: A Critical Review of the Work of John Dominic Crossan', *Journal of Religion* 64 (1984), p. 532.

mediating Being through shattering of world, parable subverts all world and all master concepts, relativizing world in the most 'absolute' sense.

> [I]f we are now to rediscover any sense of God and transcendence, this can, in Crossan's view, come only through events of language whereby order and security are undermined: at those limits at which one is conscious of the boundaries and constraints of language rather than preoccupied with its specifiable referents, all of which turn out to be intralinguistic.[31]

The themes of the Wholly Other, and subversion as the key whereby this is experienced, are continued in this work. But the subversion is not limited to shattering of world in view of temporality and the 'idolatry of time'. Subversion is now more radical. Jesus' parables subvert one's entire world, one's reality, which is created by myth.[32] The parables upset the expectations of the hearer and thereby serve to relativize the hearer's world, the hearer's structured story, that is, the hearer's reality.[33] This relativization makes the hearer vulnerable and open to God. 'It is only in such experiences that God can touch us, and only in such moments does the kingdom of God arrive. My own term for this relationship is transcendence.'[34] Only by the relativizing of the hearer's limited world can the hearer experience the unlimited transcendent.

There are several significant features at this stage of Crossan's work. First, a minor point of clarification. Crossan here identifies as structuralist the notion that reality is constituted by language, that one cannot get outside the structure of story, and that 'reality is language and we live in language like fish in the sea'.[35] Though Crossan's techniques of analysing the recovered parables of Jesus at this point can be said to fit within a structuralist conception, complete with diagrams,[36] in the history of structuralism and its successor, post-structuralism, the kind of ontological implication Crossan associates with structuralism is not seen as integral to structuralism at all, but is more appropriate to what we would today call post-structuralism. The early Crossan's work in fact becomes increasingly post-structuralist, though he had no terminology available at the time to distinguish his work from that of structuralism proper.

There are significant trends begun in *In Parables* that are continued here. I noted in the earlier work that the discussion of historiography was brief but seminal, and

---

31. Brown and Malbon, 'Parabling as a *Via Negativa*', p. 532.

32. See Crossan's discussion of myth and parable as opposite poles in the continuum of story. Myth functions as the attempt to reconcile binary opposites (following Lévi-Strauss), to offer security to the individual's storied reality. Parable, on the other hand, functions 'to create contradiction within a given situation of complacent security but, even more unnervingly, to challenge the fundamental principle of reconciliation by making us aware of the fact that *we made up* the reconciliation', *Dark Interval*, p. 57. Because parable subverts the world created by myth, 'it is a story deliberately calculated to show the limitations of myth, to shatter world so that its relativity becomes apparent', p. 60.

33. Crossan, *Dark Interval*, p. 77.

34. Crossan, *Dark Interval*, p. 122.

35. Crossan, *Dark Interval*, p. 11.

36. Crossan, *Dark Interval*, p. 10.

the discussion of hermeneutics was extensive and pregnant. What we encounter in *The Dark Interval* continues this trend. The historiography of the earlier work is mostly assumed, following the tradition-critical orientation, but is discussed even less than it was before. Attention is devoted almost exclusively to discussion of a (post-)structuralist hermeneutic as the appropriate method for interpreting the authentic words of Jesus. (It is left to later works to explain why this is so.) But the basic concern to first uncover the authentic Jesus material and then interpret it according to structuralist theory or technique continues the approach begun in *In Parables*, though in that earlier work the interpretation was more existentialist.[37]

There is another continuation of earlier trends in the present work, but within the context of a new development. Here Crossan extends his understanding of 'parable' in Jesus' ministry to include parabolic deeds, and not just words. Modern examples of parabolic deeds would be the protest demonstrations in the United States in the 1960s and 70s: a black minister sitting at a segregated lunch counter, a rabbi pouring blood over draft files, a priest burning the US flag. Certain actions of Jesus were also parabolic, such as his consorting with tax collectors and sinners. Crossan suggests that this action of Jesus was not intended to motivate repentance, but to be parabolic in that 'It was intended to raise questions of who was right and wrong before God and of how securely or self-righteously such decisions could be rendered.'[38] The parabolic deed, as parabolic, serves to subvert ethics, 'reminds everyone that God is even more important than ethics and that God may not always approve our moral judgments'.[39] Crossan thus introduces a new element in his examination of the historical Jesus, the allowance of Jesus' actions in addition to his words for understanding him; but Crossan continues the relativizing of ethics begun in *In Parables*. Both parabolic words and deeds subvert one's reality, including one's sense of right and wrong, subordinating all to the experience of the transcendent.

3. Raid on the Articulate *and* Finding Is the First Act

Crossan opens *Raid on the Articulate* with a clue to the reason for the ascendancy of hermeneutic concerns in his historical Jesus work. He recognizes a general displacement of the primacy of historical criticism in biblical studies with the rise of literary criticism. The latter is of course represented especially by structuralist criticism, and, he says, will be the focus of the present book. Interestingly, he admits that he is engaged more by structuralist philosophy than by structuralist methodology. He confesses, 'The theory fascinates me although the practice often

---

37. Crossan notes in the Preface to *The Dark Interval* that structuralism has replaced existentialism as the current intellectual rage, p. 10. It could well be that between *In Parables* and *The Dark Interval* Crossan had made a conscious paradigm shift of his own, exchanging the existentialism that could easily be inherited from the New Quest for a (post-)structuralism that is more congenial to his sense of subversion that is characteristic of Jesus' proclamation.

38. Crossan, *Dark Interval*, p. 92.

39. Crossan, *Dark Interval*, p. 93.

bores me.'[40] But structuralist theory, for Crossan, has the effect of challenging and placing qualifications on historical criticism. Since structuralism reminds us that language is our reality, the medium of our living, the historian is reminded that it is only language and text that binds him to the historical subject. What this challenge amounts to for Crossan is a call to balance historical and literary work in New Testament criticism and especially in historical Jesus studies:

> [This book] presumes, acknowledges, and appreciates the results of historical investigation into the teachings of Jesus. It will never use texts except those supported as authentic by the vast majority of the most critical historical scholarship. But the book claims that such texts are best understood not only within their own contemporary situation by comparative historical criticism but also, and indeed especially, in confrontation with texts within our own world which are functionally, generically, and philosophically on the same literary trajectory, that is, through comparative literary criticism.[41]

One can get an idea of the nature of historiography for Crossan at this point by looking at a discussion in which he considers the possibilities for recovering the historical Jesus. He identifies four problem areas that any historical method must deal with when facing the sources on Jesus: (1) the general problem of the uncertainty of all historical research; (2) the fact that the events pertaining to the life of Jesus are quite removed, in place and time, from the contemporary historian; (3) the fact that the sources are confessional witnesses rather than 'uncommitted chronicle'; and (4) 'the problem of constant adaptation, application, and interpretation which offers us multiple versions of the same unit within successive or even simultaneous layers of the tradition'.[42] He notes that it is in this last problem that we can hope to find the best solution to the problem of the historical Jesus. In view of the existence of parallel units and various versions of the same tradition, the problem of uncovering authentic tradition becomes the problem of finding the original version that had been variously reinterpreted by the tradents in their efforts to find application in their own situations. The original version is isolated by charting the trajectory of adaptation and reapplication of the tradition by the community. It is only by recognizing the presence of continual reinterpretation of an original tradition, which resulted in the occurrence of parallels and variations, and by tracing the trajectory of reinterpretation, that one can hope to find the original tradition that required such reinterpretation. This necessitates the criterion of dissimilarity as the basic criterion for authenticity in historical Jesus research. 'The principle is logically persuasive *only* if one has decided that creative change is what strikes one most forcibly in any careful reading of our texts.'[43] Dissimilarity with regard to form, before content, is Crossan's focus in this book. The forms of Jesus' language were slowly changed by the early church, but these forms put up a certain resis-

---

40. Crossan, *Raid on the Articulate: Comic Eschatology in Jesus and Borges* (New York: Harper & Row, 1976), p. xiv.
41. Crossan, *Raid*, p. xv.
42. Crossan, *Raid*, p. 176.
43. Crossan, *Raid*, p. 177.

tance to mutation that draws our attention and isolates them as possibly historically authentic material.

In this explication of historical method, one can see consistency with and development of Crossan's similar statement in *In Parables*. In that earlier work there were three items that most warranted our attention. These items recur here. (1) Earlier, the existence of parallel traditions was the major factor in the data that calls for historiographic attention. This continues to be the case, and more so, inasmuch as parallels are now the one problem area in which the historian has most hope of finding a solution to the historical Jesus problem. (2) Crossan had earlier described the 'classic methodological model' in Jesus studies as tradition criticism followed by application of criteria of authenticity to the earliest recovered form of the tradition. This conception remains basically unchanged in the present work, though there begins to emerge an increasing attention to the historical process of reinterpretation itself, which later becomes the problem of the 'hermeneutical Jesus' for Crossan. The criterion of dissimilarity, previously given primacy, continues to be the most important criterion for determining the authenticity of early forms of tradition. (3) He had previously noted that dissimilarity should be applied not just to content, but also to style and form. The importance of the form of Jesus' speech (i.e., parables) had engaged Crossan the most then, and it continues to do so now. He had noted then that attention to form requires discussion of hermeneutical and philosophical issues, and the trajectory begun by that observation, which led Crossan to take up structuralism in *The Dark Interval*, is sustained here. To the present discussion of hermeneutics and philosophy we now turn.

What Crossan considers the structuralist tendency to see reality as 'story', reality exhausted by language, is continued in this work. So is the need to relativize that reality. But this relativization is undertaken in light of a new dimension to story, which Crossan identifies as 'play'. Play is the human imaginative activity that creates world; the totality of played world is what we call reality. 'This reality is the interlaced and interwoven fabric of our play. It is layer upon layer of solid and substantial play and in this and on this play we live, move and have our being.'[44] Crossan also introduces comedy as the means whereby world is subverted by manifesting world as the creation of play. 'Comedy…is the epiphany of play. Comic play is play made manifest.'[45] Along this line, comic eschatology is an eschatology unlike either the prophetic or the apocalyptic. Comic eschatology serves to subvert world, to remind the players of the relativity of the world as play. In this, comic eschatology is effectively the ending of the endgame.[46] Comic eschatology relativizes world by manifesting it as the creation of play, and thereby opens the gate to transcendence.[47] So what Crossan had previously described as Jesus' prophetic and permanent eschatology, he now understands to be more properly comic.

Crossan relates comic eschatology to Jesus' experience of God by introducing the idea of God's 'aniconicity'. God cannot be captured in any image, including the

---

44. Crossan, *Raid*, p. 27.
45. Crossan, *Raid*, p. 30.
46. Crossan, *Raid*, p. 45.
47. Crossan, *Raid*, pp. 47-49.

images or concepts of language. Because of God's aniconicity, all such icons which would be used to represent him must be subverted. Crossan illustrates this iconoclastic message in scripture. The book of Ruth is iconoclastic of law and Ecclesiastes is iconoclastic of the Sapiential tradition: 'God cannot be caught in the nets of Wisdom any more than in the nets of Law.' Jesus' message is also aniconic: 'The content of Jesus' message is a comic eschatology of forms and genres. In his teachings the aniconic God of Israel escapes not only wood and stone, silver and gold, but also eludes the images of human imagination and the forms of human language. Jesus represents the full flowering of Israel's aniconic faith, the consummate creativity of Israel's iconoclastic imagination.'[48] For example, Jesus' injunction to 'turn the other cheek' (Mt. 5.39b-41 and Lk. 6.29a-b) is not an ethical example, but rather a subversion of case law as found in the Book of the Covenant (Exod. 20.22–23.33), a challenge of the legal tradition. Jesus offers here what amounts to a parody of case law; this parody reminds us that even the most necessary laws are only play. Jesus thereby points to a more fundamental morality behind the morality of case law, that is, the necessity to abide with the Holy.[49]

Crossan also adds a new and integral dimension to his understanding of Jesus' parables in a discussion of allegory. *In Parables* maintained the distinction between parable and allegory, with the latter being merely informative but the former creating participation in its referent. Crossan now rejects this distinction as 'romantic'.[50] He praises allegory for its ability to generate a plurality of interpretive levels and to convey paradox and differing paradoxical interpretations.[51] 'An allegory is a story whose plurality of interpretive levels indicates that the original is itself a metaphor for that multiplicity… These various levels developed by analysis are but the obedient reflection of the multiplicity imaged in and by the story itself.'[52] Allegory is plot at play, or, allegory shows plot to be essentially playful. Paradoxical interpretations of an allegory are its salient characteristic. Paradox is also the heart of comic eschatology, for paradox is 'language laughing at itself', language revealing itself to be always and only play. Jesus' parables are narrative paradox, paradox in the form of a story.[53] Their paradoxicality manifests the played nature of reality, subverts the hearer's reality and thereby makes possible the experience of the transcendent, which cannot be captured in our played language and reality.

The introduction of the notions of play and the multiplicity of interpretations (polyvalence) indicates even more strongly Crossan's post-structuralist sensibilities. In his introduction of play Crossan quotes extensively from deconstructionist philosopher Jacques Derrida. It would be helpful at this point to identify very briefly some important elements of the deconstructionist brand of post-structuralism, as

---

48. Crossan, *Raid*, p. 60.
49. Crossan, *Raid*, p. 69.
50. Crossan, *Raid*, p. 116.
51. David H. Fisher, 'The Pleasures of Allegory', *Anglican Theological Review* 66 (July 1984), p. 302.
52. Crossan, *Raid*, p. 125.
53. Crossan, *Raid*, p. 93.

we did previously for structuralism.[54] Derrida capitalized on the Saussurean observation that in language signifiers are distinguished only by their difference from all other signifiers in the linguistic system. He drew from this the conclusion that there are no signifieds (no 'transcendental signifieds', as he termed them), only signifiers. Signifiers are distinguished only by what they are not, that is, by an *absence* rather than a *presence*. No element of language is present in itself; each is present only in relation to something that it is not, and neither is that something present in itself. Language is all an infinite play of differences. Derrida calls this essential difference *différance*. Note that this *différance* cannot be a concept, because there are no positive entities in Derrida's understanding. *Différance* is the possibility that creates differences between signifiers.

Derrida opposes the binary oppositions that have always characterized Western thought, e.g., transcendent/immanent, intelligible/sensible, spirit/body, presence/absence, necessary/contingent, masculine/feminine, sane/insane, identity/difference, object/representation, objective/subjective, content/form, speech/writing, etc. This opposition privileges the first term at the expense of the second. He 'deconstructs' the opposition, showing how the terms are actually joined in intimate relation, and the line drawn between them is ultimately political. Since single elements are not simply present in and of themselves, but are present only in relation to what they are not (*différance*), opposing terms carry in themselves traces of each other, just as they carry traces of all other things that they are not.[55] Deconstruction involves a recognition of this essential difference that causes all 'things' to contain in themselves traces of what they are not. Applied to texts, deconstruction recognizes that what is stated explicitly contains traces of what is not stated, so what appears to be stated is a deceptive covering for its opposite. Deconstruction effectively turns a text upon itself. In denying any transcendental signified, the possibility of any fundamental order of being, it attacks a text from the inside, showing that its 'inside' is unreal, to be debunked: 'it is a violent science utilizing others' strength against themselves'.[56]

Some elements in *Raid on the Articulate* undoubtedly betray a deconstructionist or generally post-structuralist influence at this stage. (1) Crossan's identification of play as the activity that creates world is a case in point. Deconstruction also stresses that reality, which is linguistic, is constituted by *différance*, the play of differences, being radically differential. (2) Deconstruction turns a text against itself, debunking its illusion of transcendental signifieds. The spirit of this enterprise fits well with Crossan's concern with subversion as the gateway to the experience of the transcendent, though Crossan here sees paradox as the key to subversion. (3) Crossan's suggestion of the polyvalence of the parables is a general post-structuralist concern, inasmuch as post-structuralism seeks to go beyond the systemic orientation of structuralism which seeks a univalent reading of texts, and insists on an endless reading not dictated by author, text, or even interpreter.

54. As with structuralism, most of our summary of deconstruction is drawn from Moore, *Poststructuralism and the New Testament*, pp. 18ff.

55. Moore, *Poststructuralism*, p. 31.

56. John P. Leavey, 'Four Protocols: Derrida, His Deconstruction', *Semeia* 23 (1982), p. 45.

At the end of this examination of *Raid on the Articulate* there is a greater sense of the need to coordinate our findings in historiography and hermeneutics. I have noted Crossan's express desire in historical Jesus studies to balance the findings of historical investigation, consisting largely of tradition criticism, with literary work, consisting of (post-)structuralist interpretation. But I have also noted his expressed interest in structuralist theory over structuralist method. What one can see emerging in *Raid* is a rationale for a pattern that was begun in *In Parables*, the pattern of an *assumption* of the need for historical work, behind a greater devotion of space to discussion of hermeneutical issues. The rationale is what would seem to be a completely reasonable conception of the historical Jesus enterprise as consisting of a two-stage process: historical work on the data, followed by interpretation. This rationale is stated most explicitly in Crossan's next book, *Finding Is the First Act*. This book can be seen as a smaller, pivotal work between the two larger works, *Raid on the Articulate* and *Cliffs of Fall*.

The relation between historical and literary studies was described in *Raid* as one of balance: both areas of study need the requisite attention for proper understanding of the historical Jesus. In *Finding Is the First Act*, balance should still generally characterize the two disciplines, but their relation is now more nuanced. Crossan here depicts that relation first of all in terms of one between diachronic and synchronic study. His particular object of study here is Jesus' Treasure Parable (Mt. 13.44). A complete analysis of the parable should employ the diachronic and genetic methods of historical criticism as well as the synchronic and systemic study of thematic and generic parallels, specifically the parallels found in the Jewish treasure parables and the entire treasure tradition in world folklore.[57] Crossan says that the diachronic or historical dimension of study is oriented to establishing the corpus of authentic Jesus material, and his own work has always begun *after* and been based *upon* this corpus as established by historical scholarship that removed the interpretive traditions from original Jesus material. The interpretive work that follows historical reconstruction is necessary because the scholars who had been involved in recovering the historical data base of Jesus material had failed to understand and interpret correctly the material they had recovered. The crucial cause of this failure was 'the fact that *historical* thinking was required for reconstructing the corpus but *literary* appreciation was required for interpreting its meaning'.[58] Here is a rationale for the ever-extensive attention to hermeneutical issues in Crossan's historical Jesus work. He has always (up to this point, at least) seen his work as consisting of interpretive efforts *following upon* the historical work that is preliminary. (I would point out, however, that the historical work has not been absent from his published studies, as we have seen since *In Parables*, though one can see now that it has been a preliminary and subordinate interest.) The historical methods established by generations of scholars investigating the historical Jesus are the time-tested tools that have allowed authentic Jesus tradition to be reconstructed, but these tools have been inadequate to grasp the message contained in those recon-

---

57. Crossan, *Finding Is the First Act: Trove Folktales and Jesus' Treasure Parable* (Philadelphia: Fortress Press, 1979), p. 1.
58. Crossan, *Finding*, p. 2.

structed traditions. Crossan has found in structuralist theory the means to understand the proclamation of the historical Jesus as found in the established historical corpus.

The idea that accurate interpretation follows upon and assumes the results of historical scholarship is illustrated in Crossan's outline of the actual course of historical Jesus research in the years leading up to *Finding is the First Act*. Crossan sees in Jesus research three consecutive, developmental phases.[59] The first phase was the Historical Phase, summarized by Norman Perrin in 1967.[60] In this phase, based upon an understanding of the nature of the Jesus tradition in the Gospels and a requisite application of the criterion of dissimilarity, scholars have reached a consensus on what materials are to be included in the corpus of authentic Jesus data. Crossan's work presumes the general validity of these conclusions. The second is the Literary Phase. Once the corpus of authentic material is established, there remains the task of interpreting it in comparison with itself rather than in the traditional and evangelical contexts in which it has been dispersed and reinterpreted. Crossan reiterates his earlier comment, that historical scholars had largely failed in their interpretation of the authentic material, and he now specifies that that failure was in the area of explaining the radicality of the images of Jesus' speech and the formal and material strangeness of his language. This quality of strangeness is present in all forms of Jesus' language and in many of his actions, and requires some literary sophistication to be attentive to its full presence and to resist the tendency to translate it into normal language and to conclude that it was saying something that could easily have been said in other terms. The quality of strangeness in Jesus' communication is recognized by many scholars and includes traits such as hyperbole, paradox, ridiculous caricatures, or hilarious incongruity. Such descriptions of Jesus' speech force the discussion of historical Jesus research into the third phase, the Philosophical Phase. The special linguistic and semiotic aspects of the historical Jesus' communication require appreciable philosophical and theological attention. Crossan cites the examples of W.A. Beardslee's use of A.N. Whitehead, Dan Via's and Paul Ricoeur's use of phenomenological and/or structuralist analysis on the parables, and Crossan's own use of 'the Nietzsche-Heidegger-Derrida tradition'. He points out that presently (in the 1970s), historical Jesus research is in transition between the second and third phases; scholars are gradually coming to recognize the need for attention to the kind of hermeneutic and philosophical issues that Jesus' communication raises.

It would seem then that the early Crossan sees historical Jesus studies as moving beyond purely historical work, but not in the sense of leaving a historical orientation behind to move on to other, non-historical interpretive arenas, as we have noted is the position of most structuralists, i.e., exchanging the diachronic for the synchronic. For the early Crossan, synchronic assumes diachronic, and literary and philosophical analysis goes beyond historical in the sense that the historical forms the necessary basis for the latter work of interpretation. Interpretive work reaches its philosophical apogee in Crossan's *Cliffs of Fall*. But we have noted that *Finding Is the First Act* serves as a pivotal point to that work. The former is pivotal in its

---

59. Crossan, *Finding*, pp. 99-102.
60. In Perrin, *Rediscovering the Teaching of Jesus*.

interpretation of Jesus' Treasure Parable as radically paradoxical metaparable, an interpretation that prepares the way for *Cliffs*.

What Crossan sees in this parable is a paradoxical metaphor of the finder's selling all his possessions to obtain something which was not his to take, the treasure hidden in the field of another; Jesus thereby gives a metaphor for transcendence and the Kingdom. One *gives up* absolutely everything to obtain the *gift* of God, *even the parable itself* is given up. 'One must give up even the advice to give up everything.'[61] The advice to give up even the advice, and the parable as teaching the giving up even of the parable, makes this as metaparable. Crossan proposes that the prefix *meta-* be used for any form of communication that so deliberately turns on itself in self-negation. 'Jesus' treasure story is thus a metaparable, a paradoxical artifact which succeeds precisely to the extent that it fails. I will tell you, it says, what the kingdom of God is like. Watch carefully how and as I fail to do so and learn that it cannot be done. Have you seen my failure? If you have, then I have succeeded. And the more magnificent my failure, the greater my success.'[62] The parable as metaparable is an example of language genuflecting, 'not just talking about doing it in content, but actually doing it in form...[In Jesus' Treasure Parable] "The speaker begins by declaring his willingness to give up all that he has for God and he ends by giving up the giving up".'[63] This giving up includes surrendering practical morality. Crossan notes that paradox always carries the danger of nihilism. It is true that Jesus' parables do not reflect any moral sensitivity or ethical concern, compared to contemporary Jewish parables. The Treasure Parable presents the special problem that the finder, in buying another's field to obtain the hidden treasure, seems to give up morality as part of the 'all he had' given up to obtain the field and the treasure: the treasure in the field would have been the rightful property of the field owner, so the buyer's purchasing the property for the express purpose of obtaining the treasure was unscrupulous at best. This would seem to teach nihilism. Crossan's response, echoing observations he has made since *In Parables*, is that Jesus was concerned not with practical morality, but with fundamental morality. Crossan repeats his earlier point that fundamental morality has to do with our 'dwelling' with God, similar to Heidegger's 'dwelling with Being', while practical morality has to do with our 'dwelling' with one another. Jesus comes close to ignoring the latter to establish the primacy of the former. The notion of God's aniconicity is relevant here. This aniconicity is negative in force rather than positive: 'It robs us of our absolutes and in the space cleared by their absence offers us a freedom for human responsibility, personal and social decision, and the creation of those conventions which make us what we are.' This negation generates restlessness which disturbs answers, and creativity, which is 'the most precious gift of aniconicity'.[64]

This interpretation of the Treasure Parable precipitated Crossan's point on the Philosophical Phase of historical Jesus work. Seeing the parables as expressing this

---

61. Crossan, *Finding*, p. 94.
62. Crossan, *Finding*, p. 120.
63. Crossan, *Finding*, p. 122.
64. Crossan, *Finding*, p. 117.

form of radical paradox would not have been possible without the kind of philosophical and structuralist analysis that Crossan had undertaken in this work. This type of analysis and its consequent interpretation culminate in *Cliffs of Fall*.

4. Cliffs of Fall

Cliffs of Fall consists of three essays written between 1977 and 1979. That it is Crossan's most post-structuralist-sounding work is well attested.[65] Throughout the work he takes up themes that we have seen running through previous works, and gives them post-structuralist extension. In the first essay, he takes the presence of metaphor in parable as the point of departure for explicating his view on the ubiquity of metaphor. He denies a clear distinction between figurative and literal language, advocating the metaphoricity of all language. He cites Derrida's observations on the absence that is the ground of reality, and draws implications for the metaphoricity of language. The absence of a fixed, literal, univocal, referential language leads to the inevitability of metaphor. Since there is no absolutely literal language against which metaphor may be identified, all language is metaphorical. This carries the implication of the polyvalence of language. The absence of a fixed univocal language also means that there is a *void of meaning*, an essential absence, at the core of metaphor. It is this void that allows for polyvalence in readings.

In the second part of the essay Crossan focuses on Jesus' parables in particular. He notes Paul Ricoeur's qualifications on the definition of parable as used by Jesus. Religious language consists of 'limit-expressions': 'intensification, transgression, and going to the limit' of language.[66] Language becomes religious when it 'transgresses', when it points beyond its immediate signification to the Wholly Other. The parables are limit-expressions in their extravagance of expressing the extraordinary in the ordinary. Crossan agrees with this, but uses the term *paradoxical* for what Ricoeur would call limit-expression. Crossan reiterates his observation from *Raid on the Articulate* and *Finding Is the First Act*, that Jesus' paradox is an extension of the aniconicity of Israel's God. Formerly in Israel's history this aniconicity was against law, wisdom, or anything that could be an idol; but with Jesus it was turned against language itself, which for Crossan is potentially an idol. 'Jesus' language is simply language genuflecting before Israel's aniconic God... What does it do to the human imagination to imagine an unimaginable God? Is it possible to proclaim figural aniconicity and still assert linguistic iconicity? Must not iconicity, however long it may take, turn eventually on language itself?'[67]

Of the three essays, the second focuses the most on actual exegesis using historical method. Crossan proceeds along traditional historical-critical lines, comparing the extant versions of the parable of the Sower and attempting to determine what

---

65. Stephen Moore uses the work as 'an entry into the universe (or multiverse) of poststructuralist thought', if not post-structuralist method. *Literary Criticism and the Gospels: The Theoretical Challenge* (New Haven: Yale University Press, 1989), p. 139.

66. John Dominic Crossan, *Cliffs of Fall: Paradox and Polyvalence in the Parables of Jesus* (New York: Seabury, 1980), p. 13.

67. Crossan, *Cliffs*, p. 20.

was probably the original version, spoken by the historical Jesus. When he recon-structs the original, he offers an interpretation. His stated purpose in this essay is to explore the question of hermeneutical presuppositions, especially the problem of univalence and polyvalence in interpretation. Crossan suggests that some parables are windows, showing us a world, others are mirrors, showing us ourselves as interpreters. The latter are metaparables, parables about parables. As was the Treasure Parable in *Finding*, so is the Sower Parable of this type. As a parable about parables, the Sower parable reveals the deliberate self-negation of the sower, or the parabler, and the polyvalent nature of the seed, or the text of the parable. 'Jesus' text negates the sower to concentrate on the seed and thus the text and its metaphoric and polyvalent destiny take precedence over the author.'[68] Crossan also mentions divine aniconicity in this essay, offering it as the source of paradox (as in *Raid* and *Finding)*, and also of polyvalence. An aniconic monotheism can only express itself in paradoxical or multiple images. This aniconicity is the root from which Jesus derived his parable of the 'absent sower and the polyvalent seed'.[69]

In the third essay Crossan provides the theoretical basis for polyvalence of texts. This he calls a metaphor of metaphors. He repeats his assertion of the first essay, that all reality is metaphorical. Here he offers a metaphor to account for all meta-phors. He recognizes that such an undertaking is ultimately paradoxical, however; if all reality is metaphorical, any metaphor to account for all metaphors would itself be subject to an explanatory metaphor, since according to Kurt Gödel's incompleteness theory, no deductive system can be proven from within. The series of explanatory metaphors could be extended infinitely. Crossan welcomes this paradox 'as a destiny to be enjoyed rather than as a difficulty to be avoided'.[70] He considers this evidence that paradox necessarily and permanently exists at the heart of the human.[71] The fundamental paradox is that the player himself is played, the perceiver is perceived.

The metaphor of metaphors that Crossan offers, what he also calls the megame-taphor (preferred over the clumsy 'metametaphor'), is play. He reiterates the point he made concerning play in *Raid on the Articulate*, that play constitutes world or story. Play is the ultimate paradigm of reality. In the context of parable, ludic (playful) allegory, which amounts to polyvalent narration, is plot rendered self-conscious, manifesting itself as play. The supremely self-manifestive allegory, the allegory which is most fully aware of its playful essence and manifests that aware-ness, is the metaparable, as Crossan sees in the parable of the Sower. Metaparable manifests that all, including itself, is relative play, and this reveals the 'paradoxical core that makes story polyvalent or allegorical since it both invites, permeates, and relativizes each and every reading. Only violence to the paradox can present a final or official reading.'[72]

---

68. Crossan, *Cliffs*, p. 58.
69. Crossan, *Cliffs*, p. 59.
70. Crossan, *Cliffs*, p. 70.
71. Crossan, *Cliffs*, p. 71.
72. Crossan, *Cliffs*, p. 101.

We see that Crossan takes the notion of play and storied world to their post-structuralist limits. We finish this summary of *Cliffs* with notice of veiled references to negative theological expression in the third essay. Crossan gives a name, '[chaos]', to the unspeakable that lies outside words and signs. This [chaos] is the ground of play. I call attention to this naming of the unnameable to show that, even in his most deconstructionist expressions, Crossan maintains a concern to articulate the ineffable transcendent.

5. *Evaluation*

The twin trajectories of historiography and hermeneutics that we have been tracing through the early works of Crossan have each developed consistently, in their respective spheres. Historical method has been founded upon the 'classic methodological model': (1) tradition criticism, reconstructing stages in the transmission of a tradition to recover the earliest version, followed by (2) application of criteria of authenticity, particularly the criterion of dissimilarity, to this earliest recoverable form to determine if it is authentic to Jesus. This model has remained essentially unchanged in the early Crossan. He discusses it little, but he is always careful to acknowledge it as the assumed means for establishing the historically authentic corpus with which he works.

Though there is more development, and much more discussion, of hermeneutics, this development is also consistent along the course charted from the opening pages of *In Parables*. Recall that in the Preface to that work, Crossan commented on the nature of parables as understandable only within their own world, and on the nature of reality as parabolic, as 'images projected on the white screen of chaos'. While it may be true that the analysis of *In Parables* remained mostly within traditional historical-critical methodological bounds,[73] Crossan at this point was already looking forward to what would later become not only a full use of structuralist method, but an even more intensive interest in structuralist and post-structuralist theory in interpreting the message of Jesus' parables. From an understanding of parables as subverting world and the 'idolatry of time' in favour of permanent eschatology, Crossan moves to seeing parables as paradoxical metaphors relativizing all reality in view of the linguistic nature of reality and the aniconic nature of God. Ultimately, Jesus' parables are radically paradoxical, in that they subvert all reality, including themselves. We have in the early statement of *In Parables* the germ of not only a hermeneutic, but the latter as a result of an epistemology and an ontology, or, in a more post-structuralist spirit, an anti-ontology.

It may be that the hermeneutic is a function of an ontology, but it seems just as likely that the ontology is bound up with a theology, specifically a negative theology, for Crossan seems always concerned with the parables of the historical Jesus as relativizing their hearers' reality to prepare for an experience of the transcendent

---

73. That according to Scott, 'to impose is not / To Discover', p. 23. But notice that even in *In Parables*, p. 33, Crossan sees a need, citing Lévi-Strauss, to interpret any one of the parables of Jesus in the context of all his parables as a system.

that cannot be contained within that reality. The theological tradition of the *via negativa* is based on the conviction of the utter transcendence of the divine. Negative theological discourse is concerned with its own inadequacy both to express and to comprehend the Holy, which is inexpressible and not capturable in finite conception. This is as much a commentary on the limitations of language as on the transcendence of the Wholly Other. To the degree that any theology maintains some sense of God's transcendence, that theology will involve a moment of the *via negativa*. But for theologies which conceive the divine-human relation in sharply dualistic terms, for example, in terms of the completely inexpressible Wholly Other over against the utterly linguistic and self-referential world of the human, negative theology becomes radically negative, constituting the whole of the theological enterprise. This tendency is seen in Crossan, prepared in his early expressions of the Wholly Other experienced in metaphor, and eventually worked out in more explicitly negative terms. The experience of transcendence necessitates relativization of all reality. The aniconic Wholly Other resists the specifications of an eschatology, a law, a wisdom, an ethic, or a language. The transcendent is that Absence beyond the limits of language, that unspeakable [chaos] that cannot be named, but the experience of which is prepared for by the paradoxical parable and the ludic allegory.

Whether or not a larger negative theological orientation is integral to Crossan's hermeneutic here, there is a significant point that could be raised regarding the relation between the hermeneutic and the historiography that may have already become evident to the reader. I have pointed out a rationale for Crossan's attention to hermeneutics to the virtual exclusion of historiographic discussion, that rationale being that his declared purpose is the interpretation of Jesus' proclamation that *follows upon* and *assumes* the work of history, in a conception of historical Jesus studies as a two-phase process of historical work with the data followed by interpretation of the authentic data. Hence the subtitle of the present chapter, 'post-historiographic structuralism'. Now, whether the historical study of Jesus, or any historical study for that matter, is legitimately conceived as such a two-phase process is a question I will take up in due course (I said above that the conception *seems* perfectly reasonable, and it is not without a pedigree). What I would point out here is that the hermeneutic involved in the interpretation seems to have little if any bearing on the formulation of the presumed historiography. Crossan formulates a structuralist hermeneutic, which as we have seen usually brackets the question of history in relation to the interpretation of the text, because language is seen as a closed, self-referential system. Any reference to historical persons or events is imposing an illegitimate extra-linguistic referent onto language. Crossan even goes beyond typical structuralist claims in adopting an ontology that confines reality to language, a move usually characteristic of some post-structuralists, as we have seen. But Crossan's historiography seems impervious to these hermeneutical and ontological moves, and continues to operate on the assumption that what is sought is a real historical, extra-linguistic referent, the authentic words of the real historical Jesus of Nazareth. He embraces a hermeneutic that denies the historical referent, and an ontology that denies extra-linguistic reality, along with a historiography that assumes both such a referent and a reality. Brown and Malbon note that Crossan moves from history to language and back to history in these early works. He identifies the authentic words of Jesus in order to analyse them linguistically (synchronically), but then wants to determine the function of the language in its historical, and current, situation. It may be that there is an attempt on Crossan's part at a genuine dialectic between a structuralist hermeneutic and a historical method that is typically foreign to it.[74] But the theoretical justification for the connection of history with literary theory is at best unclear.[75]

In the works where post-structuralist concerns come more explicitly to the fore, polyvalence of texts is an essential feature. But several commentators have pointed out difficulties between this theory and historical method in Crossan. In the essay on the Sower parable, for example, Crossan proceeds to uncover univalence in this parable in order to illustrate its message of polyvalence. That is, he offers a univocal interpretation while insisting on an essential polyvalence.[76] This seems to amount to the rooting of the notion of polyvalence in the univalence of the historical figure of Jesus and a univalent interpretation of his parables: 'In the name of paradox and freeplay [Crossan] actually presents a normative and "canonical" interpretation. If one is really willing to follow ludic semiotics and freeplay wherever they lead, one must be willing to follow them away from the attempt to create an origin, away from a reconstruction of the historical Jesus.'[77]

It is difficult to avoid the impression that Crossan himself became aware of difficulties encroaching upon his historical method as a result of his post-structuralist hermeneutic. After *Cliffs* we find his most explicit reliance upon Derridean deconstruction in a 1982 essay.[78] But after this, post-structuralist theory effectively disappears from Crossan's historical work.[79] In a later interview he was asked about

74. David Fisher makes a case for this being precisely Crossan's strength, 'The Pleasures of Allegory', pp. 298-307.

75. Brown and Malbon, p. 535. Crossan recalls in his memoirs an exchange he had with Norman Perrin in 1976. Upon reading *Raid on the Articulate* Perrin noted, to Crossan's chagrin, that Crossan was leaving New Testament studies for literary criticism. This, Crossan says, caused him to reconsider his long-range plans for experimentation in literary theory. See *Tipperary*, p. 172.

76. See Moore, *Literary Criticism*, p. 145: We see in *Cliffs* 'a plurivocity of premises on the part of its author that subverts the univocity of his own argument'. Moore says this results in a deconstructionist criticism that is weak compared to most American deconstructors, and a historical criticism that many would see as irresponsible, p. 148.

77. Mary Ann Tolbert, 'Polyvalence and the Parables: A Consideration of J.D. Crossan's *Cliffs of Fall*', *SBL 1980 Seminar Papers* (ed. Paul J. Achtemeier; Chico, CA: Scholars Press, 1980), p. 67.

78. Especially Derrida's notion of *différance*: Crossan, 'Difference and Divinity', *Semeia* 23 (1982), pp. 29-40.

79. Stephen Moore and Susan Lochrie Graham note the post-modernist Jesus of the early Crossan, as well as the change in course: 'After *Cliffs of Fall* Crossan adjusted his tie, smoothed down his hair, and began the more respectable line of research that would eventually result in *The Historical Jesus*, with its correspondingly serious protagonist', Moore and Graham, 'The Quest of the New Historicist Jesus', *Biblical Interpretation* 5 (1997), p. 455. Their evaluation of the change is of course meant to be ironic, coming as they do from a New Historicist perspective.

the relationship of his later historical Jesus work to his earlier structuralist work on the parables of Jesus. He insisted, consistent with what we have observed, that his interest had always been in the historical Jesus, and he used structuralist method as long as it was helpful in trying to understand Jesus' parables. When the method ceased being useful, he abandoned it.[80] 'Methods are helpful only to the extent that they help us understand. If you have to spend more time explaining the method than you do putting it to use, it's probably not a good method.'[81] But we have noted more than a superficial use of a structuralist *method* in the early Crossan. He seems to have had much more at stake in (post-)structuralism than a useful tool for understanding a historical figure, a negative theological orientation being one possibility.

But whatever investment Crossan had in his early hermeneutic, and whatever his reasons for quitting it, we can take away from this early phase two features that endure and tie the two phases of his historical Jesus work together: (1) His historiography remains intact. In fact, we will see in the later Crossan that it gains the ascendancy that previously belonged to hermeneutics, and develops in a direction that is consistent with the course set from the beginning of *In Parables*. (2) Though the (post-)structuralist character of his hermeneutic disappears, his two-part conception of historiography as (a) historical work followed by (b) interpretation (which conception may well have been responsible for his development of a hermeneutic in *isolation* from his historiography) sets a course that will continue to pervade his historiography through *The Historical Jesus* and beyond.

80. In his memoirs, Crossan says that he began his work in the early 1970s, when historical Jesus research focused almost exclusively on Jesus' words; he took up his work in such a milieu, and followed suit. But in the 1980s he began to shift to a wider emphasis not just on Jesus' words, but on his life. See *Tipperary*, pp. 173-74. Whether this wider focus was a cause or a consequence of his abandonment of (post-)structuralism is difficult to say. But the changes are certainly of a piece.

81. Crossan, 'The Historical Jesus: An Interview with John Dominic Crossan', *The Christian Century* 108 (December 18-25, 1991), p. 1200.

Chapter 2

THE LATER CROSSAN: THE INTERDISCIPLINARY APPROACH

Continuing an essentially diachronic analysis of Crossan's work, I will now change course and, rather than structuring the presentation according to the chronological sequence of individual published works as in the early Crossan, will treat his work in two large groups. Within each group, historiographic and hermeneutical issues will be viewed more or less synchronically. I have noted that Crossan's works between *Cliffs of Fall* and *The Historical Jesus* can be treated as a transition phase. This will be the first group, followed by the works including and after *The Historical Jesus*. In the latter group we find the 'later Crossan', the mature expression of Crossan's historiography, and while it is further explained and defended throughout that period, within it we find no new methodological developments.

1. *Transition*

The period between the early and later phases opens with a study of Jesus' aphorisms bearing a title (*In Fragments*) reminiscent of Crossan's first work on the historical Jesus (*In Parables*). Crossan says the resemblance is deliberate. His earlier studies of the parables had shown their polyvalent nature. The original parables of the historical Jesus were such that their subsequent reinterpretation in the tradition was in a sense the inevitable response to the parabolic challenge. The radical paradoxicality of the parables positively invoked the divergent versions of them that later came about. In view of this, 'the problem of the historical Jesus thereby translates and transforms itself into the problem of the hermeneutical Jesus. Instead of the multiplicity of textual interpretations cutting the tradition off from the parabler himself, its very plurality links it most fully to the creative matrix from which it came. Polyvalence is not the parable's failure or betrayal, but rather its victory and success.'[1] What was the earlier Crossan's quest for interpretation of the authentic parables of Jesus is now a quest to understand the process of transmission that resulted from Jesus' words; and the transmission was in a very important sense a *result* of the original. The paradoxical and polyvalent parables necessarily resulted in variety in their transmission.

I noted in the last chapter that, after *Cliffs of Fall*, Crossan seems to abandon a structuralist method of literary analysis and a post-structuralist hermeneutic and

---

1. Crossan, *In Fragments: The Aphorisms of Jesus* (San Francisco: Harper & Row, 1983), p. vii.

ontology. Yet in this 'transition' phase, the conclusions he had drawn earlier from such a methodological and philosophical milieu continue to inform his understanding of the nature of Jesus' speech and actions, and turn his attention to the ramifications of that nature for the character of the subsequent Jesus tradition. Indeed, his stated focus in *In Fragments* and the other major work of the period, *Four Other Gospels*, is not the recovery and interpretation of the original words of Jesus, but examination of how the tradition handles its materials.[2] With *In Fragments*, this amounts to a typology of the aphoristic tradition, recalling the broader categorization of forms that Bultmann had laid down in his *History of the Synoptic Tradition*. In *Four Other Gospels* Crossan examines four sources outside the canon (*Gospel of Thomas*, Secret Mark,[3] Egerton Papyrus 2, *Gospel of Peter*) for their relation to the canonical Gospels, by means of source-critical analysis of key passages. In *The Cross that Spoke* he locates the origin of the canonical passion narratives in the Cross Gospel, a source that he finds embedded in the Gospel of Peter.[4]

So the nature of the historical Jesus' speech transforms the problem of the historical Jesus into the problem of the hermeneutical Jesus, or the problem of how Jesus was variously interpreted. The resulting focus on the process of transmission Crossan calls 'transmissional analysis',[5] though it seems not to differ substantially from what is usually called 'tradition criticism', which is what we saw in the early Crossan, in his determination of the authentic form of Jesus' parables, in a historical criticism that was prior to literary or philosophical interpretation. As we have seen, uncovering the history of transmission of a piece of tradition has always been central to Crossan's historical method. That it is the transmission itself that he is most concerned with at this stage, does not mean that he has simply bracketed his interest in the historical Jesus. Transmissional analysis is always done with an eye to the historical Jesus, inasmuch as analysis of how traditions are handled in transmission assumes an original version of the tradition that was transmitted, revised and reinterpreted. At one point Crossan stresses that his practice of transmissional analysis assumes an emphasis that distinguishes it from two other transmissional emphases. There is the *primal* emphasis, which seeks to recover the original word or deed by removing layers of tradition. There is the *final* emphasis, which focuses on the final form of the tradition in its current context; transmissional analysis is here done in order better to understand the final author's redaction. Then there is the *hermeneutical* emphasis, which is concerned with the process that connects the

---

2.   Crossan, *Fragments*, p. viii; also *Four Other Gospels: Shadows on the Contours of the Canon* (Minneapolis: Winston Press, 1985), pp. 9-10.

3.   Crossan's evaluation of the legitimacy of Secret Mark is based on the work of Morton Smith, whose conclusions on that source are controversial; many scholars doubt the document's authenticity. Jacob Neusner, who had previously praised Smith's work on Secret Mark, has lately pronounced the document a fraud. See Neusner's foreward in Birger Gerhardsson, *Memory and Manuscript: Oral Tradition and Written Transmission in Rabbinic Judaism and Early Christianity with Tradition and Transmission in Early Christianity* (Grand Rapids: Eerdmans; Livonia, MI: Dove Booksellers, 1998), p. xxvii.

4.   Crossan, *The Cross that Spoke: The Origins of the Passion Narrative* (San Francisco: Harper & Row, 1988).

5.   Crossan, *Fragments*, p. 9; *Four Other Gospels*, p. 7.

primal with the final. Crossan says the hermeneutical emphasis, which is his chosen emphasis, absorbs the other two as it discovers interpretations and applications that arose in the traditioning process.[6] Of course, interpretations and applications can be identified and appreciated only in relation to an original. The notion of an authentic form is inherent even in an analysis that is primarily occupied with the traditioning process itself.

In Crossan's analysis of the aphorisms of Jesus, the underlying concern for an original reveals itself in a description of the nature of the transmission of aphorisms. Jesus' aphorisms were both initially spoken and eventually transmitted in a context of oral sensibility, as opposed to scribal sensibility. Scribal sensibility is oriented to exact sequence of words and precise syntax, while oral sensibility is oriented to *sense* over sequence, and *structure* over syntax. Oral repetition remembers and repeats structures, not words, *ipsissima structura* not *ipsissima verba*. In the sources on Jesus we are dealing with a transition moment between an oral and a scribal sensibility, 'with the mechanics of a *writer* for whom *orality* is still quite dominant',[7] or, with scribal transmission within a basic oral sensibility. In such an environment, the basic unit of transmission is not the *ipsissima verba* of an aphoristic saying, but the *ipsissima structura* of an aphoristic core. Aphorisms uttered and passed on in this oral sensibility consisted of, not precise words, but a structure or core that was subject to multiple variations. So in analysing the transmission of Jesus' aphorisms, the original against which variations are seen to be such, is a core or structure, rather than a complete saying. An example of such a core is *For and Against* (in Mark, appearing as 'He that is not for us is against us'), a core which has three independent attestations, in Mk 9.40, Q 11.23, and Oxy P 1224. In all, Crossan identifies a corpus of 133 aphoristic cores with attestation in Mark and Q.[8]

On the one hand, the handling of aphoristic material in terms of a core from which variations are identified is simply a necessary tradition-critical move at this stage in Crossan's work. His previous work on parables could handle parabolic material by means of tradition criticism with little concern for identification of something like a 'parabolic core'. Parables lend themselves to tradition-critical analysis in that, generally, the various versions of a parable can easily be seen to be such. A parable is relatively simple to identify throughout its variations, so examining the variations for determination of the original form requires little specific effort at determining what counts as a version of the parable. But with aphorisms, identification of 'versions' is not so clear-cut. This situation is borne out by Crossan's insistence that it is not appropriate to identify an original saying behind versions of an aphorism, but rather an original core or structure; and even the original core does not contain a determinate original meaning from which the versions deviate.[9] Versions vary enough in form and content that they must be grouped according to a discernible core before they can be subject to transmissional analy-

6. Crossan, *Four Other Gospels*, p. 9.
7. Crossan, *Fragments*, p. 39.
8. Due to the abundance of Jesus' aphorisms in many sources, Crossan limits his analysis to aphoristic cores attested in these sources for the sake of time and space, *Fragments*, p. viii.
9. Crossan, *Fragments*, p. 41.

sis. The aphoristic core is a necessary methodological tool for Crossan as he takes up tradition criticism in relation to the aphorisms.

But there are other significant developments in method taking place here. The notion of grouping sayings according to core structure is the beginning of what will become for Crossan the important device of working with traditions in *complexes*. We will see in *The Historical Jesus* that complexes are a key feature of Crossan's mature method. *In Fragments* includes an index of the aphorisms treated in that work, listed according to an assigned number and aphorism title (like that mentioned above, 71, *For and Against*, and others such as 19, *Kingdom and Children* and 27, *Blessed the Poor*). This is something like an early version of the inventory of complexes found later in appendix 1 of *The Historical Jesus*. But it is clear here that complexes are a necessary device if one is to handle all the traditions fundamentally in a tradition-critical manner. Analysing material for the purpose of determining an original version behind extant variations (or similarly, for the purpose of determining how the extant variations reinterpreted an original) requires an initial grouping of materials that are more or less similar in form, structure, or content, on the assumption that similarities reflect an original to which the extant materials are, as it were, genetically related. So, since tradition criticism applied to aphorisms necessitates the aphoristic core, so the latter development presages what will result when tradition criticism is applied to the whole tradition: the organization of material into complexes.

If a tradition-critical approach to the data results in complexes, the approach is in turn a result of what Crossan sees as a basic historiographic problem in the data on Jesus, the existence of parallels. I have noted that in the early Crossan the presence of multiple versions of the same unit of tradition is a feature in the sources that cries out for explanation. *In Parables* presents that feature as the point of departure for Crossan's description of historical method;[10] in *Raid on the Articulate*, it was the problem area that offered the best hope for a solution to the problem of the historical Jesus.[11] In this transition period, where tradition criticism in the form of transmissional analysis is being further developed, the fact of parallels is prominent, and its role as the impetus for Crossan's tradition-critical orientation emerges most strongly. It is in this period that he designed and edited a compilation of *Sayings Parallels*, consisting of sayings of Jesus arranged according to their parallel attestations in various sources, both intra- and extracanonical, in a form similar to a Gospel synopsis. In the Preface he notes the book's 'existence and structure derives from one basic postulate: *the exact same unit often appears in different sources, genres, and versions within the Jesus tradition.* That is what is meant by parallel sayings.'[12] After being read holistically for nearly two thousand years, the recognition of parallelism of the same unit in different sources, genres and versions calls for the sources to be read horizontally, across the entire corpus, rather than vertically, down each source individually. The arrangement of *Sayings Parallels* is

---

10. See above, p. 20.
11. See above, p. 30.
12. Crossan, *Sayings Parallels: A Workbook for the Jesus Tradition* (Philadelphia: Fortress Press, 1986), p. xiii.

intended to facilitate discussion of an explanation for these parallels. Though Crossan does not wish to offer in this work any particular explanation for the existence of parallels (it is a *work*book, not a textbook), that he would compile and publish an exhaustive listing of them indicates their significance for him as a phenomenon in the data (which I will comment on below). If his methodological developments up to this time are any indication, parallels are to be accounted for at least partly by means of tradition criticism: different versions of a tradition are variations on a single historical core, either a core structure as with the aphorisms, or an original narrative form of the parables. The answer that Crossan offers to the parallels' cry for explanation is the one found in a tradition-critical orientation to the data.

Before we leave the transition period, one other significant development requires our attention. In the early Crossan we saw the prominence of the criterion of dissimilarity, used in conjunction with tradition criticism, the classical methodological model as outlined by Perrin. The various versions of a unit are analysed for how they made adaptations and changes to an original version, and to the original is applied the criterion of dissimilarity, to determine if it originated with Jesus and not with an early Jesus community. But by the late 1980s Crossan had become sceptical of the usefulness of the criterion of dissimilarity in Jesus research, due to the character of early Judaism and Christianity with which the criterion would compare Jesus. Research had come to show that ancient Judaism and Christianity were both too variegated to serve as foils from which Jesus could be seen to be dissimilar. For example, both apocalyptic and sapiential interpretations of Jesus can be detected in the earliest traditions. This being the case, one could not legitimately posit dissimilarity of either of these interpretations from the other as a support for their historicity. Since there is not enough continuity in early Christianity or Judaism to see Jesus as clearly dissimilar from either of them, Crossan instead proposes a criterion of *adequacy* as an alternative 'first principle' in Jesus studies. In view of the given multiplicity that characterizes the tradition, 'that is original which best explains the multiplicity engendered in the tradition'.[13] Crossan is seeking to uncover what Jesus could have originally said and done that would have engendered such multiplicity. 'I am trying to imagine words and deeds that could have been, plausibly and persuasively, sincerely and honestly, interpreted in [opposing] directions by different followers at the same time.'[14] This revision of the criterion of dissimilarity is clearly of a piece with the problem of the 'hermeneutical Jesus', the problem of how Jesus was variously reinterpreted in the tradition, and the consequent focus on the process of transmission that emerges in this stage of Crossan's thinking. At the same time, as a criterion for Jesus research it reflects a refocusing onto the historical figure who is always in the background, always assumed in Crossan's transmissional analysis. But as a means of recovering the original figure that engendered the traditions, the criterion of adequacy represents a certain explicit relinquishment of Crossan's earlier interpretation of Jesus' parables. The earlier interpretation would explain the multiplicity in the tradition by

13. Crossan, 'Divine Immediacy and Human Immediacy: Towards a New First Principle in Historical Jesus Research', *Semeia* 41 (1988), p. 125.
14. Crossan, 'Divine Immediacy', p. 125.

positing a polyvalence in the original, rooted in a post-structuralist void of meaning. It would see the multiplicity as the inevitable and appropriate response to the radical paradoxicality that characterized Jesus' speech, the self-reversing nature of the metaparable that negates not only the hearers' world but also the parable itself and the parabler himself, in view of the aniconic transcendent God who must be experienced since he cannot be captured in law, wisdom or language. But the newly formulated criterion of adequacy appears to look for a new understanding of Jesus' proclamation and deeds, some other way of explaining the multiplicity than by suggesting a self-negating original. I noted in Chapter One that Crossan has acknowledged abandoning (post-)structuralist method when it ceased being useful for interpreting Jesus' parables. It would appear that this new criterion signals the abandonment of their resulting understanding of Jesus as well.

2. *Mature Method*

In a discussion of methodology in *The Birth of Christianity*, Crossan describes his work on the historical Jesus, begun in 1969, as taking place on two fronts: materials and methods. 'On materials, I have studied parables and aphorisms, as well as intracanonical and extracanonical gospels. On methods, I started with historical criticism, next incorporated literary criticism, and finally added macrosociological criticism to form an integrated interdisciplinary model.'[15] We have seen the developments in materials through the early and transition periods: beginning with Jesus' parables, later moving to the aphorisms, always open to all sources without regard for canonical status (the *Gospel of Thomas* has been included in the inventory of traditions since *In Parables*), but later intentionally expanding the inventory of possible sources (*Four Other Gospels*). But methodological developments have been our particular concern, and we have noticed the consistent but increasingly sophisticated use of tradition criticism, along with methods of literary criticism in the early phase that seem to drop away by the end of the transition period. What Crossan now describes as an integrated interdisciplinary model represents the culmination of his methodological development. I will describe the details of that model, along with Crossan's portrait of the historical Jesus that it produces, and the model's relation to Crossan's stated hermeneutic at this stage.

2.1. *The Interdisciplinary Method*
Though Crossan's work since *In Parables* has always sought refinement of method, his most explicit expression of the need for methodological attention is found in the work in which he most clearly outlines his fully developed method, *The Historical*

---

15. Crossan, *The Birth of Christianity: Discovering What Happened in the Years Immediately After the Execution of Jesus* (San Francisco: HarperSanFrancisco, 1998), p. 139. Of course, the 'literary criticism' that Crossan refers to here is the type associated with form and redaction criticism and the determination of genetic relations among the sources. Such was the sense of the term 'literary' before the development of the properly literary methods in the 1970s, such as structuralism, post-structuralism and narrative criticism. Crossan certainly experimented with the latter, but, as we have seen, did not keep up the experimentation.

Jesus. In that work he notes the variety among current portraits of the historical Jesus, a situation that is a cause for academic embarrassment. This diversity demands attention to questions of method, and for Crossan, the answers to those questions are rooted in a conception of historiography modelled on an archaeological dig, with chronological stratification of materials as the necessary organizing principle. Without such organization, individual traditions, like artefacts from a dig, can be taken to support whatever conclusion the historian/archaeologist wishes. It is within this general stratigraphic conception that Crossan proposes his three-tiered method.

His method recognizes three levels of historical work. The broadest is the *macrocosmic* level, utilizing contemporary research in the area of cross-cultural and cross-temporal social anthropology. Crossan draws on several anthropological models, two of the most significant being the pan-Mediterranean models of patronage and clientage as the basis of Mediterranean political life,[16] and honour and shame as fundamental Mediterranean values.[17] Next is the *mesocosmic* level, consisting of the immediate historical context of Jesus of Nazareth, the situation in first-century Greco-Roman history. The *microcosmic* level consists of the literature concerning Jesus. It is to this level that Crossan devotes most of his methodological discussion. What makes these three areas of investigation 'levels' is the contextual function of each higher level in relation to the next lower level, such that the three operate as concentric circles. Work on the lowest, textual level (the innermost circle) reveals data relevant to the historical Jesus; these data are then interpreted within the outer circles, in light of first-century Greco-Roman history, and of the most universalizable anthropological models, in a way appropriate to the historical contextualization of data. This procedure is clearly operative in Crossan's presentation in *The Historical Jesus*, though for effect of presentation the three levels are reversed. Parts I ('Brokered Kingdom') and II ('Embattled Brokerage') establish the broadly Mediterranean and specifically first-century historic context for locating Jesus, followed by Part III ('Brokerless Kingdom'), in which the traditions on Jesus are set within this context and read in light of it. But the levels can also be seen as independent and mutually reinforcing 'vectors'. At one point, Crossan says his method 'locates the historical Jesus where three independent vectors cross. That triangulation serves as internal discipline and mutual corrective, since all must intersect at the same point for any of them to be correct.'[18] This understanding of the three areas as independent and mutually supportive is crucial, and will form an important part of our analysis.

The level of textual analysis is most significant, such that 'any study of the historical Jesus stands or falls on how one handles the literary level of the text itself'.[19] Closest attention to the handling of the sources is necessary because of the existence of parallel traditions, and in this we see the orientation that has always driven

16. Crossan, *The Historical* Jesus, pp. 65ff.

17. Crossan, *The Historical Jesus*, pp. 9ff.

18. Crossan, *Jesus: A Revolutionary Biography* (San Francisco: HarperSanFrancisco, 1994), p. xi.

19. Crossan, *The Historical Jesus*, p. xxix.

Crossan's method. But there is also the theological nature of the sources on Jesus. Crossan presents as the basis for his textual work the long-recognized observation that the Gospels were written for the purpose of proclaiming 'good news'. They were the theological interpretations of the tradition by the early Jesus communities, and as such reflect three major layers: *retention* of authentic data on the historical Jesus, *development* of those data by application to new situations, and the eventual *creation* of new traditions. The problem the historian faces in handling the sources on Jesus is how to search back through the sedimented layers of the gospels to find what Jesus actually said and did. This search is facilitated by specific methodological moves.

These moves involve first of all compiling an inventory of all relevant sources and texts (those sources both inside and outside the New Testament canon), in their historical and literary relationships. The latter qualification involves specifying not only extant sources, but also one's view of the interrelationships among those sources, e.g., Markan priority and the existence of Q. These interrelationships necessitate the positing of non-extant but recovered sources such as Q and the Cross Gospel (as recovered in Crossan's earlier *The Cross that Spoke*). Once the inventory of possible sources is specified, it is established within four chronological layers, based on the discernible date of composition of each source. Crossan specifies the dates of the layers, or strata, as CE 30–60, 60–80, 80–120, 120–150. Finally, the traditions from the stratified sources are grouped according to complexes (rather than individual units of tradition), and each complex is noted for the number of times it is attested in *independent* sources (e.g., Mark, Q, *Gospel of Thomas*).[20]

This inventory of stratified and multiply attested complexes is handled according to three principles, which produce the database of Jesus tradition with which Crossan works. The first principle is attention to the *sequence of strata* attested in the complexes. This is mostly recognition of the importance of the first stratum; Crossan limits himself to complexes with attestation in this stratum when formulating a working hypothesis on the historical Jesus, which can then be tested against the subsequent strata. Any judgements on complexes attested no earlier than the second, third or fourth strata are made only in light of the judgements made on the basis of attestation in the first stratum. The second principle is *hierarchy of attestation*. This is the recognition of the importance of those complexes having the highest count of independent attestation, based on the sources as specified in the initial inventory. The more highly attested a complex, the greater claim it may have to authenticity. Crossan's initial inventory of sources is important at this stage, because it largely determines whether parallel versions of a complex are independent attestations of the material in question, or whether they are dependent and so do not qualify as multiple attestations. For example, much of the double-tradition material in the synoptics (parallel material in Matthew and Luke) is counted not as double attestation of a single unit, but as a single attestation in the one source Q. Similarly, much of the triple tradition material (parallels in Matthew, Mark and Luke) is considered not triple attestation of the given tradition, but single attestation

---

20. Crossan, *The Historical Jesus*, p. xxxi.

in the one source, Mark.[21] Closely related to hierarchy of attestation is the third principle, the *bracketing of singularity*. Crossan completely avoids any complex that is only singly attested, even if that attestation is in the first stratum. He considers this an important safeguard, since a unit found in at least two independent sources in the first stratum could not have been created by either of the sources.[22] Ultimately, Crossan identifies a corpus of 522 complexes, about a third of which are more than singly attested.

Examining each complex according to these three principles yields results that can be specified by a pair of numbers, the first indicating the earliest stratum in which the complex is attested, and the second indicating the total number of independent attestations of the complex throughout all strata. For example, complex 20 *Kingdom and Children* is attested in the first stratum (*Gos. Thom.* 22.1-2) and is independently attested four times (once in each stratum), and so is designated [1/4]. This tabulation allows one to note quickly for a given complex what are the key indicators of its authenticity for Crossan: date of earliest attestation and number of independent attestations. The lower the first number, and the higher the second, the more likely the complex reflects material authentic to Jesus.[23] In addition to designating each complex with an attestation index number, Crossan also specifies his determination of authenticity on the complex with one of three signs: +, –, or ±. The first indicates a positive judgement of historicity: the core of the complex derives from the historical Jesus (though of course the same could not be said of all its various versions within the complex; only the core theme is judged to be from Jesus). The second sign indicates that the core of the complex does not derive from Jesus but from later Jesus tradition. The third sign is intended to show that 'the action or happening did not occur as an event at one moment in time or place (hence –) but that it represents a dramatic historicization of something that took place over a much longer period (hence +).'[24] Material in this last category reflects processes that were dramatically incarnated in events.

2.2. *The Resulting Portrait*
Crossan uses this three-level model of historical method to paint a portrait of the historical Jesus that has by now become well known among Jesus scholars. In a sketch of that portrait we can see how aspects of his model are applied.[25]

---

21. Much of the double- and triple-tradition material is so treated by Crossan, but not all of it. A few examples: Complex 19 *What Goes In* is found in Mk 7.14-15 and in Mt. 15.10-11. But Crossan does not take these two occurrences as only one attestation, that of Mark upon which Matthew is dependent, but rather as two independent attestations, one in the second and one in the third stratum. Complex 20 *Kingdom and Children* is found in the unit in Mk 10.13-16 and its parallels as one attestation, but is in fact multiply attested by the similar saying on children in Mt. 18.3. Complex 22 *Prophet's Own Country* is a triple tradition passage in the synoptics (Mk 6.1-6 pars.) but Crossan counts the Mark–Matthew versions as one attestation, and the Luke version as an independent attestation. See the inventory in *The Historical Jesus*, p. 436.

22. Crossan, *The Historical Jesus*, pp. xxxii-xxxiii.

23. Crossan, *The Historical Jesus*, pp. xxxiii-xxxiv.

24. Crossan, *The Historical Jesus*, p. 434.

25. This sketch is drawn from *The Historical Jesus*. The popular version of that work, *Jesus: A*

Based on triple independent attestation of the *John Baptizes Jesus* complex, and a reasoning similar to the 'criterion of embarrassment',[26] Crossan concludes that Jesus' baptism by John is one of the surest things we know about them both.[27] But John's message and baptism had nothing to do with Jesus; rather, John was announcing imminent apocalyptic intervention by God and not Jesus. Jesus originally endorsed John's message, but later changed his view, after John's death, to the importance of being in the kingdom. Crossan suggests two possible contexts for a first-century understanding of 'Kingdom of God' (the exact phrase most likely used by Jesus): apocalyptic or sapiential. The apocalyptic option was real, as first-century sources demonstrate. But so was the sapiential option. He notes references to wisdom in association with kingdom in Philo, Wisdom of Solomon and Sentences of Sextus.[28]

Crossan creates a fourfold typology of Kingdom of God conceptions among Jews in the first century, based on the crossing of apocalyptic and sapiential conceptions with the anthropological class distinctions of peasant and retainer. The result is the apocalyptic and sapiential options existing in both classes. Here Crossan clarifies the distinction between apocalyptic and sapiential. Apocalyptic is concerned with a future kingdom brought about solely by divine action, which will be visible to all. Sapiential is concerned with an ethical kingdom in the present, characterized by a style of life rather than a hope for the future. Crossan insists that both conceptions can be 'eschatological', by which he means that both can be radically world-negating. The justification for the class distinction among kingdom conceptions is based on the distinction between *proclaimed* and *performed* apocalypses. The proclaimed apocalypses were the written ones of the retainer class; the performed apocalypses were the enactions of the millennial prophets and possibly even the messianic claimants, all of whom were apparently of the peasant class. On the basis of this distinction, Crossan concludes 'those twin modes of the millennial vision should be matched with twin modes of the sapiential dream.'[29]

Jesus' proclamation of the kingdom of God is located in this typology, as a peasant, sapiential kingdom; that is, the kingdom not as apocalyptic event but as sapiential mode of life, and as a kingdom of 'nobodies'. Based on analysis of the complexes *Kingdom and Children*, *Blessed the Poor* and *Kingdom and Riches*, Crossan determines that Jesus' conception of the kingdom was a kingdom of the Unclean, Degraded and Expendable classes. He notes in both forms of *The Feast*

Revolutionary Biography, contains a condensed version, but even briefer sketches by Crossan can be found in Crossan, *Who Killed Jesus? Exposing the Roots of Anti-Semitism in the Gospel Story of the Death of Jesus* (San Francisco: HarperSanFrancisco, 1995), pp. 211-12; and Crossan and Richard G. Watts, *Who Is Jesus? Answers to Your Questions about the Historical Jesus* (Louisville, KY: Westminster/John Knox Press, 1999), pp. 135-36.

26. Jesus' being baptized by John would imply that the Baptist was superior to Jesus, so preservation of the tradition speaks in favour of its authenticity, particularly since later tradition tended to employ theological 'damage control' by highlighting Jesus' subsequent epiphany and giving explicit theological reasons for Jesus' baptism.

27. Crossan, *The Historical Jesus*, p. 234.

28. Crossan, *The Historical Jesus*, pp. 287-91.

29. Crossan, *The Historical Jesus*, p. 292.

parable (Q [Lk.] 14.15-24 and *Gos. Thom.* 64) a common plot structure and a common concern to invite the poor, maimed, lame and blind. Crossan sees this as advocating an egalitarian commensality, in the midst of the honour and shame ideology of Mediterranean society. Jesus practised open table fellowship that enacted his message of an egalitarian kingdom, disregarding distinctions of purity and hierarchies of power. Since it was possible for early Christians to debate about whether Jesus was for or against ritual food laws, Crossan proposes that Jesus' position in itself must have been unclear on them. Jesus must have simply *ignored* the food laws; but such would have been a fundamental subversion of them. 'Open commensality profoundly negates distinctions and hierarchies between female and male, poor and rich, Gentile and Jew. It does so, indeed, at a level that would offend the ritual laws of *any* civilized society. That was precisely its challenge.'[30]

Jesus enacted his egalitarian kingdom not only in his open commensality, but also in his performance of miracles, which Crossan classifies as 'magic' to connote their subversive nature vis-à-vis established religious hierarchies. He notes that magic is to religion as banditry is to politics. Banditry calls into question the assumed moral basis of aristocratic and structural violence. It takes from the rich and gives to the poor, if not wealth, then at least the monopoly on violence. It forces the question of what the moral difference is between an official army and an outlaw gang. 'As banditry challenges the ultimate legitimacy of political power, so magic challenges that of spiritual power... Religion is official and approved magic; magic is unofficial and unapproved religion. More simply: "we" practice religion, "they" practice magic. The question is not whether magicians are for or against official religion. Their very existence, totally apart from such intentions, is a challenge to its validity and exclusivity.'[31] Magic is subversive, unofficial, unapproved and lower-class religion. So magic and religion are political and prescriptive terms, not descriptive terms. By curing people with his magic, apart from official religious structures, Jesus challenged those structures. In a wider sense, he challenged the system of brokerage between patron and client that characterizes Mediterranean society.[32] He offered direct, unmediated access to God in divine healing.

The three texts of the 'mission discourse' (*Gos. Thom.* 14.2, 1Q, Mk 6.7-13) are where the heart of the Jesus movement is seen most clearly. Here an explicit connection is made between the Kingdom's unbrokered egalitarianism on the one hand,

30. Crossan, *The Historical Jesus*, pp. 262-63.
31. Crossan, *The Historical Jesus*, p. 305.
32. Without a middle class, Roman society was based on patronage, with the power wielder employing clients, who in turn attract clients, resulting in pyramids of power. The relationship between patron and client could be brokered, with a middleman distributing goods to the clients, and in turn representing the clients to the patron. Crossan cites anthropological studies that find patronage to be the bedrock of political life in the Mediterranean, co-existing with any and all types of government, amounting to 'submission to patron in order to gain access to resources', *The Historical Jesus*, p. 65. Patronage and clientage can be religious and theological as well as social and political, and is in fact usually both. Crossan cites studies of the conjunction between mortal and immortal patrons and brokers. 'Both types seem to have thrived in periods when power was concentrated in the hands of a few, when economic and political uncertainty prevailed, when widespread poverty induced dependency', p. 68.

and miracle and table fellowship on the other. Jesus directed his disciples in a mission of radical itinerancy (carrying no purse, living on the donations of others in exchange for healings), as a symbolic representation of unbrokered egalitarianism. It is in this context that Crossan applies his now well-known model of the Cynic to Jesus. The Cynic philosophers of Greco-Roman antiquity were, for Crossan's purposes, characterized particularly by their counter-cultural and itinerant profile. Among Jesus and his followers, open table fellowship and free healing were practised in the context of an itinerancy that would not settle in one place and establish a brokered presence. Free, unbrokered access to God and to one another is the heart of the Kingdom.[33]

Jesus' radical egalitarian message made him the functional opponent of the Temple. His offer of access to God not mediated by temple or priesthood was a lived threat to established religious structures. Jesus' challenge, like the Baptist, was in the form of an independent individual replacing the Temple; but Jesus' itinerancy symbolized his challenge, and made him even more radical than the Baptist. Crossan sees Jesus' Temple 'cleansing' as a symbolic destruction, in which his egalitarianism 'exploded in indignation at the Temple as the seat and symbol of all that was nonegalitarian, patronal, and even oppressive on both the religious and the political level'.[34] This action, performed in the 'confined and tinder-box atmosphere' of the Temple at Passover, was the immediate cause of Jesus' execution by Pilate.

So Crossan interprets Jesus against the background of an inclusive Judaism, and not a literary or sophisticated philosophical inclusivism, but rather a 'peasant, oral, and popular philosophical praxis' form of inclusivism that Crossan calls 'Jewish Cynicism'. Cynics were clearly 'hippies in a world of Augustan yuppies'. Jesus and his followers fit against that counter-cultural background, but not against the specific background of Greco-Roman Cynics. The latter were urban and individualistic, while Jesus was primarily rural, and egalitarian. Jesus was also a magician, which does not fit the Cynic model. In bringing together these disparate elements of magician and Cynic, Crossan offers an effective summary of his portrait of Jesus:

> The historical Jesus was, then, a *peasant Jewish Cynic*. His peasant village was close enough to a Greco-Roman city like Sepphoris that sight and knowledge of Cynicism are neither inexplicable nor unlikely. But his work was among the farms and villages of Lower Galilee. His strategy, implicitly for himself and explicitly for his followers, was the combination of *free healing and common eating*, a religious and economic egalitarianism that negated alike and at once the hierarchical and patronal normalcies of Jewish religion and Roman power. And, lest he himself be interpreted as simply the new broker of a new God, he moved on constantly, settling down neither at Nazareth nor Capernaum. He was neither broker nor mediator, but, somewhat paradoxically, the announcer that neither should exist between humanity and divinity or between humanity and itself. Miracle and parable, healing and eating were calculated to force individuals into

33. Crossan, *The Historical Jesus*, p. 346.
34. Crossan, *The Historical Jesus*, p. 360.

unmediated physical and spiritual contact with God and unmediated physical and spiritual contact with one another. He announced, in other words, the brokerless kingdom of God.[35]

There is a dimension of this representation of Jesus that is immediately obvious, and is worth noting because it parallels certain developments we have seen in Crossan's method. In Crossan's early work, we saw that Jesus' parables were intended, to one degree or another, to subvert or shatter the hearers' world, to allow for the experience of the transcendent. All of reality, all absolutes, including ethical ones, are relativized by radical paradox. Paradox carries with it the real danger of nihilism, and Jesus' parables as paradoxical suffer the danger of nihilistic misinterpretation. Jesus in fact came close to ignoring practical morality, in favour of fundamental morality, which is a dwelling with God that is morality's proper ground. This negation of the ethical is of a piece with the aniconic nature of God, who cannot be captured in any image, language, concept, or morality. When all of world is subverted and relativized, then the Wholly Other God can be experienced.

Clearly, the relativizing of the ethical is no longer a characteristic of Crossan's Jesus portrait in *The Historical Jesus*. Rather than offering an experience of the transcendent, albeit one that serves as a 'fundamental morality', Jesus is here offering an alternative social vision, though one that is not without a religious dimension. Jesus' Kingdom proclamation in the later Crossan is about the brokerless Kingdom of God, particularly, what the *world* would look like if God were in direct, immediate control.[36] This later understanding of Jesus can be seen as a revolutionary social programme growing out of Jesus' understanding of God's immediate presence, as opposed to an experience of God that grounds but also fundamentally relativizes ethical norms. There is no danger of a nihilistic misinterpretation of Jesus in the later Crossan. Indeed, his moral vision is so explicit that it threatens and challenges the honour/shame and patron/client/broker structures of Mediterranean society.

This considerable shift of emphasis, from a mostly asocial experience of the transcendent to revolutionary social vision, is as difficult to account for as is Crossan's abandonment of his earlier (post-)structuralist orientation.[37] There is a certain theological consistency between the earlier negative-theological emphasis on God's aniconicity and the later understanding of God's presence as unmediated or unbrokered. Both have to do with absence of mediators between humanity and God. But the later emphasis on egalitarianism and unmediated contact between people is as thoroughgoing as it is unprecedented in Crossan. He comes to express

---

35. Crossan, *The Historical Jesus*, p. 422.

36. See Crossan's description in 'The Historical Jesus: An Interview with John Dominic Crossan', p. 1203.

37. In a response to Franz Josef van Beeck, who claims that Crossan's Jesus studies must be understood as originating in the New Hermeneutic, Crossan insists that the New Hermeneutic is not helpful as the immediate background to his work. 'My understanding of the social and the political is exactly the opposite to its emphasis on the personal and the existential', 'Responses and Reflections', in *Jesus and Faith*, p. 160. His emphasis in *The Historical Jesus* may be opposite, but, as we have seen, van Beeck's assessment is apropos of the early Crossan.

the ethos behind this social emphasis as a 'sarcophilic' as opposed to a 'sarcophobic' understanding of human being. The sarcophobic understanding sees the human
being as a soul enclosed in a body, resulting in an anthropological dualism that
is dehumanizing, whereas the sarcophilic understanding sees human being as
enfleshed spirit, holding soul and body together in a monistic interaction in which
they can be distinguished but not separated. In *The Birth of Christianity* Crossan
declares that this distinction is the basis for his understanding of Christian origins.
Jesus, along with the traditional Judaism within which he arose, was sarcophilic,
while Paul was sarcophobic. In spite of the fact that he preached that there was no
distinction between Jew and Greek, male and female, slave and free (Gal. 3.28),
Paul gave only spiritual significance to the latter two distinctions; he did not carry
them out to their full 'fleshly' or social implications. Paul was influenced by Pla-
tonic dualism to the point where he could not but compromise the sarcophilic
understanding that characterized Jesus' proclamation.[38] The sarcophilic, in refusing
to separate flesh and spirit, also refuses to separate religion and politics, ethics and
economics, divinity and humanity. Each member of these pairs can only be understood in their interaction with the other.[39]

The social implications of the sarcophilic understanding may help to account for
the shift in Crossan's interpretation of Jesus and his abandonment of (post-)structur-
alism. The latter resulted in an interpretation of Jesus that did not allow for serious
consideration of a social dimension to Jesus' message. The radical negation that
results from radical paradox subverts world in a way that for Crossan now seems to
be inappropriate, for radical negation neglects the ethical by relativizing it. There is
yet an element of negation for Jesus, as we saw in the counter-cultural posture of
the Cynic; but in *Birth of Christianity* this negation becomes even more explicitly
social in its implication, as Crossan comes to describe Jesus' *ethical eschatology*.
Whereas in *The Historical Jesus* Jesus' eschatology is thought best described as
sapiential, now his kingdom proclamation is marked by 'a divinely mandated and
nonviolent resistance to the normalcy of discrimination, exploitation, oppression,
and persecution'.[40] The element of subversion and negation that Crossan has always
seen in Jesus is still present, but it now takes the form of an ethical eschatology that
'negates the world by actively protesting and nonviolently resisting a system judged
to be evil, unjust, and violent'.[41] One can see in the later Crossan a working out of
the social dimension of Jesus' career that Crossan had previously neglected, perhaps because of an overly narrow focus on Jesus' parables, which at the time he
said best encapsulated Jesus' proclamation. Crossan's expanding of his work to the
aphorisms and other materials in the transition phase resulted not only in refinement of method but also in a consequent refinement of his understanding of Jesus.

---

38. Crossan, *Birth*, pp. xxii-xxvii. He presents a similar argument in 'Historical Jesus as Risen
Lord', in *The Jesus Controversy: Perspectives in Conflict* (Harrisburg, PA: Trinity Press International, 1999), pp. 36-43.
39. Crossan, *Birth*, p. xxxii.
40. Crossan, *Birth*, p. 317.
41. Crossan, *Birth*, p. 284.

Chapter 3

THE METHOD CONSIDERED

I have two preliminary observations on Crossan's interdisciplinary model. First, it is called 'interdisciplinary' by virtue of its work in three equally important areas: literary analysis, historical context and social anthropology. These areas and their designation as interdisciplinary require some qualification. Of course, the 'literary' analysis is specifically of the tradition-critical kind, as distinct from the structuralist literary analysis of the early Crossan. This needs to be pointed out because Crossan's observation, with which we began this consideration of his mature method,[1] seems to imply that the literary criticism of the later Crossan is a continuous development from the literary criticism of the early Crossan. We have seen that this is not the case. What in the later Crossan is classified as 'literary criticism' is what was customarily so called in New Testament studies (that is, source, form, redaction and tradition criticism) before the advent of the more widely recognized methods of literary criticism (e.g., structuralism, post-structuralism, narrative criticism, etc.). But possibly more significant is that a perusal of the course of historiography throughout the twentieth century leaves the impression that only in the relatively insular world of New Testament studies could Crossan's method be called 'interdisciplinary'. The social sciences have been featured in historiography generally since the turn of the twentieth century.[2] The status of their use has not been uncontested, as we will see later in our examination of Ben Meyer. But their prominence in twentieth-century historiography has been undeniable.[3] This is not

---

1. See above, p. 48.
2. A standard historiographic text of the early twentieth century (C.V. Langlois and C. Seignobos, *Introduction to the Study of History* [trans. G.G. Berry; New York: Henry Holt and Company, 1898]), describes historical synthesis as 'an application of the descriptive sciences which deal with humanity, descriptive psychology, sociology or social science', p. 224. For these authors, the categories formed by observation in social sciences constitute the a-priori questions by which the facts of history will be ordered.
3. See Georg G. Iggers, *Historiography in the Twentieth Century: From Scientific Objectivity to the Postmodern Challenge* (Hanover, NH: Wesleyan University Press, 1997), who characterizes twentieth-century historiography, at least before the 'postmodern challenge', as aiming for scientific rigour with a social-science orientation that replaced the nineteenth-century concentration on politics and major figures, p. 8. An important constituent in the rise of the social sciences in historiography was the so-called *Annales* school, centred on the French journal of that name (see Iggers, ch. 5). A major contributor was Fernand Braudel, whose *The Mediterranean and the Mediterranean World in the Age of Philip II* Crossan praises as 'huge and magnificent', and valuable for its study of Mediterranean ecology (*The Historical Jesus*, p. 5).

to detract from Crossan's important use of the social sciences in his own work. He is contributing to a significant trend that includes figures such as Gerd Theissen,[4] Richard Horsley[5] and Bruce Malina,[6] among others. But in the context of the larger world of historiography, this trend merely amounts to historically oriented New Testament studies trying to catch up. The social sciences have been a part of historiography for long enough that their use can hardly be considered 'interdisciplinary'. My point in all this is not that Crossan has mischaracterized his method; rather, in the effort to situate historical Jesus studies within the wider historiographic field, one would do well to acknowledge that certain tools are more or less standard, and the sooner we recognize this by routinely incorporating them into our studies the sooner we will benefit from all the tools at our disposal.

My second preliminary observation is more integral to an evaluation of Crossan's method, and has to do with the use of *complexes*. We have seen that their development as a tool for handling the data arose in Crossan's transition phase, as a consequence of a tradition-critical approach to the data. If one is to compare traditions for the purpose of determining an authentic core upon which the different traditions are greater or lesser variations, the traditions will have to be grouped according to common theme or some other similarity or commonality. We see now that the grouping of traditions into complexes is foundational to Crossan's mature method. Rather than trying to demonstrate that Jesus said or did what is contained in any individual unit of tradition, Crossan asks whether the core of a given complex goes back to Jesus, whether Jesus said or did something like what is contained in the complex.[7] But some recent commentators have criticized Crossan's use of complexes, and their criticisms ultimately have to do with how complexes are constituted. Dale Allison has observed Crossan's use of the criterion of multiple attestation in relation to complexes. In Crossan's method, authenticity is supported by multiple attestation of a complex, but Allison argues for its applicability to themes or ideas as well. He notes that even Crossan argues for the authenticity of some singly attested sayings (against his stated intention to bracket those) on the grounds that the sayings attest a common *theme*, even if they are not part of the same complex.[8] Allison takes this as evidence that multiple attestation is legitimately applied to broader themes and motifs, and not just to complexes.[9] I would

---

4. *Sociology of Early Palestinian Christianity* (trans. John Bowden; Philadelphia: Fortress Press, 1978).

5. *Sociology and the Jesus Movement* (New York: Continuum, 2nd edn, 1994).

6. Malina and Richard L. Rohrbaugh, *Social-Science Commentary on the Synoptic Gospels* (Minneapolis: Fortress Press, 1992); also Wolfgang Stegemann, Bruce J. Malina and Gerd Theissen (eds.), *The Social Setting of Jesus and the Gospels* (Minneapolis: Fortress Press, 2001).

7. Crossan, *The Historical Jesus*, p. xxxiii.

8. Dale Allison, *Jesus of Nazareth: Millenarian Prophet* (Minneapolis: Fortress Press, 1998), p. 23.

9. An example of a broader theme that is multiply attested, even if no single traditions bearing the theme are, is that of the apocalyptic Son of Man sayings. Crossan's case against Jesus' eschatology being apocalyptic is built on the fact that none of the complexes that link the Son of Man designation to apocalyptic (six of which are multiply attested) specifically have the Son of Man designation in more than one of their attestations (*The Historical Jesus*, pp. 254-55). However,

conclude that what raises the issue of complexes versus themes in the first instance is the very constitution of complexes. In his analysis of Crossan's method, Christopher Tuckett has noted that complexes are difficult to define, and so problems arise when trying to tabulate numerically how a complex is attested. Complexes seem to be material that is thematically related, but some complexes contain material whose thematic relation is amorphous, and others consist of singly attested sayings which may in fact be thematically related to other complexes to form one multiply attested complex.[10] The consequence of all this is the fact that Crossan's results depend a great deal on what goes into a complex, and what goes into a complex is not a simple matter. Complexes are foundational to Crossan's method because their attestation in terms of both chronology (earliest stratum) and frequency determines what is authentic material, and how a complex is attested depends on what material is allowed into the complex.

Crossan would surely recognize that the determination of a given complex is a matter of scholarly judgement, as are all the 'material investments' that one would make in response to the methodological 'formal moves' he has outlined.[11] But he seems to treat the judgements made in relation to formation of complexes as self-evident: what goes into a complex is simply a matter of what the constituent traditions have in common, and this is more or less plain on its face.[12] But it is in fact not so plain, and is a matter of a type of judgement that leads to a major criticism of Crossan's method. The judgement at work in the determination of what goes into a complex is a judgement involving interpretation and meaning. To determine what goes into a complex, one must engage in certain interpretive judgements regarding the traditions that may be included in the complex. When one observes data in the sources that seem to share some elements, one makes comparative judgements that are bound up with determinations of the data's meaning and significance in relation to the historical object under study. The discussion over 'complexes versus themes' reflects this issue of the role of interpretation when handling the data: how one handles the data (e.g., how one groups complexes or recognizes themes) is bound up with how one understands them. The ramifications of this apparently obvious statement are far-reaching and not so obvious. We will consider them in relation to some details of Crossan's method.

Allison is saying, across all the traditions in all the complexes, the apocalyptic theme is so widely and early attested that it would speak in favour of its presence in Jesus' career.

10. Christopher M. Tuckett, 'The Historical Jesus, Crossan and Methodology', in Stefan Maser and Egbert Schlarb (eds.), *Text und Geschichte* (Marburger Theologische Studien, 50; Marburg: Elwert, 1999), p. 267. Like Allison, Tuckett also notes that Crossan allows for multiple attestation of themes among different singly attested complexes (p. 268).

11. Crossan, *The Historical Jesus*, p. 426.

12. In *Birth of Christianity*, p. 87, he responds to the above kinds of criticisms of his complexes by noting that what he is getting at in forming them is what generally associates terms with one another in the context of an oral sensibility. His complexes identify a *matrix* or *core structure* among traditions, which necessarily exists insofar as it serves to distinguish one tradition from another. This reasoning is similar to what we saw in *In Fragments*, where complexes were first identified.

1. *The Existence of Parallels*

From the earliest stages of Crossan's historical Jesus work, I have noted a feature of the sources that he sees as central to the problem of the historical Jesus: the existence of parallel material. The presence of multiple versions of the same unit is a feature in the sources that cries out for explanation. It would probably not be an exaggeration to say that accounting for parallel materials is the essence of a historical method for Crossan; if it is our best hope for a solution to the problem of the historical Jesus, then it is certainly basic to historical method in that area at least.

The explanation that Crossan offers for the existence of parallels is that of the relations among the sources, particularly relations of literary dependence. Parallel material is accounted for by positing the dependence of one source upon another, or the dependence of both on a common source. On the one hand, such explanations are no different than the efforts over the last two hundred years to deal with the 'synoptic problem'.[13] For example, on the most widely accepted account, the parallels among Matthew, Mark and Luke are best explained by the Two Source Theory, that Matthew and Luke used Mark and Q as sources. But Crossan sees such theories not only as possible explanations of parallels, but as the *necessary presupposition* of any investigation of the historical Jesus. He acknowledged in a published exchange with N.T. Wright, 'The validity of one's Jesus-conclusions stand or fall with that of one's gospel-presuppositions. If mine are wrong, then all is a delusion.'[14] Later, he devotes considerable space in *Birth of Christianity* to explaining the nature of source relationships as foundational to one's historical method and so to one's portrait of the historical Jesus.[15] Due to parallel material, decisions about source relations must be made, and these will affect all subsequent historical work, because source relations reveal genetic relations among traditions. Traditions that are genetically related represent not separate and independent attestations of an event, but actually only one attestation, inasmuch as later traditions simply rely for their information on earlier ones. If we assume that the nature of the sources and their relations to one another are such that later sources used earlier ones, and in such a way that they absorbed them or 'swallowed them whole' then 'the problem of the historical Jesus pushes you back and back along that absorptive path to the earliest stratum of the tradition'.[16] After stating his own presuppositions on the source relations among both intra- and extracanonical material, Crossan notes that those presuppositions form the foundation of that book, and '[N]o scholar who

---

13. Though the problem is usually conceived as a function of the historical consciousness that did not arise until modernity, it has been a problem in one form or another since earliest Christianity. See the exhaustive treatment of the problem in David Laird Dungan, *A History of the Synoptic Problem: The Canon, the Text, the Composition, and the Interpretation of the Gospels* (New York: Doubleday, 1999).

14. Crossan, 'What Victory? What God? A Review Debate with N.T. Wright on *Jesus and the Victory of God*', *Scottish Journal of Theology* 50 (1997), p. 351.

15. Crossan, *Birth*, chs. 7 and 8.

16. Crossan, *Birth*, p. 101.

works on the reconstruction of the historical Jesus or earliest Christianity can avoid making a decision on each of those items. Wrong anywhere there, wrong everywhere thereafter. And that holds for *everyone*.'[17]

I have noted how Crossan's orientation toward a tradition-critical approach to the sources is rooted in the fact of parallel traditions.[18] Not only can parallel material be accounted for by literary source relations, but it also can be explained as variations on a historical core. The difference between these explanations is mostly one of degree: parallels with a high degree of similarity (e.g., verbatim parallels) are explained as genetically related, as literarily dependent. Parallels with less than verbatim similarity can possibly be seen as independent variations on a single historical theme, depending on the degree of similarity. Encompassing both forms of explanation is a tradition criticism that examines the extant versions of a tradition to determine the historical core behind them all. I would also point out that the orientation to tradition criticism is what gives rise to a 'stratified' conception of the data. Tradition criticism observes how an historical core is changed throughout its successive versions, on the assumption that the extant versions are best explained as successively later editions of an original, historical core. These later editions can be thought of as layers, or strata, that the historian must dig through to arrive at the core upon which they have accumulated. This is precisely how Crossan puts the historical problem when he describes the Jesus tradition as containing the three layers of retention, development and creation, requiring that the historian search back through those layers to determine what Jesus actually said and did.[19]

Now, in the world of New Testament studies, the need for an explanation of parallel materials is largely self-evident. An historical approach to the data would seem to demand such an explanation, and the explanation that Crossan offers (literary source relations and tradition criticism) is in fact mostly standard in the field. But there is an important historiographic reason for what seems to be such an obvious need. In the early part of the twentieth century the French historian Marc Bloch noted that there is a problem of *comparison* that is at the bottom of nearly all historical criticism.[20] Judgements on things like the date, authorship, provenance, or authenticity of a document or testimony depend ultimately on comparisons of that testimony with others. A measure of similarity is required to vindicate, say, the

---

17. Crossan, *Birth*, p. 120.

18. See pp. 46-47.

19. Crossan, *The Historical Jesus*, p. xxxi. Our point in noting the relation of stratification of the data with tradition criticism is not that this is unique to Crossan. It is of course as old as tradition criticism itself, from the latter's earliest days in the genesis of form criticism, and is probably of a piece even with source criticism. Bultmann cannot help but refer to the 'strata' of Mark that must be separated (i.e., historical from redactionary), since Wrede identified Mark's theological agenda. See *History of the Synoptic Tradition* (trans. John Marsh; Oxford: Basil Blackwell, rev. edn, 1963), p. 1. My point is that, where tradition criticism is practised, stratification is assumed. See also Crossan and Jonathan L. Reed, *Excavating Jesus: Beneath the Stones, Behind the Texts* (San Francisco: HarperSanFrancisco, 2001), pp. 12-14, where Crossan presents the conception of layers in the Gospels as prerequisite to using them as historical sources.

20. Marc Bloch, *The Historian's Craft* (trans. Peter Putnam; New York: Vintage Books, 1953), p. 110.

authenticity of a document that claims to be of a certain period and to bear witness to a certain event. The document must be similar enough to other documents known to originate from the period and to witness to the event to be considered authentic to that period and possibly itself a witness. But too much similarity discredits a document; e.g., if it is exactly like another document, or very close, it is probably copied from it and not original. If one of two documents is established as a copy, the original is considered the only authentic witness. So authenticity depends upon a principle we could call 'limited similarity'. Both too much similarity and not enough serve to discredit the authenticity of a witness. Bloch explains why this is so:

> [C]riticism oscillates between two extremes: the similarity which vindicates and that which discredits. This is because there is a limit to coincidence, and social unity is made up of links which are, on the whole, rather weak. In other words, we estimate that the universe and society possess sufficient uniformity to exclude the possibility of overly pronounced deviations. But, as we picture it to ourselves, this uniformity is confined to some very general characteristics. It includes, we think upon delving further into reality, a number of possible combinations so nearly infinite that their spontaneous repetition is inconceivable: there must be a voluntary act of imitation. And so, to add it all up, the criticism of evidence relies upon an instinctive metaphysics of the similar and the dissimilar, of the one and the many.[21]

This 'metaphysics of the similar and the dissimilar' makes perfect sense of the focus on parallel traditions. Seeing the fact of parallels as the heart of the historical problem, the situation that demands explanation if we are to handle the texts historically, is a disposition that grows out of this instinctive metaphysics that Bloch says drives historical criticism. Seeing the relationships among the sources as the necessary presupposition for historical work is a conclusion that fits with our assumptions of both the uniformity of the universe and the inconceivability of spontaneous repetition among the nearly infinite possible combinations. It is quite natural and reasonable to expect similar materials to be explained, and for that explanation to be key to determining the authenticity of the materials as historical witnesses. So Crossan's demands in this area, demands which he shares with much of the history of New Testament scholarship,[22] are vindicated by something that appears to be fundamental to historical criticism.

However, in spite of the notion of limited similarity, the focus that is found in Crossan, and in much historical Jesus work, on parallel materials and their implications, is in fact mitigated by two important factors. The first of these has to do with the oral nature of the traditions on Jesus. The second regards the nature of the data as evidence versus testimony.

---

21. Bloch, *The Historian's Craft*, pp. 115-16.

22. Crossan appeals to the scholarly consensus when expounding on the importance of source relations, 'It is the scholarly conclusions of *tradition-criticism*, hard won by gospel scholarship over the last two hundred years (but also confirmed by my own personal study), that separates me from the simplicity of common sense...', *Birth*, p. 93. See source relations, tradition criticism and stratification bound together most explicitly in Perrin, *Rediscovering the Teaching of Jesus*, pp. 32-34.

A certain recognition of an oral stage of transmission of the Jesus traditions is almost universal among New Testament scholars. We have seen that Crossan himself, in the transmissional analysis of his transition period, sought to take account of the aphorisms of Jesus circulating within an oral sensibility, which is reflected even in their written form.[23] For Crossan, orality implies that extant traditions should be seen as reflecting a common oral, historical core. But some scholars have recently criticized Crossan for his handling of the data in terms of source relations and especially of literary dependence among parallel traditions, claiming that Crossan does not take seriously enough the oral nature of the tradition. Werner Kelber notes that Crossan has not taken account of the nature of the traditions as oral performance. Crossan's organization of traditions into complexes, which can then be quantified in terms of attestation, reflects an application of a logic that is appropriate to 'a long and intense experience with the written and printed word. But if spoken words 'cannot be "broken" and reassembled', logic cannot take possession of the performative poetics of Jesus' proclamation. We are bound to conclude that the oral performance of his words is unknowable through formal thought based on literary or typographical sensibilities.'[24] The specific nature of oral performance that Kelber has in mind is the *variability* of *initial* performance. In an oral sensibility, a similar saying is performed in a plurality of ways, such that each 'version' of the saying is an autonomous act, with none of them appropriately being thought of as either 'original' or 'secondary'. Since original rendering is essentially variable, what is ruled out for the historian is the search for the original form of a saying, or even a common structure or core for similar sayings. The oral nature of the initial performance of the traditions by the historical Jesus mitigates the demand for an explanation of parallel traditions, particularly an explanation that centres on literary dependence and tradition criticism.[25]

J.D.G. Dunn has joined Kelber in noting that orality heavily qualifies how the historian can account for similar traditions. He insists that the narrative traditions on Jesus have too many oral features to be ignored.[26] The earliest tradition was characterized by oral performance, which was a matter of the *shared* memories of Jesus' impact on the community. This was a communal process, not a matter of individual isolated recollections. Orality is communal, while literality is individualistic. But the character of shared memory means that we cannot know with precision what Jesus said or did in many cases. We have the shared memory of Jesus' shared impact on the disciples. There is of course a historical figure who made this impact, but not a single, original, pure form of tradition which the historian can recover in each case.[27] Dunn fundamentally opposes the imagery of layers for understanding the tradition. This, he says, is essentially a literary paradigm, with

---

23. See above, p. 45.

24. Werner Kelber, 'The Quest for the Historical Jesus', in *The Jesus Controversy*, p. 108.

25. See also Kelber, 'Jesus and Tradition: Words in Time, Words in Space', *Semeia* 65 (1994), pp. 139-67; and Kelber, *The Oral and the Written Gospel* (Philadelphia: Fortress Press, 1983).

26. J.D.G. Dunn, 'Jesus in Oral Memory: The Initial Stages of the Jesus Tradition', in *SBL 2000 Seminar Papers* 39 (Atlanta: Society of Biblical Literature, 2000), p. 306.

27. Dunn, 'Jesus in Oral Memory', pp. 318-19.

each retelling of a tradition being like a new 'edition', a new layer on an original. Dunn's alternative is to see the oral tradition not as layers but as new performances or retellings; traditions are performed and not edited.[28] So what we encounter in the sources is not the top layer of a series of layers on an original, but a lived tradition, a record of an ongoing performance.[29]

These observations speak to the heart of a method oriented to tradition criticism and rooted in the need to explain parallel materials. As much as limited similarity and a 'metaphysics of the similar and the dissimilar' may compel historians to offer an explanation for similar materials, and to account for them in terms of source relations and variations on a historical core, orality compels historians to mollify these kinds of conclusions as a basis for historical work. Crossan has responded to the types of criticisms we see in Kelber and Dunn, and his response indicates that he appreciates how detrimental to his method these criticisms can be.[30] For his method, from the beginning, has been situated squarely within the time-honoured tenets of historical-critical New Testament studies that base historical investigation of Jesus on literary relations among the sources and tradition criticism, and 'If it is wrong, any historical reconstruction of Jesus and his followers built upon it is methodologically invalid.'[31]

The second factor that mitigates a focus on parallels and the resulting tradition criticism is the nature of historical data as *evidence* rather than *testimony*. This

---

28. The implication of this, which Dunn details in his study, is that 'the stabilities of the tradition were sufficiently maintained and the variabilities of the retellings subject to sufficient control for the substance of the tradition, and often the actual words of Jesus which made the first tradition-forming impact, to continue as integral parts of the living tradition, for at least as long as it took the Synoptic tradition to be written down. In other words, whereas the concept of literary layers implies increasing remoteness from an "original", "pure" or "authentic" layer, the concept of performance allows a directness, even an immediacy of interaction with a living theme and core even when variously embroidered in various retellings', pp. 322-23. Dunn seems to hold an optimistic view of the reliability of the tradition as memory of Jesus' words and deeds. Whether or not one agrees with his view on reliability, his point remains that accounting for similar traditions in terms of layers on an original is an essentially literary conception which is heavily qualified by the oral nature of the traditions.

29. Dunn, 'Jesus in Oral Memory', p. 326. Sean Freyne makes a similar point: Stratification of the sources is an inadequate historical method in view of the oral nature of the tradition. The traditions existed in living contexts: 'Nothing is frozen in time, awaiting the arrival of the modern historical critic with his or her trowel to release it from the later "fill" that has obscured it from view for centuries', Freyne, 'Galilean Questions to Crossan's Mediterranean Jesus', in William E. Arnal and Michel Desjardins (eds.), *Whose Historical Jesus?* (Studies in Christianity and Judaism, 7; Ontario: Wilfrid Laurier University Press, 1997), p. 64.

30. In *The Birth of Christianity* he devotes over forty pages (47-89) to refuting orality, which he links closely with memory, as an explanation for parallel materials in the sources on Jesus. Similarly, in his memoirs he notes the temporal gap that existed between Jesus' life and the first written records of him. 'Many of my scholarly colleagues fill those yawning chasms by claiming oral tradition and especially preliterate memory. I agree, or course, that both exist, but I am much more skeptical about its retentive accuracy or even whether it is a good general explanation of the ongoing Jesus tradition.' He then discusses for three pages why memory is not reliable and orality is not a sufficient explanation for Gospel parallels, *A Long Way from Tipperary*, pp. 153-56.

31. Crossan, *Birth*, p. 93.

distinction requires some explication. Philosopher-historian R.G. Collingwood criticized what he called 'scissors-and-paste' historiography. This approach amounts to
the excerpting and combining of the testimonies of different sources to reconstruct
the historical object.[32] Such a process does not necessarily mean that all testimonies are equally accepted as trustworthy and true. Contradictory testimonies still
have to be scrutinized, and one or all of them rejected; the sources giving such
testimonies will be criticized for their relative degree of trustworthiness, based
largely on what we have called the principle of limited similarity. In scissors-and-
paste history, the historian decides what he or she wants to know about, and then
collects statements about it from sources (actors, eyewitnesses, second- or third-
hand information, etc.), forming a pool of potential data on the subject. From this
pool the historian decides which statements to include and which to omit, based
upon judgements of authenticity. That scissors-and-paste is concerned with collect-
ing and collating testimony does not imply that it omits reasoned inference on the
part of the historian. Scissors-and-paste, despite the pejorative connotations, does
not mean that the historian does not need to reason from the data. All history is
inferential, in that the historian must infer, on the basis of the evidence, what went
forward in the past. But the inference characteristic of scissors-and-paste treats the
data fundamentally as *testimonies* about the object, to be judged true or false and
either used or discarded on that basis. Its inference is inference from testimonies to
conclusions about what happened.

Against scissors-and-paste, which handles the data as true or false testimonies,
Collingwood proposed that the important question to ask about a given statement
in a source is not whether it is true, but what it means. 'What light is thrown on the
subject in which I am interested by the fact that this person made this statement,
meaning by it what he did mean?' In other words, statements are not treated as
testimonies but as evidence, 'not as true or false accounts of the facts of which they
profess to be accounts, but as other facts which, if [the historian] knows the right
questions to ask about them, may throw light on those facts'.[33] The scissors-and-
paste historian is interested in the content of statements-as-testimony; but the
historian's interest should rather be in the very fact that the statements are made.
When a statement is determined not to be useful on its face, as a testimony, it may
yet be useful if the historian asks the right questions of it.

The distinction being drawn here is between taking the data as true or false witnesses to the event under investigation, and taking the data as evidence in a much
broader sense than whether or not they give authentic testimony to the event. What
is to be asked of data is not *primarily* whether they are *true*, but what is their *significance*, because a datum's significance in relation to the event can extend beyond
the mere giving of testimony. Put another way, testimony or witness is only one
class of datum, only one way in which a datum may be significant in relation to an
object. This idea is borne out in the basic historiographic principle of what we can
call the 'unintentional witness'. According to this principle, statements are often

32. R.G. Collingwood, *The Idea of History* (New York: Oxford University Press, 1946), p. 257.
33. Collingwood, *Idea*, p. 275.

more valuable for what they tell the historian *apart* from what they intend to say; this is based on the assumption that intentional statements are often clouded by the agenda and bias of the author, but what comes out of his statement apart from what the author intended to relate is not so filtered.[34] Authors are often unwilling or unable to tell the truth about what they are interested in, but may tell us something else that they are not saying intentionally.[35] Of course, the unintentional information imparted by data can only loosely be called 'witness'. It is better to think of it as the result of the *impact* of the event, and so to treat it as evidence by which we may infer something about the event.

It is clear that in Crossan's approach, and in the methodological tradition within which he works, the data on Jesus are handled strictly as testimony.[36] Crossan's emphasis on explaining parallels, and the resulting source relations that he says are the necessary presupposition of historical Jesus work, are based on the assumption that the data are either true or false testimony to the words, deeds and events of the life of Jesus. Source relations, and their stratification, are fundamental because later and dependent sources are not independent testimonies to the events they describe; only the earliest and independent sources can be considered valid testimony. This is seen clearly in a recent work, in which Crossan presents the fundamental need for a layered or stratified conception of the Gospels when handling them as sources on the historical Jesus, and that because they are four purported testimonies to the events under consideration. He illustrates the situation with a scenario of four witnesses to a traffic accident. As long as the four witnesses are known to be independent and relatively disinterested, and their stories are complementary or roughly similar, all is well for the attorneys who are trying to make a case for what happened based on their stories. But if one witness is discovered to be a reporter who

---

34. Among the many statements and versions of the principle, see Bloch, *The Historian's Craft*, pp. 89-90; Louis Gottschalk, *Understanding History: A Primer of Historical Method* (New York: Alfred A. Knopf, 1958), pp. 163-64; Michael Stanford, *A Companion to the Study of History* (Oxford: Basil Blackwell, 1994), pp. 146-47, 161-62.

35. We can see this principle at work in New Testament studies at the foundation of form criticism. The latter values the Gospel data not for what they *intend* to say about Jesus, but what they say *unintentionally* about their own *Sitze im Leben*. That the Gospels do tell us about the early church would seem to be a historiographically reasonable expectation, but so would the possibility that they tell us about Jesus, in the same broad capacity as evidence rather than witness. There is no historiographic reason for a priori admitting the former possibility (church) but excluding the latter (Jesus).

36. One aspect of Crossan's presentation can be seen to reflect an implicit recognition of data serving as evidence beyond mere testimony. The signs that Crossan uses to designate tradition complexes as either authentic (+) or inauthentic (−) do not serve to handle all the possible historical significance of all the traditions, he admits. He introduces the third symbol (±) as a way to indicate that the complex is useful for indicating something historical, though his method does not permit that the complex be allowed as testimony. This third category of judgement is for data that symbolize or dramatize processes that took place over a long period of time in Jesus' career (see *The Historical Jesus*, p. 434). Crossan seems to be trying to reckon here with data as evidence beyond testimony, the type of evidence that his method as he outlines it does not accommodate. His method is designed to handle only testimony, and so he must introduce a category of judgement that adjusts his method to other types of evidence that impinge on the investigation.

got his knowledge second-hand, and the other three are found to have gotten their stories from the reporter, the attorneys in fact have not four, corroborating accounts but only one, and that one is not even an eyewitness. All this reduces the strength of any case made on the testimony of those 'witnesses'.[37] So the relations of possible dependence among the sources must be established first, because those relations in turn establish which sources can be used as valid testimony.

To see (as tradition criticism does) similar data among the sources as all variations on a historical core is to handle those data simply as testimony of greater or lesser accuracy. Clearly, to apply criteria of authenticity to the data is to scrutinize them for their value as *witnesses* to the events in question. All this is most often employed in Jesus studies in disregard of the larger category of evidence to which the data rightly belong.

Before we leave this discussion of data-as-evidence, I should point out that nothing I have said is intended to deny the value of the comparisons that are at the heart of historical judgements. As I will show further in a later chapter, comparisons still must be made among the several sources on Jesus; similar and different data must still be accounted for. Nor does taking the data as evidence require that the tools designed to deal with the data as testimony all be discarded, for testimony is a valid category of evidence; but it is not the *only* category. My observations above, on orality, see the data primarily (though arguably not *exclusively*) as testimony to their object. So we are not disregarding testimony as such. But the distinction between testimony and evidence injects an important element into an analysis of the way Crossan's method approaches the historical data. Source relations and consequent stratification are not the absolute presupposition that he understands them to be, parallel materials are not the crux of the historical problem that he takes them to be, and tradition criticism is not the sine qua non of a historical handling of the data.

2. *Data and Interpretation*

At the conclusion of Chapter Two I noted a feature of Crossan's early phase that ties the two phases of his work together. There he operates with a conception of historiography as a two-phase process of historical work followed by interpretation. In the early Crossan, the first phase is handled by means of tradition criticism, the second by application of structuralist and post-structuralist analysis. We can see that same two-phase conception operative in the interdisciplinary method of his later period. The interdisciplinary model sees historical investigation taking place on three levels, the macrocosmic level of social anthropology, the mesocosmic level of local (Greco-Roman) history, and the microcosmic level of the sources themselves. It is to the microcosmic level that Crossan devotes most of his attention in methodological discussion, because, as he says, method stands or falls with how one handles the sources. These three levels can be seen to play the role of the two phases of Crossan's early historical method. The first phase, in which the data

---

37. Crossan and Reed, *Excavating Jesus*, p. 13.

are examined for their authenticity as data on Jesus, is taken up by the microcosmic level, which is a sophistication of the tradition criticism of the early Crossan. In this phase the sources are sifted by means of stratification and multiple attestation (based on prior decisions of source relations and dating), to yield a database of authentic material on Jesus. As we saw, the core of authentic material consists of complexes that are both attested in the earliest stratum and attested at least twice throughout the strata. In the second phase, the data that have been established as authentic are interpreted. In the later Crossan, the work of interpretation is done by setting the authentic materials into the contexts of Greco-Roman history and social anthropology, the meso- and macrocosmic levels of historical work. These wider contexts shed necessary light on the meaning of the authentic data. I would suggest capturing this two-phase understanding of historical method as 'data control' followed by 'data interpretation'.[38]

In *The Birth of Christianity* are found comments from Crossan that substantiate the observation that he continues to operate with an understanding of historical method as consisting of basically two distinct and isolated phases, and also an argument that gives a rationale for this understanding of method. In his methodological discussion in that work, he illustrates how the data on the historical Jesus should be handled by comparing the study of Jesus to the study of a text of Paul, namely, Romans. With Romans, the inventory, or database, relevant to the object under study is set, in the epistle itself. There is more or less complete agreement on *what* is to be interpreted. But this is not the case with Jesus. 'We cannot act here as if we all had the same inventory of materials – the same "text", as it were – in our hands or on our desks. And of course our results and conclusions will be different when we start with different data-bases or inventories of first-stratum materials.'[39] If historians are working with different databases of materials to be interpreted, as is often the case with historians of Jesus who do not specify beforehand exactly what their database consists of, then of course historians will come up with different interpretations. Agreement must be reached on *what* is to be interpreted before there can be any basis for comparing the *results* of interpretation. '[I]*nventory precedes interpretation* and *method precedes inventory*. We must always begin by asking: What texts are you using to understand the birth of Christianity, and why those rather than some others?'[40] Of course, related to the historical Jesus, the question is not just 'which texts?' but 'which data within those texts?' It would seem that nothing could be more obvious: the data to be interpreted must be established before they can be interpreted, or else there would be nothing to interpret.

Like his work with tradition criticism and source relations, this understanding of historical method is something Crossan shares with many New Testament scholars. In fact, it seems to be a common understanding of the nature of historical investigation, not only in New Testament and historical Jesus studies, but also in some

38. I borrow the former term from Ben Meyer; see below, Chapter 6.
39. Crossan, *Birth*, p. 141.
40. Crossan, *Birth*, p. 143.

wider historiographic circles. We will note just a few illustrative examples from historiography and from historical Jesus studies.

Langlois and Seignobos divide the work of history into 'analysis' and 'synthesis'. Analysis derives facts from documents, which are then constructed in synthesis into a picture of the historical object. The work of analysis results in an 'incoherent mass of minute facts, with detail-knowledge reduced as it were to a powder'.[41] This metaphor is vivid. Analysis establishes the raw materials with which the historian must work, the authentic 'powder' that the historian extracts from the possible sources. This powder is then reconstituted by the historian in the work of interpretation. Similarly, Louis Gottschalk identifies four 'bare essentials' of all historical work: (1) the collection of the surviving relevant materials; (2) the exclusion of materials, or parts of materials, that are unauthentic; (3) the extraction of credible testimony from the authentic material; 4) the organization of the credible testimony into a meaningful narrative or exposition.[42] The first three of these phases we can classify under 'controlling the data', followed by the final phase of organizing the data into a meaningful whole. Gottschalk also divides the historical process into analysis and historiography, the latter being his equivalent of the 'synthesis' described by Langlois and Seignobos.[43]

Among historians of Jesus, Norman Perrin is typical. He devotes the first chapter of his *Reconstructing the Teaching of Jesus* to methodological issues, where he considers separately the tasks involved in 'reconstruction' and 'interpretation' of Jesus' teachings. The former is Perrin's version of our 'data control', and involves first, determining the history of transmission of the particular tradition under consideration, to isolate the earliest form, then applying criteria for verification that the earliest form is from Jesus.[44] This is followed by the work of interpretation of that authenticated tradition: 'Once we have arrived at a reconstruction of an aspect of the teaching of Jesus, our next task is to seek to understand it, by which we mean to interpret it in its original setting and to arrive as closely as we can at its original meaning.'[45] Marcus Borg has recently described historical Jesus work in a way that fits neatly with the two-phase process: 'The first step is discerning what is likely to go back to Jesus. The second step is setting this material in the historical context of the Jewish homeland in the first century.'[46] That the second step of contextualization is the means of interpretation is clear: 'Historical context is crucial, for words spoken have meaning only in context. They mean little, or remain ambiguous, apart from context'.[47] First, determine authentic data, then determine what the data mean,

---

41. Langlois and Seignobos, *Introduction*, p. 214.

42. Gottschalk, *Understanding History*, p. 28.

43. Gottschalk, *Understanding History*, p. 52.

44. Perrin, *Rediscovering*, pp. 38-39.

45. Perrin, *Rediscovering*, pp. 49-50. For Perrin, interpretation is to be guided by the context of first-century Judaism, the context of Jesus' ministry, and the nature of the sources as freely creative and based on the experience of the resurrected Lord and not on historical reminiscence, pp. 51ff.

46. Borg, 'Seeing Jesus: Sources, Lenses and Method', in Borg and N.T. Wright, *The Meaning of Jesus: Two Visions* (San Francisco: HarperSanFrancisco, 1999), p. 11.

47. Borg, 'Seeing Jesus', p. 13.

what they tell us about Jesus. E.P. Sanders's work is different from that of Perrin and Borg, in both approach and resulting portrait of Jesus,[48] but he still reflects a general understanding of establishing authentic data first, before deciding what the data mean. His methodological proposal is that we begin with a set of 'virtually indisputable facts' when investigating Jesus.[49] Such facts constitute the most reliable historical bedrock from which we can go on to construct a portrait.[50] We see a similar orientation in Paula Fredriksen. Upon noting the diversity of emphases among contemporary portraits of Jesus, a diversity resulting partly from historians' emphasizing different sources in their reconstructions, she wonders if there is a way through this diversity. Her answer: 'We have facts... Facts are always subject to interpretation – that's part of the fun – but they also exist as fixed points in our investigation. Any explanation, any reconstruction of Jesus' mission and message must speak adequately to what we *know* to have been the case. If it cannot...that reconstruction fails as history.'[51] The facts are first established, or at least a handful of the most crucial facts, and from there we can proceed possibly to determining other relevant facts, and ultimately to interpreting all the facts.[52]

48.   See appendix 1 on Sanders's view of tradition criticism and criteria of authenticity applied to the sayings of Jesus.

49.   Sanders, *Jesus and Judaism*, p. 11.

50.   Sanders, *Jesus and Judaism*, p. 10.

51.   Paula Fredriksen, *Jesus of Nazareth: King of the Jews* (New York: Vintage Books, 1999), p. 7. The facts that Fredriksen says must be our starting point are that Jesus was crucified as a political insurrectionist, and that his followers were not.

52.   In noting details of the synoptic problem, as well as the evangelists' apparent creation of material using Old Testament allusions, Fredriksen concludes, 'In light of these complexities, all Gospel material must be weighed and judged before it can serve as evidence of the historical Jesus', p. 27.

See also the first volume of John P. Meier's multi-volume work on the historical Jesus. Meier seeks to limit his investigation to something resembling the determination of the facts on Jesus. In discussing the use of social science tools for interpretation, Meier notes that such interpretive tasks are legitimate, but are not his concern. 'This book operates on a very fundamental level as it asks what within the Gospels, and in other sources available, really goes back to the historical Jesus. The primary goal of this book is the detection of reliable data... Our goal will be primarily the ascertaining of reliable data, not sophisticated sociological interpretation of the data via models', *A Marginal Jew: Rethinking the Historical Jesus*. I. *The Roots of the Problem and the Person* (New York: Doubleday, 1991), pp. 10-11. Meier insists that, though an absolutely interpretation-free presentation is unattainable, he will attempt as much as possible to keep interpretation to a minimum. It is not clear from his comments whether he intends his entire multi-volume presentation to be limited to detection of reliable data, or whether the initial volume alone will have this focus; and he is speaking of 'interpretation' here specifically in terms of that derived from application of social science tools. But in any case, it seems clear that Meier is conceiving the historical task as principally the determination of authentic data or facts, the interpretation of which, via sociological models or any other means, is a secondary and subsequent matter.

We can finally note one well-known contemporary historian who seems to operate with this conception when he comments on whether historians' presentations are 'personal': '[H]istorians give visions of the past. The good ones are not merely plausible; they rest on a solid base of facts that nobody disputes. There is nothing personal about facts, but there is about choosing and grouping them. It is by the patterning and the meanings ascribed that the vision is conveyed',

I would not want to deny that historical investigation involves both of these activities, controlling the data and interpreting the data. That both of these operations are required of the historian is a truism. But it may be that there is too much common sense among the descriptions of these operations as distinct and isolated, and not enough consideration for how the relation between them may be more properly nuanced. I would suggest that there is in fact a reciprocity between the tasks of data control and data interpretation. *Whether* data are usable in an investigation cannot be determined apart from *how* they are usable. The first determination cannot be established prior to and in isolation from the second. This is a point that I will develop in some detail in later chapters; it is a major contribution of the other Jesus scholar I will examine, Ben Meyer. For now I will describe some of the highlights.

Collingwood illustrates his point about historical data being evidence (and not simply testimony) by comparing the historian's work to the rather grisly example of the detective investigating a homicide.[53] For the detective, what counts as evidence in the investigation is anything that is *used* as evidence. It is only when the detective has had occasion to use a datum in the reconstruction of the crime that the detective can know whether that datum is actually going to be useful.[54] What the detective cannot do is first survey the crime scene and determine exactly what will and will not be of use in determining what happened there. Every fingerprint, every fibre on the victim's body, the placement of every article in the scene, every word of 'testimony' from possible witnesses, all is potential evidence, and none of it can be either admitted as useful or ruled out as useless until the detective has had opportunity either to use it or to discard it, based on the role that the datum plays in the detective's reconstruction of the crime. The pool of evidence does not consist of a set of previously fixed points, whose status as valid evidence the detective has determined once and for all, and which the detective must then arrange, using interpretive powers, into an account of what happened. The valid data are not 'fixed' or settled upon before the reconstruction begins, because the reconstruction partly determines what will count as valid data.[55] For the detective, there is a reciprocity between determining what will be valid data and interpreting those data, between deciding what data are relevant and deciding what is the significance of the relevant data in relation to the crime under investigation. *Whether* a datum is

---

Jacques Barzun, *From Dawn to Decadence: Five Hundred Years of Western Cultural Life* (New York: Harper Collins, 2000), p. xiv. Once again, established facts are the bedrock, to be *followed* by interpretations.

53. Collingwood, *The Idea of History*, pp. 266ff.

54. Collingwood, *The Idea of History*, p. 280.

55. I say the reconstruction 'partly' determines what will be valid data, because there are general principles applied by the detective; for example, when a homicide victim is a woman, the spouse or romantic partner is usually a suspect. These kinds of generalities are guidelines that the detective uses, and the historian has guidelines as well, but none of these are absolute means of determining what will count as valid data. I will discuss such general rules, and their relation to the 'criteria of authenticity', in Chapter 8, below.

useful and *how* it is useful are the two decisions the detective must make, but they are not made in isolation from one another.[56]

As with the detective, so with the historian. The historian cannot determine the status of a historical datum, as useful or otherwise, until he or she has had opportunity to use it in the investigation. The datum must have a sense (or fail to have a sense) in the context of an inquiry before its status as valid can be determined. It must be emphasized that what I am describing here is a genuine *reciprocity* between data control and interpretation, and not simply an inversion of the two phases, i.e., interpretation before data control. Such an inversion would amount to the claim that we must determine what a datum says about our object *before* we can determine whether the datum will be used. This would be a convenient way to justify our forcing the data into an a-priori picture of Jesus, using that picture as the criterion for determining what the data will mean and which data will be allowed. The data are not to be forced by an interpretation undertaken prior to their control; but neither can the data be controlled prior to being used in an interpretation.

One other caveat is appropriate here. An insistence on the reciprocity of data control and data interpretation does not reduce to the simple argument that 'there are no uninterpreted facts'. Much is often made of the idea that there are no 'brute facts' in history; all the facts that are discovered (or, more properly, inferred) by the historian are already interpretation-laden. The implications drawn from this idea are various, including the reaction against a positivist spirit that would do history by discovering the facts and allowing them to 'speak for themselves'; against this there is the insistence that facts have no voice of their own, the historian's personal involvement is necessary for their discovery and interpretation.[57] There is also the implication that, since historical facts are bound up with interpretation, all history is necessarily interpretive, and therefore the interpretations that are found in the Gospels are not necessarily ruled out as history simply because they are interpretations, albeit theological ones.[58] As true as these implications may be, the basic notion that there are no 'brute facts' in history is today as much of a truism as is the idea that history involves both data control and interpretation (although the impli-

---

56. Notice a similar point made by Appleby, Hunt and Jacob: 'Historians' questions turn the material remains from the past into evidence, for evidence is only evidence in relation to a particular account. (Think of the detective who notices a telltale streak of shoe polish on a doorjamb; a perfectly ordinary trace of passage becomes a clue.) But once a story is told, an argument made, or an interpretation advanced, the objects that compose the supporting evidence come under scrutiny', Joyce Appleby, Lynn Hunt and Margaret Jacob, *Telling the Truth about History* (New York: W.W. Norton, 1994), p. 261. Notice that the 'scrutiny' of the evidence is not performed independent of an argument or interpretation.

57. In Jesus studies, see the 'new understanding of history' that characterized the New Quest, including the historian's existential encounter with history. See James Robinson, *A New Quest of the Historical Jesus*. A different understanding of the historian's 'subjective' involvement with history will be observed below in our examination of Ben Meyer.

58. Something like this is the argument of Ronald H. Nash, *Christian Faith and Historical Understanding* (Grand Rapids: Zondervan, 1984), esp. ch. 6. Of course, this argument has the effect of leveling *all* interpretations, and so does not amount to a defence of the Gospel portraits in particular, but only a relativizing of all portraits.

cations of the truisms are rarely thought through by historians). I would not deny either point. But what I would offer is rather the more concrete proposal that, in historiography, the data cannot be evaluated for their *usefulness* in isolation from their *use* in the course of historical investigation. I have cast this issue as the reciprocity of data control and interpretation, and have avoided too much discussion of the problematic notion of historical 'facts'. My position is more properly related to the issue of interpretive judgements that were raised in relation to the use of complexes in Crossan. I noted the difficulty in determining what units properly form a particular complex, and how themes relate to complexes. Regarding these kinds of difficulties, Christopher Tuckett has suggested that it may not be possible to pin down the traditions into formulae and statistics that are independent of the theories we wish to develop about the traditions.[59] Decisions about things like complexes are difficult because complexes are fuzzy things; those decisions are bound up with decisions about how to interpret the data. The data are shaped by the historian's interpretive decisions, which contribute to ultimate decisions on their validity. This illustrates the interpretive problems that are of a piece with the reciprocity between control and interpretation.

To conclude this section on data control and interpretation, I would point out that the preceding account is in the first instance descriptive: historical enquiries work this way in any case, even in those investigations that do not acknowledge the reciprocity or seem designed to resist it. We can see in Crossan's own work how an important historical judgement is made on data in interaction with an interpretation of their significance in his account of the events. Crossan discusses the *Temple and Jesus* complex[60] and its relation to Jesus' 'cleansing' of the Temple (Mk 11.15-18). Crossan draws two significant conclusions from his analysis of this material: (1) He suggests that the presence of the tradition that Jesus would destroy the temple came from Jesus' temple action, which was a symbolic destruction. In addition, since the word 'house' appears in all three sources (*Gos. Thom.*, Mark, John), and in the latter two it is appended to explain Jesus' temple action, Crossan concludes provisionally that the action was originally accompanied by a saying about 'house'. He finally proposes a tradition-historical reconstruction, consisting of a first stratum of action-accompanied-by-house-saying; these two elements were later separated from one another in diverging lines of interpretation.[61] 2) He offers Jesus' temple action as the immediate cause of his crucifixion.

These two conclusions are important parts of Crossan's portrait of Jesus. The second conclusion is Crossan's explanation for Jesus' death, which would be difficult to explain on any other basis given Crossan's portrait of Jesus as a Jewish Cynic. The first conclusion supports the historicity of Jesus' temple action, as well as its character as a symbolic destruction, making the action intelligible in Jesus' programme of an egalitarian social vision of unbrokered religion and relationships.

---

59. Tuckett, 'The Historical Jesus, Crossan and Methodology', p. 279.

60. In this complex Jesus is said to have threatened the destruction of the Temple (*Gos. Thom.* 71; Mk 14.55-59; 15.29-32a; Jn 2.18-22).

61. Crossan, *The Historical Jesus*, pp. 355-59.

Both conclusions provide a way of accounting for Jesus' death as cohering with the picture Crossan has drawn of his life. However, the difficulty with these conclusions, in terms of Crossan's method, is that neither the association of the *Temple and Jesus* tradition with Jesus' temple action, nor the association of Jesus' temple action with his death, is allowed by the method. Crossan has said that his method limits him to materials at least doubly attested, and attested in the first stratum. But the temple action is not attested in Crossan's first stratum,[62] and the association of the action with Jesus' death has no plural attestation at all. Crossan freely admits the second point, and acknowledges that his conclusions regarding Jesus' death are somewhat unmethodological. But he offers a full explanation of Jesus' death along these lines[63] and points out that the reason such a non-methodologically grounded explanation is justified is that, 'Without it...we are reduced to even greater guesswork in answering why then, why there, why thus?' In other words, this explanation seems best to account for the data, but it cannot be supported by Crossan's own method of stratification and multiple attestation. So there is a major feature of Crossan's presentation that is not supportable by his stated method.

That Crossan has to account for some data by an explanation and argument, rather than by his stated method, is not in itself necessarily problematic. It simply shows that decisions on the historicity of data are not made apart from a consideration of how those data are used in the investigation. Crossan posits Jesus' temple action as of a piece with his egalitarian programme, and as the immediate cause of his death, not because Crossan's method has established the temple action as historical or has established the historicity of it as a symbolic destruction, but because Crossan ultimately finds in the course of his investigation that these explanations are required for a cogent accounting of the data. These data are allowed not because he has *first* controlled them, but because he has controlled them in interaction with his interpretation of their significance for a coherent portrait of Jesus. Even a method that would deny the reciprocity of data control and interpretation cannot simply eliminate it; its presence in historiography is ubiquitous and shows through in any case.

3. *Interactivism*

Our examination of historiography and hermeneutics in the later Crossan is turning out to be the mirror image of our examination of the early Crossan. It was noted that the early Crossan was more heavily weighted toward hermeneutical discussion, whereas the later Crossan has been occupied almost exclusively with historiographic issues. But there is one hermeneutical point that surfaces in the later Crossan that is explicit enough to deserve special attention. He is careful to point out in his methodological discussion in *The Historical Jesus* that by outlining his

62. The temple action is found only in Mk 11.15-18 pars., and Jn 2.14-16.
63. 'I think the symbolic destruction was but the logical extension of the miracle and table conjunction, of open healing and open eating; I think that it actually happened and, *if* it happened at Passover, *could* easily have led to arrest and execution', *The Historical Jesus*, p. 360.

method he is not pretending to a 'spurious objectivity' but is rather concerned with an 'attainable honesty' in his investigation of Jesus.[64] Crossan is sophisticated enough in his hermeneutic to know that history cannot be done without the self-involvement of the historian. But acknowledging that self-involvement does not require that the historian give up all claims to be getting at a real historical object. Crossan suggests a middle way between the illusion of narcissism or historical solipsism (that history is the mere projection of oneself and one's own concerns) and the delusion of positivism (the assumption that history can be viewed without self-involvement). Crossan's middle way, which he says is how he understands 'postmodernism',[65] Crossan calls *interactivism*. 'The past and the present must interact with one another, each changing and challenging the other, and the ideal is an absolutely fair and equal reaction between one another.'[66] Historical reconstruction is not a naively objectivist apprehension of a historical object, but is always the interaction of the present with the past. This issues in Crossan's definition of history: 'the past reconstructed interactively by the present through argued evidence in public discourse'.[67]

It seems that the most practical result of this interactivism, for Crossan, is a certain inevitable plurality in understandings of the historical Jesus. But the extent of this plurality is not clear. At times Crossan seems to express it as a general plurality that relativizes all historical results, along with all understandings of the historical Jesus and of the Christ of faith that are built upon those understandings.[68] But in other contexts Crossan seems to be referring simply to the fact that history can never be done once and for all. Each new generation must do history anew, because each generation will be interacting with the historical object from a new historical location.[69] He is even careful to guard against relativizing all historical results, and that for ethical reasons: '[O]ur decency, morality, and humanity demand that we never say it is all relative, perspective, hype, and spin, or that, since we cannot know for sure, it does not matter at all.'[70] It seems we could conclude that for Crossan interactivism means that historical results will be relative across generations, but not within generations.[71] Or perhaps there would be some inter-generational relativizing

---

64. Crossan, *The Historical Jesus*, p. xxxiv.

65. Crossan comments at one point on the philosophical basis of the Third Quest of the historical Jesus, as 'more postmodern than positivistic, rationalistic, romantic or existential', in contrast to the first two quests. See 'Responses and Reflections', in Jeffrey Carlson and Robert A. Ludwig (eds.), *Jesus and Faith: A Conversation on the Work of John Dominic Crossan* (Maryknoll, NY: Orbis Books, 1994), p. 160.

66. Crossan, *Birth*, p. 42.

67. Crossan, *Birth*, p. 20; also 'Historical Jesus as Risen Lord', p. 3.

68. Crossan, *The Historical Jesus*, p. 423.

69. Crossan, 'Historical Jesus as Risen Lord', p. 5; see also *Who Killed Jesus?*, p. 217: 'It is not (in a postmodern world) that we find once and for all who the historical Jesus was way back then. It is that each generation and century must redo that historical work and establish its best reconstruction, a reconstruction that will be and must be in some creative interaction with its own particular needs, visions, and programs.'

70. Crossan, 'Historical Jesus as Risen Lord', p. 4.

71. Crossan certainly is not willing to relativize portraits of Jesus within the *current* generation,

that would be appropriate, say, within a generation but across wide cultural gaps. But we can only speculate because Crossan is short on drawing specific consequences of his 'interactivism' for his own historical work. This leads us to consider what his interactivist hermeneutic has to do with his historiography.

What does the interactive nature of historical enquiry have to do with the formulation of historical method for Crossan? Historical reconstruction is indeed a dialectic of past and present, but this dialectic is kept 'honest' by one's method. Method does not guarantee truth, but it is our only means of discipline, 'our one best hope for honesty'.[72] Crossan sees his notion of interactivism as parallel to N.T. Wright's *critical realism* but he notes that they differ on how that concept works in practice.[73] Crossan says his method protects the historical object from 'violation' and 'disfigurement', though not from discussion or interaction. His stratification and inventory of attestation do not provide a positivist foundation for his Jesus portrait that is timelessly definitive, they just keep the interaction of past and present honest. 'A postmodern sensibility – that is, an equal awareness of your own and your subject's historicity – does not *preclude* but *demands* attention to method.'[74]

In fact, one has a difficult time drawing any connection between 'interactivism' and Crossan's stated method. It seems that the only real implication of the former for the latter is the fact that we can never stop doing history, including a history of Jesus. Crossan is thus willing to relativize *overall historical results* in the name of historical location, as I noted above, but draws no implications for how history is actually undertaken. Crossan's notion of interactivism seems to be a theoretical concession, with little or no practical consequence for the way he does history.[75] The fact that he discusses method in terms of 'honesty' and 'protecting the historical subject from violation and disfigurement' bears this out. Method is the means by which one applies a check on the 'interactivism' by which one cannot help but be afflicted.

No doubt Crossan says method is how we remain honest because a method such as he outlines, with statistical tabulation of the attestation of complexes according to stratum and frequency, makes historical judgements public, and therefore repeatable. Method, as he says, does not guarantee the validity of results, but it makes

---

when he claims that the current variety of portraits is an 'academic embarrassment' and may reflect the historians' covert agendas as they 'do theology and call it history, do autobiography and call it biography', *The Historical Jesus*, p. xxviii.

72. Crossan, *Birth*, p. 44.

73. Wright suggests that historiography be based on a critical realist epistemology, as opposed to either naive realism or idealism. We will discuss Wright, along with other versions of critical realism, particularly that outlined by Ben Meyer, in Chapter 4 below, and in appendix 2, 'Varieties of Critical Realism'.

74. Crossan, *Birth*, p. 45.

75. *Pace* Clive Marsh, who sees in Crossan's comments in the Preface of *The Historical Jesus* an 'insightful handling of his own procedure' and a 'postmodern sensitivity to the historian's interpretative task' ('Quests of the Historical Jesus in New Historicist Perspective', p. 406). From this Marsh concludes that Crossan is representative of 'The Postmodern Quest' of the historical Jesus (p. 412).

fully accessible the means by which one reaches those results, and anyone else who uses the same method can reach the same results, or else take up the methodological challenge by posing a different, preferable, but still public, method. But my consideration of Crossan's method has shown that historical judgements, on matters of both data control and interpretation, are dynamic. Even within a method that claims to put on display every step involved in every historical judgement, pivotal decisions are still made that are based on arguments not reducible to rules of thumb. Such is the nature of historical knowledge, as will become evident in the succeeding chapters of this study.

Historical method should account for how we know the historical object. Method must take seriously the dynamic nature of historical knowledge, as well as the interactivity between historian and history. Crossan's method does not account for either. We have seen how data control and interpretation are separated in his method; and he has neither appreciated nor demonstrated how interactivity affects the very *doing* of history. His method does not account for its own interactive nature; rather, it is meant to curb it.

This fact reflects what we have seen occurring in Crossan since his early phase. There it was noted that his post-structuralist hermeneutic seemed to have no effect on his historiography. In the later Crossan, we still have a historiography that seems unaffected by the stated hermeneutic. In his historiographic work we have seen considerable development, within a consistent orientation to tradition criticism. It is my conclusion that there is no historian of Jesus working today who has refined tradition criticism in a way more sophisticated than Crossan. His work represents the apotheosis of a methodological tradition that has developed over the course of two centuries. But it seems that, as a matter of principle, Crossan has always shielded his method from infringement by his then-current understanding of the nature of understanding.

We can take from Crossan the important gains that are reflected in his macro- and mesocosmic levels of historical work. There is a particular need in Jesus studies to catch up with the larger historiographic world in accounting for the data within the contexts provided by sociology; Crossan's attention to this area is an example to emulate. He is successful in interpreting the data in light of sociological models, without reducing historical events or actions to instances of ideal types. This latter danger is enduring wherever the generalizations of sociology are applied to particular historical objects. The challenge is to apply the generalizations meaningfully to historical situations, without assuming that the situations are explained exhaustively and exclusively by those generalizations and thereby compromising the nature of the events as historically particular. Crossan is among the best of historical Jesus scholars in meeting this challenge. Within pan-Mediterranean sociological constructs, Jesus remains a first-century religious figure with genuine religious sensibilities and a historical agent whose actions are intentional, and not reducible to a confluence of environmental factors.[76] But it is to this area

---

76. This is not to say that Crossan's chosen sociological models or contexts are necessarily accurately conceived or applied in the case of Jesus. Whether they are is the type of debate that

of his method, where I believe Crossan is most successful, that he devotes the least amount of methodological discussion. The area where he is most careful to outline his method, because he believes that this area is where historical method stands or falls, is the area where Crossan actually provides us with the least help in advancing historical method. When it comes to understanding the nature of data control, we find greater help from other sources, such as Ben Meyer.

historians ought to have among themselves. Crossan's understanding of Jesus' Jewishness is a matter of some debate; it may be that his focus on Greco-Roman culture is exclusive of thorough consideration of the context of Second Temple Judaism as most significant for understanding Jesus.

Part II

BEN MEYER AND CRITICAL REALISM

Chapter 4

Epistemology and Hermeneutics

We now turn to Meyer's work on historiography and hermeneutics, and its basis in his critical realism. I will eventually consider the outlines of Meyer's work on the historical Jesus, and observe how his historiographic and hermeneutical theory come to fruition there. I will begin with a discussion of the epistemology of critical realism, considering how Meyer's version of it assumes Bernard Lonergan's cognitional theory. I will consider the meaning and significance of the key notions of 'objectivity' and 'subjectivity' in Meyer's epistemology, and the role of 'horizons', followed by application of these in Meyer's hermeneutics. The goal in all this is exposition of Meyer's historiography in Chapter Five, where I will observe the role of critical realism and certain key notions, such as the reciprocity between data control and fact establishment. I will conclude, in Chapter Six, with a consideration of how Meyer's hermeneutics and historiography come into practice in his investigation of the historical Jesus, along with preliminary suggestions for how his method can be supplemented by recent recognition of the role of narrative in historiography.

In some ways the course of development in Meyer's works is the reverse of that of Crossan. I noted in Chapter 1 that Crossan's work on the historical Jesus began with his early *In Parables*, in which he voiced explicit reliance on tradition criticism. Over the next twenty years his subsequent Jesus works offered adjustments and refinements of method, through a structuralist and post-structuralist hermeneutic and their eventual abandonment, later dropping the criterion of dissimilarity but still by and large following 'transmissional analysis', while incorporating the social sciences. These developments in method culminated in his major Jesus work, *The Historical Jesus*. Meyer, on the other hand, entered onto the scholarly historical scene with his major study on Jesus, including extensive explication of issues of historiography, hermeneutics and method; he followed up over the next 15 years with further explication of the hermeneutical and cognitional basis for his early work. Rather than published explorations of method leading up to a full portrait of the historical Jesus, as in Crossan, Meyer's Jesus study comes first, and is followed by increasingly detailed study of method.

Why this apparently inverted sequence in Meyer's work? There are two possible reasons. First, the basis of Meyer's work in the cognitional theory of Bernard Lonergan poses some practical difficulties. Lonergan is little known in the field of New Testament studies, and Meyer's approach can be neither fully understood nor appreciated without some familiarity with Lonergan. As we will see, Meyer's New

Testament hermeneutics in fact amounts to a re-presentation of Lonergan in this area. Lonergan is a formidable thinker who requires not a little unpacking. Upon publication of *The Aims of Jesus*, more than one reviewer commented on the prominence of Lonergan in Meyer's method and the difficulty in grasping the former's relevance for Meyer's hermeneutics and historiography.[1] Though he never explicitly responded to these criticisms, some of Meyer's later work can be seen as an implicit response to them, in the form of an attempt at a remedy.[2]

Second, Meyer's work, while finding application in the areas of the historical Jesus and the early church, was always centred on hermeneutical and epistemological issues grounding these investigations or other readings of the New Testament. As we will see, Meyer considered the most profound differences among interpretive strategies and results to be rooted in conflicting hermeneutical and epistemological assumptions. He sought above all to forge a way through the apparent impasses among New Testament interpreters by clarifying the nature of the conflicts as he understood them, and offering solutions where these were available. So if the sequence of Meyer's works appears inverted, this is partly a reflection of Meyer's ongoing interest in fundamental hermeneutical matters, an interest which undergirded his early Jesus work but was not exhausted in this context, and in fact extended beyond it and outlived it, to be pursued throughout his career.[3]

1. Critical Realism

Meyer's work consistently employs a hermeneutic that assumes and builds upon the work of Jesuit philosopher and theologian Bernard Lonergan. I noted above that Meyer's work cannot be fully appreciated without some familiarity with Lonergan. It would not be an exaggeration to say that Meyer everywhere assumes Lonergan's cognitional theory as the epistemological world within which he conducts his enquiries. In *The Aims of Jesus*, explicit reference to Lonergan is infrequent, but Meyer cites Lonergan's 'generalized empirical method' as the philosophical presupposition of his entire study.[4] The essays of *Critical Realism and the New Testament* consist of a conscious exposition of Lonergan's critical realist hermeneutic and its application to New Testament studies. Meyer's debt to Lonergan is nowhere

1. See, for instance, the reviews of John Reumann *Journal of Biblical Literature* 100 (1981), pp. 296-300; James D.G. Dunn, *Scottish Journal of Theology* 34 (1981), pp. 474-76; I. Howard Marshall, *Journal for the Study of the New Testament* 7 (1980), pp. 67-69; and C.L. Mitton, *Expository Times* 90 (1979), pp. 346-47.

2. E.g., 'Lonergan's "Breakthrough" and *The Aims of Jesus*', in Dikran Y. Hadidian (ed.), *Critical Realism and the New Testament* (Princeton Theological Monograph Series, 17; Allison Park, PA: Pickwick, 1989), pp. 147-56.

3. Something of both these reasons can be seen together in the preface to *Critical Realism and the New Testament*, where Meyer comments on a source of his impulse to write those essays: he appropriated Lonergan's philosophic achievement in pursuit of his personal drive ('obsession') to make philosophical sense of his own literary and historical work. *Critical Realism*, pp. ix, x.

4. *The Aims of Jesus* (London: SCM Press, 1979), p. 18. Similarly in *The Early Christians*, p. 15.

more evident than in *Reality and Illusion in New Testament Scholarship*, where Meyer identifies the position he presents there entirely with that of Lonergan, with no attempt at originality on his part, 'no attempt to improve upon the master'.[5] Other examples could be mentioned,[6] but the point is already established: it would be difficult to overestimate the extent of Meyer's reliance on Lonergan, or the ubiquity of the latter's influence in Meyer's work.[7]

1.1. *Lonergan's Transcendental Method*
It becomes clear as Meyer's work progresses that he employs Lonergan's ideas under the general label of 'critical realism'.[8] The wider significance of this label will be discussed below, but I will generally use it as Meyer does, as a catch-all for Lonergan's cognitional theory, as we observe how Meyer appropriated that theory in his historical work. Lonergan's critical realism is in the first place a description of human cognitional operations, the spontaneous functioning of the mind in the process of knowing.[9] Lonergan described these operations as fundamentally *conscious* and *intentional*: conscious in that they are self-aware, and intentional in that they are directed towards an object.[10] These conscious and intentional operations occur in a multi-level process.

---

5.   *Reality and Illusion in New Testament Scholarship: A Primer in Critical Realist Hermeneutics* (Collegeville, MN: Liturgical Press, 1994), p. viii.

6.   See for example the collection of essays edited by Meyer and Sean McEvenue, *Lonergan's Hermeneutics: Its Development and Application* (Washington: Catholic University Press, 1989); and Meyer's acknowledgment of the Lonerganian foundation to his historical method and hermeneutic in *Christus Faber: The Master Builder and the House of God* (Allison Park, PA: Pickwick, 1992), pp. 2-5.

7.   Several former students and colleagues have noted the pervasive influence of Lonergan in Meyer's work, an influence which showed through in both his instruction and everyday conversations on scholarly topics. One former student describes Meyer's respect for Lonergan's work that approached a 'reverence', (Brice Martin, Arthur, Ontario, to the author, Glendale, CA, 21 August 2001). Other students and colleagues concur (Jo-Ann Brant, Goshen, IN, to the author, Glendale, CA, 22 August, 2001; John Martens, St Paul, MN, to the author, Glendale, CA, 22 August 2001; John Robertson, Hamilton, Ontario, to the author, Glendale, CA, 30 August 2001). But Meyer was specifically concerned with Lonergan's critical realist cognitional theory and hermeneutics; he sought to distance himself from the group he considered Lonergan devotees, whom he jokingly referred to as the 'Lonergan mafia' (Hans Rollmann, St John's, Newfoundland, to the author, Glendale, CA, 22 August, 2001). In any event, Meyer was convinced enough of the importance of Lonergan's work that he had his New Testament students read Lonergan's *Method in Theology* and other works as part of their instruction in New Testament interpretation (John Martens, 22 August 2001; Brice Martin, 21 August, 2001).

8.   The term does not appear explicitly until the essays of *Critical Realism and the New Testament*, but even in *Aims* Meyer notes that Lonergan's 'generalized empirical method' grounds a 'rigorously critical epistemological realism', *Aims*, p. 16.

9.   Meyer, *Reality*, p. 41.

10.   See Bernard Lonergan, *Collected Works of Bernard Lonergan* (ed. Frederick E. Crowe and Robert M. Doran, vol. 3), *Insight: A Study of Human Understanding* (Toronto: University of Toronto Press, 5th edn, 1992), pp. 344-46. *Insight* was Lonergan's major work on cognitional theory. For a concise summary, see also the first chapter of *Method in Theology* (New York: Herder & Herder, 1972; reprint, Toronto: University of Toronto Press, 1990), pp. 3-25. Secondary

In this process, ocular vision is involved, as are all the senses. The senses provide the data for knowledge. But these data in themselves do not constitute 'fully human knowing'. They are the lowest level of cognition, which Lonergan calls the level of 'experience'. It is on this level that the infant, as well as the non-human animal, 'knows' and relates to the world. The world of the infant consists solely of the data of experience. But in fully human knowing, these data provide only the raw materials for operations of a higher order which lead to knowledge.[11] On these data the knower operates. Prompted by his or her own wondering the knower puts questions to the data, and in the answering of those questions comes to grasp an intelligible unity in the data, in the act of understanding or insight. 'Understanding' is the second level of cognitional operations.

But the act of understanding is not the terminus of the process of knowing. The knower scrutinizes his or her understanding in the third level of cognitional operations, the act of judgement. Just as the knower is prompted to understand data by his or her questions, the knower is prompted to judgement by a desire to check the answers provided by understanding. In judgement, the knower determines what are the conditions required in order to judge the understanding to be true or false. The knower determines whether those conditions are met, and pronounces a judgement of true or false on the understanding. Only when this judgement is passed can the knower properly be said to 'know'. Fully human knowing involves this three-level cognitional operation of experience, understanding and judgement, which terminates in a grasp of the 'virtually unconditioned', Lonergan's technical term for an understanding whose truth conditions are known and are verified as fulfilled.[12] On this account, then, knowledge is ultimately a matter of grasping the virtually unconditioned, and what is known is defined as what is so grasped.

Lonergan was concerned to give an account of cognition (which answers the question 'what are we doing when we are knowing?'), and eventually of epistemology ('why is doing that knowing?') and metaphysics ('what do we know when we are doing it?'), that he saw as an alternative to a predominant misconception. The common misconception in cognition is the assumption that knowing is like seeing, peering, perceiving, looking, or intuiting. That is, knowing, at least on the level of perception, is a passive reception. Lonergan called this misconception

sources on Lonergan are numerous, but some standard expositions of his thought include David Tracy, *The Achievement of Bernard Lonergan* (New York: Herder & Herder, 1970); Hugo A. Meynell, *An Introduction to the Philosophy of Bernard Lonergan* (New York: Barnes and Noble, 1976); and Frederick E. Crowe, *Lonergan* (Collegeville, MN: Liturgical Press, 1992).

11. Meyer, 'The Challenges of Text and Reader to the Historical-Critical Method', in Wim Beuken, Sean Freyne and Anton Weiler (eds.), *The Bible and Its Readers* (Concilium 1991/1; London: SCM Press, 1991), pp. 5-6, 7.

12. Lonergan's initial exposition of his cognitional theory, in *Insight*, outlined these three levels. To these he later added a fourth, the level of *decision*, in which the knower takes action on what is known (though this level was arguably hinted at in *Insight*). See the description of these developments in a biographical context in Frederick Crowe, *Lonergan*, pp. 95-99. For effective summary of the first three levels, see *Insight*, ch. 9. For a summary of all four levels, see *Method*, ch. 1.

'picture thinking'.[13] One receives knowledge of an object by simply attending to the object, as one would look at a picture. Lonergan insisted, alternatively, that knowing, including perception, is not like seeing but is an active process of understanding and judging.

So critical realism is first of all these conscious and intentional cognitional operations, by which one comes to know. These operations are spontaneous in human knowing; they are the universal means by which knowledge is acquired.[14] But critical realism is in the second instance the objectification of these operations, making them explicit in the type of cognitional analysis that Lonergan undertakes in *Insight*. Objectifying the operations of cognition makes them into a usable philosophical tool. As one becomes aware of the process by which one comes to know, a heightening of consciousness occurs with respect to the nature of knowledge.[15] One comes to realize that knowing is not like 'taking a look' at an object but is rather a function of insight and judgement upon experiential data. The integral roles of insight and judgement are recognized, placing knowledge on a new footing.

In one respect, the point that knowledge involves the spontaneous operations of insight and judgement seems trivial. It appears to be a rehearsal of what in our day is self-evident to common sense, that normally functioning human beings cognitively process data in order to understand. But in another respect it is not trivial because common sense would often short-circuit the understanding and judging operations, most often in the area of perception, and assume that knowledge springs ready-made from data. In addition, most formal epistemologies overlook the roles of understanding and judgement.[16] Lonergan frequently pointed out that both a naive realist and a Kantian idealist account of knowledge assume that the senses immediately relate the knower to the object of knowledge. For the naive realist, that object is reality; for the idealist, that object is not reality but only appearance, distinct from the thing-in-itself. But Lonergan maintained that the senses do not immediately relate the knower to the object of knowledge, for the senses alone do not provide *knowledge*, but only *data*.[17] To assume that we have immediate contact with the objects of knowledge (whether real or apparent) through the senses is to assume that the senses themselves provide us with a kind of knowledge; but they do not. They provide only data, which in Lonergan's thinking seem to be little more than neural impulses.[18] Knowledge only comes when the data are acted upon

---

13. See 'Cognitional Structure', in Frederick E. Crowe and Robert M. Doran (eds.), *Collected Works of Bernard Lonergan. IV. Collection* (Toronto: University of Toronto Press, 2nd edn, 1988), p. 219; also 'The Subject', in William F.J. Ryan and Bernard J. Tyrrell (eds.), *A Second Collection* (Toronto: University of Toronto Press, 1974), p. 76.

14. For this reason Lonergan called these operations 'transcendental method', i.e., universal method. See *Method*, pp. 4, 13-25. Meyer picks up on this designation, but uses it sparingly: *Critical Realism*, pp. 68ff.; *Reality and Illusion*, pp. 110, 190.

15. Meyer, *Reality and Illusion*, p. 190; *Critical Realism*, p. 68.

16. Eugene Webb makes a similar point, in *Philosophers of Consciousness: Polanyi, Lonergan, Voegelin, Ricoeur, Girard, Kierkegaard* (Seattle: University of Washington Press, 1988), pp. 62ff.

17. Lonergan, 'Cognitional Structure', p. 218.

18. 'A datum of sense may be defined as the content of an act of seeing, hearing, touching,

by the operations of insight and judgement. This is true of knowledge of the most abstract and rational sort, as well as perceptual knowledge of the most concrete and mundane. I acquire my knowledge that there is a tree outside my window not simply by adverting to the tree. To believe that I acquire my knowledge simply by adverting is to assume that knowledge is like looking at an object: either looking in the sense of exercising ocular vision toward the real object, or else looking 'mentally' at the phenomenal object, the appearance of the object in the senses. On the contrary, I know that there is a tree outside my window by the exercise of understanding and judgement upon the data I experience. At this mundane level, the understanding and judgement are so spontaneous that they are easily overlooked; but it is Lonergan's contention that, without such operations, there would be no knowledge of the tree. Knowledge of every sort is a matter of these active operations.

I noted above that the knower is not immediately related to the object of knowledge by the senses, by the level of experience. Lonergan maintained that the knower is in fact only mediately related to the object by all the operations of cognition, including understanding and judgement. The world is mediated to the knower by these operations, such that Lonergan called the world so known 'the world mediated by meaning'.[19] But he held that there is indeed immediate relation to the world, and that relation is by 'the intention of being'.[20] By 'intention of being' Lonergan meant the inherent notion of and drive towards being, or the real, that constitutes the dynamism of human enquiry. As Lonergan described it, 'Deep within us all, emergent when the noise of other appetites is stilled, there is a drive to know, to understand, to see why, to discover the reason, to find the cause, to explain.'[21] This drive to know being, to know everything that is, is manifested in questioning.[22] The above description of cognitional operations pointed out that the knower is prompted from experience to understanding by wondering and questioning, and from understanding to judgement by the desire to check and affirm the

tasting, smelling', Lonergan, *Insight*, p. 96. Yet Lonergan is quick to point out that these data do not occur in a cognitional vacuum. They already have their context in the flow of perception, which is determined by the perceiver's interests and preoccupations. This flow of perception can be seen as the level of understanding or insight spontaneously following on the level of experience, the data of sense. Despite similarities, Lonergan's 'data of sense' are not to be identified with the sense-data of phenomenology. In the latter, sense-data constitute the foundation from which knowledge is inferred; they seem to constitute in themselves a basic form of knowledge. In Lonergan's theory, data of sense seem to be neither more nor less foundational or essential than are the other operations of consciousness, and are not *in themselves* knowledge. Hugo Meynell's description is apt: 'Experience only gives us uncoordinated scraps of data', *An Introduction to the Philosophy of Bernard Lonergan*, p. 3.

19. Lonergan, 'Unity and Plurality', in Frederick E. Crowe (ed.), *A Third Collection: Papers of Bernard J.F. Lonergan* (New York: Paulist Press, 1985), p. 240; 'Insight Revisited', in *A Second Collection*, p. 269; *Method*, pp. 76-77. See also Meyer's exposition in *Reality and Illusion*, pp. 189-90.

20. Lonergan, 'Unity and Plurality', p. 240; 'Cognitional Structure', p. 218; *Insight*, p. 379.

21. Lonergan, *Insight*, p. 28. This drive is described by Lonergan as 'the eros of the human spirit', *Method*, p. 13.

22. Lonergan, *Insight*, p. 372.

answers. All this wondering, questioning and desire to know is the varied manifes-
tation of the fundamental human drive to the true, the real and ultimately to the
good. This drive is detached, disinterested and unrestricted and is the immanent
source of transcendent knowledge.[23] By the questioning that this drive produces,
the knower is immediately related to the world, because the world, or being, is
what the knower strives for, what his or her questions intend, and being is what is
known when the questions are successfully answered. Our original contact with the
objects of our knowledge is not through our senses, nor through our understanding
and judgement, but through our questioning that is oriented to and intends those
objects, that drives all these cognitional operations to know the objects.[24] In Lonergan's words, 'There is the object in the world mediated by meaning: it is what is
intended by the question, and it is what becomes understood, affirmed, decided by
the answer. To this type of object we are related immediately by our questions and
only mediately by the operations relevant to answers, for the answers refer to
objects only because they are answers to questions.'[25]

Critical realism, then, in Meyer's usage, is specifically Lonergan's cognitional
theory, but it is also a broader hermeneutic that can be derived from this, a hermeneutic that controls Meyer's approach to New Testament studies and historical
Jesus research.[26] Much of this hermeneutic was worked out by Lonergan himself,
but much of it is also the result of Meyer's specific application of Lonergan in
Meyer's chosen field. At one point Meyer identifies two specific areas where a
critical realist understanding of historical-critical method is evident in his work.[27]
1) In his heuristic definition of the 'historical Jesus': 'the Jesus of ancient Palestine
insofar as, intended by historical questions, he comes to be known through satis-
factory answers to those questions'. This is, conversely, the rejection of those
definitions of the historical Jesus that abstract from the actual historical figure, e.g.,
the historical Jesus defined as 'the historian's image of Jesus'. The latter definitions
Meyer finds to be 'tinged with positivism or idealism'. Critical realism can be seen
to be at work here in the primacy given to questions in defining the object of knowl-

---

23. Lonergan, *Insight*, p. 659.

24. Meyer's reading of Lonergan is helpful: the senses provide only data, not 'reality' nor
'appearance of reality'; but wonder (the drive to know) 'is the boundless openness whereby the
wonderer/questioner enters into relation not just to data but to reality and, in principle, to the whole
of reality. Intending is an immediate relating to the intender of whatever he intends. There is
nothing to keep him from intending the real. He could not keep himself from such intending..."object" in the context of fully human knowing is whatever is intended by questions and
known when the questions are satisfactorily answered', *Critical Realism*, pp. 85-86.

25. Lonergan, *Method*, pp. 262-63; 35.

26. It is important to identify Meyer's understanding of critical realism, because the term is
gaining increased usage in New Testament and historical Jesus studies, and not all users of it
identify so firmly with Lonergan's cognitional theory. There may be broad similarities among
those with some form of critical realist sensibility, but whether or not a given version is useful for
furthering historiographic discussion would have to be determined by examining that version. See
appendix 2 of the present work for a survey of varieties of critical realism and how they compare to
Lonergan's cognitional theory.

27. This identification is found in Meyer, *Christus Faber*, p. 3.

edge, while maintaining the object as not merely theoretical or reconstructed, not 'ideal', but real insofar as the real is what is known when questions are answered correctly. Jesus as a historical figure is known by virtue of questions posed to the data and answered. 2) In 'an indispensable contribution of history to the cause of religion: the framing of the transpositions of meaning that allow religious truths to be moved into new contexts, so surviving intact the reality of continuously changing contexts'. For Meyer, an acknowledged theological purpose for the pursuit of history, far from injecting theological bias into a critical endeavour, is in fact generously provided for by a critical realist hermeneutic. Questions of a theological or religious nature can in fact be legitimate historical questions, and the history that is known in answer to those questions amounts to a changing historical framework for persisting theological truths.

1.2. *Objectivity and Subjectivity*
What is clear throughout Meyer's work is the prominence of Lonergan's emphasis on the active role of the subject in the process of knowing. This role is seen first of all in the subject's specific operations of cognition, the three levels of the subject's conscious, intentional operations, but also goes beyond what is involved in these operations to larger issues of the subject's overall resources for acquiring knowledge. The notion that best captures the spirit of Lonergan's work as applied by Meyer is that of *objectivity as rooted in authentic subjectivity*. Meyer stresses that there is a need for both 'objectivity' and 'subjectivity' in a sound epistemology or hermeneutic.[28] Once upon a time, in the epistemological 'age of innocence', a naive objectivism discussed problems exclusively in terms of objective data and objective arguments, and considered any involvement of 'subjective' elements in knowledge to be an interference. The passing of this age was marked by attention to the thinking, deciding and doing of the subject. Philosophers such as Schopenhauer, Nietzsche, Kierkegaard and John Henry Newman were initial thematizers of the subject, and Heidegger, Jaspers and others moved it toward maturity in the twentieth century.[29] The age of innocence, when the subject could be bypassed in talk of objective knowledge, has indeed passed. But we continue to live with an objectivist, pre-hermeneutical heritage that assumes that any person, given enough evidence and intelligence, will make the proper judgements. Meyer follows Lonergan in seeing knowledge as rooted in the authenticity of the subject. This recognition of the primacy of the subject is not, for Lonergan or Meyer, a complete relativizing of knowledge, or a call for the abandonment of all notions of objectivity; but it is a recognition of the meaning of objectivity as inextricably bound with the operations of the knowing subject.

The notion that objectivity requires *authenticity* in the subject implies that not just any kind of subjectivity is valid. Authentic subjectivity is rooted first of all in the cognitional operations of experience, understanding and judgement. Objectivity requires the proper functioning of these operations, resulting in the subject's

---

28. See especially *Critical Realism*, chs. 4 and 6 and *Reality and Illusion, passim*.
29. Meyer, *Critical Realism*, p. 78.

capacity for self-transcendence, the capability of affirming what is so, beyond supposition, conjecture and wishful thinking. It is the operations of cognition that result in the grasp of truth. Though truth, once attained, is independent of the subject, truth's ontological home is the subject. Truth is reached through the process of wondering, questioning, answering, reflection and judgement that takes place through the subject's operations of cognition. 'Truth, in fine, ripens on the tree of the subject, and objectivity is the fruit of subjectivity at its most intense.'[30] Because objectivity is a function of the subjectivity that is the different operations of cognition, there are different components of objectivity.[31] There is experiential objectivity which consists in the givenness of data. There is normative objectivity which consists in meeting the exigences of intelligence (for insight in response to questions) and reasonableness (for the determination of the truth of the insight). There is also absolute objectivity, which consists in combining the results of normative and experiential objectivity in the grasp of the virtually unconditioned.

Given the primacy of the operations of cognition in the notion of subjectivity, one could get the impression that 'subjectivity' for Lonergan and Meyer is really only a naive objectivism in disguise, that identifying the operations of cognition is simply an elegant way of claiming that objectivity is found in the grasp of what any reasonable person would affirm in the face of given evidence. At times Meyer seems to confirm this impression, with such comments as 'When is subjectivity authentic? When the subject does things the right way.'[32] It would be easy to take the operations of insight and judgement as providing universal criteria for correct thinking, or a foundational standard of reasonableness. But for Lonergan, the point of considering the operations of cognition was always to show that knowledge is the fruit of an *activity on the part of the knower*, and that the known object is always and only mediated by this activity. The cognitional operations are at the core of this activity, and are thus at the core of the subjectivity that is at the root of knowledge of objects; but Lonergan also explored other dimensions of subjectivity beyond the operations themselves. After *Insight* (1957), the major work in which he outlined his transcendental method, Lonergan began to explore subjectivity in ways not unlike the hermeneutic philosophers of the twentieth century.[33] The 1960s saw a period in his work that many of his interpreters have called his 'turn to the subject'.[34] He became concerned with specific problems of historicism and the

---

30. Meyer, *Critical Realism*, pp. 139-40. As Lonergan stated it, 'Intentionally [truth] is independent of the subject, but ontologically it resides only in the subject. Intentionally it goes beyond the subject, yet it does so only because ontologically the subject is capable of an intentional self-transcendence… The fruit of truth must grow and mature on the tree of the subject, before it can be plucked and placed in its absolute realm', 'The Subject', pp. 70, 71.

31. Meyer, *Critical Realism*, p. 199. Lonergan, *Insight*, pp. 402-407; and *Method*, p. 263.

32. Meyer, *Reality and Illusion*, p. 4.

33. He cites Gadamer frequently in *Method in Theology* (1972).

34. Crowe, *Lonergan*, pp. 94ff; Tracy, *Achievement*, p. 9; Ulf Jonsson, *Foundations for Knowing God: Bernard Lonergan's Foundations for Knowledge of God and the Challenge from Antifoundationalism* (European University Studies, 23; Frankfurt am Main: Peter Lang, 1999), pp. 78ff.

social sciences, and issues of cultural relativity attendant to these. His work in this period reflects an understanding of 'authentic subjectivity' that goes beyond the operations of cognition to the broader resources within the subject, by which the subject knows; this is an exploration of all the subjective conditions for the attainment of objective truth.

Meyer capitalizes on these observations of Lonergan for the area of New Testament studies. Meyer notes that New Testament scholars utilizing historical method typically resist the appropriation of subjectivity because of long-held and well-entrenched positivist commitments. But Meyer insists that positivism does not harmonize with the practice of history; the historian draws on 'everything he knows – his whole fund of experience and range of understanding and hard-won equilibrium of judgment', and not merely on the positivist's data of sense.[35] The central role of the operations of cognition in subjectivity notwithstanding, Meyer follows Lonergan when he criticizes the assumption that all people, given enough evidence and intelligence, will make the proper judgements. No scholarly community is led to its judgements simply by the careful marshalling and weighing of evidence. What counts as evidence sufficient for a particular judgement cannot simply be the evidence sufficient to win the assent of all people,[36] for there are factors that contribute to judgement that not all people share. In the final analysis, judgement is more than a matter of 'data' and 'argument', it is a matter of subjectivity that consists of the subject's *horizons*.[37]

1.3. *Horizons and Conversion*

An early discussion of the notion of horizon in Lonergan occurs in the 1963 article 'Metaphysics as Horizon', in which he expounds on the term as used by Emerich Coreth. Here Lonergan defines horizon as 'a maximum field of vision from a determinate standpoint'.[38] From this literal definition one can derive an epistemological application, in which horizon is the boundary within which one knows. Horizon is the context that is prior to the meaning of all statements; statements, including statements of problems and of solutions, as well as questions, have their meaning by presupposing their proper horizon. For this reason, horizons cannot be proved deductively: they are the context for the meaning of any proof. Lonergan identified both subjective and objective poles in a given horizon; the subjective pole is the resources present in the subject for understanding or construing meanings, or the subject's 'intentionality-meaning possibilities'.[39] The objective pole is the 'worlds of meaning' to which the subject is open by virtue of the possibilities for understanding available to the subject based on his or her subjective resources.[40]

35. Meyer, *Critical Realism*, p. 141.

36. As seems to be assumed by, for example, John Meier, when he proposes to arrive at an historical picture of Jesus on which a Catholic, a Protestant, a Jew and an agnostic could all agree. See Meier, *A Marginal Jew*, vol. 1, 1-2; and Meyer's comments on Meier's proposal in *Reality and Illusion*, p. 108.

37. Meyer, *Critical Realism*, pp. 80-81.

38. Lonergan, 'Metaphysics as Horizon', in *Collection*, p. 198.

39. See Tracy's explication, *Achievement*, p. 14.

40. In Coreth's use, horizon is equated with metaphysics, where metaphysics is the thema-

A later statement of horizon is found in *Method in Theology*. Horizon is literally the limit of one's field of vision; it represents the boundary of the totality of visible objects for a particular observer. Metaphorically, horizon is the limit of one's knowledge and interests.

> As our field of vision, so too the scope of our knowledge, and the range of our interests are bounded. As fields of vision vary with one's standpoint, so too the scope of one's knowledge and the range of one's interests vary with the period in which one lives, one's social background and milieu, one's education and personal development. So there has arisen a metaphorical or perhaps analogous meaning of the word, horizon. In this sense what lies beyond one's horizon is simply outside the range of one's knowledge and interests: one neither knows nor cares. But what lies within one's horizon is in some measure, great or small, an object of interest and knowledge.[41]

Meyer similarly describes Lonergan's notion of horizon as the boundary, for a particular knower, between the known unknown and the unknown unknown, i.e., between the questions one can raise but not answer and the questions one cannot even raise.[42] In the context of a discussion of historiography, Meyer describes the shaping of horizons in a way that reflects their fundamental and intensely personal nature. Historians draw from many sources for their resources for formulating historical problems and solutions,

> From firsthand contact with 'the data', from diligent reading of the relevant monographs, etc., but also from the magazine that the historian ...leafed through in the dentist's waiting room, from the jingle he heard a neighbour's child singing; in short, not only from sources listed in the handbooks and monographs, but from the thousand and one additional sources of information, inspiration, wonder, feeling, conjecture that crowd the life of the individual scholar and continuously reshape his horizons.

Around the core of subjectivity constituted by the operations of cognition, there is the notion of subjectivity as consisting of the subject's horizons, all of the various and vast personal resources that shape the subject's knowledge and interests, that determine what the subject is able to know and able to be interested in knowing, what the subject can ask questions about and what sense the subject's questions can have. These horizons are in turn shaped by the subject's experiences, social location and personal development. But the fact that horizons are intensely personal does not mean for Lonergan that they are completely relative; and the fact that horizons are determinate of the subject's knowledge and interests does not

---

tization of a latent understanding of being. Lonergan appreciates Coreth's metaphysics, but resists equating metaphysics with a total horizon: 'Metaphysics, as about being, equates with the objective pole of that horizon; but metaphysics, as science, does not equate with the subjective pole', 'Metaphysics as Horizon', p. 204. The subjective pole is the concrete enquirer in his or her performance of questions.

41. Lonergan, *Method*, p. 236.

42. Meyer notes that this precise definition does not appear in any of Lonergan's published works, but only in a typescript cited by David Tracy. Meyer, 'The Relevance of Horizon', in *The Downside Review* 112 (1994), pp. 1; 12 n. 1.

mean they function deterministically. Lonergan also spoke of the possibility, and the necessity, of horizons being changed. That they *can* be changed shows that one is not simply locked into a particular set of horizons, bound to see the world within it and without the possibility of communication with those of differing horizons. That horizons at times *should* be changed shows that Lonergan did not understand all horizons to be equally adequate.

Because any argument takes place within a particular set of horizons, it would seem that to change one's horizons would require the impossibility of arguing on the basis of one horizon the preferability of another. But Lonergan points out that a change of horizon is not done on the basis of that horizon, but by 'envisaging a quite different and, at first sight, incomprehensible alternative and then undergoing a conversion'.[43] Horizons are changed, not by argument, but by *conversion* from one horizon to the other. Here, underlying the operations of cognition, is the heart of the subject's activity that promotes authentic subjectivity, for conversion is an activity of self-transformation.[44] Lonergan's description is succinct:

> By conversion is understood a transformation of the subject and his world. Normally, it is a prolonged process though its explicit acknowledgment may be concentrated in a few momentous judgments and decisions... It is a resultant change of course and direction. It is as if one's eyes were opened and one's former world faded and fell away... Conversion, as lived, affects all of a man's conscious and intentional operations. It directs his gaze, pervades his imagination, releases the symbols that penetrate to the depths of his psyche. It enriches his understanding, guides his judgments, reinforces his decisions.[45]

Lonergan distinguished three types of conversion: intellectual, moral and religious.[46] Meyer's summary of these is effective.[47] Intellectual conversion is the transition from the horizon of cognitional myth, that knowing is like seeing, to the horizon of transcendental method. Moral conversion is the transition from the horizon of personal satisfactions to the existential primacy of values. Religious conversion is the transition from the horizon of this-worldly commitments to the primacy of the love of God in one's life. There is no required order for their occurrence in the individual subject, but when all three occur the later conversions sublate the earlier (i.e., moral sublates intellectual, religious sublates both moral and intellectual), in the sense that they go beyond them and bring them forward to fuller realization.[48]

The need for the authenticity that results from a change of horizons is prominent in Meyer's application of Lonergan to New Testament studies. As I will show, Meyer considered intellectual conversion as especially relevant. In any investigation, one's understanding of data and one's judgement of what is true or false depend on one's description, either stated or assumed, of cognitional operations. In

---

43. Lonergan, *Method*, p. 224.
44. Meyer, *Critical Realism*, p. 81.
45. Lonergan, *Method*, pp. 130-31.
46. See Lonergan, *Method*, pp. 238ff.
47. See Meyer, *Critical Realism*, pp. 69-70.
48. Lonergan, *Method*, p. 241.

biblical studies, judgements of reality and illusion in historical criticism depend on some controlling view of history and of reality, and some description of cognitional operations by which these are grasped. If a biblical scholar operates simply on the assumption that his or her view of history is self-evident and adequate, he or she may in fact be operating with unconscious ideological influences derived from an unacknowledged and possibly inadequate philosophy. '[T]he functional dependence of historical criticism on some view of reality, including historical reality, pointedly illustrates the relevance of intellectual conversion to biblical scholarship.'[49]

In summary, the critical realism that orients Meyer's entire project in New Testament and historical Jesus studies is at bottom a recognition of the need for any notion of objectivity in knowledge of the real to arise from an account of authentic subjectivity. For Meyer, following Lonergan, *the resources of the subject* for acquiring knowledge are always in view. These resources consist first of all of the subject's cognitional operations, which define the knowing process and are operative in all manner of knowing, from perception to the most abstract reasoning. They also consist of the subject's horizons, the limits within which one knows and is able to know and to be interested. Subjectivity is authentic when the subject (1) recognizes that knowing is not like seeing, and objectifies the operations of cognition, allowing them to amount to a usable procedure for acquiring knowledge, and (2) attends to the horizons within which knowledge is formed. Meyer's work in hermeneutics highlights the exercise of authentic subjectivity for understanding texts and data.

2. *Hermeneutics*

The interest in hermeneutics is the defining moment in all of Meyer's work.[50] He brings to bear the resources of Lonergan's transcendental method in the form of critical realism for the purpose of understanding how one understands the biblical text. Conveniently, Meyer outlined seven salient traits of a critical realist hermeneutic. I will structure my presentation of Meyer's hermeneutic around this list.[51]

2.1. *The Structures of Conscious Intentionality*
Critical Realism puts a high premium on the structures of conscious intentionality. These structures are of course the cognitional operations that constitute Lonergan's transcendental method, the operations of experience, understanding and judgement. These are the core of the critical realism that Meyer adopts from Lonergan, and are the starting point for the critical realist account of the knowing subject. A critical

---

49. Meyer, *Critical Realism*, p. 71.

50. A former doctoral student and teaching assistant of Meyer recalls that his discussions of hermeneutics even in undergraduate courses were often confusing to students. But such discussions were inevitable because the hermeneutic process was central to interpretation for him, and ultimately fruitful for his students. Jo-Ann Brant, Goshen, IN to the author, Glendale, CA, 22 August, 2001.

51. Found in the introduction to *Critical Realism and the New Testament*, pp. x-xiii.

realist hermeneutic will take its stand on these structures, and their ubiquity in Meyer's hermeneutic will become apparent in our study.

I have pointed out the apparently 'inverted' character of the progression of Meyer's work, in which historical application of methods is presented at the outset, to be followed up by more detailed explication of those methods and their hermeneutical basis. The explication of the cognitional operations and their role in a hermeneutic is one area where this inversion is evident. In *Aims*, Meyer assumes Lonergan's cognitional theory as the basis for his method, but gives only a few pages to an abbreviated outline of that basis.[52] Discussion of hermeneutics in this early work consists of a certain working out of implications of the theory for a historical method. It is left to *Critical Realism and the New Testament*, and especially to *Reality and Illusion* to make the theory more explicit and to make further hermeneutical applications.

2.2. *The Correlation of 'True' and 'Real'*

Reality is known through finding out what is true. From the beginning of *Insight* Lonergan intended to give an account of both the knowing subject and the object of knowledge; that is, he was interested in both an epistemology and a metaphysics, and the metaphysics as based on, as a consequence of, the epistemology. This order, epistemology followed by metaphysics, Lonergan formulated specifically against his Thomist heritage which insisted on beginning philosophical enquiry with metaphysics, with enquiry into the nature of reality.[53] Lonergan insisted that epistemology comes first. An understanding of what it is to understand, will lead one to understand the broad lines of all there is to be understood.[54] If knowledge is a matter of understanding and judgement, then the object of knowledge, the real, is what is known through true judgement. The real, or being, is also the object of the pure desire to know, which is the dynamic of the operations of cognition. What we desire to know, what all our questions which drive the knowing process intend, is being. So being, the real, can be defined in terms of what we desire to know and in fact do know by the operations of experience, understanding and judgement.[55] This functional understanding of the real is in opposition to what Lonergan described as the 'already-out-there-now' real,[56] the real that exists fully constituted apart from the subject, such that it is simply an object of extroverted consciousness, or of a knowledge that resembles 'taking a look', rather than an object to be grasped in the operations of understanding and judgement. Meyer recognized and appropriated Lonergan's metaphysics as derivative of his cognitional theory, and thereby made the real as an object of knowledge correlative to true judgements.

---

52. Meyer, *Aims*, pp. 16-17.
53. Meyer, *Critical Realism*, p. 5; Crowe, p. 51.
54. Lonergan, *Insight*, p. 22.
55. See Meyer, *Reality and Illusion*, p. 23.
56. Lonergan, *Insight*, pp. 276-77; *Method*, pp. 262-63.

2.3. *Primacy of Individual Meaning*

The meaning of the text as individual and unique is given priority over understanding the text by subsuming its contents under general categories. Meyer's distinction between interpretation of texts and analysis of texts helps illuminate this point.[57] Interpretation focuses on understanding the intended sense of the text. But in addition to being interpreted, a text may be understood in other ways, i.e., analysed. Analysis focuses on what is revealed in the text aside from what was intended, or possibly contrary to what was intended. The latter reads 'between the lines', reads the text in spite of itself. Some analysis precedes interpretation and is done for interpretation's sake. Such would include textual criticism, literary analysis of the form or genre of the text, or those matters usually covered under New Testament 'introduction': author, date and provenance of a text. Some analysis, such as aspects of historical reconstruction, follows interpretation and supposes it. The latter type of analysis will usually be wrong if correct interpretation has not already been accomplished. In this sense interpretation, which grasps the unique and intended meaning of the text, must precede certain types of analysis.

Meyer insists that interpretation of the intended sense of the text is always primary and indispensable in historical work. 'It is only by rightly understanding the ransom note as a ransom note that there is any point in examining the ransom note for what it might unintentionally reveal of its own sender. It is only through understanding the encomium on its own terms and in accord with its intended sense that the social historian can use it as a resource for reconstructing the semantic network, the horizons and field of vision, the social world of the encomium.'[58] Even in those types of analysis that precede interpretation, the analyst cannot even begin unless there is some preliminary understanding of the text. But such an understanding is necessarily provisional; it is held loosely, subject to revision in light of the results of later interpretation. Meyer emphasizes the primacy of interpretation over against tendencies in New Testament studies to make analysis primary, or even to dispense with interpretation altogether in favour of analysis. He sees the latter tendency in structuralist approaches and in certain applications of social science criticism in historiography. To these one could certainly add poststructuralism and deconstruction, since, as was noted in Chapter One, these follow structuralism in the rejection of the intended meaning of the text as a legitimate object of interpretation, and go even further in insisting that determinate meaning is not to be found in any text.

The hallmark of critical realism is a full accounting of the knowing subject. As I will show, interpretation of a text is given primacy in a critical realist hermeneutic because to interpret well the subject is required to take full account of his or her subjectivity. An analysis that attempts to bypass interpretation leaves an important component of subject and subjectivity out of account, neglecting the sine qua non of knowledge and of understanding.

---

57. See his discussion in *Reality and Illusion*, pp. 98-101.
58. Meyer, *Reality and Illusion*, p. 99.

2.4. *The Intended Sense*

In Meyer's critical realism, 'the text has a *prima facie* claim on the reader, namely, to be construed in accord with its intended sense'.[59] This point is presupposed in the above understanding of interpretation as construal of the intended sense. The intended sense is, in a word, what makes the individual utterance or text to be what it is, and what makes discourse determinate.[60] The intended sense is exclusively what makes, say, a poem to be a poem, and not just a 'chunk of language'.[61]

Meyer grounds the notion of the intended sense of texts in the human drive toward the mediation of meaning to one's fellows. Language is the 'primary and peerless' resource for the mediation of meaning, encoding meaning that the communicator wishes to express. The receiver of the communication construes or decodes the transmission, and the construal may or may not correspond to what the transmitter intended.[62] In the written text, the intended message is encoded by the writer, and the reader construes the text with a view to receiving its message. So 'intended meaning' is not understood to be only in the writer, but is intrinsic to the text insofar as the text encodes the writer's message.[63]

Meyer was fully cognizant of the trend away from understanding interpretation in terms of construal of the intended sense of the text. The latter has come to be termed the 'intentional fallacy', after the programmatic essay by Wimsatt and Beardsley.[64] Though notions of intention have not been completely abandoned, and in some circles are undergoing qualified revival,[65] the tenor of today's hermeneutic environment, in which not only intention but also determinate textual meaning is often denied, seems to place the onus on the one supporting the notion of the intended sense. Meyer consistently defends the intended sense on the ground that objections to it assume that the intended sense is *extrinsic* to the written text, located in the mind of the author, which by all accounts is inaccessible to the interpreter. Meyer instead locates the intended sense *within* the text; the intended sense is both what the writer had in mind *and managed to express* in the text.[66] This intention includes all aspects of the text that contribute to the realization of meaning, going beyond simply the content of what is meant (i.e., 'the conceptual content yielded by even a good paraphrase') to how it is meant, in such aspects as tone, style and genre.[67]

59. Meyer, *Critical Realism*, p. xi.
60. Meyer, *Critical Realism*, p. xii.
61. Meyer, *Reality and Illusion*, p. 97.
62. Meyer, *Critical Realism*, pp. 18-19.
63. Meyer, *Critical Realism*, p. 19.
64. Viz., 'The Intentional Fallacy', in *The Verbal Icon: Studies in the Meaning of Poetry* (Lexington, KY: University of Kentucky Press, 1954), pp. 3-18.
65. As in the revision of the notion of intention suggested by Stephen Fowl, 'The Role of Authorial Intention in the Theological Interpretation of Scripture', in Joel B. Green and Max Turner (eds.), *Between Two Horizons: Spanning New Testament Studies and Systematic Theology* (Grand Rapids: Eerdmans, 2000), pp. 71-87.
66. Meyer, *Reality and Illusion*, pp. 97-98; *Critical Realism*, pp. 20, 40.
67. Meyer, *Reality and Illusion*, pp. 94-96.

Though much of today's hermeneutic environment is hostile to intention as relevant to interpretation, it would not seem that Meyer's defence of the intended sense is directed so much to the historically inclined interpreters who are the focus of the present study. It is arguable that some idea of an intended sense is inherent in historical investigation. Investigating the New Testament texts and other sources for information they may yield on the historical Jesus is an enterprise undertaken by historians, most of whom handle texts as historical artefacts, which means that the texts are, at least partly, products of historical agents and events. In this sense the association of agent/author with the text is intrinsic to treating the text as a piece of historical evidence. The total divorce of author from text that is characteristic of most denials of the intended sense would effectively shatter the text as a 'window' onto history, rendering it useless as a piece of evidence, a basis for inferring what went forward in the past. We will see below that this kind of denial of the text as a means of historical inference is in fact what some recent proposals want to do. But most historians of Jesus, I would say most historians generally, do not want to do this; rather, they treat the text as significant for what it reveals of the historical agents and events that engendered the text. I noted in Chapter One that the early Crossan, despite his appropriation of post-structuralist thought (which is clearly hostile to intention) for interpreting the content of Jesus' parables, assumed a discoverable, univocal message in those parables, which message was intended by their author, Jesus, and is to be discovered largely in spite of the intentions the evangelists had in mind when they recorded the tradition. In many cases the notion of the intended sense, as *intrinsic* to the text as described by Meyer, is simply assumed by the historian as he or she uses the text as a means of understanding the historical agents who produced the text. Probably the more pertinent of Meyer's observations for our purposes is his emphasis on the primacy of the intended sense vis-à-vis analysis. Among historians, although there is usually an operative assumption of an intended sense, the intended sense as emphasized by Meyer (i.e., as preceding analysis) tends to be not so much denied as neglected. Some of the further points below will illuminate how, in Meyer's hermeneutic, a certain attention to the intended sense is necessary for understanding the text on its own terms, and such an understanding is necessary for proper historical analysis.

2.5. *The Necessity of Judgement*

A critical realist hermeneutic 'distinguishes between understanding and judgement and makes judgement integral to the task of interpreting'.[68] Interpretation is an instance of knowledge; it is knowledge of the intended sense of the text. All knowledge involves experience, understanding and judgement. The knowledge that is interpretation has its experience in the data received as marks on paper. These marks must be understood, and the understanding must be judged to be correct or otherwise. This explication of interpretation as a form of knowledge, involving the same cognitional operations as all knowledge, is offered against what Meyer called a 'hermeneutics of innocence'. The latter is a form of naive realism that assumes

---

68. Meyer, *Critical Realism*, p. xii.

that textual meaning is 'already-out-there-now', fully constituted on the page, waiting to be read off the page. Interpretation is rather a matter of the subject's operations of understanding and judgement, and, like the metaphysics of critical realism, sees meaning as a reality defined in terms of the subject's understanding and judgement: meaning is what is construed, and judged correctly so, by the interpreter. This is an important qualification of the idea of the 'plain sense' of the text. Rather than assuming that the intended sense is the 'plain sense', obvious at first glance, this understanding of interpretation sees the intended sense of a text as an unknown to be known, to be uncovered by the operations of understanding and judgement, whether that sense be 'plain' or figurative or symbolic.[69]

I should clarify some of Meyer's comments in relation to the need for judgement in interpretation. On the one hand he insists that judgement is integral to interpretation, inasmuch as interpretation is knowledge involving both understanding and judgement, against a 'hermeneutics of innocence'. But he also says that not all texts require interpretation. Some texts in fact yield their meaning immediately, and Meyer reasons that, if that were not the case, if all texts needed interpretation, then every interpretation would in turn require its own interpretation and so on, *ad infinitum*.[70] Here it seems that Meyer's use of 'interpretation' is not altogether consistent. In most contexts he uses the term to designate the understanding of the intended sense that is necessary for the reading of any text (as in 4.2.3 and 4.2.4 above). But he also uses 'interpretation' as a technical designation for the deliberate re-presentation of the intended sense by an intepreter for a particular audience. In this sense not every text proposes a practical difficulty for its construal that requires deliberate re-presentation or 'unpacking'.[71] But Meyer certainly does not mean that some texts do not need to be understood. For Meyer, understanding and judgement are integral to the interpretation of any text, whereby 'interpretation' is meant construal of the intended sense. Even a text that does not require a technical re-presentation for a particular audience (say, the hometown newspaper for the townsfolk) requires an act of understanding and judgement (on the part of any of the townsfolk who pick up the paper and read it).

2.6. *Reader, Text and Referent*
Critical realism 'acknowledges the triangular structure of reader, text, and referent'.[72] By 'referent' Meyer means 'what the text is about'. Within these three elements there exist the two hermeneutic circles of (1) reader and text, and (2) text and referent. The latter circle is Meyer's concern here. In the circle of text and referent, or of 'things and words', 'we understand words by understanding the things they refer

---

69. Meyer, *Reality and Illusion*, p. 95.
70. Meyer, *Reality and Illusion*, pp. 90-91.
71. Lonergan makes a similar point, that members of the same community, who share the same 'common sense' mode of understanding and expression, do not need deliberately to 'interpret' one another's expressions; *Method*, p. 154. Though he does not cite this reference, Meyer probably follows Lonergan's thinking here.
72. Meyer, *Critical Realism*, p. xii.

to; we understand things by understanding the words that refer to them.'[73] The crucial point about this circle for Meyer is that words cannot be understood unless the reader has some pre-understanding of the thing to which the words refer. Any understanding of a communication supposes some such pre-understanding of the thing communicated. Understanding is a spiral from pre-understanding of the thing through understanding of the words to a better understanding of the thing. A fully appreciative and affective understanding of the words requires a pre-understanding of the thing that amounts to a 'vital relationship' to the thing. 'Only such a relationship allows one to catch tone and nuance, to savour value, to share in a sense of loss or in the élan of celebration.'[74] Now this pre-understanding that includes a life-relation is the hearer's *total relationship* to the thing – that relationship in its intellectual, moral and emotional dimensions. This relationship is given in the hearer's access to the referent independently of the text.[75]

This access and relationship to the referent in the case of the New Testament texts on Jesus is in fact found in Christianity's dogmatic tradition, though Meyer does not claim that the latter is the unique point of access to the Gospels. He cites Bultmann as one who pioneered the acknowledgment of the reciprocal mediation of things and words and the need for pre-understanding of and vital relationship to the thing. But Bultmann called for pre-understanding of the referent of the Gospels specifically in Heidegger's existentialist categories as found in *Being and Time*, i.e., in the call to decision and thereby to authentic existence. Meyer says such a pre-understanding which arises from a felt need is enough to start with when reading the New Testament texts, but the texts will eventually reveal more ultimate needs. 'In the face of the text felt need, if remaining only that, is a limiting disposition.'[76]

Though Christianity's theological tradition is not the unique point of access to a pre-understanding of 'the thing' expressed in the Gospels, for Meyer there is no escaping the fact that, since these are theological texts, the primary task in their interpretation is theological.[77] If interpretation is understood as the grasp of the intended sense, then the interpretation of religious literature will involve the grasp of religious meanings, which will require that the interpreter be alert to religious meanings and values. In the circle of things and words, a pre-understanding of the thing referred to by a religious text will require a vital relation to that thing, which for Meyer raises the question of the interpreter's personal religious authenticity.[78]

In this context Meyer almost seems drawn to claim that interpretation of the New Testament, including historical investigation of Jesus, requires that the interpreter/ historian be a Christian. This may be due partly to the milieu in which Meyer inaugurated his New Testament and historical Jesus studies, coming out of the New Quest. I will point out below some echoes of the explicitly theological orientation of

---

73. Meyer, *Aims*, p. 96.
74. Meyer, *Aims*, p. 97; *Critical Realism*, p. 22.
75. Meyer, *Critical Realism*, p. 117; *Reality and Illusion*, p. 92.
76. Meyer, *Aims*, p. 103.
77. Meyer, *Reality and Illusion*, p. 149.
78. Meyer, *Reality and Illusion*, p. 178.

the New Quest in Meyer's hermeneutic, as well as some historiographic advances that he took over from it and furthered beyond what the New Quest was able to envision. But the theological task and the religious authenticity that Meyer says are indispensable to New Testament interpretation should not be taken as a requirement of a definite confession of faith on the part of the interpreter, which would amount to a fideism that Meyer would certainly see as inconsistent with Lonergan's account of knowledge. Rather, the theological and religious dimensions of the interpretation of religious texts are simply aspects of the interpreter's subjectivity that must be attended to if the interpreter is to 'measure up' to the text. This is the area of Meyer's hermeneutic where authentic subjectivity comes to full flower.

2.7. *Measuring Up to the Text*

The reader's need to measure up to the text is a matter of the existential dimension of interpretation, which is at once the most crucial and the least immediately educable dimension.[79] It is the area where the subject's need for attention to his or her subjectivity is most acute. Meyer conceives the hermeneutic circle of text and reader as understanding oneself in order to understand the text, and understanding the text in order to understand oneself. The latter is straightforward and empirical, but the former has to do with one's existential self-knowledge, which is largely a matter of one's horizons.

For Meyer, the dynamism of interpretation is *encounter*. All interpretation is ordered to encounter. Encounter is 'vital contact' with the intended sense of the text, personal contact with and response to its meaning. Encounter as the dynamism of interpretation is of a piece with the need for a pre-understanding of and vital relation to the referent. In both cases what is needed is a personal relation such that the subject is engaged in a personal confrontation, a personal meeting with the thing or the intended sense, and the subject is thereby personally addressed and challenged.[80] Meyer echoes Lonergan in this, for whom encounter puts to the test the understanding of oneself that is necessary for interpretation. Self-understanding is a matter of attending to and possibly changing one's horizon to that of the text in order to understand the text's meaning; this is the means by which one 'locks onto the wavelength' of the text.[81] The text has its horizon, the interpreter has his or her horizon; encounter with the text involves the interpreter's being open to his or her own horizon being challenged by that of the text, with the possibility that the interpreter's horizon may require change in order for the interpreter to understand the text within its horizon. All this of course requires that the reader be *attuned* to the horizons of the text and to the reader's own horizons, for it is only within horizons that one understands a text or any communication.

In all this the influence of Hans-Georg Gadamer is evident. Both Meyer and Lonergan frequently cite Gadamer in their discussions of the existential dimension of subjectivity in interpretation.[82] Especially clear is the Gadamerian influence in

79. Meyer, *Reality and Illusion*, p. 93.
80. Meyer, *Critical Realism*, p. 22; *Reality and Illusion*, p. 208.
81. Lonergan, *Method*, p. 161.
82. Gadamer was visiting professor at McMaster University, where Meyer was on faculty, in

Lonergan and Meyer's appropriation of the importance of the interpreter's need to be informed by the history of interpretation engendered by the text. For both Meyer and Lonergan this is an important aspect of the existential dimension of interpretation, part of what is required for the reader to measure up to the text. Classic texts 'create the milieu in which they are studied and interpreted. They produce in the reader through the cultural tradition the mentality, the *Vorverständnis*, from which they will be read, studied, interpreted.'[83] Such texts 'ground a tradition' of their own interpretation, and interpreters, to interpret well, must be aware of their location within this tradition, from which they understand the text.[84] This is a form of Gadamer's historically effected consciousness,[85] which for Gadamer is the primary means by which interpreters take account of their own historicity, the historical location from within which they interpret. Historical understanding, like all understanding, takes place from within the flow of history. The interpreter is always already affected (and effected) by history, and so undertakes the interpretive task within this flow, which amounts to participation in a tradition of which both interpreter and text are a part. This is in contrast to a naive historicism which sees tradition as simply something to be bracketed. On Gadamer's understanding, the temporal distance that separates text and interpreter is less a gulf to be bridged than the ground of the course of events in which the present is rooted.[86] The object of interpretation is part of the tradition in which interpreters already find themselves; the classic text has accrued a tradition of interpretation to itself, and has effected our history and thus ourselves and all our attempts to interpret it. Here one can see the emergence of Gadamer's hermeneutics of belonging, which takes seriously our belonging to history and to a tradition, without which there would be no interpretation.

Undergirding these calls to historically effected consciousness and encounter with the text is a general hermeneutics of 'consent' or good will. For Meyer,

> Good will is an antecedent disposition of openness to the horizon, message and tone of the text. The impersonal curiosity of the physicist is not enough for the interpreter. He does not confront mute nature; he enters into 'dialogue', questioning and being questioned. He knows in advance only that without attention and sympathy he may not 'hear' the text. The orientation to consent is a condition of such hearing, as Hans-Georg Gadamer, in concert with many others from John Henry Newman to the present, has insisted. Openness to consent is ideally the openness of 'basic horizon', the horizon of the thoroughly authentic man.[87]

the Fall terms from 1970–1975. Meyer is known to have interacted frequently with Gadamer, and had public discussions with him in some formal settings (e.g., colloquia). On at least one occasion, Gadamer referred favourably to Meyer's own work in a public lecture (John Robertson, Hamilton, Ontario to the author, Glendale, CA, 5 September 2001).

83. Lonergan, *Method*, p. 161, cited in Meyer, *Reality and Illusion*, p. 93.

84. Meyer, *Aims*, p. 59; 'Historical Understanding and *Jesus and the Gospel*: A Review Article', *The Second Century* 5 (1986), pp. 168-69; *Critical Realism*, p. 23.

85. Hans-Georg Gadamer, *Truth and Method* (trans. Joel Weinsheimer and Donald G. Marshall; New York: Continuum, 2nd rev. edn, 1989), pp. 299ff.

86. Gadamer, *Truth and Method*, p. 297.

87. Meyer, *Critical Realism*, p. 92.

This fundamental posture of openness makes possible the encounter with the text that is required for genuine interpretation. Gadamer's thought is of course at the root of this notion of openness,[88] but Meyer's immediate resource in the area of New Testament interpretation is Peter Stuhlmacher. Stuhlmacher has called for a hermeneutics of consent that consists of openness to tradition, to the present, and to transcendence.[89] This latter area is consonant with Meyer's conclusion that openness to the New Testament texts, inasmuch as they are religious and theological, will raise the question of the interpreter's personal religious authenticity, and will require that their interpretation be seen as necessarily a theological task.

The hermeneutics of consent is about the interpreter's openness to being addressed and challenged by the text, especially in the area of horizon. When this openness is present and this challenge is faced, the interpreter may discover that a conversion is required, in the Lonerganian sense, in order to understand the text. When the text is religious, openness to its horizon may challenge the religious dimension of the interpreter's horizon. When the text is theological, openness requires understanding the text on its own theological terms.

To follow up on this requirement of openness for interpretation, we would do well to recall that Meyer does not deny the need for an analysis that follows interpretation, and that has more in common with a hermeneutics of 'suspicion'. Openness to a religious text and its engendered tradition does not require that one set aside all attempts to explain the text in terms other than its own, e.g., in terms of historical analysis. As I noted above, the primacy of interpretation does not preclude analysis, but it does require *genuine* interpretation as indispensable to *adequate* analysis. It does not require a thoroughgoing faith perspective, i.e., that one be a Christian, in order to interpret Christian texts. But it does require an openness to being addressed by the meaning of the texts, and being challenged by them, in order to interpret well. For 'As "all real living is meeting"…so is all real reading and interpreting.'[90]

---

88. For Gadamer, hermeneutical openness to tradition is analogous to the I–Thou experience in human relations, and similarly results in the interpreter being challenged. 'In human relations the important thing is…to experience the Thou truly as a Thou—i.e., not to overlook his claim but to let him really say something to us… Openness to the other, then, involves recognizing that I myself must accept some things that are against me, even though no one else forces me to do so. This is parallel to the hermeneutical experience. I must allow tradition's claim to validity, not in the sense of simply acknowledging the past in its otherness, but in such a way that it has something to say to me. This too calls for a fundamental sort of openness', *Truth and Method*, p. 361. Openness means, contrary to a naive historical objectivity, that the historian's own criteria of knowledge can be called into question by tradition. Historically effected consciousness lets itself experience tradition and keeps itself open to the truth claims encountered in tradition.

89. Peter Stuhlmacher, *Historical Criticism and Theological Interpretation of Scripture: Toward a Hermeneutics of Consent* (trans. Roy Harrisville; Philadelphia: Fortress Press, 1977), pp. 83-90. Stuhlmacher's own debt to Gadamer is not explicitly acknowledged by Stuhlmacher, but is recognized by Harrisville in the introduction, pp. 13-14.

90. Meyer, *Reality and Illusion*, p. 208.

Chapter 5

HISTORIOGRAPHY

Meyer's interest in hermeneutics gives shape to all his work, but this work moves principally in the sphere of historical-critical method of New Testament interpretation. Meyer saw the roots of differences among historical interpreters of the New Testament to lie in problems of hermeneutics and ultimately in cognitional theory. We come now to the area of our main interest, where epistemology and hermeneutics find expression in Meyer's understanding of historiography. Above I noted two areas where Meyer identified a critical realist understanding of historical-critical method operative in his work: in the definition of the historical Jesus as an ancient figure accessible via questions posed to data and answered, and in an understanding of critical history as open to theological questions.[1] We now have to go behind this relatively late formulation by Meyer to examine the explicit historiographic underpinnings as formulated principally in *The Aims of Jesus* and in other works to a lesser degree.

1. *Telling Presuppositions*

In surveying the course of historical Jesus studies since Reimarus,[2] Meyer sees two distinct eras of method, dominated by what were thought to be the pressing methodological issues of the time. In the nineteenth century, source relationships among the Gospels were the focus. This was the era of 'blame the sources'. The generation of Jesus historians from F.C. Baur to H.J. Holtzmann was 'mesmerized by a siren-song: the lure of early sources, the critical importance of reducing to a minimum the time-lag between event and account'.[3] The need was for identifying the sources among the Gospels that are chronologically the closest to the events they describe, on the assumption that the earliest accounts have their historical veracity most assured, being less likely to have been tainted by the theological concerns of early Christians that accrued to the sources over time, and so more likely to be objective in their accounts. But chronological order of the sources does not establish which *traditions* are oldest. In any case, all synoptic redaction and traditions have to do with 'dogmatic' concerns; none is exempt, not even the oldest traditions. D.F. Strauss had recognized this prior to mid-century, and in this was ahead

---

1. See above, pp. 86-87.
2. Meyer, *Critical Realism*, ch. 2.
3. Meyer, *Aims*, p. 38.; see also *Critical Realism*, pp. 141ff.

of his time. He shifted the focus in Jesus studies from the event narrated in the Gospels, to the account itself, seeing this as taking priority over the question of the order of the sources. His conclusion was that the accounts, all of them, were thoroughly mythological in character. This recognition of the importance of the nature of the sources was not appreciated again until William Wrede's work at the turn of the twentieth century, to be followed by Bultmann and the form critics. Meyer notes that Strauss was right in seeing the *nature of the sources* as the crucial issue (though his understanding of that nature as 'mythological' is problematic), because it is assumptions in this area that are partly at the roots of disagreement in Jesus studies.

Once the thoroughly theological nature of the sources was recognized, the era of 'blame the sources' was succeeded by the era of 'blame the methods'. Given the theological nature of the sources, the need was thought to be for a method that would allow the historical Jesus to be found in the sources in spite of their nature. The twentieth century was marked by steady technical progress toward this end, with advances in linguistic and environmental research, form criticism, availability of rabbinic sources and great collaborative efforts such as the *Theological Dictionary of the New Testament*.[4] Meyer of course acknowledges these advances as valuable historical tools. But he ultimately denies that any difficulties that have beset historical Jesus studies over the last two centuries have been a technical matter of method. Rather, the roots of problems and disagreements have lain in *presuppositions* that have tacitly guided historical work, presuppositions which are partly culturally determined. There are many kinds of presuppositions, but the kinds relevant to Meyer's analysis are two: those of the historian's purpose, which determine the questions the historian will ask; and those concerning judgements of possibility in determining answers to the questions. Presuppositions of the first kind have varied considerably in Jesus studies, but those of the second kind have been fairly consistent since the Enlightenment. Meyer identifies two presuppositions of the second kind, which have been especially prominent: history as a closed continuum of cause and effect, and the principle of analogy in historical method.[5]

The notion of history as a closed continuum is of course the presupposition underlying denial of the historicity of any account of miracle or prophecy. The historian supposes that he or she is to determine causal relations among the events of history, without recourse to the miraculous or supernatural as a category of explanation for any event. The principle of analogy was given definitive shape by Ernst Troeltsch,[6] and holds that the very possibility of historical knowledge is an assumption of analogy between the historian's experience and the historical events that are the object of knowledge. If the events in question are utterly unlike the fund of the historian's experience, then those events are utterly unknowable to the historian. The consequence of this is a strong qualification of what it would mean

4. Meyer, *Aims*, p. 48.
5. Meyer, *Aims*, pp. 14-17.
6. Ernst Troeltsch, 'Über historische und dogmatische Methode in der Theologie', in *Gesammelte Schriften II: Zur religiösen Lage, Religionsphilosophie und Ethik* (Tübingen: J.C.B. Mohr [Paul Siebeck], 1922), pp. 729-53.

for a historical event to be unique. No event can be so unique as to be without analogy in the historian's contemporary experience, because the historian's experience is the necessary framework for knowledge of the event.

Meyer sees these two presuppositions as widespread in historical work, but insists they are little more than culturally determined, reductionistic philosophical baggage that has encumbered legitimate historical method. As such, they are at the root of problems in Jesus studies, and the epistemological assessments on which they are based have been shown to be faulty by Lonergan's cognitional theory.[7] In a later exposition, Meyer observed three issues that Lonergan treats in his theory that are relevant to historical knowledge.[8] (1) Remotely relevant is the notion basic to a critical realist epistemology, that knowing is not like taking a look, but is a matter of the multiple operations of experience, insight and judgement. Critical realism debunks epistemologies that are based on the knowing-is-like-seeing fallacy, as well as any historiography that is seen to derive from such an epistemology. (2) In *Insight*, Lonergan had presented an understanding of world process in terms of emergent probability rather than necessity. Classical scientific enquiry had conceived its goal as the formulation of generalities which hold necessarily, making world process, or natural occurrence, deterministic and a matter of necessity. But contemporary science conceives its generalities as expressions of statistical probability rather than necessity, and world process is seen in terms of probabilities of occurrence rather than deterministic regularity. In short, whereas classical enquiry considered natural laws expressions of necessity, contemporary statistical enquiry considers such 'laws' to be not necessities but simply verified possibilities, whose obtaining is a matter of statistical frequency.[9] Meyer takes these observations of Lonergan to tell against the idea of the universe as a closed continuum; the latter idea is an example of the cult of necessity, and is thus inconsistent with contemporary statistical approaches.[10] (3) Lonergan understood historical knowledge to be a sophisticated specialization of common sense. He distinguished between scientific knowledge and common-sense knowledge. The former examines the relations of objects to one another, to the end of formulations of a general and universal nature. Common-sense knowledge, on the other hand, considers objects not in relation to one another but in their relation to the observer, and is ultimately interested in the particular and the concrete rather than the universal. Its domain is the familiar and the practical, rather than the theoretical.[11] Lonergan considered history to be an application of common-sense knowledge, inasmuch as history is concerned not with the discovery of universal

7. Meyer, *Aims*, pp. 16-17, 54.
8. Meyer, *Critical Realism*, pp. 150-51.
9. See the succinct summary in Lonergan, *Method*, p. 226.
10. Seeing emergent probability as offering some support for the miraculous, has some precedent in Lonergan himself. He presents his summary of a statistical understanding of the uniformity of nature in the context of a consideration of the question of the possibility of miracles, concluding that 'Evidently the scientific case concerning miracles has weakened', *Method*, p. 226.
11. On common sense see Lonergan, *Insight*, pp. 196-269, esp. 196-204.

laws or regularities but with understanding particular and concrete events.[12] History as concerned with the particular and concrete will qualify the principle of analogy. While the historian's own experience is indeed the context for an understanding of the particular event, the historian cannot extrapolate a universal law from his or her experience within which the particular event must be understood. The historian's experience is the context for understanding in the broad, horizonal sense that the historian brings his or her whole fund of knowledge and values to bear on the examination of the concrete event, while always viewing the particular as particular.

Meyer is short on exposition of these aspects of Lonergan's theory, but their effect on his historical Jesus work is evident. Meyer generally takes Lonergan's theory to require that no data can be excluded from historical consideration a priori, such as accounts of miracles, prophecy, or overtly theological or Christological formulations. Decisions about such data are as much a matter of insight and judgement as are decisions about any other potential data, or any other knowledge for that matter. One cannot simply make a decision on all miracle accounts in the sources based on analogy with one's own experience, or on laws assumed to operate in the universe as a closed continuum. Whole complexes of material cannot be dismissed on such bases, as previous Jesus studies had done, and so the task of investigating the historical Jesus becomes more demanding, because more data are allowed into the investigation. As Meyer says, 'Lonergan confirmed me in an account of history-as-knowledge that allowed me to deal with historical questions historically...I accordingly found myself in a position to consider all actual historical data as open without reservation to historical treatment.'[13]

That all data are open to historical treatment does not mean that all data are simply assumed to be historically authentic. If whole complexes of data cannot be excluded a priori on the basis of certain philosophical presuppositions, neither can the possibility be excluded a priori of the presence of legend, midrash, folklore or parable in the data, or that the Jesus tradition was subject to omissions, transpositions and additions.[14] But if Meyer's avowed stance toward the data is one of neither credulity nor scepticism, it would indeed seem that his occupation with the presuppositions guiding historical studies, and the specific ways that Lonergan's cognitional theory criticizes those presuppositions, is particularly directed toward defending miracle as a category of historical explanation. Arguments against analogy and the closed continuum are in fact the common stock of apologists for the miraculous. Meyer is such an apologist, to the degree that he shares these arguments. But outside these specific areas, Meyer does not attempt to explore the labyrinth of philosophical issues involved in miracle.[15] Though he is not unaware of the complexity of the issues, he mostly relies on whatever work of Lonergan is relevant, and then mostly assuming Lonergan's detailed arguments rather than

---

12. Lonergan, *Method*, pp. 216, 229.
13. Meyer, *Critical Realism*, p. 150.
14. Meyer, *Aims*, pp. 72-74.
15. See, for example, the detailed treatment of Colin Brown, *Miracles and the Critical Mind* (Grand Rapids: Eerdmans, 1984).

presenting them. But it would be a mistake to take Meyer's entire appropriation of Lonergan and his resulting epistemology, hermeneutic and historiography as wholly and exclusively in the service of a defence of miracles.[16] Even if one were to reject the argument for miracles, there remain important methodological resources in Meyer's historiography. It is probably the case, in fact, that no historian who is convinced that miracle is off limits as a category of historical explanation, is going to be persuaded otherwise by Meyer's presentation, limited as it is; but the argument for miracles, though it is a consequence of Meyer's position, is only one consequence, and its acceptance is not necessary for the appreciation of his larger observations on the nature of historical knowledge and investigation.[17]

So these presuppositions that Meyer sees as the source of problems in Jesus studies have resulted in the routine denial of miracle accounts, but their larger significance lies in the epistemology they reflect and the historiography with which they are bound. The epistemology is a naive empiricism, and the resulting historiography is equally unself-suspecting. These can best be explored in light of Meyer's alternative formulation.

2. *Inference and Hypothesis*

Following on and drawing from his discussion of historical method in *The Aims of Jesus*, Meyer formulates four principles of historical criticism: (1) historical investigation pursues knowledge, not simply belief or assumption; (2) historical knowledge is inferential; (3) the technique of historical investigation is the hypothesis; (4) historical hypotheses require verification.[18] These four principles can be recast into one serviceable statement of Meyer's historical method: historical investigation pursues inferential knowledge through a process of hypothesis and verification.

Now as it stands, this statement is mostly unremarkable. The idea that historical knowledge is inferential is a truism among historians. Knowledge of the past is commonly described as 'indirect', as opposed to the 'direct' knowledge of the present, or of perception.[19] Objects of perception exist, are physically present to the

---

16. In the context of a discussion of the hermeneutics of consent, Meyer notes that affective recoil from the subject matter of the biblical text has resulted in misinterpretation. The a-priori rejection of miracles is one area of such recoil, and amounts to an undiscriminating ideological stance that has had a negative impact on New Testament interpretation. 'Nevertheless, I would not wish to make the issue of the interpreter's "good will" or "orientation to consent" hinge on the resolution of the more than ordinarily complex questions of prophecy and miracle', *Critical Realism*, p. 92.

17. I would also point out that, in the course of his historical investigation of Jesus, although Meyer assumes the general validity of the miracle traditions, he makes little effort to defend any particular miracle account in the sources. He in fact insists that 'The mass of them [are] insusceptible of firm historical judgments *in individuo*' (*Aims*, p. 158), and recognizes the presence of folklore in the miracle traditions (see below, p. 142 n. 50). Miracle is a historical category for Meyer, but his acceptance of such does not result in a flat credulity toward all miracle accounts.

18. Meyer, *The Aims of Jesus*, pp. 88-92.

19. See for example Michael Stanford, *A Companion to the Study of History* (Oxford: Basil Blackwell, 1994), pp. 113-18; Alan Richardson, *History Sacred and Profane* (London: SCM Press,

observer, are fully objective in that sense, and thus are known directly. But objects of historical knowledge do not exist, at least not in the same sense as those of immediate perception. Historical objects must be inferred, by the historian's reasoning, from presently existing data, including documents and artefacts, which are the traces left by the events and agents of the past. From these traces the historian reasons imaginatively to the objects, the historical events and agents, which left the traces. The historian knows past events indirectly, only in the imaginative reconstruction. This way of understanding historical knowledge is almost universally accepted among historians, though it may be at odds with something like a common-sense view of history, which tends to see the objects of present perception and the objects of historical knowledge as of the same kind: that there is a tree outside my window is not a different kind of fact than that Abraham Lincoln was assassinated on April 14, 1865. Since both are considered 'facts', they are assumed to be similarly established and known. But historians generally do not share the common-sense view. The nature of historical investigation reveals that knowledge of historical objects is inferred from present data.

The second part of Meyer's statement of method, regarding hypothesis and verification, does not have as wide currency among historians as does the notion of inferential knowledge, but most historians would probably agree with its basic point. Historical investigation proceeds by offering a hypothesis in possible explanation of the relevant historical data; the hypothesis is tested by examination of the data, to see if they fit the hypothesis. Something like such a procedure is at work on some level of any historical investigation, and in that sense is methodologically self-evident. With this and with the common understanding of inferential knowledge Meyer would agree, as far as these go; but Meyer's formulation of these principles is much more historiographically freighted than is the prevailing usage. Three main features of Meyer's historiography can be highlighted, expanding on the notions of inference and hypothesis: (1) the goal of historical investigation is the interpretation and explanation of intentions; (2) the procedure of historical investigation is hypothesis and verification; (3) this procedure takes place on the levels of controlling the data and establishing the facts.

2.1. *Interpretation and Explanation of Intentions*
Meyer sees critical history as 'the strategically structured effort to interpret and explain' historical data.[20] Specifically, historical data are interpreted and explained in terms of the intentions of historical agents, or subjects. Historical interpretation

---

1964), pp. 191ff.; Marc Bloch, *The Historian's Craft*, p. 48; Louis Gottschalk, *Understanding History*, pp. 41ff.; R.G. Collingwood, *The Idea of History*, pp. 233, 252, 255. Of course, the Lonerganian critical realist would want to qualify the statement that perceptual knowledge is 'direct'; for Lonergan, knowledge is never direct in the sense that it is like 'taking a look', but always involves understanding and judgement. But perceptual knowledge can be distinguished from historical knowledge in that the former is not *inferential*, at least not in the same sense as is historical knowledge. The insight involved in perceptual knowledge is a grasping of an intelligible unity in the data, but is not an inference from the data.

20. Meyer, *Aims*, p. 80.

is the grasp of the intentions of the subjects of history; historical explanation is the accounting of the interaction and realization of particular intentions, explaining why certain events went forward and others did not in terms of the interaction of intentions. Historical investigation is a matter of opening a path to the intending subjects of history and to the course of events. It is the intentions of subjects that make historical events to be historical, charging them with meaning as specifically human actions. Just as the meaning of a text is a matter of intention, so the meaning of human events is the intentions of the subjects performing them, and the historian's job is to understand the intentions or goals of subjects and the events that resulted from the realization and interaction of those intentions.[21]

Now the understanding of history-as-intentions has had its detractors. Both the Old Quest and the New Quest spoke of intentions in history, and were criticized for it. After the Old Quest, a common criticism of the nineteenth-century lives of Jesus was their tendency to offer psychological portraits of Jesus. These portraits were faulted on the grounds that their authors had little understanding of Jesus' historical milieu, and even less real evidence by which to make a legitimate clinical psychological evaluation of Jesus.[22] Another reaction against the Old Quest was its understanding of Jesus as an inspiring hero, enacting a programme of eternal values of love, service, the value of the individual, the fatherhood of God and the brotherhood of man. Henry Cadbury warned against such a 'modernizing' of the historical Jesus by attributing to him a unified life purpose, aim or motive. Any unity in his life rather sprang from 'an unphrased inner quality and temperament'.[23] Any self-consciousness in him took the form of religious obedience.[24] We can see in Cadbury the tendency, in reaction to psychological or ethicist portraits of Jesus, to reject any talk of historical subjects' aims or intentions. But one need not associate intentions with anything like a unified life purpose in the classic liberal sense, or with unconscious psychological motives or forces of personality. In any case, this is not how Meyer understands intentions.

The New Quest also had its version of occupation with intentionality, which has been criticized. James Robinson's programmatic essay outlines a new understanding of the self that informs historiography in the New Quest, seeing the self as actualized in the individual's act of intention and commitment that gives historical events meaning.[25] Historiography is about grasping this intention and act of self-actualization that takes place within historical subjects, and encountering the selfhood that is revealed therein. In all contexts that Robinson describes the object of history as intentions, he clearly and easily associates those intentions with expressions of existential selfhood.[26] So the New Quest understands the significance of intentions in specifically existentialist terms.

21. Meyer, *Aims*, pp. 77-78; *Reality and Illusion*, pp. 106ff.

22. See the classic criticism by Albert Schweitzer, *The Psychiatric Study of Jesus: Exposition and Criticism* (trans. Charles Rhind Joy; Boston: Beacon Press, 1958).

23. Henry Cadbury, *The Peril of Modernizing Jesus* (New York: Macmillan, 1937), p. 148.

24. Cadbury, p. 152.

25. James M. Robinson, *A New Quest of the Historical Jesus*, p. 68.

26. See, for example, Robinson, *A New Quest*, pp. 68, 69, 71, 95, 105. With its origin among students of Bultmann, the New Quest of course adopts Bultmann's understanding of history as the

The identification of intentions with psychological portraits, classic liberal theology, or existential selfhood began with the Old and New Quests, and persists today. Stephen Fowl insists that historical Jesus studies as they have traditionally been pursued are principally occupied with the recovery of the authentic sayings of Jesus, in order to grasp his 'inner life', and for that reason have always failed. The inner life of Jesus is not a proper object of historical enquiry.[27] Clearly this categorization and rejection of history of Jesus in terms of the 'inner life' assumes the existentialist agenda of the New Quest, and even the psychological construals of the Old Quest.[28] Alan Winton has suggested that the 'new view of history' proposed by the New Quest was actually a return to the psychologizing view of the nineteenth century, but in twentieth-century language; 'intention' is essentially a psychological category, and therefore not a legitimate object of historical enquiry.[29] Sean Freyne explicitly says that Meyer's focus on Jesus' 'aims' suggests personal and existential overtones.[30] Gerd Theissen and Dagmar Winter give a brief mention of Meyer's *The Aims of Jesus*, but appear to dismiss this work as illegitimate because, as its title indicates, it is concerned with matters other than 'historical factuality'.[31]

But without the psychological and existential baggage, objections to intentionality are weakened, for intentionality can be formulated in other terms. William Farmer notes that the topic of Jesus' 'aims' has lately been regarded as off limits, because aims are conceived in terms of Jesus' self-consciousness, which is thought to be historically unrecoverable. Farmer notes that, alternatively, Meyer has recast the question of aims or intentions in a constructive way: what is under investigation is not Jesus' personality or private life, but his public career. The question for the historian is, what did Jesus do and say that can make sense out of what emerged from what he said and did?[32] Publicly accessible meanings are at issue, not a privately held consciousness. James Charlesworth is also sympathetic with efforts to understand Jesus' intentionality, which he sees in both Meyer and E.P. Sanders. Charlesworth sees this goal as preferable to any attempt at recovery of the *ipsis-*

grasp of historical subjects' self-understanding that comes to expression in their decisions, in order to comprehend one's own existence and take responsibility for the future by one's own decisions. See his expositions in, for example, *Jesus and the Word* (trans. Louise Pettibone Smith and Erminie Huntress Lantero; New York: Charles Scribner's Sons, 1958), pp. 3-15; and *The Presence of Eternity: History and Eschatology* (The Gifford Lectures 1955; New York: Harper & Brothers, 1957), chs. VIII-X.

27. Stephen Fowl, 'Reconstructing and Deconstructing the Quest of the Historical Jesus', *Scottish Journal of Theology* 42 (1989), p. 331.

28. I would note that earlier in this article Fowl commends the methodological move of describing history sympathetically, in terms of the *Weltanschauung* of the historical subject. Such a move would certainly commend some understanding of history in terms of the historical subject's perceptions, if not intentions.

29. Alan P. Winton, *The Proverbs of Jesus: Issues of History and Rhetoric* (Sheffield: Sheffield Academic Press, 1990), p. 104.

30. Sean Freyne, *Galilee, Jesus, and the Gospels* (Philadelphia: Fortress Press, 1988), p. 25.

31. Theissen and Winter, *Die Kriterienfrage in der Jesusforschung*, p. 155.

32. William Farmer, 'Reflections upon the Historical Perimeters for Understanding the Aims of Jesus', p. 59.

sima vox Jesu; he is concerned with 'the meaning [Jesus] poured forth through the words that appeared when he intended to communicate something to someone'.[33]

Meyer insists that 'the "baby" of human subjectivity is not the "bath-water" of groundless psychological conjecture.'[34] For Meyer, intentions are essentially public things because they are what give human actions meaning and intelligibility. For the significance of intentions as suppliers of meaning, Meyer borrowed from the work of R.G. Collingwood, an early-twentieth-century British philosopher and historian. Collingwood distinguished between the inside and the outside of historical events. The 'outside' of an event is 'everything belonging to it which can be described in terms of bodies and their movements'. The 'inside' is 'that in it which can only be described in terms of thought'.[35] The event is a unity of these outside and inside components. The inside is what makes a mere event to be a human action; so the historian, seeking to understand the event as an action, understands it in terms of the thoughts and intentions of the agents. Meyer follows Collingwood in this distinction between inside and outside, identifying discovery of the inside as the goal of historical investigation.[36] To discover the inside of an event is 'to grasp it as motivated in some way, moving in some direction, significant in some context'.[37]

Now I should note that Collingwood's understanding of the inside of the event is for him bound up with his general understanding of the work of history as reenactment, or rethinking the thoughts of historical agents. This understanding is in turn informed by his idealist orientation: historical knowledge is knowledge of what mind has done in the past. History is ultimately concerned with thought not in its particular manifestations, but in its universality.

> Individual acts and persons appear in history not in virtue of their individuality as such, but because that individuality is the vehicle of a thought which, because it was actually theirs, is potentially everyone's... [I]t is just the universality of an event or character that makes it a proper and possible object of historical study, if by universality we mean something that oversteps the limits of merely local and temporal existence and possesses a significance valid for all men at all times.[38]

33. James H. Charlesworth, *Jesus within Judaism*, p. 167. Charlesworth helpfully distinguishes among intentionality, self-understanding, and self-consciousness. The first two are legitimate areas of enquiry into the historical Jesus. The last is a 'Pandora's box'. 'By using "self-consciousness" we may inadvertently be guilty of approaching the traditions in light of what we know from psychoanalysis. We are also liable to slip backward inadvertently into the romantic quest of the nineteenth century. Finally, a search for Jesus' self-consciousness may indeed reflect the failure to be sensitive to the limits of our biblical traditions', p. 136.

34. Meyer, *Reality and Illusion*, p. 104.

35. R.G. Collingwood, *The Idea of History*, p. 213.

36. Meyer, *Critical Realism*, pp. 62, 148; *Reality and Illusion*, p. 106.

37. Meyer, *Critical Realism*, p. 167. Meyer is followed in this by N.T. Wright, *The New Testament and the People of God*, pp. 109ff., who distinguishes between aims (the fundamental direction of a person's life), intentions (the specific application of the aim in a particular situation), and motivations (the specific sense, on a specific occasion, that a certain action is appropriate and desirable). But for Wright, aims are individual instantiations of worldviews shared by communities, so the root object of historical investigation is the community's worldview, which is expressed in its symbols, characteristic behaviour and literature.

38. Collingwood, *Idea*, p. 303.

These thoughts of particular agents are grasped by the historian by means of rethinking them in the historian's own mind. For Collingwood, this rethinking is possible because the thoughts are numerically identical across time and among those who think them.[39] Quite literally, the same thought exists across its life in the mental activity of various thinkers. That the thought does not happen to be in the mind of anyone in particular at a given moment does not change the fact that it can be revived at any time by being thought again. Thoughts cannot be carried away by the flow of consciousness because thought, as well as the act of thinking, stands outside this flow.[40] Collingwood sees the business of history as reenacting the activities of mind in the past.

Such a preoccupation with and reification of mental activity will be of little use to most historians or philosophers today. But it is not clear that Collingwood's idealist orientation necessarily disqualifies the legitimacy of many of his points on historical method. He was very influential in twentieth-century historiography,[41] and Meyer manages to capitalize on those things in Collingwood that effected this influence, without appropriating all his idealist trappings. As I will show below, Collingwood had some important observations on the nature of historical reasoning that transcend his orientation to universal thought, and these observations can be put to good use.

There is an objection to intentionality as the object of history that we have not considered, and it is a more formidable objection than the anti-psychological and anti-existential reactions that we have noted. Some historians object to accounting for historical events in terms of intentionality because it seems that many events in history simply cannot be attributed to the thoughts or intentions of agents. In many cases, factors and forces are at work that cannot adequately be described in terms of human intentionality, purpose or motive; or, actions that can be described in terms of intention can also be understood in a way that has little to do with intention.[42] Factors of geography and climate, and social, economic and cultural factors often enter into historical explanation. Of course, a large part of the last century in historiography was taken up with the debate over the proper role of explanatory models drawn from the social sciences, vis-à-vis the particularity of individual events that is assumed to be the proper field of historical investigation.[43] Does explaining an event by subsuming it under a general model or law compromise the particularity of the event as historical? I will have more to say in a later chapter on issues of generality, particularity and the social sciences. But here we can note that the issue raises the concern of the legitimacy of limiting historical explanation to

39. Collingwood, *Idea*, pp. 283-84.

40. Collingwood, *Idea*, p. 287.

41. His popularity in the New Quest was evident, beginning with an existentialist appropriation by Bultmann in *The Presence of Eternity*; see Robinson, *A New Quest*, pp. 42 n.1; 71.

42. See Norman Wilson, *History in Crisis? Recent Directions in Historiography* (Upper Saddle River, NJ: Prentice Hall, 1999), p. 43.

43. See the history of recent historiography by Georg Iggers, *Historiography in the Twentieth Century: From Scientific Objectivity to the Postmodern Challenge* (Hanover, NH: Wesleyan University Press, 1997), especially chs. 5-9.

intentionality alone. Collingwood appears to make this kind of limitation, and Meyer tends in that direction to the degree that he follows Collingwood. But Meyer also has an appreciation of historical causation that is not limited to the 'thoughts' that occupied Collingwood. At one point Meyer emphasizes that his understanding of 'explanation' as the *interaction* of intentions is designed partly to make the point that what happens in history is the result of the interaction of purposes informing a variety of instruments, not just 'thought'.[44] For Meyer, intention is certainly not identified with the activities of universal Mind; as I pointed out above, intentions as the intelligible content of actions are public things, and Meyer has no investment in Collingwood's idealist programme. Neither does a focus on intentionality require that an event be attributed to the intentions of any one person in particular. Events often result from the complex interaction of intentions, in which some are realized, some are frustrated, perhaps none come completely to fulfilment, but all have a role.[45]

Meyer allows that individual intentions are often not adequate historical explanations; but given this allowance, he nevertheless seems to avoid any category of explanation that goes beyond intentions. In Jesus studies, the social sciences are the most obvious category. At one point, Meyer criticizes Richard Horsley's sociologically oriented studies of Jesus as limited, in that they fail to penetrate to the 'inside' of the Jesus event.[46] But it is not always clear whether Meyer offers a heavily qualified *acceptance* of social science explanations on the grounds that they are insufficient by themselves to yield a complete historical picture, or whether he *rejects* them as totally inapplicable to the data on the historical Jesus. Some of his comments can be taken in the latter sense. He seems to take sociological explanations of the data as necessarily reductionistic.[47] At least one commentator, who is himself sympathetic with Meyer's orientation to intentions and theological questions, has criticized Meyer for neglecting the social dimension of Jesus' career.[48]

---

44. Meyer, *Aims*, p. 79.

45. Meyer may be following Lonergan in this acknowledgment, though Lonergan allows for historical explanation beyond intentionality to a greater extent than does Meyer. While Lonergan sees the field of historical investigation as conscious, intentional, meaningful human acts, he also says that history is ultimately about what was 'going forward' in the particular past, and thus goes beyond what was intended by individual agents. Most individual agents in fact do not know what is 'going forward'. History is about the experiences of many, while experiences as intentional are individual (a debatable point, as I will show in Chapter Eight). Actual events result not only from intentions, but also from oversights, mistakes and failures. Historical investigation discovers issues and operative factors that together account for what went forward, including individual intentions but also much more. See *Method*, pp. 178-79.

46. Meyer, *Christus Faber*, p. 109. In *Jesus and the Spiral of Violence* (Minneapolis: Fortress Press, 1993), Horsley explains Jesus' activity and teaching in terms of a programme of non-violent social revolution within a context of a 'spiral of violence' precipitated by socio-economic conditions of the first century. He tends to criticize as 'idealist' any account of first-century conditions or events that would explain them in terms of, say, the religious beliefs of agents.

47. Meyer has little of value to note in recent sociological approaches in *Christus Faber*, pp. 13-15.

48. Sean Freyne, *Jesus, Galilee and the Gospels*, p. 25.

The danger of reducing the particularity of intentional actions to larger categories, such as social science models, is real. But I would also note the danger of 'reduction' in the opposition direction. Whatever limitations may plague Crossan's method, the meso- and macrocosmic levels of his approach seem to have at least an implicit appreciation of the role of both intentionality and larger categories of explanation in history. Some such interconnection of both would seem to be most appropriate, without conceiving either in exclusivistic terms. Focus on intentionality to the exclusion of larger factors is myopic, in view of the fact that it is often impossible to explain a given event in terms of intentionality alone, particularly when the action involved in the event is large-scale, i.e., including large social groups. But focus on larger factors to the exclusion of intentionality fails to take historical events seriously in their particularity, and as the interplay of meaningful human actions.[49]

2.2. *Hypothesis and Verification – Question and Answer*
In his early *The Man for Others* Meyer gave this simplified description of historical method: '*History is the asking and answering of questions*. The historian can ask any question he wishes. He is not limited to asking only those questions that were already asked by his sources... As for the *answering* of questions, the historian first sketches out a range of hypotheses; then he narrows the range in accord with his estimates of the possibilities and probabilities; finally, he tries to verify the best hypothesis in terms of the available evidence.'[50] In this statement are contained all the elements of Meyer's understanding of hypothesis and verification in history, and it remains essentially unchanged throughout its articulations in his later works. The technique of history is the hypothesis, which is the formulation and resolution of questions. More specifically, the historian brings a question to the data, formulates a hypothesis in answer to the question, and verifies the hypothesis by the data. In more Lonerganian terms, the historian identifies unknowns and converts them into knowns by determining if all their conditions are fulfilled.[51]

This apparently obvious statement of the technique of history in fact has deep roots, for Meyer, in Lonergan's transcendental method. Recall that the dynamism of knowledge for Lonergan is the wonder that is the eros of the human spirit, the disinterested drive to know. In the knowing process, this drive takes the form of questioning. The data of experience are questioned for their intelligibility, and as a result of this questioning an intelligible unity is grasped in insight. The insight is in turn questioned for its truthfulness, and this questioning leads to a judgment of true or false on the insight. This spontaneous process of questioning and answering is at

---

49. On the field of history as meaningful human actions, see Lonergan, *Method*, p. 178. Lonergan also has warnings on the use of ideal types in historical explanation: One must remember that types are not reality, but are theoretical constructs; history is not to be reduced to what is actually an abstraction. It is also true that 'the richer and the more illuminating the construct, the greater the difficulty of applying it; the thinner and looser the construct, the less is it able to contribute much to history', *Method*, p. 228.

50. Meyer, *The Man for Others*, pp. 25-26.

51. Meyer, *Aims*, p. 80.

work in every instance of knowledge. Now the objectification of this process in a 'method' is not meant to reduce the process to a set of directions for the knower to follow. Lonergan emphasized that 'Method is not to be confused with anything as pedestrian as a recipe, a prescription, a set of directions. For recipes, and the like, lead only to single results. They may be repeated as often as you please, but the repetition yields no more than another instance of the original product.'[52] The key instance to method, rather, is in the relation between questioning and answering. A question itself, inasmuch as it intends an answer, sets the standard that leads to the rejection of insufficient answers. Insufficient answers, though ultimately rejected, can help in the clarification of the question. This clarification may also reveal inter-mediate questions that have to be answered before the original question can be met. In all this there is an interaction between questions and answers, such that ques-tions partly determine what answers will be sufficient, and answers, even wrong ones, help to shape and clarify questions.[53] The 'method' that Lonergan sees to be 'transcendental' because it is ubiquitous (i.e., at work in all fields of knowledge), is a self-correcting process of learning driven by questions in interaction with answers. The fundamental role of questioning in this process highlights the fact that in no case is knowledge self-evident. It is never a matter of simply 'taking a look' at what is there to be seen. Knowledge always involves the questioning of the data of sense for their intelligible unity, and questioning the grasp of this unity for its truthfulness. For the historian, knowledge of the past is the result of whatever questions the historian asks of the data and to which answers are found. So a mind well-stocked with questions is the historian's a-priori priority, for questions deter-mine what the historian will ultimately derive from the data.[54]

This premium on questioning is an element Lonergan shared with Collingwood. In discussing historical reasoning, Collingwood proposed a 'logic of question-and-answer' to replace propositional logic. The latter takes propositions to be self-contained 'bearers of thought', and so to be meaningful or not, truthful or not, in isolation. But in the logic of question-and-answer, propositions only have meaning as answers to questions. One cannot know the meaning or truthfulness of a propo-sition until one knows the question to which it is an answer.[55] Meaning and truth are not predicated of individual propositions, but are relative to a complex of questions and answers.[56] Collingwood developed this understanding while working on archaeological digs of Roman ruins in Britain. In the archaeological situation, one finds out nothing from what is uncovered in the dig except in answer to a question. If one digs with a simple curiosity about what one will find, one learns nothing, except as occasional questions may arise while digging. But the more focused the questions one has in mind, the more the data that are discovered in the course of digging take on meaning and significance as answers to those questions,

52. Lonergan, 'A Post-Hegelian Philosophy of Religion', p. 204.

53. Lonergan, 'A Post-Hegelian Philosophy of Religion', pp. 204-205.

54. Lonergan, 'Method: Trend and Variations', in Frederick E. Crowe (ed.), *A Third Collec-tion: Papers of Bernard J.F. Lonergan* (New York: Paulist Press, 1985), p. 17.

55. Collingwood, *An Autobiography* (New York: Oxford University Press, 1939), p. 31.

56. Collingwood, *Autobiography*, p. 37.

and the more one learns from the data.[57] As in archaeology, so in history, and indeed in any investigation: what one finds depends on the questions one asks. The true nature of historical method is to 'put history to the question'. Sources are not read simply receptively, with the historian taking in what they choose to say (once they have been scrutinized for their reliability). Sources are read with a question in mind, the historian 'having taken the initiative by deciding for himself what he wants to find out from them'.[58] Every step in historical investigation depends on asking a question. 'The question is the charge of gas, exploded in the cylinder-head, which is the motive force of every piston-stroke.'[59] The logic of question-and-answer is in fact the best representation of the process of thought; it is to be preferred over the idea of thought as simply gaping with a blank mind, and the blanker the mind the more one will 'apprehend the facts'.[60] The similarities to Lonergan here are striking. Just as for Lonergan knowledge is not simply a matter of 'taking a look' but depends on insight and judgement driven by (in answer to) questions, so for Collingwood thought is not a matter of gaping with a blank mind but depends on asking questions of the data; for without questions, the data do not speak.

Meyer capitalizes on Collingwood's logic of question-and-answer, but for particular ends that Collingwood himself did not articulate. Meyer emphasizes the *autonomy* of the historian's questions, the fact that they are the historian's own questions and not dictated by any outside source. In pure exegesis, historical sources are understood on the basis of questions fixed by the sources themselves, related to what the author meant to communicate; this is commensurate with Meyer's understanding of the primacy of the intended sense in interpretation. But in historical analysis that follows interpretation, the historian's questions are his or her own questions, not necessarily fixed by the intention of the author of the source.[61] In the quotation above, from *The Man for Others*, Meyer emphasized that historians can pose any question they wish; they are not limited by the questions of the sources. Such is the way of analysis, which focuses on what is revealed in the text apart from what was intended. Historians are free to pose questions not found in the sources, and until they do this, they are not operating as historians. Such questions constitute historical analysis and new questions are what move historical enquiry forward. Of course, one should not pose questions that one does not think can be answered; but within that limit, all questions are fair game.[62] Meyer emphasizes this autonomy of the historian vis-à-vis the sources, but there are other specific dimensions of autonomy that for him are just as important. Since all questions

---

57. Collingwood, *Autobiography*, pp. 24-25. Compare this with Crossan's archaeological metaphor, where its significance for historiography means that the sources must be stratified. Collingwood seems to be getting at something more fundamental about the nature of historical knowledge and reasoning, whether or not stratification of sources is called for in any particular case.

58. Collingwood, *Idea*, p. 270.

59. Collingwood, *Idea*, p. 273.

60. Collingwood, *Idea*, p. 274.

61. Meyer, *Aims*, p. 91.

62. Meyer, *Critical Realism*, p. 132.

are fair game, they may reflect various interests, and most significantly, theological interests are not off limits. Theology may in fact play a creative role rather than an obstructive role in critical history. Meyer admits that historical questions drawn from theology have tended to distort the appreciation of historical data, but this is not necessarily so. Since theology, like history, is driven to know the truth, a theological motive may drive history to true conclusions rather than to distortions.[63] He offers Gustaf Dalman and Joachim Jeremias as examples. Dalman was motivated by Pietist missionary ambitions and Jeremias by the search for a grounding for theology in the authoritative voice of the historical Jesus. In neither case did historical conscience give way to theological pressure, but religious motive did remain crucial to historical practice.[64]

Meyer's basic point about the historian not being limited to the questions of the sources is an important one; and his emphasis on the legitimacy of theological questions in critical history is well taken. But I would offer two important qualifications. First, though theological *motives* may not necessarily distort critical history, what a legitimate theological *question* for history may look like should be nuanced. For this one should keep in mind that the object of history largely consists in the intentions of historical agents. Historical events are interpreted and explained in terms of agents' intentions, along with the context of larger social, cultural, economic, or other factors. As long as theological questions have these intentions and contexts in mind as the field of possible answers, they are appropriate to critical history. If, however, they require answers outside this field, they are outside the purview of historical investigation. 'Did Jesus intend to inaugurate the reign of God in his proclamation?' is a legitimate, theologically oriented historical question. 'Did Jesus in fact inaugurate the reign of God?' is a theological question, albeit one with a historical dimension in that it is partly answered by what took place in history as an outcome of Jesus' ministry. But I would maintain that it is not primarily a historical question, because ultimately it is not answerable in terms of either intentionality or context. There is no reason to think that Meyer would disagree with this qualification; as we will see, his portrait of the historical Jesus explores intentions in their explicitly theological orientation.[65] Second, it is true that Collingwood placed a premium on the historian's questions, and insisted that those questions are the historian's own, and not to be found in the sources themselves. But in his logic of question and answer Collingwood also rightly pointed out that each question and answer in a given complex must be relevant, or appropriate. That is, each question has to 'arise' and each answer has to be the 'right'

63. Meyer, *Critical Realism*, p. 152.
64. Meyer, *Critical Realism*, p. 153.
65. At the conclusion of his portrait of the historical Jesus, Meyer acknowledges the thoroughly theological nature of Jesus' intentionality as he describes it, but insists this nature is historically necessary. 'Some may suppose that to define the aims of Jesus in terms of so grandiose a vision of things is to do theology, not history. But the history of Israel in general, and above all in the centuries preceding and following Jesus, was not the prosaic affair evoked by a facile division between theology and history. All the issues and actors were immersed in religious schemes and visions', *Aims*, p. 222.

answer.[66] 'To say that a question arises, is to say that it has a logical connection with our previous thoughts, that we have a reason for asking it and are not moved by mere capricious curiosity.'[67] An answer is the 'right' answer when it enables one to get ahead with the process of questioning and answering.[68] Although the historian's questions are his or her own, not just any question will do because not all questions arise in a given context of an investigation. It turns out that the historian's questioning is in fact bound, not by the questions of the sources, but by the logic of the investigation the historian is pursuing. As Lonergan pointed out, fresh questions arise out of relevant answers.[69] Though Meyer never mentions the need for legitimate questions to 'arise', there is no necessary conflict between this logic and his stress on the autonomy of questions. The latter is, for Meyer, invoked primarily in the service of defending theological questions and motivations in critical history, and in pointing out that questions are not limited to those of the sources; but given this service, relatively autonomous questions are posed within the context of an existing line of questioning. The historian's autonomy is not absolute.

2.3. *Controlling the Data, Establishing the Facts*
Historical investigation proceeds by the historian's posing questions to the data, formulating hypotheses in answer to those questions, and verifying the hypotheses. This technique is employed on the two levels of critical history: controlling the data and establishing the facts. The data are the givens of historical research, the minimal historical materials with which the historian has to work. Now Meyer describes the nature of data differently in at least two different instances. In one illustration a datum appears to be something like a bare historical 'fact', e.g., 'that Charles de Gaulle retired from the presidency of the Fifth Republic in the spring of 1969'.[70] But in the context of a fuller explanation of the relation between data control and fact establishment, a datum for Meyer would seem to be any form of historical 'trace', a piece of evidence left by a historical event, one of the 'tracks' of history. In the case of Jesus a datum would be a saying or pericope purportedly originating from an event in his life. Such a datum would of course not be a historical 'fact' as in the de Gaulle illustration, but would be a piece of historical detritus left by some event or agent in history. This latter meaning of 'datum' appears to be the more consistently used by Meyer; for he goes on to say that a datum is 'controlled' when (1) its meaning is grasped and (2) it is determined to be

66. Collingwood, *Autobiography*, p. 37.

67. This is the explanation of John Hogan, *Collingwood and Theological Hermeneutics* (College Theological Society Studies in Religion, 3; Lanham, MD: University Press of America, 1989), p. 50.

68. Note that the 'right' answer is not necessarily a 'true' answer. 'Cases are quite common in which the "right" answer to a question is "false"; for example, cases in which a thinker is following a false scent, either inadvertently or to construct a *reductio ad absurdum*', *Idea*, p. 37. Such a case is not unlike the insufficient answer which Lonergan says is still useful in that it helps to clarify the question.

69. Lonergan, 'A Post-Hegelian Philosophy', p. 205.

70. Meyer, *Aims*, p. 88.

a datum relevant to the question the historian is asking.[71] In the case of Jesus, a datum is controlled when it is determined what the meaning of the datum is, and whether or not it is a datum on Jesus, i.e., whether it is historically authentic.

Any possible confusion over the nature of historical data is clarified when one understands the fuller meaning of historical 'facts' in Meyer's usage. In this Meyer again relies on Collingwood. A historical fact is not to be identified with a datum, but is rather related to Collingwood's notion of the 'inside' of the event. The thought or purpose making an event an intentional human act is the inside of the event, and a historical fact is defined as the event understood in terms of these intentions. On this definition, historical facts are not data, not those things with which the historian begins the investigation. Rather, historical facts emerge only at the *end* of the investigation, as its goal, as events are seen in light of their motivating intentions. Facts are the totality of what happened, seen in terms of why it happened. For this reason, for the historian there is no difference between discovering what happened and discovering why it happened.[72]

From this understanding of data and facts emerges one of the most significant aspects of Meyer's historiography, and one that sets him apart most explicitly from Crossan. Though historical investigation proceeds on the distinct levels of data control and fact establishment, progress on each level is not isolated but *reciprocal*. The levels interact spirally, with hypotheses and verifications on one level continually modified in light of those on the other. Meyer consistently stresses that decisions on the historicity of data (data 'control') cannot simply be settled at the outset of historical investigation, prior to the establishment of the facts. Of course, certain initial decisions on the data will have to be made in the beginning, or else the investigation could not even get underway. These decisions cannot be guided by a general mistrust of the data, which would have a stifling effect on all subsequent enquiry, though a selective mistrust may develop during the course of investigation.[73] In any case, decisions made on the data in the beginning are subject to revision as the investigation progresses. This is because the historian's understanding of the data is dependent on the larger frame of reference within which the data are set as enquiry continues and historical hypotheses develop. The enquiry may uncover a network of relations that shed new light on the data, giving them a sense more historically cogent than the historian could have previously envisioned.[74] As the data are further understood in the context of hypotheses bearing on the establishment of facts, decisions on the data are subject to change. So there is a genuine reciprocity between the control of the data and the establishment of facts from the data.

That the historian cannot begin the enquiry with a stance of general mistrust of the data does not entail a stance of naive credulity as the enquiry progresses. Meyer forswears both suppositional extremes in historical Jesus studies: methodical cre-

---

71. Meyer, *Aims*, p. 80.
72. Meyer, *Aims*, p. 87.
73. Meyer, *Aims*, p. 84.
74. Meyer, *Aims*, pp. 80-84; *Critical Realism*, p. 132; *Christus Faber*, p. 16; *Reality and Illusion*, p. 104.

dulity and methodical scepticism. The former assumes the data are authentic unless obviously beyond harmonization, the latter that they are inauthentic in view of their character as serving the confessional concerns of the early church. Both extremes are inadequate, unself-suspecting and self-defeating, and the 'burden of proof' is on anyone who in a given instance would make a case for either authenticity or inauthenticity. Meyer draws two practical consequences from this rejection of methodical suppositions: (1) There will be three columns for historicity judgements on the data, 'yes', 'no' and 'question mark'. The third column is necessary when neither credulity nor scepticism is assumed, because there is the real possibility that large portions of material will not yield to firm judgements either way. *Assumptions* have the effect of eliminating such historical residues, but *no mere assumption can take the place of reasoned historical judgement*. Rather than fall back on assumption, the critical historian must be ready to admit that he or she does not know.[75] (2) Historicity judgements on the data will be qualified by nuances over the scale of probability. These judgements cannot be settled by the application of a single systematic question, or even a set of questions, that are believed to settle historicity issues without remainder. 'No method will be admitted to which caution, nuance, and the admission of doubt are alien.'[76] The systematic questions Meyer has in mind in the field of Jesus studies are of course the criteria of authenticity.

Judgements of historicity on individual data are usually made in the course of investigation, in interaction with determination of the facts, as individual bits of data are or are not seen to fit in a larger historical picture. But Meyer says that such judgements should be independently verified, in either a direct or an oblique pattern of inference. In a direct pattern, the historian determines the intention, knowledgeability and veracity of the writer of the source; if these are verified, historicity may be inferred. But in the case of the Gospel data, the intention of the evangelist is often difficult to define, and 'the evidence is against presuming that either the gospels as such or the individual pericopae as such are merely recorded memories.'[77] So oblique patterns of inference are used, and these patterns take the form of what are traditionally known as the criteria of authenticity.

Now in Meyer's historiography, the criteria are generally necessary for verification of historicity judgments, but this role is different from the one the criteria play in, for example, Crossan's method and in classic tradition criticism. As I showed in Chapter Two, the criteria of stratification and multiple attestation are for Crossan the principle means of establishing a pool of usable data on the historical Jesus, and that as the *first* stage of investigation. Meyer denies that the criteria can be used in this way, as universal requisites for a tradition to be considered historical. There are in fact no such universal requisites.[78] For this reason

75. Meyer, *Critical Realism*, p. 131.

76. Meyer, *Aims*, p. 84.

77. Meyer, *Aims*, p. 85.

78. Meyer gives as example the acid-test criterion of dissimilarity, which is rooted in a methodical scepticism. This criterion supposes that the Gospel material was not only stamped by the confessional concerns of the church but was created to serve those concerns. This supposition is made thematic by the working criterion that data from the Gospels should be taken as so created unless

he prefers to call the criteria 'indices', reflecting their character as a means of gauging whether historicity is more likely than non-historicity, rather than as universal requisites to historicity.[79] In addition, the indices are to operate *in sensu aiente*: their presence favours historicity but their absence does not require non-historicity.[80] Perhaps most importantly, the indices do not operate in abstraction from the course of investigation in pursuit of the establishment of facts. Meyer roundly criticizes an approach to method that reduces evaluation of data to application of a few rules of thumb, to be followed by historical construction based on the usable data. Decisions on the data are made principally in the course of an investigation, as the data are seen to play a role in various explanatory hypotheses. These decisions are verified, or else challenged, by the indices; but the indices do not establish a judgment of historicity apart from the larger investigation. A genuine reciprocity between data control and fact establishment does not allow historicity questions to be answered before the construction begins. Again, Crossan is the prime exemplar of a method that does precisely that, and Meyer's criticism of Crossan is explicit and rather caustic. In a review of *The Historical Jesus*, Meyer suggests that there is no real historical enquiry undertaken in that work, no struggle with recalcitrant data, no room for enduring question marks, but only an unsubstantiated hypothesis proposed within an artifice of apparent surgical precision: 'All is aseptic, the data having been freeze-dried, prepackaged, and labeled with literary flair. Instead of an inquiry, what we have here is simply the proposal of a bright idea.'[81] Meyer undoubtedly also has Crossan in view in later comments, when Meyer points out the dynamic nature of historical thinking and knowing and contrasts this with a method that presumes to know the data in advance of historical enquiry: 'It just will not do, therefore, to survey in advance the mass of data, freeze-dry, package and label it, merrily go on to so-called reconstruction without further worry about historicity, and call the whole "critical". Or even an advance in method!'[82]

Meyer's stress on the dynamic nature of historical knowing, seen in the reciprocity between data control and fact establishment and in his revisioning of the criteria of authenticity, lead him to an all-out assault on the predominant understanding of method in Jesus studies and of the criteria of authenticity. Since the New Quest, the criteria had been taken to be the means of assuring objectivity in judgements of historicity. They offer a clear, publicly accessible way of evaluating the data, using

---

this assumption is implausible, i.e., unless the data are contrary to both the church's confession and to the church's possible source in Judaism. But the suppositional basis of the criterion is relativized by the fact that application of the criterion itself shows that traditions contrary to the church's concerns, i.e., 'dissimilar' traditions, were in fact preserved. That this is seen to be the case relativizes the assumption of confessional creativity by the church, and shows the criterion to be much less than the acid-test Käsemann presented it to be and it has been assumed to be in Jesus studies. See *Aims*, pp. 81-83.

   79. Meyer, *Aims*, p. 86; *Critical Realism*, p. 131.

   80. Meyer, *Aims*, p. 87.

   81. Meyer, review of *The Historical Jesus: The Life of a Mediterranean Jewish Peasant*, by John Dominic Crossan, *The Catholic Biblical Quarterly* 55 (1993), p. 576.

   82. Meyer, *Reality and Illusion*, p. 105.

a repeatable method, resulting in judgements open to confirmation or rejection based on that method. Meyer countered this understanding of the criteria, or indices, by insisting that their use does not change the fact that the historian draws on his or her subjectivity in historical knowing. The Lonerganian slogan is 'the way to objectivity is through authentic subjectivity', and objectivity in historical knowledge is no exception. The criteria are usually thought of in the context of a false dilemma: 'either the burden of objectivity must be borne by "criteria" expected to eliminate the bothersome business of the historian's "subjectivity", or we must stoically admit that answers are just products of presupposition and preju-dice, assured results are fictitious, and all parties to the critical debate may be wrong.'[83] On a critical realist hermeneutic, the historian is seen to draw on his or her whole fund of experience and range of understanding in making historical evaluations. The indices do not change this fact, but rather illustrate it. In the final analysis, the indices are understood to be 'heuristic resources epitomizing discreet, more or less useful, patterns of observation and inference'. Historical knowing is a sophistication of common sense,[84] and indices function in historical investigation the way proverbs function in common sense. They give general advice for where to look and how to proceed, but cannot be taken as absolute norms. In Lonergan's words, '[Common sense] generalities are not principles, relevant to every possible instance, but proverbs saying what may be useful to bear in mind, and commonly rounded out by a contradictory piece of advice. Look before you leap! He who hesitates is lost!'[85] When an index is seen to function as a sort of proverb, its ability to bear the weight of objectivity is relativized. Indices must work in concert with hypotheses that organize and illumine the data in answer to questions posed by the historian to the data. In the end, the weight of objectivity is borne by the whole 'subjectivity' of the historian's enquiry.

I have identified the reciprocity between the levels of data control and fact establishment as one of the most distinctive and important features of Meyer's methodological proposal. Its grounding in his understanding of critical realism is essential. Data control depends on the role the data are seen to play in historical hypotheses, and their usability in these hypotheses depends on their being con-trolled. For Meyer this grand circularity is a consequence of a critical realist understanding of historical thinking and knowing. Thinking in all cases is a matter of insight, and knowing is a matter of judgement upon the insight. The insight and judgement that are at work in data control are of a piece with the insight and judgement at work in fact establishment. The understanding and knowledge of historical data are such that the determination of the historicity of the data and the establishment of facts from the data are interdependent dimensions of one ongoing movement, one process of questioning, proposing hypotheses and verifying the hypotheses.[86] When either dimension is pursued apart from the other, this process

83. Meyer, *Critical Realism*, p. 141.
84. See above, pp. 104-105.
85. Lonergan, *Method*, p. 230.
86. Meyer clearly echoes Lonergan in this. The latter pointed out that historical facts and their interconnections form a single piece, such that one cannot first determine facts and then go on to

is either truncated and its conclusions ill-founded, or, more likely, conclusions are affected by a reciprocity that is tacitly at work but neither recognized nor acknowledged by the historian.

There are further resources that can be tapped to help fill out Meyer's stress on the reciprocity of data and facts. Another way of stating this same issue is to say that historical data and their *interpretations* are interdependent. As I showed in Chapter Three, the establishment of data and the interpretation of the established data are commonly conceived by historians as distinct processes. Meyer would agree with a distinction between these, but only a heuristic distinction. I have shown that Crossan's method holds data and interpretation apart, and in this he in fact has some company among historians. But Collingwood advanced an alternative understanding of the relation between data and interpretation that we can use to develop Meyer's ideas further.

Meyer relies principally on Collingwood's new understanding of the nature of historical fact, arising from his notion of the inside of the historical event. For Meyer, this understanding is consonant with his critical realist conception of knowledge as a matter of insight and judgement. Historical facts, understood as events seen in light of agents' intentions, are accessible by insight and judgement into the data, and are not self-evident or known by simply 'taking a look' at the data. Facts are considered unknowns that become knowns only by exercise of the knowing process. Collingwood's ideas certainly lend themselves to this critical realist appropriation. But Collingwood also gives a description of the relation between fact and interpretation that Meyer does not exploit. Collingwood notes the traditional understanding of the activity of historical interpretation, that it is a matter of stretching an imaginative web between fixed points of data. Once the data are fixed by the historian's scrutinizing them for their reliability, the historian weaves a web of interpretation among them, discovering interconnections, contexts, causes and effects, and otherwise making sense of the data in a construction of a complete historical account. On this understanding, the previously fixed points of data serve as the bedrock for the interpretation, the bar at which any interpretation must be justified. Collingwood counters this understanding by *denying that there are any fixed points*. By this he does not mean that there are no data, or that data cannot be distinguished from interpretation. But the interpretive web of the historian is not dependent on the fixed points of *independently established* data. Rather, *the fixed points are dependent upon the imaginative web*. The authenticity of the data is dependent on the role the data play in the historically cogent picture painted by the historian. The historian's construction judges the fixed points by determining whether they fit into a coherent and continuous picture, a picture which makes historical sense. The scaffolding of the truth of a historical construction is not the fixed points of data independently established, but is rather the historian's 'a priori imagination'. 'Freed from its dependence on fixed points supplied from without,

---

discover interconnections. Lonergan insisted that a clear-cut distinction between the determination of historical facts and the determination of their interconnections is a positivist/empiricism assumption, rooted in a nineteenth-century notion of natural science. See *Method*, pp. 199-202.

the historian's picture of the past is thus in every detail an imaginary picture, and its necessity is at every point the necessity of the a-priori imagination. Whatever goes into it, goes into it not because his imagination passively accepts it, but because it actively demands it.'[87] Data are accepted or rejected because of their role in the historian's cogent imaginative explanation. But even data that are rejected as not bearing directly on the historical subject at hand are not categorized as useless, for they may yet prove useful in answering pertinent historical questions. I explained in Chapter Three that data are to be handled not simply as *testimony* but as *evidence*. A statement that is not useful on its face, still may be useful if the right questions are asked. Collingwood insists that critical history does not first ask if data are true or false, but rather what they mean. The historian asks what light is thrown on the subject by the fact that this person made this statement, and meant by it what they did. Statements are treated 'not as true or false accounts of the facts of which they profess to be accounts, but as other facts which, if [the historian] knows the right questions to ask about them, may throw light on those facts'.[88]

These points on the relation of data to interpretation are further illustrated in Collingwood's celebrated example of the detective, which I drew from in Chapter Three.[89] The data of a historical investigation are to be viewed in the same manner as the evidence in an investigation of a crime. What counts as a piece of evidence for a detective depends on what question the detective is asking. Nothing is evidence except in relation to a question. When a detective enters a crime scene, say the scene of a homicide, the scene is immediately cordoned off to protect it from corruption, because everything in the scene is potential evidence. What will count as actual evidence has yet to be determined, by the questions that the detective poses as the entire scene is examined. Both what will count as evidence and what the relevant evidence will mean, depend on the questions the detective has in mind as he or she searches for clues. Collingwood's logic of question-and-answer is of course integral here. It is only as the detective/historian has occasion to use a datum in answer to a question and in reconstruction of the crime/history that they know whether and how it will be useful.[90]

So Collingwood's logic of question-and-answer gives one a firmer grasp of the nature of the reciprocity between data and interpretation. Data cannot be controlled until they are understood, and they cannot be understood before they assume some

87. Collingwood, *Idea*, p. 245. That the historical picture is imaginary does not imply for Collingwood that it is simply imposed by the historian upon the data, according to his or her fancy. On the contrary, the historical picture is imaginary in that it is inferred from the evidence, and for Collingwood this inference appears to be almost deductive, in that it has to do with logical compulsion, or what the evidence requires. A historical picture is 'imaginary' but compelling in light of the evidence. A cogent historical account will prove its point 'as conclusively as a demonstration in mathematics', *Idea*, pp. 262ff.

88. Collingwood, *Idea*, p. 275.

89. Collingwood, *Idea*, pp. 266ff. Meyer refers to the example in *Aims*, p. 14; and *Reality and Illusion*, p. 102. But he does not mention the logic of question-and-answer that I will see is integral to it.

90. Collingwood, *Idea*, p. 280.

role in a historical investigation, or are seen in light of some historical question. As Collingwood said, 'You can't collect your evidence before you begin thinking ...because thinking means asking questions (logicians, please note) and nothing is evidence except in relation to some definite question.'[91] Any evaluation of data will be done with questions in mind, and not simply questions of whether a datum is a true or false testimony. For 'thinking means asking questions', and those questions are the means of historical understanding, the stuff of historical interpretation.

3. *Historiography and the Metacritical Moment*

I began this discussion of Meyer's historiography by noting two sets of presuppositions that he said have long guided historical Jesus work: presuppositions of purpose, which determine the questions the historian will ask, and presuppositions concerning judgements of possibility in determining answers to the questions. Meyer held that the latter kind of presuppositions have traditionally been based on a faulty epistemology and reflect an inadequate historiography, which he countered with Lonergan's cognitional theory. Meyer also had some pointed observations on the former type of presuppositions, those of purpose. These have to do with the reason one undertakes historical investigation, and are related to what Meyer calls the metacritical moment.[92]

   The metacritical moment is the ulterior purpose or goal for doing history. All critical history is undertaken with some ultimate purpose in mind, which is beyond the historical investigation itself; this purpose is the value one places on doing history, one's idea of what history is 'good for'. To place any value at all on historical investigation is to acknowledge some metacritical goals; these reasons for doing history account for why it is done, but are themselves 'metacritical', transcending historical criticism. The interpretation and explanation that are the goals of critical history are in fact proximate goals, in the service of the metacritical goals that arise from the historian's presupposed value in doing history. It is of course not uncommon in critical history to forswear any ulterior purpose as inevitably corrupting on the historical enterprise.[93] Historians, in order to be objective, are to undertake their task in a disinterested manner, where 'disinterested' means denial of any purpose other than recovery of historical truth and so denial of any investment in history's results other than the recovery of historical truth 'for its own sake'. This kind of disinterest Meyer regards as a positivist illusion. All historians have basic postures and ulterior interests, and these interests figure significantly in the historical task.

---

   91. Collingwood, *Idea*, p. 281.
   92. Meyer discusses the metacritical moment principally in *Aims*, pp. 92-94 and *Reality and Illusion*, pp. 110-13.
   93. See for example Paul Merkley, who, against the specifically existentialist usefulness of history proclaimed by the New Quest, insists: 'We should make no mistake about it: history is *useless*', 'New Quests for Old: One Historian's Observations on a Bad Bargain', *Canadian Journal of Theology* 16 (1970), p. 216.

[Metacritical goals] have an impact on every aspect of the historical enterprise, including the understanding of method. Finally, the motives, values, uses, and ulterior purposes of history, be it ever so critical, are themselves metacritical presuppositions. They are not controlled by method but arise from the historian's intellectual and moral being, and in the end they account more fundamentally and adequately than anything else for the kind of history he produces.[94]

At least two examples of metacritical goals of history can be seen in Meyer. We have already noted his stress on the legitimacy of theological questions in critical history. He also stresses that historical results can and indeed must be of use for theology. In this he once again follows Lonergan, in the latter's statement of theological method, in which his critical realism requires that theology be radically empirical. Empirical, but not empiricist: for Lonergan, all knowledge begins with the data of experience, and is thus at bottom 'empirical'; but knowledge of course does not simply consist in the givenness of data, but involves operations of intelligence and judgement upon the data. Theological knowledge is no exception; it too begins with the data of experience, and thus must take account of the results of textual interpretation and of historical investigation.[95] Meyer makes theological use of historical results when he demonstrates how the history of Jesus offers the divine solution to the human problem of evil.[96]

A second, related example of a metacritical goal in Meyer is history's opening up of new possibilities of becoming. In history, historians encounter something of themselves, enter into dialogue with history and open themselves up to being challenged and questioned by history. Meyer describes historians' relations to the historical reality they discover in much the same terms as he describes interpreters' relations to the text: history ultimately involves encounter or vital contact, which is a listening to history's challenge and being confronted with its grasp of existence. I would note that it is difficult to overlook Meyer's convergence with Bultmann here. Meyer in fact offers specific approval of Bultmann's recognition that history is not merely the evaluation of facts, that history cannot be examined with impersonal objectivity as can nature. 'This is the power of Bultmann's proposal and performance: the openness to be invited, challenged, changed. Hence the metaphors of "meeting" and "listening". The value of history lies in vital contact with new possibilities of becoming.'[97] For all Meyer's criticism of certain guiding principles of Bultmann's historiography (e.g., analogy and the closed continuum) he

94. Meyer, *Aims*, pp. 93-94; repeated almost verbatim much later in *Reality and Illusion*, p. 110.

95. I should point out that, though theology has an initial empirical level for Lonergan, it is not therefore exhausted by the work of a 'natural' theology. It is not simply 'from below', for, following on the phases (Lonergan calls them 'functional specialties') of research, interpretation and history, there is the need for 'dialectic', in which the results of the first phases are examined for their horizonal implications. A conversion in horizons on the part of the investigator is often necessary in the following phase, 'foundations', before the dogmatic, systematic and communicative phases can be undertaken. Thus, though theology begins with an empirical task, it requires an existential moment as the foundation for actual doctrinal formulation. See *Method in Theology*, esp. ch. 5.

96. See Meyer, *Christus Faber*, ch. 10; and *Reality and Illusion*, ch. 7.

97. Meyer *Aims*, pp. 49-50.

praises Bultmann, as well as the post-Bultmannian New Quest, for their understanding of history as the investigation of intentionality, against a positivism that
denies that intentionality is accessible.[98] He also praises the hermeneutic rehabilita-
tion of 'subjectivity' that is seen in Bultmann.[99] It would seem that Meyer and
Bultmann, along with the post-Bultmannians, are all in fact cousins under the
skin.[100] As early as *The Man for Others* (1971) Meyer sums up Jesus' message in
existentialist-sounding language, as a 'call to decision', and describes doing history
as an 'encounter'.[101] In *Aims* he notes the explicitly theological purposes governing
the choice of questions in serious historical Jesus research today; such an observation, published in 1979, is at least consonant with the theological motivation of
the New Quest, to discover the continuities between the Jesus of history and the
Christ of the kerygma.[102] But I would suggest that Meyer's understanding of decision and of the possibilities opened up by history has more to do with his understanding of modern historical consciousness than with a Bultmannian existentialism,
i.e., an existential selfhood fashioned by one's solitary responsible decisions over
against the future.[103] For Meyer, selfhood is fashioned by decisions in the sense
that humans are the product of their own history; and modern historical consciousness has revealed that to be the case.[104] Critical history reveals the selfhood so
fashioned and opens possibilities for understanding and fashioning one's own selfhood. The selfhood fashioned by decisions is thus, once again, more Gadamerian

98. See Meyer, 'Historical Understanding and *Jesus and the Gospel*', p. 166.

99. Meyer, 'The Challenges of Text and Reader', p. 4. See the Introduction to Bultmann, *Jesus and the Word*.

100. Their commonalities are probably due to certain Heideggerian roots that can be traced in both: in Bultmann and the New Quest, directly to Heidegger from Bultmann, but in Meyer, to Heidegger by way of Gadamer. In a sense we have here two branches on a Heideggerian tree; but these branches are as different as Bultmann is from Gadamer, as different as demythologizing is from a hermeneutic of belonging.

101. Meyer, *The Man for Others*, pp. 146-47.

102. Meyer, *Aims*, p. 18. On the theological motivation of the New Quest's historical investigation, see the classic statement by Ernst Käsemann, 'The Problem of the Historical Jesus', pp. 17ff.

103. At one point Meyer explicitly rejects an existentialist hermeneutic in New Testament studies, not because of its emphasis on decision but because of its hyper-individualism. 'In no small part the power of existentialism lay in its appreciation of decision as the peak of human intentionality; its deficiency lay in attending to decision almost exclusively in its solitary moment. Though decision and, above all, conversion is intensely personal and utterly intimate, it is not so private as to be solitary (as Lonergan insisted)', *Aims*, p. 212. He was later to distance himself explicitly, by distancing Lonergan, from existentialist philosophy: 'Existentialist philosophy made the language of authenticity prominent and glamorous. As time passed and the glamour began to fade...Bernard Lonergan gave it new definition and a new lease on life. He redefined authenticity as the human excellence born of self-transcendence, that "going beyond" self that was realized in true judgment and virtuous action, and, above all, in love', 'In Tune with a World that Is Good: Variations on the Theme of Authenticity', *Toronto Journal of Theology* 6 (1990), p. 3.

104. Meyer, *Aims*, p. 76. Meyer sees historical consciousness as rooted in an understanding of human acts of meaning. By acts of meaning humans make themselves and their world. Every such act is embedded in an always-changing context. Historical consciousness is generated by humanity's awareness of its autonomy, of itself as maker of self and the world of meaning, in the ever-
changing context. See *Critical Realism*, p. 25.

than Bultmannian. The historian indeed 'encounters' history, but the object of this encounter is not the existential selfhood of historical subjects, but rather the challenge of an alternative horizon that confronts the horizon of the historian with the possible need for conversion. Meyer distances himself from the New Quest with other specific criticisms, in spite of hermeneutic similarities.[105] But in the final analysis, he is wholly sympathetic with the spirit of an ulterior purpose to history in the understanding and fashioning of oneself.

Such are the metacritical goals that, *more than anything else*, account for the historian's method and the kind of history the historian produces. This places the metacritical moment in a position more fundamental than any method, for ulterior purposes are outside the control of method. One would think that such a herme-neutically important point would receive appreciable development by Meyer, but in fact he gives relatively little attention to it, certainly far less than his attention to points of method as such. This makes it difficult for us to know just how to take Meyer here. On its face, the claim of the controlling role of the metacritical moment would appear to have the effect of radically relativizing historical results, and would therefore be subject to the same criticisms as any such claim for a totalizing relativism. If results are finally dependent on ulterior purpose, and this purpose can vary widely among historians, then results too will vary, with varying purposes, and in the end there are no means of adjudicating between results, for there are no critical controls on the choice of appropriate purposes. There would in fact be no means of even communicating among historians unless they happen to share metacritical goals, for not only their end results but also their means of enquiry will be relative to their purposes; there is no other way for purposes to exercise control over results than through the process of investigation.

Now it seems clear that Meyer does not intend to relativize historical results or methods in this way. In the first instance, he would not have devoted the attention he did to detailed discussion of appropriate method if he truly intended to radically relativize methods and results.[106] Although the immediate goals of critical history (interpretation and explanation) are only proximate and open goals to any ulterior value, ulterior values are not to be the direct and immediate concern of the histo-rian. Meyer insists that the historical task can be corrupted by the intrusion of goals like theology, social sciences, philosophy and interfaith dialogue, when these are the historian's immediate concerns. There remains a real danger of bias interfering with historical investigation.[107] So Meyer's claim that metacritical goals account

---

105. Meyer criticizes in Bultmann an existential reductionism that 'pulverizes' anything that is not existentially communicable, e.g., Jesus' historical particularity and messiahship are irrelevant to faith; past events cannot be salvific; any conception of eschatology, redeemer and redemption is mythological, *Aims*, p. 50. He notes the widespread use of Collingwood in Bultmann and the New Quest, which is actually a misuse, because Collingwood 'subverts in advance the thinking of roughly half the people who cite him favorably', *Critical Realism*, p. 53 n. 57; see also p. 150.

106. In the discussion of Meyer's hermeneutic, I noted the primacy he gives to consent or good-will in interpretation, while also recognizing the analysis that follows interpretation and is charac-terized by a hermeneutics of suspicion (pp. 50-57, 65). For Meyer, historical analysis is truly 'critical' and not blindly in the service of any ideology or theology.

107. Meyer, *Reality and Illusion*, pp. 111-12.

'more than anything else' for historical results will have to be qualified; although these goals are real and always present, they are in a sense held in abeyance for the sake of critical historical investigation.

There is one other point, which we can draw from Lonergan, that may help illumine Meyer's comments on metacritical goals, though Meyer never made this application explicitly. During the period of his 'turn to the subject' in the 1960s, when Lonergan was developing his notion of horizons and exploring concepts of meaning and the human sciences, he advanced a fourth level to his previous three levels of consciousness, the level of decision. On this level the subject advances beyond determining the true, to determining the good or the valuable. The addition of this level comes with the recognition that knowledge cannot be obtained without the personal engagement of the subject. The cognitional operations by which knowledge is obtained are operations of a knowing subject, and as the subject, driven by questioning, strives for the intelligible, the true and the real, the subject ultimately strives for the good. This is because the striving for the true and real that drives one through the levels of cognitional operations is ultimately a striving for a value. One will strive for the true only if one recognizes the value of truth. To refuse to attach any value to truth, and thus to the pursuit of truth, is to say that truth is quite literally worthless.[108] So the striving after truth as a *value* is necessary for knowledge.[109]

In this way the fourth level of conscious operations is the culmination of the progressive unfolding of the one continuous desiring that moves one up through the levels of cognition. The desire for intelligibility, truth and reality culminates in the desire for the good, the valuable, the worthwhile.[110] The fourth level sublates the lower levels, including them but going beyond them. The pursuit of the good prolongs, promotes and completes the pursuit of the intelligible, true and real. So the desire to know that was previously described as 'disinterested' is now seen to be only relatively so. A value is ultimately attached to the goal of this desire; the attainment of truth is considered worthwhile for the knowing subject. In this Lonergan insists on the primacy of the existential subject. But by 'existential' Lonergan does not mean the primacy of results or of the will (as the emphasis on 'decision' in existentialism often implies); rather, he refers to the subject as fundamentally concerned with the self as becoming good or evil.[111] The existential subject is indeed the subject as one makes oneself to be what one is by one's responsible actions. But the subject's ultimate concern is not with the results of one's actions but with what one becomes in being responsible. In addition, it is only in such responsible actions that the good or value is to be determined; just as 'being' is only known in the experience of particular instances of being, so what the good specifically is can only be seen in actions of good people.[112] So the striving for the

---

108. As Lonergan observed, 'not even the natural sciences can prescind from the question of value, for the very pursuit of science is the pursuit of a value, and the contention that science should be value-free, *wertfrei*, if, taken literally, implies that science should be worthless', 'Theology and Man's Future', in *A Second Collection*, pp. 143-44.

109. See the excellent summary in Jonsson, *Foundations for Knowing God*, pp. 79ff.

110. Lonergan, 'The Subject', p. 81.

111. Lonergan, 'The Subject', p. 84.

112. Lonergan, 'The Subject', p. 83.

good that is the culmination of the drive to the true and the real is the subject's striving for what it is to become.

It may be best to see Meyer's comments on the metacritical goals of history in light of the later Lonergan's broadly existential concerns. The pursuit of historical knowledge, like the pursuit of any knowledge, cannot be separated from the pursuit of value. This pursuit of value is of a piece with the subject's acting responsibly and so becoming good. Knowledge is a function of experience, insight and judgement, which are fully exercised only by the responsible subject. For a metacritical goal to arise out of the subject's intellectual and moral being, and thereby to control the subject's enquiries, is for the subject to recognize and acknowledge the ultimate value of its enquiries and to conduct them responsibly in light of that value, because responsibility only obtains when a value is recognized. In this way, Meyer's metacritical goals, seen as values, affect method and results, in that they promote the responsible functioning of the subject's knowing operations. But those values thus have their effect as ulterior purposes and not proximate ones; they affect the enquiry specifically in the promotion of responsibility, without which the subject would not operate fully.

Chapter 6

MEYER'S METHOD IN PRACTICE

I will now show how Meyer's historiography and hermeneutics affect his actual historical practice. I will first offer a sketch of his portrait of the historical Jesus, followed by consideration of some specific ways he derives the portrait in the course of his investigation.

1. *The Portrait*

According to Meyer, Jesus' ministry took place in roughly three phases: (1) a ministry of baptism, performed alongside John the Baptist, which ended with the Baptist's arrest; (2) a public ministry in Galilee, which ended with Peter's messianic confession; and (3) a private proclamation to his disciples, on the way to Jerusalem, which ended with Jesus' death.

In the first phase, Jesus initially baptized alongside John and shared in his ministry. This beginning marks Jesus' horizons as 'eschatological and "preparationist"', and suggests that Jesus participated in the Baptist's aim, the restoration of Israel in view of the imminent eschaton.[1] Jesus, like John, called for repentance (which was radical, involving renunciation of exclusivist claims to be the 'true Israel' based upon membership in a group, e.g., Essenes; and the opening of the heart to others) and thus invited conflict with the religious elite.[2] The Baptist's role was to assemble by baptism the remnant of Israel destined for cleansing and acquittal and thus ultimately for restoration. Jesus first of all entered into this scheme of prophetic meaning and sharing in the Baptist's call; and he also read divine signs in the Baptist's career bearing on himself. Like the Baptist, Jesus understood his own role in terms of the scriptural promise of the restoration of Israel; and, like the Baptist, he understood this restoration as called for now and already begun. It was begun by John's baptism, and Jesus took up this mission as his own, initially as an ally of John but also seeing signs of his own role and destiny in John's mission.

After John's arrest, Jesus saw his own new career as constituting another distinct phase in the eschatological scenario of fulfilment events. This marks the second phase of Jesus' career, the public ministry, which Meyer treats in two aspects: the public proclamation and the public actions. In the proclamation, the theme of 'the reign of God' takes priority over the theme of 'the wrath to come' that character-

---

1.   Meyer, *Aims*, p. 123.
2.   Meyer, *Aims*, pp. 120-21.

ized the first phase. While the message of the Baptist called for repentance and offered restoration in view of the coming judgement, the reign of God was the central theme of Jesus' message and teaching beginning in the second phase, and is defined by Meyer as 'the triumphant consummation of God's lordship over man and events'.[3] It is most characterized by *gratuity* (offered as a free gift to all, which is a scandal) and *present realization*, but like the Baptist's message, it is still associated with the restoration of Israel.[4]

Both the Baptist and Jesus understood the restoration to take place among the remnant of Israel. Meyer is careful to qualify the notion of remnant: it is not to be understood in exclusivist terms, with demands of Torah as the requirement of admission. Meyer sees Jesus and the Baptist as 'preparationist', intending to prepare Israel for the imminent eschatological consummation of history; they did not conceive of the remnant as consisting of those with a right understanding and observance of Torah. This as opposed to the Pharisees who were 'tranformationist', intending to reform Israel through observance of Torah, or groups such as the Essenes who were 'separatist', requiring specific observance for admission to their ranks, exclusive of the mass of Israel as such. Both the Pharisees and the Essenes had an eschatology, but their eschatology was not the defining principle of their movements. For the Baptist and Jesus, by contrast, the remnant was constituted by response to the specifically eschatological demand.[5] This was a demand that, though gratuitous, also involved judgement in that it could be rejected by those to whom it was offered, and in the event largely was rejected. This possibility of rejection and judgement necessarily carried with it the possibility of the remnant as the object of restoration. The remnant envisioned by the Baptist and Jesus was thus an 'open remnant', in contrast to the 'closed remnant' of particularistic sects such as the Pharisees and Essenes.[6]

The reign of God and equivalent expressions took on an absolute, end-of-the-world sense in Jesus' use, as seen in the convergence of end-of-the-world motifs that Jesus associated with them. These motifs include reversal of conditions of historical existence in the apocalyptic beatitudes; the judgement motif in the parables of the kingdom; and the warnings that the time is short. In the esoteric traditions, which I will describe below, Jesus emphasized the shortness of time between his public career and the outbreak of the ordeal, which would itself be short, followed by the day of the Son of Man.[7]

---

3. Meyer, *Aims*, p. 130.

4. In view of the ongoing debate about the eschatological component of Jesus' message and career, it would be best to clarify in what sense Meyer understands the reign of God and the restoration of Israel to be eschatological. Meyer says that the reign of God was, for Jesus, climactically and definitively eschatological, in that it signified the end of time and the present order and the inauguration of the age to come (*Aims*, pp. 130-31). The reign of God was a free gift, and an order of things from which people could be admitted or excluded; and it was presently being realized.

5. Meyer, *Aims*, p. 234.

6. The notion of the 'open remnant' is formulated by Meyer as early as 1965, in his article 'Jesus and the Remnant of Israel', *Journal of Biblical Literature* 84 (1965), p. 127.

7. Meyer, 'Jesus' Scenario of the Future', in *Christus Faber*, pp. 43ff.

Though the reign of God and the restoration of Israel were eschatologically conceived, Meyer insists that Jesus was not apocalyptic. Meyer demonstrates this in several elements of Jesus' proclamation: in his rejection of stilted symbolism in favour of the master image of the temple; in his rejection of attempts to date the future; in his affirmation of the whole world as from God's hand and control (Mt. 10.29); and in his affirmation of nature, of the root structures of social existence, of the goodness of ordinary customs and daily occupations of the world. Jesus' eschatology, like apocalyptic, was 'absolute;' but rather than causing withdrawal of humans from the world, rather than 'diminishing the life of man-in-time', it brought the condition of life's fulfilment.[8]

Repentance, not Torah obedience, was required for participation in the restoration. This repentance was conceived by the Baptist and Jesus as the appropriate response to the gratuity of the kingdom. It was a renunciation of all claims on the kingdom, in view of God's boundless goodness. But though Torah obedience was not a 'requirement for admission', Meyer understands the content of Jesus' public teaching as Torah for a graced and already restored Israel. This was to replace the former casuistic Torah which was provisional. The Mosaic Torah was in a sense defective because it had been accommodated to a defective Israel.[9] But now is the time of the gift of the eschaton, and the new Torah is for a community of the transformed. Thus Jesus' teaching was characterized as (1) eschatological, (2) prescriptive, and (3) transcending the Mosaic Torah.[10] 'The commands of Jesus were the heart of his teaching, reflecting the revolutionary significance of the reign of God and specifying the right response to it. Nothing was to be left as it was. The eschatological reversal of fortunes (now it was to be the turn of the poor, the hungry, and the mourners) was matched by an eschatological transvaluation of values.'[11]

In Jesus' teaching Torah was transformed by reference to the new revelation of the reign of God. Jesus' Torah teaching was offered not as interpretation but as revelation. In his capacity as teacher as well as proclaimer, then, Jesus was not a rabbi but a prophet. Meyer says that Jesus understood himself to be the unique revealer of the full, final measure of God's will.[12] Meyer sees three decisive traits of Jesus' teaching that are intelligible only on the assumption that such was Jesus' self-understanding: the correlation of his teaching with his proclamation of the reign of God; its transcendence of the Mosaic economy; and authority that is personal rather than exegetical (i.e., prophetic rather than scribal).[13]

---

8. Meyer, *Aims*, pp. 249-50.

9. Meyer, *Aims*, p. 141.

10. However, the Mosaic Torah's 'inner dynamism' was not transcended but only realized. Only its external forms were transcended, and in their own direction. This is Meyer's response to what is commonly known as Jesus' 'intensification' of Torah, *Aims*, p. 142. 'The reign of God was God's supreme and climactic gift to Israel and the world, not just goodness but boundless goodness. How could the time-tested, customary, quotidian morality of the Torah be an appropriate response to boundless goodness? The bursting of limits in the antitheses [of the Sermon on the Mount] correlates with the message of the herald of salvation…', *Aims*, p. 144.

11. Meyer, *Aims*, p. 145.

12. Meyer, *Aims*, p. 151.

13. Meyer, *Aims*, p. 151.

Jesus' message was directed to an unlikely audience: sinners and the afflicted and outcast. That his message was so directed means that it had a symbolic dimension: (1) The sinners and outcasts were types of Israel-to-be-saved. The eschatological reversal of the situation of the outcasts imaged the eschatological restoration of Israel. (2) Restoration was to involve reconciliation between people as well. In this understanding, Jesus' message of restoration was consciously divisive. 'The restoration Jesus was intent on effecting startled everyone who came into contact with him–the crowds, the learned and pious, the simple, afflicted, and outcast, the disciples, the priestly and aristocratic *élite*–firing fierce allegiances and inciting deadly hostilities. This divisive impact…was perfectly conscious on Jesus' part. It externalized the incongruence of Israel's dispositions and his own distinctive aims.'[14]

The public actions of Jesus were themselves carriers of meaning, and Meyer examines them as such. The actions include the call of the disciples and their being sent to Israel; miraculous signs of salvation; table fellowship with sinners; public debate and public formulations of mission; and entry into Jerusalem to 'cleanse' the temple. I give here brief descriptions of Meyer's treatment of three of these categories. In the category of miraculous signs, the exorcisms function as signs of the eschaton, as much as do proclamation or prophecy. Meyer notes that this meaning presupposes the unity of evil and a frame of reference generated by the eschatological proclamation of the exorcist. The miracles in general were decisive signs of the imminent eschaton, the reign of God, re-creation and the defeat of Satan.[15] The category of Jesus' table fellowship with sinners had a twofold purpose: (1) the forgiveness and conversion of sinners; and (2) reconciliation of people with one another. Jesus' fellowship with sinners was a challenge to the social order,[16] and a reversing of the classic biblical structure of repentance as seen in the Baptist (conversion first, then communion): Jesus' structure was communion first, which flowered into conversion. This was the perfect translation into action of Jesus' eschatological macarisms (Mt. 5.3ff., par.): *free* and *now* and related to the restoration of Israel. The entry into Jerusalem and temple cleansing were also calculated and symbolic. In the text, these events constituted a single narrative and reflected a single continuous event. The temple was the goal of the procession into the city. The whole event signified the imminent eschaton. 'It brought the capital city and the temple into relation to the reign of God…the temple cleansing signaled the dawn of a new era and restoration of cult appropriate to it.'[17]

The third phase of Jesus' career, the esoteric teachings, relates to his public career as theme to performance (the esoteric teaching promoted the public performance at

---

14. Meyer, *Aims*, pp. 172-73.

15. Meyer, *Aims*, pp. 154-58.

16. Meyer notes that Jesus' table fellowship must be seen in its first-century socio-religious context. Table fellowship established social lines and maintained sacral character. Ritual distinction between clean and unclean, and moral distinction of righteous/sinner, was concretely expressed in table fellowship. According to Meyer, 'the tendency of Torah piety was to regard the ordinary run of men (Lk. 18.11) as greedy or dishonest or adulterers', *Aims*, p. 159. Habits of table fellowship expressed this tendency, and it was challenged by Jesus' practice.

17. Meyer, *Aims*, p. 170.

the level of explicit thematization) and as solution to riddle (the esoteric teaching presented the full scheme of meaning in which the disciples were to grasp the whole of Jesus' words and acts).[18] In the esoteric traditions, Jesus' teachings are not public but private, directed to the disciples alone.[19] The esoteric teaching is characterized by Jesus' presentation of himself as the messianic builder of the house of God. This was the image that communicated the final sense of his work, and specifies the comprehensive aim of his mission. Inasmuch as the core of the esoteric teaching was spoken after Peter's confession of Jesus as the Christ (Mk 8.29; Mt. 16.16; Lk. 9.20), Meyer sees the image of Jesus as messianic builder as spoken only in response to faith that had already grasped the secret of his supreme role in the eschatological plan.

The messianic 'temple' of the eschatological kingdom consists of the remnant of Israel and the gathered gentiles. Jesus saw himself as 'builder' of this temple, in that his death was expiatory for the remnant and the world, and also in the larger sense of his work as the final revealer of God's will in preparation for the reign of God.[20] As seen in the connection between Peter's confession and the first Passion prediction (Mk 8.27-30 parr.; Mk 8.31-33 parr.) Jesus conceived his imminent death as a constituent element of the messianic event. The way to enthronement was through suffering and death. But though his death was to have a positive significance at this point (as 'baptism', i.e., eschatological vocation, Lk. 12.50; Mk 10.38f.), what that significance was remained hidden. But in Mk 10.45 its significance as ransom is articulated, alluding to the ransom theme in Isaiah 43.3f., assimilated to the expiatory suffering of the Servant for 'many' in Isa. 52.13–53.12. This was ransom not just for Israel but for the world.

---

18.   Meyer, *Aims*, p. 174. Meyer sees public and esoteric dimensions to the Baptist's career as well. The esoteric dimension involved fasting, prayer and teaching; 'the heart of John's esoteric instructions was surely his prophetic expectations of the messianic judge to come', *Aims*, p. 117.

19.   It is important to note that Meyer does not identify the esoteric tradition with the 'messianic secret'. He says the 'messianic secret' motif is Markan redaction, though the idea of 'messianic mystery' is historical (the latter being the idea of the messiah's destiny of suffering, which has atoning significance). But Meyer does identify a certain historical *background* to Mark's 'secret' motif: 'As a trait of the historical career of Jesus, the so-called secret was Jesus' refusal to set an explicit messianic claim before Israel. This, however, was not designed to keep his messianic identity unknown to Israel. It simply reflected a realism about the decisive factor, the intimate personal orientation, which conditioned each man's response to revelation. Faith would not win out over unfaith if only the appeal for it were more explicit and spectacular (Luke 16.30f.). Hence Jesus' refusal of the demand for a "sign" (Mk 8.11f.; Mt. 12.38f. par.; Jn 6.30-36), the lack of public titles whether for himself (Mk 8.30 parr., etc.) or his following (Mk 4.30-32 parr., etc.), the thanksgiving for revelation to the simple (Mt. 11.25f. par.), the macarism on Peter (Mt. 16.17), the indirection of the response to the Baptist's question ("Tell John what you hear and see", Mt. 11.4 par.)', *Aims*, p. 309 n. 119.

20.   The metaphor of temple, with messiah as its builder, is reflected in such traditions as Jesus' response to Peter's confession, 'on this rock I will build my church' (Mt. 16.18); and in Jesus' word on destroying and rebuilding the temple, as related in the trial (Mt. 26.61; Mk 14.58). Meyer sees a background to this accusation in the oracle of Nathan (2 Sam. 7.12-14) and its use in Qumran texts (4Q174: 10-13). See *Aims*, p. 180.

Jesus shared the contemporary belief that a prophet's vocation entailed violent death, and Meyer refers to the existence of the tradition that such death was also considered expiatory.[21] Jesus did not aim to be rejected and killed. He offered a universal message of restoration to Israel in the coming reign of God, but when he was rejected and saw his death as imminent, he did aim to charge his rejection and death with meaning.

> Outside the ambit of his own saving mission there was only death and the dead (Mt. 8.22 par.). The standing resources of Israel could not effect eschatological life. It was not that the Mosaic dispensation had been a failure from the start; it was simply that the concluding revelation had been reserved for the eschaton. This was not the revelation of some ineluctable necessity structurally intrinsic to salvation. It was rather the revelation of God's pleasure, wisdom, will. The motif of the Servant's universal expiation revealed that it pleased God to restore Israel and save mankind – by Jesus' death.[22]

Meyer suggests that the expiatory death can be understood historically as the result of the emerging rejection of Jesus by Israel. The prediction of Jesus' death is historically intelligible in view of Jesus' rejection.[23] Jesus' message was not presented as optional; it was an offer of acquittal and life that called for a response, and could thus be rejected. When it was rejected, the refusers were offered salvation through Jesus' offering of his own life for them. But even this offer could be rejected, thus implying the post-Jesus mission to Israel.

Meyer finally offers a structuring of Jesus' view of his mission and destiny, as seen in the esoteric teachings, in terms of thesis, antithesis and synthesis. Thesis was Jesus' presentation of himself as the messianic builder of the eschatological house of God. Antithesis was the coming ordeal that would be inaugurated by his death, appearing to frustrate his mission, and involving trial for the remnant. Synthesis was the eventual consummation of the reign of God, the day of the Son of Man, inaugurated by Jesus' resurrection, in which the new temple would be built in the form of the restoration of Israel in the remnant.[24] Meyer follows the line of scholarship from Wilhelm Weiffenbach through Dodd and Jeremias, which says that in his teaching Jesus thus did not distinguish between his resurrection, his parousia, and the imminent eschatological restoration. All these were held together in Jesus' understanding of the unfolding of events bearing on the end. The future in Jesus' conception consisted first of crisis begun by his own rejection, suffering and death and eventually including the disciples and all Israel. This would be ended by the appearance of the Son of Man, which would bring resurrection, judgement and the banquet of the saved.[25]

---

21. Meyer, *Aims*, p. 310 n. 126.
22. Meyer, *Aims*, p. 218.
23. Meyer, '"Phases" in Jesus' Mission', in *Christus Faber*, p. 34.
24. Meyer, *Aims*, pp. 221-22.
25. Meyer, *Aims*, p. 204. In view of the fact that Jesus predicted the imminent eschatological restoration of Israel, and the parousia, in association with his resurrection, and the former did not come about, it would seem that Jesus was mistaken in his understanding of future events. But Meyer suggests that we understand Jesus' teaching about the future as the symbol-charged language of a

In summary, Jesus' message was the proclamation of the imminent and 'absolutely' eschatological kingdom of God, God's long-hoped-for restoration of Israel. When it was accepted only by a 'little flock' (the simple, afflicted, outcast), the messianic restoration would find fulfilment only in this *open remnant*. He saw his death as inaugurating the time of the eschatological ordeal, and serving an expiatory function for the remnant and the world. The time of the ordeal would be ended with the eschatological resurrection (including his own) and the inauguration of the eschatological kingdom. He saw himself as the builder of the messianic 'temple' of the eschaton, consisting of the remnant of Israel and the gathered gentiles.

> The national restoration that Jesus proposed he first of all incarnated in himself... He expressed the major aspects of this restoration in words...but in acts as well as in words. His proclamation said: salvation, free, now... The beneficiaries of these actions included the likely and the unlikely, the rich and the poor... His task was to prepare Israel for the consummation, so fulfilling all promises, prophecies and types. It was to prepare the nation for judgement by winning the remission of sins for all who wanted it. It was, finally, to create the conditions in which human bonds of affection could flourish without hindrance; in which the Father, his name hallowed by the nations, would reign supreme; and in which, restored to his friends, Jesus himself would end his abstinence, drinking wine 'new' on 'that day'...when his work would be wholly done.[26]

2. *Hypotheses, Indices and the Handling of Data*

As one examines Meyer's presentation of the historical Jesus, one thing is immediately obvious, especially in comparison with Crossan's presentation. Meyer's actual procedure of investigation is not nearly as clearly outlined as Crossan's. We saw that Crossan organizes his investigation on three levels, and gives the most methodological attention to the 'microcosmic' level, that of handling the data in the sources. Crossan gives explicitly defined criteria for determining the historicity of data, which takes place on this level. Given Crossan's specificity for determining historicity, along with his articulation of presuppositions that he considers necessary prerequisites to any historical investigation of Jesus,[27] one can see that his

---

prophet. The prophet knows his symbols, but not necessarily how they will be realized in history. Only the course of history will reveal what the symbols symbolize. The correlation between prophetic word and actual event may appear before the eye of faith, but the correlation is ambiguous. 'If God speaks in prophecy, he speaks in the history that follows on prophecy, and it is history, history grasped within the perspective of faith, that does what the prophet cannot do – namely, decipher prophetic symbol, translating image into event, schematic sequence into actual sequence, and symbolic time into real time', *Aims*, p. 247. All this commends the view of eschatological fulfilment referred to as 'eschatology in process of realization'. So Jesus himself identified resurrection, exaltation and parousia in his view of the future. They were differentiated *ex eventu* by the early church, in view of the fact that Jesus was raised but the restoration did not come. But Jesus' presentation, as prophetic, was not necessarily 'mistaken', for the above reasons.

26. Meyer, 'Jesus and His Mission: Finding the *Gestalt*', in *Christus Faber*, p. 123.

27. These prerequisites are the specifications of sources relationships, described above, Chapters 2 and 3.

results on this level are easy to duplicate, or at least to evaluate in relation to his method. Granted the validity of his conclusions on this level, the results that he derives on the level of Palestinian and Greco-Roman history ('mesocosmic') and cross-cultural and cross-temporal social anthropology ('macrocosmic'), are lucid and compelling.

In spite of his extensive discussion of historiographic and methodological issues, Meyer's actual presentation is not so neatly outlined. He does offer a large-scale structure to his material, in the form of organizing the traditions on Jesus into three broad categories, which correspond with the three stages of Jesus' career (traditions related to the Baptist, public traditions and esoteric traditions); he examines each group of traditions for the indications they give of the historical shape of Jesus' career, and examines the three sets for their convergence on a total portrait of Jesus' aims. But Meyer's decisions on the historicity of data, and on interpretation of the data so scrutinized, are not reducible to a procedural outline. The reason for this is seen in his methodological observations, as discussed above. I noted that for Meyer, historical investigation proceeds by means of hypothesis and verification, on the levels of 'controlling the data' and 'establishing the facts'. To say that the technique of history is the hypothesis is to recognize the central role of the historian's questions in history. Data speak only in answer to questions, and those questions must be posed by a historian. Questions drive both the determination of the historicity of data, and the interpretation of those data to the establishing of facts.[28] Data are not judged for their authenticity prior to and apart from an interpretation of them; data control and interpretation are necessarily reciprocal. Data must be understood in light of an interpretation advanced by questions and answers, in order to be judged accurately as authentic or not.

The centrality of the historian's questions and the reciprocity of data and interpretation are both rooted in a Lonerganian critical realist understanding of knowledge, and particularly in Lonergan's description of the nature of historical knowledge. Recall that for Lonergan, knowledge is ultimately a matter of the subject's resources, including insight and judgement upon the data of sense operating within a set of horizons. This is true of historical knowledge as it is of any knowledge, but the former also has the characteristic of resembling the workings of common-sense knowledge. The development of historical understanding does not admit systematic objectification, unlike mathematics, the natural sciences and philosophy.

> [T]he historian finds his way in the complexity of historical reality by the same type and mode of developing understanding, as the rest of us employ in day-to-day living. The starting-point is not some set of postulates or some generally accepted theory but all that the historian already knows and believes. The more intelligent and the more cultivated he is, the broader his experience, the more open he is to all human values, the more competent and rigorous his training, the greater is his capacity to discover the past. When an investigation is succeeding, his insights are so numerous, their coalescence so spontaneous, the manner in which they complement or qualify or correct one another is so immediate and so

28. Recall that Meyer uses 'fact' in the Collingwoodian sense, as events understood in terms of the intentions by which they were performed.

deft, that the historian can objectify, not every twist and turn in the genesis of his discovery, but only the broad lines of the picture at which eventually he arrives.[29]

We must see the form of Meyer's historical presentation in light of all these observations on the nature of historical knowledge. Steps in a procedure are not easily identified in Meyer, but if we were to try to clinch a discernible process, we may note that in *Aims* he usually advances the discussion by first making a statement or description of historical explanation, and backing this up, usually in the notes, with judgements of historicity or non-historicity of the relevant data. True to his principle,[30] Meyer uses the indices of authenticity to make positive judgements, in support of his interpretation, but never to make negative ones. Negative judgements are advanced usually in the context of a larger argument, but we can identify two bases on which they are commonly made: (1) the material is seen to be redactional, or (2) the material does not fit a coherent picture in light of historical parallels. But the important point in both positive and negative judgements is that neither are passed apart from the work of interpretation, apart from fitting the data into a larger explanatory picture.

We would do well to note a few details about how Meyer makes these supporting determinations of historicity. The indices, which support positive judgements, are variously listed in four of Meyer's works. In *Aims*, he mentions seven basic indices which can be listed as follows.[31]

1.   discontinuity – 'Historicity is inferred when a tradition about Jesus is discontinuous with the tendencies of the community which transmits it.'[32]
2.   originality – this amounts to discontinuity with Judaism. Such is not requisite to historicity but is a positive index to it. An example would be Jesus' fellowship with publicans and sinners.
3.   irreducibly personal idiom – distinctive linguistic markers in Jesus' speech, such as his use of *abba* and *amen*.
4.   resistive form – particular forms of discourse that resist modification, or else make it easily liable to detection. An example from Jesus would be the parable form: 'The gospel parables, thanks especially to their organic, self-contained structure…offer a royal road to authentic sayings-material and a particularly solid base from which to assess the historicity of parallels.'[33]
5.   multiple attestation – similar material attested in multiple independent sources.[34]

29. Lonergan, *Method*, p. 216. Meyer follows Lonergan's position on this closely in *Reality and Illusion*, p. 108.
30. See above, p. 120.
31. Meyer, *Aims*, pp. 86-87.
32. This index differs from the classic 'criterion of dissimilarity' in four ways: it is not the exclusive determination of historicity, it is not a 'criterion' but an 'index', it distinguishes between the contradictory and the discontinuous, and it omits the dimension of discontinuity with Judaism. *Aims*, p. 86.
33. Meyer, *Aims*, p. 87.
34. See the discussion of criteria of authenticity in appendix 1.

6.   multiform attestation – similar material attested in various forms, e.g., as narrative and as saying.[35]

7.   Aramaic substratum – Aramaic elements discernible in the Greek text, possibly indicating an Aramaic original from which the Greek was translated, reflect origination of the material with Jesus since Aramaic was most likely Jesus' spoken language.[36]

This list is modified somewhat in later works. In *Critical Realism and the New Testament*, Meyer discusses the indices in the context of a consideration of the roles of objectivity and subjectivity in historical criticism.[37] There he lists only multiple and multiform attestation, along with general 'linguistic indices', which he describes as 'ways of speaking preferred by Jesus'. Such would include the previously mentioned 'personal idiom'.[38] In *Christus Faber* he lists discontinuity, originality, personal idiom, multiple attestation and multiform attestation. He says at this point that his use of the indices relies mostly on discontinuity and originality. When neither of these yield results, he uses multiple and multiform attestation and personal idiom.[39] In *Reality and Illusion* he lists discontinuity, originality, personal idiom, multiple attestation and multiform attestation.[40] Throughout all these lists we can see he consistently prefers discontinuity, originality and multiple and multiform attestation; he always has linguistic indices in view as well, most often in the form of personal idiom.

We may note some specific instances where Meyer applies the indices to support his decisions on historicity of data. Historicity of Jesus' baptism by John is established by the index of discontinuity, or what is sometimes called the criterion of 'embarrassment'. 'Jesus' baptism crossed the grain of primitive Christianity in so far as it could suggest subordination to the Baptist and need of repentance.'[41] The words of Jesus on the Baptist in Mt. 11.16-19b are historical ('For John came neither eating nor drinking, and they say, "He has a demon"; the Son of Man came eating and drinking, and they say, "Look, a glutton and a drunkard, a friend of tax collectors and sinners!"'). Meyer supports this by several indices.[42] According to *discontinuity*, the saying is historical because it places Jesus and the Baptist on a par, and the substance of the charge itself is discontinuous with the sensibilities of the post-Easter Christian tradition, particularly when seen in light of Deut. 21.18-

35.   See appendix 1, p. 194.
36.   See appendix 1, p. 194.
37.   Meyer, *Critical Realism*, pp. 133-36.
38.   Interestingly, Meyer also lists here possible indices of non-historicity, such as rejection of material out of harmony with Jesus' horizons, perspectives and purposes as reconstructed; and rejection of material known to be derivable from the history of earliest Christian communities, as these have been recovered. He also mentions negative linguistic indices, especially with regard to the parables (e.g., Jesus' explaining his parables is unhistorical, as Jeremias has shown). There is no other mention of such negative indices in any other of Meyer's published works.
39.   Meyer, *Christus Faber*, p. 15.
40.   Meyer, *Reality and Illusion*, p. 103.
41.   Meyer, *Aims*, p. 283 n. 21.
42.   Meyer, *Aims*, p. 285 n. 37.

21 with its description of the 'rebellious son' who warrants execution. *Resistive form* is seen in the parabolic form of vv. 16-17 ('But to what will I compare this generation? It is like children sitting in the marketplaces and calling to one another, "We played the flute for you, and you did not dance; we wailed, and you did not mourn"'); also, the *difficulty* of applying the image of the children exactly to 'this generation' speaks to the originality of the image. Aramaic substratum in the passage has been identified by Jeremias; Meyer refers to the case as presented in the latter's *New Testament Theology*. Finally, some aspects of the passage are multiply attested, as seen in Mk 2.16 and Lk. 7.27f.

Jesus' prohibition of divorce is historical, based on discontinuity and originality. Discontinuity is suggested by the disciples' response to the prohibition, indicating it was problematic for them (Mk 10.10; Mt. 19.10), as well as by the issues of divorce in the early church that indicate that flat prohibition was nuanced in later contexts (1 Cor. 7.10ff.). Originality is indicated by the fact that divorce was generally permitted under Torah.[43]

Jesus' word 'I am sent only to the lost sheep of Israel's house' (Mt. 15.24) is historical on the basis of discontinuity with the Gentile mission. Meyer notes the saying's 'glaring discontinuity with the universalist mission of the church from pre-Pauline times (Acts 11.19f.) through the mid-forties, when the Christian community of Antioch launched its mission (Acts 13.1-3)'.[44]

I have said that Meyer often makes negative judgements of historicity on one of two bases: discounting material that is redactional, or discounting material that is seen not to fit a coherent historical picture based on historical parallels. Now this précis of the bases of negative judgements is our own analysis, and not explicitly owned by Meyer. But it is warranted by specific observations on his investigation, beginning with a comment found in the opening of the second section of *Aims*, where Meyer's Jesus portrait is constructed. He notes there that his practice in handling the traditions is systematically to detach pre-redactional traditions from their redactional contexts, where these latter can be discerned. He says such an approach is justified because 'To detach traditional data from their special uses in one or other or all redactions is simply to undo something only the redactors have done.'[45] What is at work here is something like the criterion of 'discounting redaction'.[46] Any material that is seen to serve the specific purpose of an evangelist is necessarily considered unhistorical accrual to traditional material. Meyer says that in his strategy, redaction criticism remains always in the background; sometimes explanation will be given for the factors involved in detaching a given tradition from redaction, but often such explanation is not warranted, when the detachment presents no special problems. Presumably detachment will generally not present problems because disregard of redactional materials is historiographically self-evident. We can see that many of the negative judgements of historicity that Meyer

43. Meyer, *Aims*, p. 289 n. 38.
44. Meyer, *Aims*, pp. 297-98 n. 129.
45. Meyer, *Aims*, p. 112.
46. See the discussion of criteria in appendix 1, p. 194.

makes are based on the policy to discount redactional material.[47] This policy is not without its problems, as I will argue below.

The second basis of negative judgement can be illustrated with an example. The editorial comment of Mk 7.19b, that Jesus 'declared all foods clean', Meyer says reflects an early Christian understanding of the preceding authentic saying of Jesus ('Nothing that goes into a man from outside can defile him but [only] what comes out of a man [speech] defiles him'). But Mark's editorial comment is not a correct interpretation of Jesus' saying because a better interpretation (foods do not defile in the deepest and most significant sense) is supported with historic parallels that express a similar concern but do not easily seal off ritual observances from the moral order. This latter interpretation is in fact reflected in a similar, though not precisely parallel, tradition of Jesus' saying in Mt. 23.26-27.[48] In addition, if Jesus had in fact 'declared all foods clean', one would expect to see that conspicuous pronouncement more prominently displayed throughout the tradition. Here Meyer makes a negative judgement of historicity on the basis of the lack of ability to fit the material into a cogent picture of Jesus' teaching on ritual observance and the moral order. No single criterion or even a set of criteria are called upon to make the decision against historicity (though a semblance of a negative application of multiple attestation may be playing a supporting role). The material in question simply cannot be seen to make historical sense, in light of the weight of other Jesus traditions and similar historical material. A line of argument makes this case rather than an applied rule of thumb.

What should be emphasized here is that both positive and negative judgements on the data are made in the context of larger interpretations of the data.[49] As Meyer

47. A couple of examples will suffice. In his treatment of the 'miraculous signs of salvation' in Jesus' career, Meyer says the texts are to be questioned concerning the original *context* in which Jesus' *intentions* were incarnated. The best sources for discerning Jesus' intentions in performing miracles are not the narratives in which the miracles are related, but rather separate sayings of Jesus that refer to the miracles (*Aims*, p. 155). It seems that for Meyer, the latter are traditions not redactionally associated with the miracles, and therefore are not as susceptible to redactional intrusion in what they convey about the miracles. The Baptist's question to Jesus (Mt. 11.2; Lk. 7.18-19) Meyer takes to be, not an expression of doubt by one who previously had believed, but the *beginning* of the Baptist's faith in Jesus. Meyer says the former interpretation is excluded because it is based on Mt. 3.14f. (the Baptist's expression of his need to be baptized by Jesus) a passage which is redactional (*Aims*, p. 295 n. 96).

48. Meyer, *Aims*, pp. 149; 291 nn. 64, 65.

49. In a discussion of Jesus' scenario of the eschatological future, Meyer mentions the value of what he calls a 'holistic' approach: 'beginning by bringing all the relevant data together and searching for an intelligible pattern therein' (*Aims*, p. 204). This allows one to find the whole in terms of which otherwise baffling parts become intelligible. He comments on the effectiveness of the holistic approach in Dodd and Jeremias, both of whom proposed a 'whole' scenario of Jesus' eschatological vision to account for the various traditions: 'access to an intelligible whole grounds an effective approach to historicity judgments amid just such that mass of data which had so often and so thoroughly defeated the merely atomistic approach (as the chaotic critical literature of Jesus' view of the future attests)' (*Aims*, p. 205). See appendix 1 below for a discussion of the history of the criteria of authenticity, and the development in this 'holistic' direction. I will draw on this notion in Chapters Seven and Eight, when I argue for the narrative whole as the necessary context for intelligibility of the data.

offers interpretations and backs them up with detailed arguments of historicity, he relies on no index or general principle *in itself* to establish conclusively the status of data. This approach has as a practical result the allowance of more data as historical than does Crossan's approach. But Meyer's work can hardly be said to suffer from a systematic credulity that does not require scholarly argument. He formulates many determinations of non-historicity that would make such a blanket charge unwarranted.[50] But the larger point at issue in our observations of his method, the point that I have been stressing throughout this discussion of Meyer's historiography, is that historical decisions and interpretations are made in a process in which understanding of the data advances as the historian poses questions to the data and formulates answers. Data are made to 'speak' only under these conditions, and so can only be understood with a view to both control and interpretation when this process is underway. In this process data control and interpretation interact; they are symbiotic movements in one process of understanding, and are only heuristically separable.

We have noted the role of indices that support the historicity of data used in interpretations, but Meyer also makes positive decisions of historicity without the use of indices, just as he makes negative decisions without them. For example, the historicity of the Baptist's subordination of himself to the 'one to come after' (i.e., the messianic visitation) as well as his general message of repentance, is not demonstrated by the use of indices. Rather, Meyer makes sense of that message in terms of Old Testament prophetic motifs and contemporary apocalyptic expectation, citing Qumran.[51] That Jesus baptized alongside the Baptist is demonstrated by explaining how the Fourth Gospel account of Jesus' initial baptism ministry in Judea fills in gaps left by the synoptics' data on this same period, i.e., that Jesus remained in Judea until after John's arrest, but with no explanation why.[52]

At one point Meyer explicitly says that he has actually 'resisted the temptation to specify grounds for every instance of a historical judgment'.[53] The 'grounds' to which he refers in this context are the indices. In many cases it is the force of a larger argument, and not indices, that presents a cogent case for both control and interpretation. All this demonstrates the nature of historical knowledge that Meyer captures under the rubric of hypothesis and verification.

---

50. He sees Mark's device of the 'messianic secret' as redactional and therefore unhistorical, though it has a certain historical basis in Jesus' career, in his refusal to make explicit, public messianic claims (*Aims*, p. 309 n. 119). The traditions of the baptism narrative, the temptations, and the transfigurations are treated by Meyer as 'early Christian interpretations of Jesus and his mission' (*Aims*, pp. 240-41). The narratives of Peter walking on the water (Mt. 14.28-33), the command to find the coin in the fish's mouth (Mt. 17.27), Judas's betraying Jesus for gold pieces (Mt. 27.3-10), and the dead rising after Jesus' crucifixion (Mt. 27.52f.) are all considered by Meyer to be 'practically indisputable instances' of folklore (*Aims*, p. 274 n. 63), though he offers no specific arguments against them.

51. Meyer, *Aims*, p. 282 nn. 10, 12.

52. See Meyer, '"Phases" in Jesus' Mission'.

53. Meyer, *Christus Faber*, p. 15.

3. *Summary and Evaluation*

3.1. *Critical Realism and Historiography*

Ben Meyer took the cognitional theory of Bernard Lonergan, which he called 'critical realism', as his epistemological starting point for development of a historiography, with the intention that such an explicit development would ground legitimate historical investigation of Jesus. This critical realism is above all an attempt to reckon with the subjective resources of the knower in the knowing process, captured in the slogan 'the way to objectivity is through authentic subjectivity'. The implications of this were several for Meyer. One can understand this subjectivity first of all as having two important dimensions.

First, at the core of this subjectivity is the structure of cognition, the three levels of conscious operations that constitute knowing: experience, understanding and judgement. Every instance of knowledge, including historical knowledge, is a matter of the functioning of these operations. The data of experience are questioned for their intelligible unity, and such a unity is grasped in answer to those questions, in the level of understanding. This unity is questioned for its truthfulness, and the truthfulness is affirmed in the level of judgement. The knowing process is thus driven by questions, by the questions posed by the knower to the data of sense and to his or her own understanding of the data. It is in answer to questions that data have their sense and knowledge is gained. For Meyer, this questioning is the key instance of historical knowledge and comes to be formulated in historiography as the process of hypothesis and verification. Historical data come to be known as the historian poses questions to them, formulates answers to those questions, and verifies the answers. Because of the nature of historical understanding and knowledge as dependent on the questions of the historian, judgements of the usability of data cannot be made apart from the role that those data are seen to play in the historian's investigation, i.e., in the historian's question-asking-and-answering process. A principle that was emphasized in the analysis of Crossan, Meyer's understanding of historical investigation seeks to exemplify: *whether* data are usable cannot be determined apart from *how* they are usable. The role of the knower's questions in the knowing process means for historiography that data are only known in the context of the investigation; and 'knowing' data means both controlling them and interpreting them, so control and interpretation are inseparable parts of the one ongoing movement of historical investigation, the one process of historical knowing.

A second dimension of the knower's subjectivity has to do with all the manifold resources from which the knower draws for knowledge. The historian, particularly in light of the idea that historical knowledge is a sophistication of common-sense knowledge, knows the object out of the whole fund of his or her personal resources, intellectual, moral and religious. The historian does not begin the investigation with a blank mind, or with a set of postulates universally requisite for proper historical enquiry. The historian operates with a dimension of subjectivity that has to do with horizons, which are the limits of all the historian knows and is able to be concerned about. This is the largest context of knowledge, and as such is not subject to argument or proof but to change through 'conversion'. Meyer explored this dimension of subjectivity particularly in his hermeneutic, where he emphasized the existential aspect, the interpreter's 'measuring up' to the text. Valid interpretation requires that the interpreter have a pre-understanding or vital relation to the text's subject matter, which in turn requires a basic posture of goodwill or consent toward the text, with the interpreter open to having his or her horizons addressed, confronted, challenged and possibly changed by the horizon of the text. It is in this highly personal dimension that subjectivity is most 'subjective', and where the largest questions of the historian's hermeneutical involvement with the object come to the fore.

Meyer sought above all to come to terms with these two dimensions of subjectivity, what may be called the *epistemological* and the *hermeneutical* dimensions, in his critical realism. He sought to understand and to articulate how critical realism shapes the task of New Testament interpretation and especially of historiography. On the basis of this summary of Meyer we can compare his approach to historical Jesus studies with that of Crossan.

3.2. *Crossan and Meyer: 'Atomism', 'Holism' and Contexts*

Crossan and Meyer can be seen to manifest two large trends in historical Jesus studies. Crossan's approach is the culmination of a methodological tradition that has been developing at least since Bultmann, and through the post-Bultmannians, but probably has roots in the historical Jesus work of the nineteenth century. This tradition of course takes the contemporary form of form - and tradition criticism. What is most distinctive about this method is its rigorous handling of the data by subjecting individual units of tradition to examination, and that as a necessary first stage of historical investigation. As we have seen in Crossan, the examination consists mostly of reconstruction of the history of the transmission of a tradition by comparing parallel materials, and application of the criteria of authenticity to the earliest form of the tradition to determine if it will qualify for consideration as historically authentic data on Jesus. The methodological option offered by Meyer most obviously contrasts with this approach in its handling of the data in larger contexts, particularly in the context of the historian's hypotheses and attempts to verify those hypotheses. For Meyer, data are scrutinized for their historicity not first of all as individual units, but as functional parts in the larger picture of the historians' hypotheses. It is only as the data are seen in this light that indices are applied, and then strictly as support for decisions of historicity made on the basis of how the data fit, or fail to fit, in the hypotheses. This surface feature of their respective methods is what most readily distinguishes Crossan and Meyer. It is sometimes expressed as the difference between 'atomism' and 'holism'.

But there are deeper and more substantial differences that I have identified, differences in which it seems their 'atomistic' and 'holistic' approaches are rooted. Crossan, like many historians, conceives historiography as a two-phase process of data control followed by interpretation. Data must be verified as authentic before they can be used in reconstruction. Crossan would probably concede the general point that there is some interpretation at work in the first stage, but it is mostly to be consciously bracketed, as far as the historian is able to do so, only to come into deliberate use in the second phase. Data control conceived in this way requires that the data on Jesus be handled as individual units. Meyer on the other hand sees data control and interpretation as both ongoing and reciprocal tasks throughout histori- cal enquiry. Data cannot be controlled prior to understanding the role they play in the historian's questions and answers, because they have their sense only in the latter context. To attempt to verify the usability of data *before* they are actually used is to reduce the control of data to a few rules of thumb, circumventing the actual process of historical knowing which involves the historian's use of hypothe- ses for understanding *how* data might be usable in order to determine *whether* they are usable. Such is the dynamic nature of historical knowledge for Meyer.

I would suggest that what Meyer is approaching in his stress on understanding the data via hypothesis and verification is partly the recognition of the contextual nature of knowledge. Particulars are known and understood in the context of some larger whole, some sense-making frame of reference without which the particulars would have no sense. The context that Meyer's critical realism emphasizes most in relation to Jesus studies is the context of the historian's questions for understanding the data. Individual data are not understood (i.e., controlled or interpreted) except in the context of the hypotheses that the historian floats and seeks to verify in the course of investigation. The nature of historical knowledge, and of knowledge generally, reveals that individual data are known only in the context of the sense- making hypotheses that the historian poses in answer to his or her own questions in the hypothesis-and-verification process. Meyer also wrestles with another con- text, what I call above the hermeneutical dimension of his critical realism. He attempts to incorporate in his method the largest context in which all knowledge has its sense, the horizonal context. But in insisting that interpretation must precede analysis, and by exploring what valid interpretation entails, Meyer endeavoured to take account of the historian's hermeneutic involvement in his or her history, and in this Meyer was taking up one of the great challenges of our time. He recog- nized that historical method, if it is to take account of the 'authentic subjectivity' required for genuine knowledge, must find a way of articulating the role of the her- meneutic moment in historiography. This is what Meyer was about in what I have identified as the hermeneutic dimension of critical realism; also relevant are his discussions of the metacritical goals of history and autonomy of the historian's questions, the latter offered particularly to make room for theological questions in historical investigation.

Meyer's efforts in this area are another point of distinction between his approach and Crossan's. We have seen that Crossan, partly as a result of his separation of data control and interpretation, always wields his hermeneutic in a way that allows his historical method to remain mostly untouched by it. Crossan rightly sees the 'interactive' nature of the historian's work; but he offers his method, not taking account of that interactivism, but as a means to check it. Method for Crossan is a way to keep at abeyance the historian's hermeneutic involvement, to prevent it from disfiguring the historical object. The result is a historiography that is some- what lacking in self-awareness, incapable of accounting for its own interactive nature. For all his hermeneutic sophistication in recognizing the contemporary 'postmodern' challenge, Crossan seems, especially in comparison to Meyer, not to be up to the challenge, at least when it comes to formulating a historiography.

3.3. *Narrativity and the Context of the Sources*
So one can see Meyer's contribution to historiography to involve the appreciation of the contextual nature of knowledge, and the two contexts that Meyer most recognizes are the historian's hypotheses and the historian's horizons. I would suggest another context for understanding the data, one that Meyer seems to neglect. That context is the narrative context of the sources in which the data come to us, the context of the Gospels.

One can see in Meyer a singular lack of appreciation for the narrative context of the sources as a necessary context for understanding the data. I have noted his policy of systematically discounting redaction when handling the data. The redactional context is disregarded, often without any comment or explanation, because to ignore redactional material is simply to undo what the redactor has done. Many of Meyer's negative determinations of historicity are made on this basis. He seems to treat as self-evident that redactional material is without value for historical study. Why this is so for him is difficult to determine. It may be that in his pioneering work there remain vestiges of a form-critical approach to the data as discrete units. As much as Meyer argued against handling data atomistically, his milieu was still very much the post-Bultmannian one of application of criteria to individual traditions. Sean Freyne has criticized Meyer for 'still operating within a form-critical framework that pre-dates recent interest in the gospels as narratives'.[54] It may be that for Meyer, as is probably the case for many New Testament historians, talk of narrativity is usually felt to be antithetical to historical purposes. Narrative in New Testament studies continues to be associated almost exclusively with structuralism, narrative criticism, or other approaches that deliberately bracket the historical referent. But narrative actually has an important role in historiography, as I will show in a later chapter.[55]

---

54. Freyne, *Jesus, Galilee and the Gospels*, p. 25.

55. There may be another reason for Meyer's neglect of the narrative context of the sources, one that we can more readily see in his stated hermeneutic. Meyer seemed to have a particular understanding of language that does not allow for aspects of meaning that narrativity includes. Specifically, Meyer seemed bound to ideational and denotative understandings of language. (On these see the helpful discussion in A.C. Grayling, *An Introduction to Philosophical Logic* [Oxford: Basil Blackwell, 1997], pp. 191-95, 202-207.)

An ideational understanding sees language as primarily an encoding resource; language is meaningful by virtue of its encoding meanings that exist prior to language, in the mental acts of the speaker. On this theory, linguistic meaning is essentially a matter of private mental acts or ideas that the speaker or writer expresses in the chosen words. The listener or reader understands the words by decoding them, by rethinking the thoughts that they represent. A denotative understanding holds that words are meaningful by denoting or pointing out objects in the world. Now both of these theories have merit in that they speak to what seem to be legitimate aspects of language, but the theories are problematic as they stand. The ideational theory rightly recognizes that there is an intentional aspect to language, that it is meant to communicate meanings among speakers and writers, and that these meanings are intended meanings. But recognizing intentionality does not

What I would suggest at this point is that the narrative context of the sources allows us a context for understanding the data that is concrete and publicly accessible. Meyer's observations on the contexts of the historian's hypotheses and the historian's horizons are important, but in the sources themselves we have an additional context that is usable, and is in fact the necessary initial context for understanding the data. To Meyer's recognition of two important contexts, then, I would add a third; I will argue for this context in detail in the following chapters.

require that intentionality be understood in terms of *private mental acts* that give language meaning. Meyer himself articulated an understanding of the intended sense of texts that denied that they are to be thought of as inside the mind of the author; rather, the intended sense is something public, what is contained in the text itself. The ideational theory has been shown to be flawed by Ludwig Wittgenstein's demonstration of the essentially public nature of linguistic meaning; meaning is a matter of the shared use of language among users of the language, and is not a matter of private mental acts (see Wittgenstein, *Philosophical Investigations* [trans. G.E.M. Anscombe; Englewood Cliffs, NJ: Prentice Hall, 3rd edn, 1958], esp. §§256-275). The denotative theory (I would maintain) is getting at something valid about language, viz., that it has a referential dimension. Language is meaningful partly because it refers to things in the world. But limiting linguistic meaning to this dimension is problematic, for there are many words whose referents are far from clear, such as universals, abstract nouns and nouns with no article or demonstrative attached (what is the referent of the word 'table'? no table in particular, but only the 'idea' of the word table?); and two terms can have the same referent, yet have different senses (e.g., 'President of the United States' and 'husband of Laura Bush' have the same referent, but different senses; these two terms are not identical in meaning).

These are just a few of the difficulties with limiting linguistic meaning to denotation and ideation. But in his hermeneutic, Meyer seems to want to do just that, and in that he follows Lonergan. In *Insight* (pp. 576-80) and *Method* (pp. 254-57) Lonergan sees linguistic meaning as a function of prior mental acts, with knowledge and so meaning existing prior to and apart from expression in language. He responds to Wittgenstein's theory of the essentially public nature of linguistic meaning by insisting that the ordinary meaningfulness of ordinary language is indeed public, but the original meaningfulness of any language is private, a matter of expressed mental acts. Lonergan ultimately seems to take Wittgenstein to mean that there is no thought, or that thought is philosophically inconsequential; but I would insist that such is not a necessary conclusion of Wittgenstein's theory. It would seem that neither Meyer nor Lonergan have taken account of the linguistic turn in philosophy; in *Critical Realism and the New Testament*, Meyer presents his critical realist hermeneutic as a 'far cry' from 'the game but misguided effort to make linguistics the interpreter's main resource' (p. xiii). From there, Meyer goes on to discuss his hermeneutic without reference to any notion of linguistic meaning beyond the ideational or denotative.

One can see in narrativity that meaningfulness of language includes important dimensions beyond these. Narrative is a way of expressing that is not limited to simple reference to events, though it would certainly include that. I will show in Chapter Eight that narrative is meaningful as a way of making sense of our present experience by 'grasping it together' in a temporal unity along with our remembered past and our anticipated future. Narrative is the means by which we make sense of our experience and action as temporal. In this way narrative has a sense-making role in our experience, and so is meaningful not simply by referring to objects or events, but as an aspect of human intentionality. Present actions are meaningful by virtue of the background of our past and future against which those actions are performed; there is a sense in which we 'tell' ourselves the 'story' of our past and our future as we act in the present, giving our present actions a sense in the flow of that story.

3.4. *Critical Realism and the Miraculous*

I have shown that in Meyer's presentation of critical realism he had a significant stake in the miraculous as a category of historical explanation. Meyer argued specifically against the notions of the universe as a closed system of cause and effect, regulated by necessary laws, and the principle of analogy in historical criticism. He said that both of these assumptions of modern historiography are shown by critical realism to be erroneous. Since this is so, much more of the Gospel data on Jesus are allowed for historical consideration. There can be no a-priori exclusion of materials that involve accounts of miracles or fulfilment of prophecy; these are as subject to historical scrutiny as any other. But for all his defence of miracles in theory, Meyer's actual presentation of the historical Jesus seems to have little concrete investment in miracles, or in exploration of the transcendent in history that sometimes accompanies defences of miracles and theological interests in historical Jesus studies.

To be sure, Meyer accepts the Gospel miracle tradition in general. In *Aims* he spends four pages explicating the miracles and exorcisms in Jesus' ministry as 'signs of salvation', pointers to the fact and nature of the imminent restoration of Israel.[56] He warns against a minimizing attitude toward the miracle tradition in historical interpretation; in Jesus' ministry they were decisive signs of the eschaton, to be understood only in such a context, and are not to be equated with the popular prodigies of either the Jewish or the Greek world. Though he makes no specific argument for historicity, in his Jesus portrait Meyer accepts Jesus' resurrection as historical, and even deals with the question of whether Jesus was in fact mistaken, since his resurrection did not coincide with the parousia and the eschatological restoration as he had implied it would in the esoteric tradition.[57] The closest Meyer comes to an apologetic for the resurrection is in a later discussion of the issue of the continuity between the disciples' resurrection experiences and the church's confession of the resurrection. He argues for the nature of those initial experiences as 'meeting', i.e., as individual persons present to one another.[58] Jesus was present to the disciples in much the same way as any individual is present to any other in a meeting between them; this against, for example, reductionistic interpretations of the resurrection that see the disciples' experience as an experience of 'light' (with Paul's Damascus Road experience as the paradigm), divested of its quality as a meeting between persons.[59] Meyer insists that, if stripped of this quality of 'meeting', the very existence of the texts of Jesus' appearances becomes inexplicable. There is no other way of accounting for the texts' describing the disciples' experience as a meeting, than that there was a meeting-experience that gave rise to the texts.

---

56. Meyer, *Aims*, pp. 154-58.
57. See above, p. 135 n. 25.
58. 'A meeting is an instance of co-subjectivity in which "I" am the subject and my friend, the co-subject, is present to me as an object', Meyer, 'The Easter Experience Interpreted and Secured', in *Christus Faber*, p. 137.
59. Meyer, 'The Easter Experience', p. 138.

There is no question that Meyer's investment in miracle as a historical cate-gory is serious, because it is clear from his first presentations of critical realism to his later discussion of the resurrection that in his historical Jesus portrait he accepts the miracle tradition in general as genuine. But it seems that we are in a position with regard to miracles similar to that with regard to the metacritical goals of history.[60] I have noted that Meyer insisted that the historian's metacriti-cal goals account more than anything else for the kind of history produced. It would seem that such a freighted aspect of the historical enterprise would be given considerable attention in his historiography. Yet Meyer gave very little space to exploration of these goals and how they affect the doing of history. Similarly, one significant reason for his grounding historiography in critical realism is that it justifies serious historical consideration of claims of the miraculous as such; but he sat rather loose with the miracle traditions in his actual historical investigation. He did not argue for the historicity of any particular miracle account, as he would often do for various sayings or narrative material. He seems to have had more investment in the idea of miracles and their general role in Jesus' minis-try than in any specific miracle claims.

We have noted that Meyer's defence of miracles lacks the philosophical sophis-tication that accompanies many discussions in this area. Such a level of sophisti-cation ultimately would be required for a full-orbed analysis of the reality and significance of miracles in history in general, not to mention in a portrait of the historical Jesus. This is probably an area where Meyer has given us some impor-tant initial historiographic soundings, but much further work is required.

3.5. *The Social Sciences*

One final area of Meyer's work that warrants comment is his posture toward the social sciences in historiography. We have seen that Meyer shared Collingwood's understanding of historical enquiry as seeking to penetrate to the 'inside' of the event. By 'inside' Collingwood meant the thoughts of the agents involved in the event, such that history is about rethinking the thoughts of historical actors. Meyer took Collingwood's notion to have more to do with *intentionality* generally than with *thought* in particular. As in his hermeneutic, so in his historiography, Meyer identified intentions as what gives texts and actions their sense; and for Meyer, intentions are not strictly private things, in the head of the author or agent. Inten-tions are the purposes discernible within the text itself, and so the rationale of the intended sense of the text is similar to that of the 'implied author'. Intentions are the purposes discernible in the actions of historical agents, what makes the actions to be human actions and not just random movements of objects. In both cases, get-ting inside minds is not necessary to discover intentions.

We have also seen that Meyer's focus on intentionality was sometimes ex-pressed to the exclusion of factors in historical explanation that cannot be captured by intentionality.[61] The social sciences are the most common mode of explanation

---

60. On the latter, see above, pp. 124ff.
61. See above, p. 112.

in historiography that goes beyond the intentions of agents to explain events. Now Meyer at times acknowledged the usefulness of such tools, as long as they are adopted moderately, 'without extravagant expectations or claims'.[62] But it is generally the case that he resisted pronouncements that seemed to him to rely too much on social-scientific models. In this he was probably following Lonergan, who warned of the dangers of the use of ideal-types in history, by which he seems to have meant social science models, since he cited sociologist Max Weber as the name with whom they are usually associated.[63] Lonergan gave qualified acceptance of such tools. But if Meyer saw room for them in theory, it seems his concern for intentionality had little use for the social sciences in practice. His stance seems to have been that, if history has to do fundamentally with human intentionality, then larger structures or factors are mostly irrelevant to historical explanation and their use will probably be reductionistic. But this reasoning simply begs the question of whether there are in fact regularities that can be observed in social groups, that we should honestly acknowledge and about which we can constructively generalize. It does not take seriously the notion that there are social structures larger than the intentions of individuals, and that while human action has its sense primarily in light of individual intention, intention in turn has its sense in light of shared practices, beliefs, and attitudes that form its background. I will demonstrate in a later chapter that an understanding of intentionality informed by the narrativity of lived experience allows us to broaden the notion of intentionality to include group experience and not just individual experience. But even if we can so stretch intentionality to include the actions and experiences of groups, it remains the case that, the larger the groups we are investigating, the more difficult it is to speak in terms of intentionality, and the more we have to rely on law-like generalizations and regularities to help explain events. The courses of ancient empires, modern nation-states, or cultural groups can only with great difficulty, and rather artificially, be recounted in terms of interacting intentions alone. But even when we do have to employ social science tools, it also seems to be the case that their generalizations and models will have to be applied loosely, in view of the particularity that is at the core of historical events. I will consider in Chapter Eight the dialectical relation that best characterizes the use of the social sciences versus human intentionality in history. I have stated that Crossan has been able to use social science constructs of Mediterranean society without compromising the particularity and the intentionality that informed Jesus' own career. Whether Crossan's constructs are accurate and useful, and whether he uses them successfully, is a matter of some debate; but historical debate rightly deals with these very types of things. All factors that will potentially illumine the first-century context are open to consideration for the light they shed on the data we have on Jesus.

The contextualization that is integral to historical investigation is illustrated by Crossan in his description of micro-, meso- and macrocosmic levels of research.

---

62. Meyer, 'Jesus and His Mission', p. 109.
63. Lonergan, *Method*, pp. 227-28.

With this broad outline Meyer's own conception of historiography would fit, but Meyer takes appreciation of contextualization to a different plane, with his exploration of the contexts of the historian's investigation and the historian's horizons for understanding the data. In the next section I will make some historiographic proposals that seek to advance this concern for contexts.

Part III

HISTORIOGRAPHIC PROPOSALS:
FROM HOLISM TO NARRATIVE INTELLIGIBILITY

Chapter 7

HOLISM AND ITS IMPLICATIONS

In the work of Crossan and Meyer I have identified different approaches to the historical investigation of Jesus, grounded in contrasting historiographies and hermeneutics. I have described Meyer's approach as an advance over that of Crossan. Meyer's method seeks to take full account of the nature of knowledge in general, and of historical knowledge in particular; it is also formulated to incorporate Meyer's hermeneutic, rather than acting as a check on the historian's hermeneutic involvement. But I have also noted the strength of Crossan's organization of historical investigation on three levels, and the significance of his effort to locate the data on Jesus within the wider context of Palestinian and Mediterranean social constructs.

As legitimate as all these contributions are, there is room for further progress. Though Crossan appreciates the value of sociological tools that Meyer never saw fit to embrace fully, the latter's overall proposal is a considerable advance over Crossan's tradition-critical orientation. But, as I suggested in the last chapter, there are ways one can move even further in the direction Meyer's historiography has oriented us. There are resources in recent observations of the role of narrative in historiography that are consonant with some basic concerns we have seen in Meyer, but that also allow us a firmer purchase on the sources in which we find data on Jesus. These same findings on narrative assist us in incorporating Meyer's hermeneutic concerns.

Throughout this study I have cast our two protagonists, Crossan and Meyer, as exemplars of distinct approaches to historiography in Jesus studies. I will now culminate the study with a final characterization of these approaches. The present chapter will make a concluding case for the preferability of 'holism' over tradition criticism. The following chapter will suggest an improvement on a holistic method with the recognition of the narrative intelligibility of historical objects. I will offer an outline for a methodological proposal for Jesus studies in light of the observations on narrative and a new understanding of the criteria of authenticity. Finally, I will note hermeneutic resources implicit in this proposal.

I pointed out a reference in Meyer to what he described as a 'holistic' approach to historical data. Such an approach begins by surveying the mass of available data and noting intelligible patterns within it.[1] These patterns serve as the larger context within which to understand the individual pieces of data, particularly those pieces

1.   See above, p. 141 n. 49.

that would seem intractable when considered alone, but can be seen to make historical sense in a larger context. I have suggested that this approach is consistent with Meyer's emphasis on historical judgement and interpretation of individual data being made in a larger context. For Meyer, this context has to do mostly with the historian's autonomous questions that drive the investigation, and so is as much hermeneutical as historiographic. But the general concern to contextualize in order to understand is becoming more widespread among historical Jesus scholars.

1. *Holism*

'The meaning of any phenomenon or proposition depends on the "whole" of which it is a part or, in other words, it depends on the "context" in which it has a "function".'[2] This is a serviceable definition of holism as applied to historiography and hermeneutics. Holism, or contextualism, recognizes that the intelligibility of individual things depends ultimately on the context in which those things are perceived and in which they play a part. Individual phenomena are *necessarily* seen to be what they are within some larger whole. Viewing historical objects contextually is not optional for historians; they do not simply choose to situate data in a context in order to illumine them. Some context is *always* operative in *any* viewing, analysis, interpretation or judgement. Now the term 'holism' is not widely used by Jesus scholars, but we can see various types of contexts, or wholes, that are receiving increased emphasis among them.

We can consider N.T. Wright as a prominent advocate of holism in historiography. He bases this on his version of Critical Realism, which emphasizes the reciprocity between the knower and the known object, as well as worldview and its expression in narrative as the ultimate context in which knowledge takes place.[3] Prominent in Wright's historiography is the notion that historical facts, like all objects of knowledge, have their sense in the context of a larger whole. The whole that Wright has in mind is that of an overarching explanation of the interacting intentions of historical actors, as well as the largest context of worldview in which those intentions are expressed.[4] The concrete historiographic result of this contextualism is a method Wright describes in terms of 'hypothesis and verification', in a way similar to Meyer.

> The reseacher, after a period of total and sometimes confusing immersion in the data, emerges with a hypothesis, a big picture of how everything fits together. The hypothesis is proposed, spelled out as fully as possible. In the process, it is tested against three criteria: Does it make sense of the data as they stand? Does it have an appropriate level of simplicity, or even elegance? Does it shed light on areas of research other than the one it was designed to cover?[5]

---

2. Brice R. Wachterhauser, 'History and Language in Understanding', in *Hermeneutics and Modern Philosophy* (New York: State University of New York Press, 1986), p. 12.
3. See appendix 2, 'Varieties of Critical Realism'.
4. See Wright, *The New Testament and the People of God*, pp. 83, 91.
5. N.T. Wright, 'Knowing Jesus: Faith and History', in Marcus Borg and N.T. Wright, *The*

Such a method of beginning with a hypothesis Wright contrasts with one that analyses small bits of data then puts them together like a jigsaw puzzle. Wright says that the historiography of the Third Quest (as he defines that movement) understands the first task of the historian of Jesus to be not something like tradition criticism, which operates on individual data to determine their place in the early church, but rather 'the advancement of serious historical hypotheses – that is, the telling of large-scale narratives – about Jesus himself, and the examination of the prima facie relevant data to see how they fit'.[6] An adequate hypothesis will meet three demands: it will include as much of the data as possible, it will be as simple as possible, and it will prove fruitful in other related areas.[7]

The concern to begin historical investigation with a hypothesis, rather than with evaluation of individual data, is continuous with what is seen in Meyer in contrast to Crossan. I have shown the hallmark of Crossan's method, consistent with a general tradition-critical orientation, to be the initial establishment of a database by means of stratification of the material and the application of the criterion of multiple attestation to the earliest stratum. More than anything, Crossan's method calls for a public handling of the data based on principles such as these, so that the authentic material can be established to prepare for the work of interpretation. Robert Funk has generalized such a method in terms of the functions of historical enquiry. Funk identifies as the first function, 'to isolate and establish the particular… Particulars are isolated by distinguishing one thing from another, by the close comparison of reports. Particulars are established by attempting to verify each item, either by the confirmation of independent sources or by comparative evidence.'[8] What Funk is describing reflects the work of comparisons that I have identified as the heart of critical history (as seen in Crossan's orientation to literary relations and stratification), and the technique of applying criteria to establish authentic material (as seen in Crossan's multiple attestation).[9] Funk says that the second function of historians is to group the established particulars into arrays or constellations, putting together things that belong together.[10] So following on the establishment of particulars, the work of interpretation or reconstruction begins.[11] Holism challenges this method's orientation to the establishment of particulars as the necessary first step in critical history, an approach that is often characterized by its opponents as 'atomistic'. It challenges this orientation by insisting that the particulars are always

---

Meaning of Jesus: Two Visions (San Francisco: HarperSanFrancisco, 1999), p. 22. See also Wright, *The New Testament and the People of God*, pp. 99ff.

    6.   Wright, *Jesus and the Victory of God*, p. 88.

    7.   Wright, *The New Testament and the People of God*, pp. 99-100.

    8.   Robert Funk, *Honest to Jesus: Jesus for a New Millennium* (San Francisco: HarperSanFrancisco, 1996), p. 60.

    9.   See Chapters 2 and 3 above.

    10.   Funk, *Honest to Jesus*, p. 61.

    11.   Interestingly, Crossan must undertake certain measures to 'group' the material (into complexes) even within the first function. As I pointed out above (Chapter Three, pp. 59, 74 and *passim*), there is work of interpretation that Crossan must undertake within data control, even in his determination to control the data *prior* to interpretation.

already examined within a context, and the context will not wait for the authentic particulars to be established first.

Dale Allison has described the context in terms of a paradigm, a notion he borrows from Thomas Kuhn.[12] In *The Structure of Scientific Revolutions* Kuhn posits that the empirical observation that characterizes normal science is done within a larger framework, or paradigm.[13] The paradigm is the accepted context within which scientists conduct their observations of phenomena; this context establishes the rules of observation as well as the expectations for what the scientists will find and how they will order and make sense of what they find. Similarly, Allison says the historian's first move should be to look for a paradigm, an explanatory model by which to order the data on Jesus, rather than to discover which sayings or complexes are authentic.[14] 'The initial task is to create a context, a primary frame of reference, for the Jesus tradition, a context that may assist us in determining both the authenticity of traditions and their interpretation.'[15] Because the paradigm is the necessary context for viewing the data, Allison points out that most scholars have been doing this sort of thing all along, even when they claim to rely on criteria of authenticity as the first step for establishing a database; in such cases the paradigm is not stated, but rather remains tacit. By contrast, the starting paradigm or initial hypothesis on Jesus should be consciously selected by the historian, as it will serve to arrange the data into coherent patterns.

Allison suggests that the source of such paradigms or models for Jesus is all the options offered in contemporary scholarship, i.e., eschatological prophet, Zealot, magician, Cynic, etc. Now the historian is not free simply to select from among these which paradigm he or she likes best. The key is to begin with the *right* paradigm. But a paradigm's validity cannot be established through the criteria of authenticity, or through creating tradition-histories, or through any other similar means of observation, because such operations depend upon the prior assumptions the historian brings with him or her in the form of a paradigm. So beginning paradigms must be established independently of, and prior to, such operations.[16] Allison does

---

12. See Dale C. Allison, *Jesus of Nazareth: Millenarian Prophet* (Minneapolis: Fortress, 1998), pp. 36ff.

13. Thomas S. Kuhn, *The Structure of Scientific Revolutions* (Chicago: University of Chicago Press, 2nd edn, 1970).

14. Allison's general point about beginning with hypotheses is sound, but his reliance on Kuhn may be problematic. Kuhn's *paradigm* (so called in *The Structure of Scientific Revolutions*, elsewhere called 'theory', see Kuhn, 'Logic of Discovery or Psychology of Research?', in Imre Lakatos and Alan Musgrave [eds.], *Criticism and the Growth of Knowledge* [Cambridge: Cambridge University Press, 1970], pp. 1-23) seems to function on a level further removed from conscious attention than Allison's hypotheses on Jesus. The Kuhnian paradigm/theory is a constellation of background assumptions that controls how any investigation is conducted as well as the types of things it will find; it does not take the form of chosen hypotheses on the object under study. Kuhn's paradigm is more like the holism described by Hubert Dreyfus, 'Holism and Hermeneutics', in R. Hollinger (ed.), *Hermeneutics and Praxis* (Notre Dame, IN: University of Notre Dame Press, 1985), pp. 227-47. The organizing whole in this case is either a set of background beliefs or of background practices, neither of which constitute conscious hypotheses.

15. Allison, *Jesus of Nazareth*, p. 36.

16. Allison, *Jesus of Nazareth*, p. 39.

not describe how a paradigm is so established, but he presents his preferred one, Jesus as apocalyptic prophet, as justified by certain 'indisputable facts' that point in that direction.[17] He also points to several consistent themes, motifs and rhetorical strategies in the Jesus tradition.[18] It is in such consistencies that we should look for a big picture of Jesus and for possibly accurate memories. Allison notes that if these consistent themes do not preserve authentic memories of Jesus, it is pointless to look elsewhere, for it is unlikely that the tradition is mistaken in its consistent themes while preserving individual details accurately. If the big picture of Jesus in the early tradition is wrong, then the individual details are likely wrong as well.[19] All these factors lead to a paradigm or working hypothesis whose 'claim to truth lies in its explanatory power as time goes on and it is applied to ever enlarging arrays of texts and observations'.[20] We can see all this in terms of the hypothesis-and-verification method as described by Wright, or what I am calling holism. Allison first looks for patterns in the mass of data, in the form of 'indisputable facts' or consistent themes and rhetorical strategies. It is these patterns that suggest to him the appropriate beginning paradigm within which to examine the whole tradition. But the paradigm must be in place (in any case, it is in place) at the outset of historical investigation, as the means of ordering the data.

Another contemporary scholar who works with something like paradigms is William Herzog. After reviewing some of the traditional criteria of authenticity in Jesus studies, Herzog notes that their usual application fails to consider the funda-mental relationship between the part and the whole. Those who apply the criteria to individual units as a first stage in historical work fail to recognize that such appli-cation is always done with a complete construct of the historical Jesus informing the application and the resulting decisions. The historian works with a gestalt of Jesus that guides the handling of the data from the beginning. Herzog recommends that the historian identify this gestalt and handle it as a proposal to be tested against the materials. '[T]he necessity of positing a "hypothesis" about the historical Jesus and then testing it by analyzing the pieces of the Jesus tradition in the context of recent work on ancient Palestine would keep the relationship between the parts and

17. The facts include: 'That Jesus was baptized by an eschatological prophet and had among his followers people who proclaimed a near end, that certain followers of Jesus proclaimed his resurrection soon after the crucifixion, that his passion and vindication were associated with eschatological motifs, that many first-century Jews expected an apocalyptic scenario to unfold in their near future, and that our sources compare Jesus with others who believed in such a scenario or at least expected God soon to rule Palestine', *Jesus of Nazareth*, p. 44.

18. Themes and motifs include: the kingdom of God; future reward; future judgement; suf-fering/persecution for the saints; victory over evil powers; a sense that something new is here or at hand; the importance of John the Baptist; reference to 'the Son of Man'; God as Father; loving/serving/forgiving others; special regard for the unfortunate; intention as what matters most; hostility to wealth; extraordinary requests/difficult demands; conflict with religious authorities; disciples as students and helpers; Jesus as miracle worker. Rhetorical strategies include: parables; antithetical parallelism; rhetorical questions; prefatory 'amen'; the divine passive; exaggeration/hyperbole; aphoristic formulation; the unexpected or seemingly paradoxical.

19. Allison, *Jesus of Nazareth*, pp. 45-46.

20. Allison, *Jesus of Nazareth*, p. 51.

the whole at the center of the inquiry.'[21] The historian begins the enquiry with a gestalt, but the latter should remain open to alteration as individual pieces of tradition are examined. Ultimately, the gestalt and the pieces, the whole and the parts, will be in dialectical relation, each changing the other, resulting in a portrait of Jesus that is partial. Herzog's gestalt functions in the same way as Allison's paradigm, but Herzog adds to the gestalt the context provided by the social sciences.[22] Sociological study reveals aspects of the context of ancient Palestine against which any gestalt of Jesus should be tested. So for Herzog, the interpretive contexts that holism recognizes are two: the gestalt of Jesus, and the context revealed by the social sciences. He does not articulate the relation between these contexts, but it would appear that the social science context is the larger, within which the picture of Jesus is situated; and both are the context within which the data on Jesus are set.

The need for a context for understanding discrete data is a concern I have noted in Meyer, with his emphasis on the context of the historian's questions and the resulting context of the overall investigation. When it came to controlling the data, Meyer stressed above all that decisions on that level could not be made apart from decisions on the level of interpreting the data (or, 'establishing the facts'). This orientation to contextualization is also seen in Meyer's suggestion of the practice of beginning with a survey of the data to establish a framework for managing all the data. This suggestion, though a natural outworking of Meyer's methodological orientation, received little explication in his work, yet has become conspicuous among some historical Jesus scholars.[23] One scholar in particular, J.D.G. Dunn, bases a similar procedure on the nature of the sources on Jesus.

Dunn has offered two points for proceeding with the Third Quest, one point of principle and one of procedure. The point of procedure is very much like what I have called holism. Dunn emphasizes the 'need to attend first to the broad picture, otherwise we are liable to become quickly bogged down and lost in a mire of details over individual sayings'. He notes that the authenticity criteria are usually conceived in application to individual sayings; but there is a criterion which should be applied to the data before anything like authenticity criteria are applied: 'any feature which is *characteristic of and relatively distinctive within the Jesus tradition* is likely to go back to Jesus, that is, to reflect the original impact of Jesus on several of his first disciples.'[24] He notes that when this criterion is applied to the

21. William R. Herzog II, *Jesus, Justice and the Reign of God: A Ministry of Liberation* (Louisville, KY: Westminster/John Knox Press, 2000), p. 43.

22. Herzog, *Jesus*, pp. 88-89.

23. We should note some objections to a holistic approach that have been voiced. William Telford has wondered whether the data that we have to work with will bear the weight of a holistic construction. The nature of the sources seems to obviate the possibility of working with an overarching hypothesis to account for diverse bits of tradition, 'Major Trends and Interpretive Issues', pp. 58, 69. John Meier has questioned the possibility of a holistic approach. He admits that the notion is attractive, but 'until we have at least a vague idea of what parts might qualify as belonging to the historical whole, a "holistic" approach remains a distant ideal', *A Marginal Jew, Vol. 1*, p. 195 n.66.

24. J.D.G. Dunn, 'Can the Third Quest Hope to Succeed?', in Bruce Chilton and Craig Evans

Jesus tradition, we end up with a remarkably full portrayal. It is within this larger, pre-established framework that individual sayings and particulars are evaluated. This principle of procedure that Dunn has formulated is essentially the same as what we have seen in Wright and Allison: the data are surveyed for intelligible patterns, and these patterns serve as the context within which to view all the data, or the hypothesis against which to test the data. But rather than basing his point of procedure on an epistemology, Dunn bases it on a point of principle for Jesus studies. 'The synoptic tradition provides evidence not so much for what Jesus did or said in itself, but for what Jesus was *remembered* as doing or saying by his first disciples, or as we might say, for the impact of what he did and said on his first disciples.'[25] In both the sayings and narrative material, we have to do not with Jesus himself, but with the remembered Jesus, with Jesus as he can be seen to have impacted his followers. Dunn's point of principle reminds us that the data on Jesus are not in the first instance testimonies of events in the life of Jesus, but evidence of the impact of the life of Jesus.[26] It is this character of the data, as evidence of the impact of a historical event (or, in this case, a life or career), that warrants our handling them by searching for characteristic and distinctive emphases rather than true or false testimony. With this observation we are led back to a point I made in relation to Crossan's handling of data basically as testimony; data are not simply true or false testimony, but are first of all evidence.[27]

2. *Data-as-Evidence*

Collingwood suggested that the important question to ask about a given datum in a source is not whether it is true, but what it means, or what its significance is in relation to the historical object. Data are to be treated not as true or false testimonies of the facts they ostensibly relate, but rather as facts themselves, which may shed light on the other facts as they are seen to constitute the impact of those facts. Bernard Lonergan has similarly noted that the study of history is not concerned with testimonies but with 'traces'. 'Everything that exists in the present and had its origin in the past constitutes a trace of the past.'[28] The historian seeks to account

---

(eds.), *Authenticating the Activities of Jesus* (New Testament Tools and Studies, 28/2; Leiden: E.J. Brill, 1999), p. 46.

25. Dunn, 'Can the Third Quest Hope to Succeed?', p. 44.

26. Leander Keck makes a similar point, when he considers how to approach the question of authenticity of particular sayings of Jesus: '[F]or the task of portraying the Jesus of history, answering the question Is it true to Jesus? is as important and as useful as deciding whether a saying came from his mouth or not. Distinguishing the genuine from the nongenuine does not necessarily entail the judgment that the latter distorts Jesus. It does, however, imply that the perception of Jesus that he catalyzed is part of who Jesus was', *Who Is Jesus? History in Perfect Tense* (Colombia, SC: University of South Carolina Press, 2000), p. 20.

27. See above, pp. 64-67.

28. Lonergan, 'The Philosophy of History', in Robert C. Croken, Frederick E. Crowe and Robert M. Doran (eds.), *Philosophical and Theological Papers* (Toronto: University of Toronto Press, 1996), p. 56.

for data as traces of the past that are existing in the present.[29] The events of the past have left the marks of their impact in the form of these traces, and it is the historian's task to determine the possible significance of the data as traces. Past events leave their traces in a variety of forms, reports on those events being only one of them. When historians limit their handling of the data to treating them as potential sources of testimony, they use a monolithic understanding of the nature of historical data to discard systematically the other potentially valuable, multifarious traces left by historical events.

Dunn reminds us that the sources on Jesus are primarily traces, results of the impact of Jesus' career. As such they require a handling in a way that appreciates this character, and not simply as true or false testimonies. As we saw in Crossan, an approach to the data on Jesus that begins by scrutinizing and sorting them according to authenticity handles the data strictly as testimony. But their character as evidence demands that we find a way to handle them that is appropriate to that character; we must find a way to approach the data that can appreciate them as reflecting the impact of Jesus' career. Dunn proposes that a (what I would call) holistic procedure appreciates the data-as-evidence. Beginning by identifying broad themes and distinctive emphases in the sources allows one to consider the value of data that may not pass the test of authentic testimony, but may yet shed light on the historical object.[30] Dunn is not alone in this among Jesus scholars.

Dale Allison points out that it is often impossible to label a particular tradition authentic or inauthentic, because the contributions of Jesus and the church are inextricably combined in the sources. Many of the contributions of the church probably found their way into the tradition precisely because they agreed with already existing elements of the tradition, so the task of distinguishing later additions from earlier material in many cases becomes nearly impracticable. Or what could possibly be shown to be a late accretion may be a useful 'historical fiction', an episode that may not have taken place but reflects authentic elements in the

29. 'Just as the physicist considers all the colors he sees in the spectroscope and all the measurements obtained, and so on, as so much data in which he seeks an understanding and as the start of the hypothetico-deductive process, so in somewhat similar fashion the historian is not simply a believer of what other people have told him, a shrewd believer sizing up, accepting some, discounting others, but something like a scientist seeking an understanding of all the traces of the past that are existing into the present', Lonergan, 'The Philosophy of History', p. 56.

30. I should acknowledge that a method like Crossan's, that begins with scrutiny of individual sayings in order to establish a database of authentic material, *approaches* an appreciation for data-as-evidence in its use of the 'criterion of coherence'. This criterion states that a tradition can be considered authentic if it coheres in some way with the corpus of already-established authentic material (see appendix 1). Crossan uses this principle when he allows as historical many tradition complexes that are not attested in his first stratum (recall that attestation in the first stratum is requisite for inclusion in his core database), on the basis of the coherence of that lately attested material with his established core (see *The Historical Jesus*, pp. 443-49, for inventory of these later strata). The criterion of coherence is a tacit acknowledgment that there are historically useful data that do not meet the criteria of authentic *testimony*. These data are sometimes admitted because they reflect similar themes and traits as found in authentic material. But even the criterion of coherence is usually applied with the assumption that coherent material is such because it is authentic testimony.

life of Jesus.[31] Allison concludes from this that the assumption that a given tradition originated *either* with Jesus *or* with the church is facile. I would say that the assumption reflects an orientation to data-as-testimony, but that Allison shows an appreciation of data-as-evidence.[32]

3. *Reciprocity*

A holistic approach to the data is a result of an appreciation of the contextual nature of particulars, as well as of historical data-as-evidence. It is also a concrete historiographic application of the principle of reciprocity between data control and interpretation. I have identified the principle of reciprocity as a major contribution of Meyer to Jesus studies.[33] He stressed that decisions on the historicity of individual data (data control) cannot be settled apart from decisions on how to interpret the data, because the historian's understanding of the data depends on how they function in a larger frame of reference. For Meyer, this frame of reference is principally the role that the data begin to play in the historical investigation. In support of this I have drawn on Collingwood's illustration of the detective, and his notion that the 'fixed points' of history are not established independently of and prior to the interpretive web.[34] In the holistic approach there is a recognition that the relation between interpretive, big-picture contexts and discrete data or facts is symmetrical. N.T. Wright has pointed out, in holistic fashion, that historical facts are actually an inseparable part of a larger whole involving the interplay of human intentions and motivations. So the move from fact to interpretation is not a move from the clear to the unclear, contrary to popular assumption.[35] Questions of fact and interpretation are integral. Seeing individual facts or data as necessarily contextual requires that data and their interpretive contexts be treated together.

All this is consistent with what has been identified as a coherence theory of historical truth (not to be confused with the 'criterion of coherence'), as opposed to a

---

31. Allison, *Jesus of Nazareth*, pp. 58-60. Allison gives an example of an episode that may not be historical, but reflects authentic information. Though Q 4.1-13 is often considered haggadic fiction, 'whoever composed it clearly did so in the knowledge that Jesus was (a) a miracle-worker who (b) sometimes refused to give signs, (c) thought himself victorious over demonic forces, (d) was steeped in the scriptures, (e) had great faith in God, and (f) was a person of the Spirit. So what we seem to have in Q 4.1-13 is an illustration of the obvious fact that historical fiction can instruct us about history', p. 60.

32. I might also note that Theissen and Winter have proposed a new criterion of authenticity in Jesus studies, the criterion of double plausibility. See appendix 1. Traditions are likely historical which can be explained in terms of Jesus' Palestinian Jewish context and the historical impact he had upon his followers which resulted in the early church. See Theissen and Winter, *Die Kriterienfrage in Der Jesusforschung*, p. xi and *passim*. Now this criterion is formulated in the context of the traditional application of the criteria, i.e., as applied to individual traditions. There is no indication that Theissen and Winter have thrown their hats in the ring on behalf of methodological holism. But I would point out that even in an 'atomistic' context there is some recognition of a category of data broader than simple testimony.

33. See above, p. 118.

34. See pp. 71-72 and 122-23.

35. Wright, *The New Testament and the People of God*, p. 91.

correspondence theory. These are similar to coherence and correspondence theories of truth generally. Correspondence in historiography sees historical statements as justified because they correspond to past events, and such correspondence is verified by the historian's establishing a foundation of hard facts upon which to base an interpretation, or around which to build a historical reconstruction. On this view, historical progress can be made only when some such 'factual' foundation is established. In the coherence theory, historical statements are justified because they cohere with other statements. Though some statements may be taken as more firmly established than others, no statements serve as a foundation. Like holism, coherence recognizes that statements and 'facts' exist in dependence upon larger wholes.[36] Coherence is consistent with the contextualism that characterizes holism. This can be contrasted with not only the 'atomistic' approaches in Jesus studies, but with any approach that claims to begin with a foundation of 'indisputable facts' and from this foundation to move to an establishment of other facts and eventually to an interpretation of all of them. We have seen this orientation in E.P. Sanders, Paula Fredriksen, and echoes even in Dale Allison, an advocate of holism, who points to certain 'facts' as the partial justification of his chosen paradigm of Jesus.[37]

I have presented holism as an approach that discerns the contextual nature of individual data, and so appreciates the nature of data-as-evidence and the reciprocity of data control and interpretation. Data are *always* seen within a context, and an approach that attempts to evaluate the data apart from a context has the effect of distorting the data, and that usually on the basis of a tacit context that the historian brings to the data. A tacit context, unlike a public one, is not subject to scrutiny as it guides the process of data control. In a historical method that begins by scrutinizing discrete data for their authenticity, the reciprocity that should characterize the relation between context and particulars is stifled, and what should be the historian's conscious control over context and particulars becomes remote control of context over particulars. Such is the nature of a context that is not a public part of the investigation.

4. *An Objection*

This idea of tacit contexts and their control over enquiry leads us to a problem with the holistic approach as we have seen it formulated. All the holists agree that individual data are evaluated and interpreted only within a context. The historian should

36. See the discussion of W.H. Walsh, *Introduction to the Philosophy of History* (London: Hutchinson University Library, 5th edn, 1958), pp. 72-93. Walsh ultimately rejects both coherence and correspondence in favor of a supposed middle way, but the latter seems to be mostly coherence along with the insistence that historical reconstructions still have to do with the past in having past events as their referents. I would suggest that a web of historical statements 'hooks onto' the past by virtue of its relation to the evidence, as in Collingwood, *Idea of History*, p. 246.

37. Van Austin Harvey has objected to a coherence theory of historical truth on the basis that it reflects a 'hard perspectivism' that is used by some apologists to defend the content of the canonical Gospels as necessarily historical (Harvey, *The Historian and the Believer*, pp. 222ff.). I would point out that coherence does not entail a stance of systematic credulity toward any source, nor does it amount to a rejection of critical history.

begin the enquiry with a consciously chosen context, in the form of a paradigm, or gestalt, or hypothesis, or some larger whole which amounts to an overall understanding of Jesus to be tested against the data. In this way, the context within which data are necessarily viewed will be a deliberate part of the investigation from the beginning. But where does the historian find this beginning context? We have seen in Meyer, and in Wright, that the context comes from a cursory examination of the mass of data. All the data are brought together, and intelligible patterns are observed within it; these patterns constitute the context. Similarly, in Allison we saw that the context, or paradigm, comes from consistent themes, motifs and rhetorical strategies that the historian sees in the sources. This would seem to be a more sophisticated expression of the 'intelligible patterns' that Meyer and Wright suggest the historian should identify. Dunn has specified what is characteristic of and relatively distinctive within the tradition as constituting the larger whole within which particulars are examined. Presumably, the historian looks for characteristic and distinctive material within the data at large, so Dunn seems to be suggesting the same source for a context as what we see in Meyer, Wright and Allison. What is problematic about this way of defining a context is that even a preliminary, cursory examination of the mass of data will be done in some context. A holistic approach will establish a larger framework for examining discrete data, but what of the context by which the framework itself is established? It seems the holists have only put the problem of context on hold. I have noted that a holistic approach appreciates that *all* observation is contextual; but this would include the observation involved in a cursory examination of the data to identify intelligible patterns, consistent themes, or what is characteristic and distinctive. Formulations of a holistic approach apparently assume that the patterns and themes will simply present themselves in the initial examination, apart from a context of their own.[38] The larger whole that is required for understanding individual historical data is not required for identifying patterns and themes.

On the one hand, what I am getting at here is the largest context within which all observation takes place, the context of the observer's *horizons*. Both Crossan and Meyer are aware of the hermeneutic significance of this ultimate context of all knowledge, the sense-making frame of reference for all questions and statements made by the historian (though they differ on how the fact of horizon impinges historical method). A holistic method is right to insist, in the name of contextualism, on a public context (and by 'public' I mean here an accessible and demonstrable frame of reference), for understanding the data; and when I insist, on the basis of the same contextualism, for a context for formulating the frame of reference, what I am insisting on is *ultimately* the *non*-public horizonal context. As we saw in Lonergan, horizons are not demonstrable and are not subject to proof or disproof,

---

38. Herzog recognizes this. He says that Marcus Borg acknowledges the process of forming an initial gestalt from the data, but that Borg assumes that this initial forming is 'inductive', that the data suggest their own gestalt. Herzog denies that the data can so 'constellate itself', but he does not propose a context in alternative to a bare induction. He simply says that the gestalt should be subject to revision during the process of examination. See *Jesus, Justice and the Reign of God*, pp. 43-44.

because they are the context of all proof and of all demonstration.[39] In that sense we can call horizons 'non-public'. Since horizons are the largest context within which the historian observes anything, they will be a relevant factor in formulating frames of reference for understanding the historical data on Jesus. We will discuss horizons in the context of hermeneutics in the next chapter.

But on the other hand, there are other, public contexts that we can yet discuss. The conceptions of holism that we have considered all call for a public framework for understanding the data, but have no recourse to any public context for formulating *that* framework and so are left with the horizonal context as the only one. It would seem, then, that there is no way of arguing for the preferability of any one framework over any other. If Dale Allison is right, that the data can be made to fit *any* paradigm and so the *correct* paradigm must be chosen to construe the data rightly, we must have some way of adjudicating between starting paradigms. Holism as it has been formulated provides no means for adjudicating, because the context for formulating paradigms is not public, but only horizonal.

I would suggest that there is another starting context for understanding the data on Jesus, and that it is public and therefore avoids the problems of the holistic conceptions we have seen. That context is the context of the sources. If the historian begins the enquiry by understanding the data within the sources as we have them, the challenge of contextualism will be met, and the formulation of the contexts will be given, and not subject only to the contextual control of individual historians' horizons. In the next chapter I will present a case for beginning with the sources, but at this point we may note a proposal by Bruce Chilton for an approach to historical study of Jesus that heads us in the right direction.

39. See above, pp. 153-54. Contrast Wright, who says that 'All worldviews, the Christian one included, are in principle public statements', *The New Testament and the People of God*, p. 135. Wright makes this comment in contrast to the idea that worldviews are 'a matter of private language, a secret of arcane mystery which is of interest only to those who themselves profess the [worldview]'. By 'worldview' Wright seems to have in mind what we are calling 'horizon', inasmuch as worldview is the broadest framework within which all perception and all knowledge take place (see Wright, pp. 32, 37, 43 and *passim*). But Wright insists that worldviews are 'public' in the sense that they are shared by groups and capable of being articulated (as they are in stories and symbols, p. 123) and discussed (p. 117). On this definition, nothing that is capable of being expressed in language is truly *non*public, because the very possibility of linguistic meaning is its 'publicness', the shared language-games by which language-users communicate. But I would maintain, following Lonergan, that the horizon, as the broadest context for all demonstration, is itself beyond demonstration, though it is certainly not beyond articulation. Horizon as the limit of what one knows and cares about can be expressed, but cannot be argued for in the same way as can things that have their sense within the horizon. It may be that Wright would not disagree with this, for he says that when one is confronted with the question of the validity of one's worldview, one usually responds with something like 'That's just the way the world is', i.e., one does not offer an argument for one's worldview (see *Jesus and the Victory of God*, p. 138). But there can be a *conversion*, or a change, between worldviews or horizons, as both Lonergan and Wright would agree; for Lonergan, this conversion happens on some other ground than the type of argument that characterizes discussion within the horizon. But in his insistence that worldviews are public, Wright seems to want to hold out more possibility for proof of them than I think possible; and he seems generally to want to deal with worldviews in a way that treats them as pieces of the furniture of our thinking rather than the largest framework in which our thinking takes place.

Chilton is critical of the type of textual stratigraphy we have seen in Crossan, along with the assumption, arising out of a notion of a genetic, literary relationship among the Gospels, that there is a 'real' Jesus *behind* the Gospels, to be got at by getting to the most primitive layer of tradition. Chilton insists, on the contrary, we only have access to earlier meanings of Jesus *through* later meanings. Jesus is known historically only to the extent that the texts which claim to present him make good on this claim. 'There is no "primitive", "historical", "authentic", or otherwise real Jesus apart from what texts promulgate. In the first instance, therefore, Jesus is only knowable as a literarily historical phenomenon: what the Gospels point to as their source.'[40] That is, 'the literary reference of the Gospels must be the point of departure for critical reflection'.[41] The Gospel texts refer back to Jesus as their source, so any historical reading of the Gospels must take account of the 'literarily historical' Jesus, or the historical Jesus as he is understood and presented in the sources.

We cannot understand the sources unless we understand what *they believe they are referring to*. 'That reference constitutes the literarily historical Jesus for a particular document, and the community of tradents which produced it.'[42] The historian's first concern is to determine what must be presupposed of Jesus in order to explain the shape of a given text. By means of the sources we have (which Chilton identifies as five: the canonical Gospels and Thomas), we infer a description of the historical Jesus that would have produced those sources; 'that is, in a process akin to triangulation in mapping, we may infer from our reading of texts what his position must have been to produce what we read'.[43] This amounts to a 'pentagulation' in order to locate the historical Jesus. What is taking shape in Chilton's description is what he calls 'generative exegesis'. In this method, we first infer from the sources the literarily historical Jesus that is constituted in them, which seems to be the understandings of the historical Jesus reflected in the sources. From this Jesus, we infer, by 'pentagulation' among the sources, to the historical Jesus that would have given rise to the Jesus as constituted in the sources, the Jesus we would have to posit to explain the sources as they exist.[44] Chilton credits Ben Meyer with preparing the way for this approach.[45] There are in this proposal of Chilton some important soundings in the area we are exploring: beginning with the

40. Bruce Chilton, 'Assessing Progress in the Third Quest', in Bruce Chilton and Craig Evans (eds.), *Authenticating the Words of Jesus* (New Testament Tools and Studies, 28.1; Leiden: E.J. Brill, 1999), p. 16.

41. Chilton, 'Assessing Progress', p. 17.

42. Chilton, 'Assessing Progress', p. 22.

43. Chilton, 'Assessing Progress', p. 23.

44. Chilton says this process of reasoning from consequent to antecedent derives from C.S. Peirce's notion of abductive reasoning, which is often described as 'reasoning to the best explanation'. Peirce proposed abduction as a way of describing the type of inference that characterizes scientific reasoning; it is neither purely inductive, nor deductive, but is a sort of shuttling back and forth between these. A hypothesis is formed and held 'on probation', always subject to revision in light of further observation on the data. See Peirce, 'Abduction and Induction', in J. Buchler (ed.), *Philosophical Writings of Peirce* (New York: Dover, 1955), pp. 150-56.

45. Chilton, 'Assessing Progress', p. 24.

sources as the necessary initial context for understanding the data on Jesus, but not simply staying in the sources. To remain there would not be to do history, but only to recover the 'literarily historical' Jesus. From the sources we infer back to the events that gave rise to them (thereby seeing the sources as the impact of those events, or data-as-evidence), and so see the historical Jesus through the sources, rather than peeling the sources away to see Jesus behind them.

I will now make a further case for beginning with the context of the sources, based on the use of narrative in historiography. What has been opened up for us by a holistic approach can be furthered and perfected by an appreciation of narrative intelligibility.

Chapter 8

NARRATIVE INTELLIGIBILITY

Narrative has a history in historiography. I will first review some of the issues surrounding the use of narrative in history, followed by some recent discussion of
what I call narrative realism.[1] I will then apply some observations on narrativity in
support of beginning with the context of the sources, and offer an outline of a historical method for Jesus studies.

1. *Narrative in Historiography*

The nineteenth century is most often identified as the period of the rise of critical
history, the time when historiographic tools came to be developed that made history scientific. The historian was to approach the subject with a concern for objectivity, to get at 'what actually happened' without value judgements and without
partiality. But this concern for objectivity was not, contrary to now-popular conception, a deluded preoccupation with unadorned historical 'facts'. In its German
origins, with Leopold von Ranke, the new conception of history held that history
revealed human meaning, and that meaning revealed itself only in history. So
history became a way of studying human affairs and their meaning. All spheres of
human activity were thought to be opened up to historical study in this understanding of history.[2] As this model of history was adopted, its focus became increasingly
narrowed, restricting historical interest and study to nations and the political life of
nations, concentrating on archives and official documents of state. In this context,
history was conceived as the Grand Narrative of great personalities and of the
course of nations and political entities. Nineteenth-century historiography became
identified with this type of narrative history, telling the stories of national crises
and political figures, and usually in a way that maintained the political status quo.
Narrative history was considered to be just this sort of thing.

By the turn of the twentieth century, there was concern to expand the subject
matter of history and give more attention to things like the role of society, the
economy and culture; the grand narratives of politics and great figures were challenged in the name of making history even more scientific by linking it more closely
to the social sciences.[3] The debate between narrative history and the quantitative

---

1. For an anthology of key texts on the use of narrative in historiography, see Geoffrey
Roberts (ed.), *The History and Narrative Reader* (New York: Routledge, 2001).
2. See Georg Iggers, *Historiography in the Twentieth Century*, pp. 28-29.
3. Iggers, *Historiography*, p. 31.

approach of the social sciences occupied much of twentieth-century discussion in historiography. A quantitative historical method typically sees narrative as either an ancillary tool for 'writing up' the results of investigation properly produced by quantitative and analytical methods, or else a rudimentary and primitive form of knowledge that actually hinders a truly critical history. In the 1970s narrative history saw a revival, documented by Lawrence Stone.[4] Narrative historiography now reacted against the macro-structures and quantification of social science history, in favour of interest in varied aspects of human existence, with the conviction that 'the culture of the group, and even the will of the individual, are potentially at least as important causal agents of change as the impersonal forces of material output and demographic growth.'[5]

The revival of interest in narrative history is driven partly by the concern to account for human intentionality in historical events. The social science approach of the mid-twentieth century applied what has come to be known as a 'covering-law' model of historical explanation, by which historical events are thought to be explained exclusively and exhaustively by application of ideal sociological types and law-like generalizations on human behaviour.[6] This approach tended to be reductionistic, accounting for human actions in a way that disregards the intentions of the agents involved. Narrative history resists such reductionism and takes human intentions seriously, as well as the individual character of historical events. It sees narrative not as an incidental means of writing up the findings of research, but a way of knowing and of describing experience that cannot be reduced to other terms (e.g., the generalizations of analysis). But it is important to note that narrative in this sense is not necessarily of a piece with the Grand Narratives of the nineteenth century. More recent concern with narrative does not limit its focus to politics or great figures. As we will see below, certain practitioners of 'microhistory' employ narrative on a scale much smaller and more modest than the Grand Narrative.

Much of the narrative revival has to do with renewed concern for intentionality and the integrity of individual experience. But there are some advocates of narrative historiography whose interest in narrative is more properly literary. Hayden White is an example of the latter.[7] White defends the character of history as integrally and irreducibly narrative, but not because he sees historical experience itself as requiring narrative description. Rather, for White the narrative quality of written history constitutes an 'emplotment' of historical events, a means by which the historian makes sense of events in history that have no sense of their own. The

---

4. Lawrence Stone, 'The Revival of Narrative: Reflections on a New Old History', *Past and Present* 85 (1979), pp. 3-24.

5. Iggers, *Historiography in the Twentieth Century*, p. 97.

6. See Hempel, 'Explanation in Science and History' in R. Colodny (ed.), *Frontiers of Science and Philosophy* (Pittsburgh: University of Pittsburgh Press, 1962); and 'The Function of General Laws in History', *The Journal of Philosophy* 39 (1942), pp. 35-48.

7. See Hayden White, *Metahistory: The Historical Imagination in the Nineteenth Century* (Baltimore: The Johns Hopkins University Press, 1973); *Tropics of Discourse* (Baltimore: The Johns Hopkins University Press, 1978); and *The Content of the Form: Narrative Discourse and Historical Representation* (Baltimore: The Johns Hopkins University Press, 1987).

historian uses certain standard emplotting devices that are found in literature (e.g., comedy, romance, satire, tragedy) and by these imposes order on the events of history. In this way, as White says, 'history is as much invented as discovered'. There is no continuity between the narrative history written by the historian and the events as they occur in history. The distinction between history and fiction is effectively collapsed.[8] We might call this orientation to a narrative historiography 'narrative anti-realism'.

At least one commentator has criticized Crossan from this perspective, claiming that Crossan is 'positivist' because he believes himself to be getting at, or discovering, a real historical object when he investigates the historical Jesus.[9] Though this position is not impervious, I will not devote space to refuting it here. I will simply note that neither of the Jesus historians I am examining are anti-realists, though they both appreciate the significance of hermeneutical nuance. For that matter, the world of historical Jesus studies would have little sympathy with any form of anti-realism in historiography.[10] But perhaps it is for this reason that Jesus historians have given little attention to narrativity in history. Narrative in New Testament studies has mostly been associated with tendencies to bracket the historically referential dimension of the text.[11] My brief review of narrative in historiography is

8.   For good summaries of this understanding of narrative historiography, see Alun Munslow, *Deconstructing History* (New York: Routledge, 1997); and Keith Jenkins, *On 'What Is History?': From Carr and Elton to Rorty and White* (New York: Routledge, 1995).

9.   Hal Childs follows the position of White, as well as Paul Veyne and Peter Munz, which he classifies under the general label 'critical historiography'. See Childs *The Myth of the Historical Jesus and the Evolution of Consciousness*, esp. ch. 3. Childs relies on Carl Jung's analytical psychology to suggest that history is pure projection of the historian's archetypes, that is, the mythic world of meaning that constitutes the psyche.

10.   Of course, the same would not be true for recent advocates of New Historicism in New Testament studies. New Historicism is at least a couple of decades old in historiography, but has had a life less than half that in biblical studies. It can be seen as an application of post-structuralist sentiments to the doing of history, occupied with such matters as the historian's cultural location and the plays of power that figure into things like the preservation of historical texts (sources) as well as their investigation. In post-structuralist fashion, New Historicism greatly qualifies any claim to 'truth' in historical investigation, suspicious of bids to power. On New Historicism in New Testament and historical Jesus studies, see the dedicated issue of *Biblical Interpretation* 5 (1997); and Gina Hens-Piazza, *The New Historicism* (Minneapolis: Fortress Press, 2002). On New Historicism generally, see John Zammito, 'Are We Being Theoretical Yet? The New Historicism, the New Philosophy of History, and "Practicing Historians"', *Journal of Modern History* 65 (1993), pp. 783-814.

11.   Such has been the case at least since the work of Hans Frei, arising out of a New Critical orientation: *The Eclipse of Biblical Narrative: A Study in Eighteenth and Nineteenth Century Hermeneutics* (New Haven, CN: Yale University Press, 1974), and *The Identity of Jesus Christ: The Hermeneutical Basis of Dogmatic Theology* (Philadelphia: Fortress Press, 1975); and continuing through the work of structuralists. Some comments of Robert Funk represent the conflicted understanding in New Testament studies of the role of narrative in historiography. At the end of his structuralist work on *The Poetics of Biblical Narrative*, Funk wonders how history can 'break into' the network of language. He is concerned to distinguish between fiction and history, and insists that there is some relation between historical events and historical narratives about them, but the relationship is unknown, and not univocal (but he cites ethical reasons for distinguishing fact from

meant to show that talk of narrative does not equate with the bracketing of history, nor with a denial of real historical referents; neither is it necessarily associated with the type of Grand Narratives of the nineteenth century.[12] There is a conception of narrativity that recognizes the significant role of narrative in human action, and thus in historical events and our understanding of them.

2. *Narrative Realism*

Within this revival of narrative, but in contrast to narrative anti-realism, is what I call a 'narrative realism'. This understanding of narrativity can be seen in the work of David Carr. Carr is concerned to account for narrativity in historiography by focusing on the narrative character of lived experience.[13] So his concern for narrative is not specifically literary or text-centred, but rather experience-centred.[14] He shows that the narrative expression that historiography takes is an extension of the features of historical experience. Narrative structure inheres in the events of history and human living.

Carr bases his case on a phenomenological analysis of temporal experience. He notes Husserl's observation that all our temporal experience involves the retention of the immediate past and the anticipation ('protention') of the future. Nothing can be experienced except against the background of what preceded it and what we anticipate will succeed it. Merleau-Ponty held that the figure-background scheme is basic in spatial perception; supposedly distinct units of sensation must be grasped as a configuration to be experienced at all. So discrete sensations are not basic units of actual experience but are only abstract products of analysis. What is true of temporal and spatial experience is certainly true of active human living generally. The present is experienced as a passage between a remembered past experience and an anticipated future. Action has a means-end structure which is similar to the beginning-middle-end structure of narrative. Events of life, far from being a mere sequence, 'constitute rather a complex structure of temporal configurations that interlock and receive their definition and their meaning from within action itself'.[15]

But any comparison of temporal experience with narrative has to consider that a narrative is not simply a sequence of events with beginning-middle-end, but also has a storyteller and audience. It would seem that these elements are not found in the events but are imposed upon them as a form of organization. To be narrated,

---

fiction). See Funk, *The Poetics of Biblical Narrative* (Sonoma, CA: Polebridge Press, 1988), pp. 295-300.

12. Peter Novick seems to reduce issues of narrativity to these two terms, a relativistic anti-realism versus the traditional Grand Narratives. See *That Noble Dream: The Objectivity Question and the American Historical Profession* (Cambridge: Cambridge University Press, 1988), pp. 622-23.

13. A concise statement is found in 'Narrative and the Real World: An Argument for Continuity', *History and Theory* 25 (1986), pp. 117-31. A fuller exposition is in *Time, Narrative and History* (Bloomington, IN: Indiana University Press, 1986).

14. Carr, *Time, Narrative and History*, p. 16.

15. Carr, 'Narrative and the Real World', p. 122.

the events must be transformed by one who knows more than the characters experiencing the events. So narration is not just telling, but telling from a superior point of view. Those experiencing the events are confined to the present, and are denied the authoritative, retrospective point of view of the narrator, who, among other things, can eliminate the extraneous elements, the 'static' of real life, and tell only what is necessary to further the plot.

But Carr points out that in our experience we are not 'confined to the present', but experience the present and recall the past in anticipation of the future. Present action is teleological in nature: acts and movements derive their sense from a projected end they serve. Action can be said to have a quasi-retrospective character, in that 'the elements and phases of an action, though they unfold in time, are viewed from the perspective of their having been completed.'[16] We view present events in terms of their relation to possible later events. So in our temporal experience we are constantly striving to occupy the narrator's position with respect to our own lives.[17]

Narrative is thus a *constitutive* part of action, not just a commentary or accompaniment. In this narrative the individual may assume any of three roles: storyteller, agent or audience. 'The actions and sufferings of life can be viewed as a process of telling ourselves stories, listening to those stories, acting them out, or living them through... Sometimes we must change the story to accommodate the events; sometimes we change the events, by acting, to accommodate the story... The retrospective view of the narrator, with its capacity for seeing the whole in all its irony, is not in irreconcilable opposition to the agent's view but is an extension and refinement of a viewpoint inherent in action itself.'[18] Narrative does indeed create meaning, but it does so in the course of life, and not simply after the fact. Our experiences and actions are thus lived as structured sequences of temporal phases. These sequences have beginnings and endings and are thus separated from their temporal surroundings. They are also 'internally articulated in relations of suspension-resolution, departure-return, means-end, problem-solution, etc'.[19]

In summary, the structure of sequences of our experiences consists of a temporal grasp,

> which can be described as protentional-retentional at the pre-reflective level of short-term or simple experiences and actions, and as reflective and explicitly narrational at the level of more complex experiences and actions. In both cases temporal multiplicity is spanned, gathered, or held together; in the latter case this takes on the character of assuming a story-teller's point of view on the action performed or the experience had. The result is that in the complex actions and experiences of everyday life we are subjects or agents, narrators, and even spectators to the events we live through and the actions we undertake.[20]

---

16. Carr, 'Narrative and the Real World', p. 124.
17. Carr, 'Narrative and the Real World', p. 125.
18. Carr, 'Narrative and the Real World', p. 126.
19. Carr, *Time, Narrative and History*, p. 64.
20. Carr, *Time, Narrative and History*, p. 64.

Everything described so far has to do with the experiences of the individual. But history has to do, at some point, with social groups. For these phenomenological observations to be applicable to history, something like a phenomenology of group experience would have to be done. This would treat the group not as object but as subject. An approach to the group that is truly from the inside, while also able to incorporate phenomenological observations of the individual's experience, is the first person approach of *we*. Such an approach would not be oriented to things like ontological claims about what society *is*, or epistemological claims about how it is known by an observer. Carr's investigation of group experience and narrativity, like his treatment of individual experience, is from a first-person perspective, concerned with narrative's practical function in lived experience.[21]

Carr notes that the self is socially constituted, and also that many of our experiences are experienced as groups, in the first-person plural.[22] So, much of what is said about the individual's experience as narrative can be seen to have parallels in the experience of the group. Like individual experience, group experience consists in a grasp of a sequence of events as a temporal configuration, such that present experience derives its significance from its relation to a common past and future. 'To engage in a common action is likewise to constitute a succession of phases articulated as steps and stages, subprojects, means and ends. Social human time, like individual human time, is constructed into configured sequences which make up the events and projects of our common action and experience.'[23]

Social time, like individual time, has a narrative structure. The group configures temporal sequences in a prospective-retrospective grasp; temporal phases are given their sense of presenting a commonly experienced event or of realizing a common goal.[24] But in groups, the roles of narrator, audience and character may be played by different individuals or sub-groups in the division of labour. Some sub-groups may take the role of narrators, articulating what 'we' are experiencing to the others in the group who are the audience and the characters in the narrative.

A 'community' exists by virtue of a shared experience articulated as a story. The group shares an account of its origin and destiny and interprets its present experience in light of these. One can see here that narrative again has a practical function prior to a cognitive or aesthetic one; narrative makes coordinated, group action possible while it maintains the continuity of the group subject which acts. Carr says that we must go even further and say that narrative is literally *constitutive* of the group.[25]

So historical existence and historical understanding/thought are of a piece. We understand ourselves and constitute ourselves, as individuals and as groups, by the prospective-retrospective consciousness. We experience and act out of a grasping

21. Carr, *Time, Narrative and History*, p. 124.

22. 'To inhabit a territory, to organize politically and economically for its cultivation and civilization, to experience a natural or human threat and rise to meet it' are all examples of group experiences, 'Narrative and the Real World', p. 127.

23. Carr, 'Narrative and the Real World', p. 127.

24. Carr, 'Narrative and the Real World', p. 128.

25. Carr, 'Narrative and the Real World', p. 128.

together of temporal experience, and this grasping gives our actions their sense. Carr is concerned to substantiate the continuity between a narrative historiography and the 'real world' by demonstrating the narrative quality of lived experience. His approach to this is basically phenomenological, but we can draw certain epistemological and hermeneutical implications for historiography.

First of all, the narrativity of lived experience would seem to be most relevant to what we have discussed in terms of the intentionality of historical subjects. I have shown that Meyer orients his historical investigation to understanding events in terms of the intentions of the agents involved. I have also shown in narrativity in history generally that narrative is often concerned with the integrity of individual experience. Practitioners of what has been referred to as 'microhistory' defend narrative historiography partly on this basis. They are interested in narrating the experiences of ordinary people in their local settings, in an effort to preserve the significance of the individual and unique over against the structures and generalizations of the social sciences.[26] Carlo Ginzburg sees the narrativity of microhistory focusing on close observation of particulars precisely because the particular is anomalous (rather than analogous, i.e., typical or repetitive), thereby recognizing that social structures are complex. There is a legitimate social macroscopic sphere, but the implications of it cannot automatically be transferred to the sphere of the individual and the unique. This is the recognition of the heterogeneity between the micro and the macro.[27]

In line with these orientations to history in terms of intentionality, Carr bases his defence of narrativity on individual experience; but he does not limit narrativity to the individual. He applies it to the actions and experiences of groups as well. But it seems that its most immediate application would have to do with intentionality as such. While group experiences can indeed partake of a narrative quality, even to the point where groups can be said to be narratively constituted, it is also the case that the larger the group, the more difficult it would be to detect a true narrative cohesion in its actions and experiences.[28] The societies that Carr identifies as legitimate narratively experiencing subjects, such as the Roman Catholic Church or the American South,[29] would appear to be some of the largest groups to which a conscious sense of narrativity could possibly be applied; and even with these groups, the attribution of a *single* narrative begins to be precarious. The larger the scale on

26.   See the analyses in Iggers, *Historiography*, pp. 99, 102; and Peter Burke, 'History of Events and the Revival of Narrative', in Peter Burke (ed.), *New Perspectives on Historical Writing* (Cambridge: Polity Press, 1991), pp. 233-48.

27.   Carlo Ginzburg, 'Microhistory: Two or Three Things That I Know about It', *Critical Inquiry* 20 (1993), p. 33. See also Giovanni Levi, 'On Microhistory', in Peter Burke (ed.), *New Perspectives on Historical Writing* (Cambridge: Polity Press, 1991), pp. 93-113.

28.   A similar criticism is found in William Dray, *On History and Philosophers of History* (Leiden: E.J. Brill, 1989), pp. 149-51. Dray wonders what is the epistemological status of narratives related by the historian that were not part of the lived experiences of any of the historical agents, for example an 'industrial revolution'. These kinds of narratives seem necessarily to be construed by the historian apart from the conscious, lived narratives of any individual or group. Dray seems to be raising the question of narrativity applied on the largest scale.

29.   Carr, *Time, Narrative and History*, p. 169.

which we seek to apply narrative intelligibility, the more difficult becomes the identification of a true narrative cohesiveness.[30]

A second implication I would draw from Carr is the point of the narrative intelligibility of historical objects. We saw that Carr was not immediately concerned with such epistemological questions as how historical events are known or understood. But it can legitimately be inferred from his observations of the narrativity of historical experience that historical objects have an irreducible narrative dimension to them, a dimension which can only be understood narratively. Historical events, and the data from which they are inferred, have an intrinsic narrative intelligibility. The intentional actions of historical agents are performed in the context of a sense-making story by which the agents grasped their experience in a temporal unity. The historian's goal has to do with the recovery of the narrativity by which actions were performed, to the extent that the historian has to do with intentionality. This is consonant with the basic conviction of holism, that individual parts have their sense within a larger whole. The whole within which the actions of historical agents have their sense is the narrative whole of individual intentionality, as well as the narrative whole that makes up the configurational efforts of social groups.

N.T. Wright has approached this understanding of narrative intelligibility, on an epistemological basis. For Wright, the prior framework within which all knowledge and perception take place consists fundamentally of worldview, which is characterized by stories. All individual 'facts' and 'objects' come with theories attached, which are stories; facts are perceived and verified within stories. Objects are only intelligible within events; events have to do with intelligible actions.[31] Stories invest events with meaning. The implication of narrativity for history is that the individual historical agent should be understood as retelling a received story, the story received from the group of which the agent is a part. In the case of Jesus, his stories, as well as the controversy between Christianity and Judaism in the first century, were about '*different retellings of the story of Israel's god, his people, and the world*'.[32] Wright reflects a certain concern with the narrative intelligibility of lived experience, which requires that the historian seek to recover the narratives within which agents acted.

The concrete historiographic conclusion that I want to draw from the idea of narrative intelligibility is that historical events, with their inherently narrative quality, must be understood in the context of narrative. The ultimate narrative context is that by which the agents of history themselves made sense of their actions. Such a

---

30. Of course, this does not address the issue of whether there might be a necessary narrative quality even in historical descriptions on the largest social level, but on some basis other than Carr's narrativity of experience. Appleby, Hunt and Jacob point out that there is a narrative cast even in histories that are not deliberately narrative. This is the case because every work of history has the structure of a plot, with a beginning, middle and end. So calls for a return to narrative miss the point that narrative has always been part of history writing; history has never been 'non-narrative'. See Appleby, Hunt and Jacob, *Telling the Truth about History*, p. 231. But I would point out that this type of defence of narrative historiography would be congenial to narrative anti-realists as much as to narrative realists.

31. Wright, *The New Testament and the People of God*, pp. 43ff.

32. Wright, *The New Testament and the People of God*, p. 76 (emphasis original).

context would include the individual's narratives, as well as those of the group(s) to which the individual belonged. The historian seeks to understand the events of history, so far as these events have to do with human agency, in the context of the narratives by which agents acted. But what is true of historical events is also true of the data by which we know those events. The holists have reminded us that data have a sense only in a context; I would posit that, in light of narrative intelligibility, *the context of the sources in which we find the data is the necessary context for an initial understanding of the data.*

3. *The Context of the Sources*

I am proposing that the historian must begin an investigation into the historical Jesus by understanding individual data in the context in which they come to us, the context of their respective sources. This approach obviously contrasts with that of Crossan and tradition criticism, which requires as the first step that the historian make determinations of authenticity of each datum, and that apart from how any of the data function in the sources. We have seen that Crossan arranges the data of the various sources into complexes based loosely on common themes or motifs, irrespective of their roles in the sources. These complexes are evaluated for their authenticity based on the number of times they are independently attested in the various sources, and on the stratum in which they receive their earliest attestation. Only those complexes which are attested in the first stratum, and at least doubly attested throughout the strata, are considered possible data for inclusion in the core database of authentic Jesus material. Crossan's is a prime example of a method that presumes to understand, and evaluate, data apart from any public context. The context of the sources in which the data are found is systematically, and as a matter of principle, disregarded.

Ben Meyer's major advance over the method represented by Crossan is his insistence that the data be evaluated in a context, specifically, in the context of the role that the data play in historical hypotheses. Meyer was a pioneer in Jesus studies in recognizing that the data are only understood in a context, and his early suggestions of a holistic method have come to be widely appreciated. But Meyer, like Crossan, deliberately discounted the context of the sources for understanding the data. For Meyer, to ignore redaction is simply 'to undo what the redactor has done'.[33] The holists have followed Meyer in seeking a context for understanding the data, but they give little attention to the narrative context of the sources as a possible public context with which to begin historical work. A holistic approach as we have seen it formulated begins by, as it were, dumping the data into one large pile, and within this pile attempting to discern patterns and themes. The major difficulty with this is, as I have said, that the initial discernment of patterns itself takes place within a context, and for holism, this context is tacit. But contexts should be as public as one can make them, so that they and the sense that they lend the data can be subject to analysis and control. Since the Gospel sources

---

33. See the discussion above, p. 146.

are the context in which the data come to us, they are the only public context that we can use for an initial understanding of the data that will not be chosen arbitrarily, by means of some prior, tacitly operating, context by which the historian makes choices.[34] I would point out again, as I have already acknowledged and will address below, all historians, like all knowers, have a tacit context within which all choices are made and all things are perceived and known. But there are also public contexts, and the more public we can make our contexts, the more they and the interpretations we make within them will be subject to scrutiny by ourselves and others, and the more we will be able to communicate about the results we derive by them.

I have seen some promise in Bruce Chilton's generative exegesis, which requires that the 'literarily historical' Jesus be the point of departure for critical reflection. The historical Jesus can only be seen *through* the understanding of Jesus that is our given, or what we have to work with in the sources. The historian must begin with this understanding as presented in the sources, and from there determine what must be presupposed of Jesus in order to explain what is in the sources, or what the historical reality was that generated the data that we have. There can identified two strengths of Chilton's method. First, understanding Jesus as he is presented in the sources meets the requirement that the data be viewed within a public context. The 'literarily historical' Jesus is a Jesus that can be established from the data by appeal to a context that is completely accessible to any interested observer: the literarily historical Jesus of Matthew is Jesus as he is portrayed in the confines of Matthew's Gospel; the literarily historical Jesus of Mark is Jesus as we find him presented in Mark, and so on. What constitutes the literarily historical Jesus for each source is a matter of how the data are construed within that source. In this way, all the data of all the sources have a context already provided for their interpretation, and the parameters of that context are entirely public. Second, by beginning with Jesus as he is understood and portrayed in the sources and reasoning back to the historical figure that would have given rise to this understanding, the data are treated as evidence and not simply as testimony. True to the nature of historical reasoning, the sources are handled as tracks left by the movement of a historical phenomenon. The historian begins with the sources and reasons back to what the historical event would have been that gave rise to those sources as evidence, including but not limited to how the sources may function as testimony.[35]

---

34. Don Hagner has recently argued for the sources as the necessary context for understanding the data. The sources provide the interpretive framework, without which 'the discrete data become too fragmentary and too capable of various construals. It is as though one were confronted with a large number of dots to be connected together to form a picture but lacked the numbers that indicated which way the lines were to be drawn. What happens is that each person connects the dots in his or her own way', 'An Analysis of Recent "Historical Jesus" Studies', p. 90.

35. Similarly, Jens Schröter opposes attempts in historical Jesus studies to separate too easily the historical Jesus from later interpretations of him. Historical study should rather first of all be about how early Christians variously understood the historical Jesus. We seek to understand the features of our texts as interpretations of historical events. 'Every approach to the historical Jesus behind the Gospels has to explain how these writings could have come into being as the earliest

Another scholar who reflects a similar concern for beginning with the source contexts, rather than discounting them, is Sean Freyne. Freyne proposes beginning a study of the historical Jesus with the texts themselves, in a form of reader-oriented approach to narrative that pays attention to constructs in the text such as implied author, narrator, narratee and ideal reader. He suggests that 'At the end of such a reading of the gospels it appears that certain questions are likely to arise that are historical as well as literary in character, namely those of the relationship between the various accounts and their possible extra-textual referents.'[36] Beginning with the Gospel texts in fact allows the researcher's historical questions to be set by the text, and helps guard against the researcher's own interests, or, as I would say, his other tacit context, from setting the agenda for historical investigation. Freyne sees the latter tendency reflected in those historical studies that begin with particular judgements concerning, e.g., what is to be counted as evidence. Beginning with the texts allows such judgements to be based on what is reflected in the data rather than the historian's personal interests. Freyne explicitly contrasts his approach to Crossan's method of stratification, characterizing the former as a narrative realism as applied to the final Gospels, in an attempt to see how literary and historical concerns might cooperate.[37] I should point out, though, that Freyne's 'narrative realism' has to do not with the continuity of historical narrative with historical experience that we have been considering, but with the verisimilitude that is a feature of literary works, that striving for realism that makes fiction believable. Freyne acknowledges that a focus on the verisimilitude of the text in doing history leaves him open to the charge of confusing the realism of narrative fiction with historical fact. But he cites the work of Paul Ricoeur which shows an overlap between narrative fiction and history writing that may 'assist in freeing us from the objectivist fallacy without thereby abandoning a critical historical perspective'.[38] In this I take Freyne to be saying that narrativity qualifies the nature of historical knowledge, and thus of historical investigation, but does not require the sort of anti-realist perspective that often accompanies discussion of narrativity in New Testament studies and historiography.

---

descriptions of this person', 'The Historical Jesus and the Sayings Tradition: Comments on Current Research', *Neotestamentica* 30 (1996), p. 153 and *passim*.

36. Sean Freyne, *Jesus, Galilee and the Gospels*, pp. 26-27.

37. Freyne, 'Galilean Questions to Crossan's Mediterranean Jesus', in William E. Arnal and Michel Desjardins (eds.), *Whose Historical Jesus?* (Studies in Christianity and Judaism, 7; Waterloo, ON: Wilfrid Laurier University Press, 1997), p. 66.

38. Freyne, 'Galilean Questions', p. 66. The most relevant work of Ricoeur to which Freyne refers is his three-volume *Time and Narrative* (trans. Kathleen Blamey and David Pellauer; Chicago: University of Chicago Press, 1984–88); see also Ricoeur, 'The Narrative Function', in *Hermeneutics and the Human Sciences: Essays on Language, Action and Interpretation* (ed. and trans. John B. Thompson; Cambridge: Cambridge University Press, 1981). David Carr classifies Ricoeur among the narrative anti-realists. It is true that Ricoeur does not attempt to demonstrate the continuity of historical narrative with historical experience, but he seems to take the referential dimension of historical narrative more seriously than do the anti-realists. I would place Ricoeur somewhere between the anti-realists and Carr.

N.T. Wright has been with us at every step in our discussion of historiography since Meyer's critical realism. He has contributions that help us round out our discussion of beginning with the sources. Wright suggests that since worldview is the necessary context for all understanding, and since worldview is expressed in narrative, narrative is the primary context for understanding a text, including the Gospel texts.[39] He recommends beginning historical Jesus work with composition criticism of the Gospels, rather than with issues of literary dependence (arguing specifically against Crossan). 'The only safe place to begin is with the documents we have. When we have done our composition-critical analysis of these documents in their own terms, we *might* find that their main thrusts and emphases were consistent with a particular line of literary dependence.'[40] This is in full agreement with what I am suggesting is the necessary first step in Jesus studies. It also reflects an appreciation of the point I am going to make in the next section, about the critical comparative work that must follow the understanding of the source contexts if we are to do history. Wright's entire programme in Jesus studies is among the most congenial to what I have been claiming is the nature of historiography and its implications for historical Jesus work.[41] But that being said, I have two points of criticism of Wright.

In the first place, Wright's concern for narrative as a communication of worldview is similar to my point about the narrative dimension of lived experience. But it seems that the latter more clearly articulates how narrative inheres in actual experience and so in the historical object as something that the historian can know. In his focus on worldview, Wright appears to deal with narrative at a rather high level of abstraction, something like the horizon or ultimate context for one's experi-

39. Wright, *The New Testament and the People of God*, p. 371. He surveys the narratives of each of the Gospels for their general worldviews in ch. 13.

40. Wright, 'Doing Justice to Jesus: A Response to J.D. Crossan: "What Victory? What God?"', *Scottish Journal of Theology* 50 (1997), p. 364.

41. There is some indication among holists of at least a nascent recognition of beginning with source contexts. In his emphasis on beginning with a gestalt of Jesus and testing it as a hypothesis against the data, William Herzog comments: 'it seems important to acknowledge that it is neither possible nor desirable to separate Jesus from the theological and religious readings of his work found in the Gospels, although they may not always be helpful for reconstructing the historical Jesus', *Jesus, Justice and the Reign of God*, p. 44. This comment is little more than an aside in his discussion, but Herzog is getting at the significance of the gestalt of the sources themselves for understanding the data on Jesus, while also recognizing that the historian must move beyond the sources for a critical reconstruction. But, like many Jesus historians, Herzog later says concern for the narrative context of the gospels is not helpful, assuming that it mostly brackets the question of history (p. 88).

Though it is not clear that he is a holist, Irvin Batdorf mentions the effect that the context of one's 'hermeneutic matrix' has on one's Jesus portrait. Part of this matrix is the historian's attitude toward the overall canonical picture of Jesus. Batdorf seems to emphasize the need for, if not beginning with the context of the canonical portraits, at least accounting for them historically in any portrait that is offered. 'An ancient document can scarcely make any contribution to our understanding unless taken seriously first of all on its own terms', 'Interpreting Jesus Since Bultmann: Selected Paradigms and Their Hermeneutical Matrix', in *SBL 1984 Seminar Papers* (ed. Kent H. Richards; Chico, CA: Scholars Press, 1984), p. 212.

ence of the world. He stresses the need to uncover worldviews to make sense of the actions of historical actors, and since worldview is expressed narratively, attention to narrative is necessary for discovering and understanding worldview. But what Wright is after is difficult for the historian to get at and generalize about as a historical object. Recognizing the narrative quality of lived experience is more concrete and recoverable, inasmuch as experience is not what it is without such a context, and so experience is always related by subjects in narrative terms. All this is not to deny that some features of the horizonal kind are a necessary part of narrative experience; but to attempt to construct a comprehensive horizon is not necessary, and in many cases may not be feasible, for understanding historical actions.[42] David Carr's narrative realism deals with how we act out of 'narratives' on a more mundane level, how we make sense of experience by grasping together remembered past and anticipated future as the context for present action; it would thus seem to be more readily usable for historiography, as a means of understanding human intentionality.

My second point has to do with how Wright handles the different sources in constructing his portrait of Jesus. In spite of his recommendation that one begin with composition criticism of the Gospels, understanding each of them first on their own terms, he treats the sources in the way I have described as characteristic of holists generally: the data are all dumped into one large pile, and themes and patterns are chosen from the whole lot with little regard for how the data may have functioned differently in different sources. L.T. Johnson has noted that Wright uses the Gospels as sources somewhat uncritically. He draws data from them without a principle of selection or use, avoiding what does not fit his hypothesis as determined by perceiving patterns among the mass of data.[43] He does not take seriously the differences among Gospels, their distinctiveness as literary units. The result is a portrait of Jesus that reads like an elaborate Gospel harmony rather than a conclusion arising from critical comparisons.[44]

But Wright must have anticipated this criticism. Even before his Jesus work was published, he commented on the suspicion of narrativity by many historically oriented New Testament scholars on the grounds that narratives tend to contain unwarranted harmonization. Wright's proleptic response: 'Of course there is to be harmonization... A good historical account offers precisely a harmonious treatment of the whole; that, as we have seen, is one of its tasks, if it is to be taken seri-

42. L.T. Johnson has a similar criticism. He sees Wright as pronouncing on worldview contexts that he is not able to generalize on in a historically legitimate way (especially a first-century Jewish worldview). See Johnson, 'A Historiographical Response to Wright's Jesus', in Carey C. Newman (ed.), *Jesus and the Restoration of Israel: A Critical Assessment of N.T. Wright's Jesus and the Victory of God* (Downers Grove, IL: InterVarsity Press, 1999), p. 217.

43. Johnson, 'A Historiographical Response', pp. 217-18.

44. See the criticism of Robert Gundry, who says Wright merges 'the plural Jesuses of Matthew, Mark and Luke into one synoptic Jesus. Thus the distinctive lineaments of the various portrayals are blurred almost to the vanishing point; Wright's main interest remains historical rather than biblical and historicity is insulated against the doubt that differences between the Synoptics often raise (to say nothing about greater differences between these Gospels and the Gospel of John)', 'Reconstructing Jesus', *Christianity Today*, 27 April 1998, p. 77.

ously.'[45] But Wright is conflating harmonization of different sources with coherence. A good historical account will offer an explanation of the data that is coherent and cogent; that is, the truth of individual historical statements lies in the role they play in an overall coherent account, in light of the data. But coherence among the historian's statements does not translate into harmonization of historical sources. A satisfaction with this kind of harmonization amounts to a neglect of the work of comparisons that is the heart of critical history. Though he begins with a stated focus on narrativity, and on the integrity of the narrativity of each source, Wright appears to gloss over the true distinctiveness of sources that should follow on reading the sources on their own terms.

This brings me to the point where I must articulate a full conception of historiography, particularly as related to historical Jesus studies. I have made a case for beginning with the sources as the necessary first context for understanding the data, based on holistic-contextual issues and on the narrative intelligibility of historical objects. If the sources are our necessary starting point for historical investigation, how do we proceed?

4. *Narrativity and Historiography: Outline of a Proposal*

Some comments by L.T. Johnson will help illustrate one suppositional extreme that any method must guard against. Johnson has called for attention to the narrative context of the Gospels for understanding individual data. A method that first demonstrates the historical plausibility of individual data then arranges them for interpretation never actually gets beyond the data as discrete elements. He contends that, without the Gospel contexts, interpretation of the data is arbitrary. Once the data are removed from their Gospel contexts, they can be put together in multiple ways, and all such arrangements lack any claim to historical probability. This is because without the framework of the Gospels, we have only facts, facts without context; and facts without context are without meaning.[46] Johnson is clearly sympathetic with a broadly holistic concern to understand particulars in a larger context; and he appreciates the narrative context of the Gospels as necessary for understanding their discrete contents. But Johnson also denies the historical legitimacy of any inference or meaning for the data beyond the Gospels. This is because, he says, the 'methods of critical historiography' can only give us facts, not meanings. For Johnson, historiography cannot access meanings. 'Meanings derive from the interpretation of the facts rather than the facts themselves. And such interpretation depends on story.'[47]

Johnson seems to be in line with a narrative anti-realism, which sees the meaning of events as a matter of narrative emplotment but insists that such emplotment is not continuous with events as they occur in history. The meaning that narrative lends to events is beyond the historian's purview, as far as Johnson is concerned, so historical investigation cannot give us the real meaning of events, but only the

45. Wright, *The New Testament and the People of God*, p. 114.
46. L.T. Johnson, *The Real Jesus*, pp. 124-25.
47. Johnson, *The Real Jesus*, p. 133.

'facts'. Against this, I would of course marshal the case for narrative realism that I have been arguing. Critical history does access meanings, because the meanings by which historical actions were performed are precisely what the historian is after and what historical investigation is about, as far as it is about human intentionality. In this same vein, I would also take issue with Johnson's assumption of a dichotomy between historical fact and meaning. This kind of dichotomy seems to be characteristic of many narrative anti-realists. They usually assume the reality of historical 'facts', such as, in the case of Jesus, that he was baptized by John and crucified by the Romans. But they argue that the meaning of such 'facts' is what is imposed by the historian in the narrative emplotment. I have been arguing that, on the contrary, historical facts are not established independently of historical interpretations. This is the point I have made in the insistence that data control is not done apart from interpretation, and in the argument for a coherence theory of historical truth and verification.[48]

Johnson and Wright together show us what we need for a critical historiography. Wright sees the need for historiography to understand data in a narrative context, but he neglects the comparative work that history requires. Johnson also recognizes the need for a narrative context, but says this context has nothing to do with critical history. If my observations on the difficulties of both these positions are correct, it seems that historiography calls for us to begin with the narrative context of the sources for understanding the data, but not to remain there. Inasmuch as comparisons are crucial for doing history, we must move on to such comparisons *after* an initial understanding of the data within the integrity of the narrative context of the sources. Simply to remain with the sources as our only context for understanding the data would not be to do history, but to do something on the order of New Testament theology. It would give us a description of the understanding of Jesus contained in each source, but would not tell us how those understandings compare to one another, nor how other contexts may shed additional light on the data. It is in this regard that Crossan's identification of meso- and macrocosmic levels of investigation is crucial.

I can suggest, then, an approach to historical Jesus studies along these lines. The historian must begin by understanding all the data in the context of their respective sources, keeping in mind the fact of the narrative intelligibility of historical events and thus of historical data. The historian grasps the total picture of Jesus presented in each source, in its narrative unity and also in its distinctiveness. The narrative context of the sources can be illumined by several tools. Wright has mentioned composition criticism, which can be considered a holistic version of redaction criticism, and looks for the author's overarching purpose that informs the work.[49] Freyne suggests discerning literary constructs such as implied author, narrator and narratee, which are proper to narrative criticism. These types of approaches, and

---

48. On the latter, see above, pp. 162-63.

49. See the apt description of composition criticism by Stephen Moore, *Literary Criticism and the Gospels*, pp. 4ff.

many others, may help elucidate the narrative intelligibility of the data.[50] What must be borne in mind in any approach to the sources is that they are ultimately being treated as pieces of historical evidence. As much as some techniques of narrative analysis may bracket the historical referent, they will eventually have to accommodate the setting of data in wider contexts that is a necessary part of historical work. This leads us to a second part of historical investigation. As the data are understood in their source contexts, other contexts are brought to bear, including information on Crossan's meso- and macrocosmic levels. What is known of first-century Greco-Roman and Palestinian history is brought in to shed light on the significance of the data in a properly historical context. The tools and resources in historical Jesus studies are numerous, including archaeology, sources such as the Dead Sea Scrolls, Josephus, various canonical and non-canonical sources which help establish the wider historical context within which to view the data. Constructs that are derived from these sources, as well as from sociological studies, would be a part of this wider contextualization: models of apocalyptic, sapiential and prophetic traditions, messianic claimants, healers, holy men, Cynic philosophers, examples of banditry or other subversive elements. All are fair game for testing against the data; none can be eliminated a priori if we are doing critical history. In this respect, what I am proposing is a historiography that does not differ from contemporary approaches in its allowance of what can be brought in to further the investigation. But any wider context or historical or sociological model is employed only *after* the data have been given their primary sense by the sources. In this way, the data are handled in relation to such models within a public context with which any investigation must reckon; besides taking account of the narrative intelligibility of the data, this helps guard against models being applied to the data in procrustean fashion, in a method that simply selects the preferred model, applies it to the data, and eliminates any data that do not fit the model.

In the process of applying wider contexts and models to the data, the proposed method will make full use of the comparative tools that drive critical history. The historian will compare the pictures of Jesus that are discerned in the sources with one another, asking how they may fit with each other, or fail to fit, and what this fit tells us about the historical figure behind them, in a way similar to Chilton's 'pentagulation'. In this way the method is clearly not about discovering Jesus as he is portrayed in the sources and simply remaining with these portraits.[51] Comparisons are very much a part of this proposal, but how these comparisons operate is very

---

50. Another possibility is certain uses of 'intertextuality' appropriate to historical investigation. On the various uses of intertextuality, including the historical, see James H. Charlesworth, 'Intertextuality: Isaiah 40.3 and the Serek he-Yahad', in Craig A. Evans and Shemaryahu Talmon (eds.), *The Quest for Context and Meaning: Studies in Biblical Intertextuality in Honor of James A. Sanders* (Leiden: E.J. Brill, 1997), pp. 197-224.

51. *Pace* Funk in his censure of all methods but tradition criticism: 'For third questers there can be no picking and choosing among sayings and acts as a way to determine who Jesus was. Instead, one must present a theory of the whole, set Jesus firmly within first-century Judaism, state what his real aims were, discover why he died, when the church began, and what kind of documents the canonical gospels are', *Honest to Jesus*, p. 65.

different from how they are conceived in a method like Crossan's which we saw above.[52] Because we are understanding the data first of all within their narrative contexts, any further analysis of the data beyond those contexts will be analysis, not so much of discrete units of tradition, but of broad outlines of portraits of Jesus. What we are left with after we see the data in narrative context is an overall picture of Jesus as portrayed in the source in which we find the data. Each source has its picture, and the data are handled in the context of this picture as they are set in wider historical contexts, compared with various models, and compared with one another. The approach to data in this method thus handles them as broad outlines of a portrait and not detachable units of tradition. Such a handling is inevitable when we recognize the narrative intelligibility of historical data. The data *begin* to have their sense in the narrative contexts in which we find them, but this sense is subject to elaboration and alteration as historical investigation proceeds beyond the sources themselves. The sense is elaborated, altered, some of the data are possibly set aside as of lesser historical use, but the narrative context for the data is never simply re-placed. The data function from the beginning in a context of a larger picture, and it is the lineaments of this picture that are the elements which the historian works with in the tasks of wider contextualization and comparisons. So in this method, historical Jesus studies paints with a broad brush. It works primarily with outlines of portraits, not with individual units.

If this method paints with a broad brush, then (to change the metaphor) its work of comparisons will wield blunt tools. In this way the method contrasts with one that uses the criteria of authenticity as surgical instruments for carving out authentic pieces of data. We saw in Crossan that his use of criteria, which revolves primarily around stratification and multiple attestation, reflects a legitimate orientation to critical comparisons among data. Meyer sought to qualify the criteria by considering them indices, which are not invariable rules of thumb for determining authenticity, but are rather patterns of observation and inference that operate in concert with the formulation and testing of hypotheses. In both these approaches, however, the criteria are applied to individual units of tradition. Alternatively, I am suggesting that, since individual data are only understood in the context of a broad outline, the criteria are applied to the outlines as global principles reflecting maxims proper to the work of comparisons. I can illustrate this by considering how Crossan's criteria reflect such principles.

The procedure of stratification, coupled with the criterion that only a tradition attested in the earliest stratum can be considered authentic, reflects the principle of what we can call proximity. The closer in proximity the material is to the event the historian is investigating, the better the chance the material will yield useful information about the event.[53] This is a legitimate supposition, and an axiomatic truth for the purpose of comparisons. We can distinguish material that is closer or further in proximity in a temporal sense, or in a communicative sense. Temporal proximity has to do with how soon after the event the source was recorded; communicative proximity has to do with whether the source was recorded by an

---

52. See Chapter 3, pp. 60-61 and *passim*.
53. See the formulation in Gottschalk, *Understanding History*, p. 150.

eyewitness, or passed along second- or third-hand. Material that is recorded soon after the event is less likely to be subject to the contingencies of memory; material that is recorded by an eyewitness is not subject to the multiple 'filters' of those who passed along the information. Crossan's searching for traditions in the earliest stratum reflects this valuing of material in closest proximity to the event. But in my method, the principle does not become a self-contained criterion. This is especially the case in view of the nature of the data as evidence and not simply testimony. Proximity has its greatest force when the data are being considered as testimony on an event. When the data are handled more generally as evidence, proximity continues to be relevant, but since the data that are not testimonial are not simply discarded, proximity becomes a useful principle for comparing outlines in the sources that may otherwise reflect historical phenomena. Material from what we may identify as a later source would be weighed against material from an earlier one; the relative proximity of the material is *one* factor in an overall argument for preferring an aspect of one source over a competing aspect in another.

The criterion of multiple attestation, by which Crossan counts as likely authentic those traditions which are at least doubly independently attested throughout the strata, reflects the principle of corroboration. According to this principle, the more independent sources that verify an event, the higher the event's claim to veracity, because it was likely not simply created by any of the sources. As Gottschalk states, 'the general rule of historians…is to accept as historical only those particulars which rest upon *the independent testimony of two or more reliable witnesses*.'[54] Again, Gottschalk is treating data specifically as testimony, but corroboration would also apply to data as evidence beyond testimony. Outlines of a portrait that are found in multiple sources generally reflect a more widespread effect or impact resulting from the historical event. Of course, for Crossan, application of this criterion depends heavily on prior decisions of literary dependence among the extant sources. It would appear that the principle of limited similarity[55] would require that we account for similarities among the sources (the synoptic problem) with some explanation of interrelationships. But I have also given factors mitigating the role of such theories in historical investigation of Jesus.[56] The result is that the principle of corroboration is indeed affected by source relationships, but given the qualified role that the latter play in data control and interpretation, and given the need to handle the data as evidence and not simply testimony, genetic relations among the sources cannot be the sine qua non of adequate application of corroboration, as they are for Crossan.

What I am offering here is nothing like a complete taxonomy of criteria of authenticity in terms of principles of comparison. It is simply the recognition that many of the criteria that have been formulated in historical Jesus studies reflect legitimate comparative standards, albeit at a considerable methodological remove

54. Gottschalk, *Understanding History*, p. 166 (emphasis original).
55. See above, pp. 61-62.
56. See above, pp. 62-66.

from how those standards legitimately function.[57] They function properly when they are applied as global principles that guide historians in making judgements in their comparisons, showing them where to look and providing counterbalances for weighing evidence, rather than empirical tests for conclusively establishing usable discrete data.

What Crossan seems to be after in his emphasis on adequate method is the formulation of a public means for evaluating and understanding the data. The disposition behind this emphasis can only be applauded. The more public our decision-making, the more it will be subject to scrutiny by ourselves and others, and the more we will be able to communicate among ourselves about our decisions and their results. But Crossan, like many in historical Jesus research, proposes to make his method public by elevating general critical principles to the status of fixed formal moves that constitute a repeatable method; Crossan does not say so, but it seems that this method, as public, is expected to produce identical results when *identical material investments* are deposited into it. It is my contention that the principles cannot bear this methodological weight. Judgements of the usability of data will have to be made by means of arguments demonstrating that the data support, or else fail to support, a coherent picture; rules of thumb cannot make such decisions on their own. What Crossan suggests is a public method is in fact not as public as he claims, principally because it disregards the contextual nature of the data and of our understanding of them. Beginning with a given, identifiable context for the data (i.e., that of their respective sources), and offering an *argument* (using principles of comparison and many other tools) in pursuit of a coherent picture: this is as 'public' as a method can hope to be.

5. *Narrativity and Hermeneutics*

It is probably his concern for 'public-ness' that is behind Crossan's conception of method as a means of curbing the historian's hermeneutic involvement. I have shown, from his earliest historical Jesus work, that Crossan works with a hermeneutic that does not impinge upon his stated historical method. From his structuralist period to his mature interdisciplinary approach, Crossan seems to formulate and employ historical method in isolation from hermeneutic, and he ultimately relies on method as a means of minimizing the historian's hermeneutic involvement in historical investigation. For this reason, Crossan's formulation of method never takes account of the very presence of the historian as the one doing the investigating. Crossan indeed acknowledges the fact of 'interactivism', a fact which he is too hermeneutically astute to deny: the past and the present interact, changing and challenging one another. Historical method, he says, does not change this interaction,

---

57. Many of the criteria reflect comparative principles, but not all of them. Some of the criteria do not involve comparisons at all, but rather the application, by means of a distilled rule of thumb, of an assumption of what the historical Jesus must have been like. In this way, those criteria are ways of authenticating traditions that happen to cohere with a particular understanding of Jesus. Such criteria would include dissimilarity, and things like distinctive idiom and Aramaic substratum.

but protects the historical object from disfigurement by making enquiry 'honest', which I have taken to mean 'public'.[58] While I agree that making things public is important, as far as it can be done, it is just as important that our method be able to account for its own interactive nature. Otherwise, we will be employing a method that is lacking in self-awareness and thereby also lacking in the capacity for self-criticism.

I have made quite a lot in this concluding historiographic discussion of the contextual nature of observation, knowledge and meaning. I have identified the approach of the holists, as well as narrative realism, as significant methodological appropriations of contextualism. We can in fact identify many different types and levels of contexts that figure into historical investigation. There is the narrative context of the sources that I have been discussing. There is also the context of the historical object, in its many dimensions; this is the context most often referred to and thought of when one speaks of 'historical context': the social, economic, political, environmental, cultural contexts of the historical object that contribute to the historian's grasping the full historical sense and significance of the object. Then there is the specifically narrative context of the object itself, which is not identical to but not completely separate from the various dimensions of the 'historical context'. The object's narrative context is that dimension of narrative intelligibility that we have seen explicated by narrative realism, the narrative that was inherent in the lived experience of the historical agents. This is the narrative context by which the agents acted, that gave their actions and their experience their sense as distinctly human actions. Besides these basic contexts, we could probably think of many others, but the one I would mention here as most significant for a consideration of hermeneutics is the context of the historian's horizons, that broadest of contexts within which the historian lives and observes the world.

The interaction that Crossan describes probably has to do with this broadest context. The horizons that historians carry around with them are what make their history an interaction of themselves with their objects, since the objects cannot but be seen within the horizons. But if Crossan tries to minimize the horizon's presence with his method, Meyer made the most of the horizon in his. We have seen that Meyer distinguished between interpretation and analysis in reading any text. Where historical investigation is concerned, interpretation must precede analysis; the text must be understood on its own terms before it can be analysed in terms other than its own, e.g., in historical analysis. The interpretation that precedes analysis has a significant existential dimension, requiring that the interpreter's horizons be open to the horizons of the text. This is a hermeneutics of goodwill or consent, in which the interpreter 'encounters' the text in a willingness to be confronted and challenged by it. This kind of openness is requisite to adequate understanding of the text. But following on interpretation is analysis, in which something like a hermeneutics of suspicion is appropriate. Meyer said that in such analysis, the historian does history out of the whole fund of his or her personal resources, intellectual, emotional, moral and religious. The course of historical investigation

58. Crossan, *Birth*, pp. 42-44.

depends on the questions that the historian brings to the sources, and these questions are autonomous, the historian's own questions, not fixed even by the sources
(unlike in interpretation). The historian's questions arise out of his or her personal
resources, which is to say that historical investigation and historical results are
what they are from within the historian's horizons. It does not seem, however, that
Meyer wanted to relativize critical history radically, in the way that some of his
comments on the role of the horizon seem to do. For not only is Meyer's hermeneutic 'critical', it is also 'realist': though understanding is a matter of insight,
judgement and horizons, it is capable of being accurate understanding of real
objects.

In Meyer's emphasis on interpretation that precedes analysis we can find common ground with an emphasis on beginning with the context of the sources for
historical investigation. In both cases, the text is necessarily understood on its own
terms before the data are seen in any other context. But to Meyer's efforts to articulate the role of horizons (which is arguably the basic hermeneutical question) in
both interpretation and analysis we can add some observations from narrativity.
These observations may help to clarify the dynamics of the historian's understanding of the historical object from within the horizonal context.

Once again, N.T. Wright has already been where we want to go, and we can
use his observations as a point of departure. Wright's version of critical realism is
fundamentally about knowledge taking place within worldview, worldview being
expressed in narrative. Known objects are only such by virtue of their being perceived within events or narratives. The worldview context makes knowledge a
dialogue or conversation between knower and known, or between humans with
their narratives, and the events with theirs. Historical knowledge is ultimately a
dialogue between the historian's worldview and the worldview of the object.[59] It
is this dialogue that Crossan echoes in his expression of 'interactivism'. This dialogue or interaction has to do with the presence of non-public horizons in the historical investigation. Horizons are non-public in the sense that they are not subject
to arguments advancing proof or disproof, because they are the necessary context
for all arguments and all proofs. But if the historian does history fundamentally
from within a horizon that cannot be demonstrated, how can historical investigation and results ultimately be justified? For by definition the horizon, the ultimate context for observation, is what the historian brings to the investigation from
his or her personal resources. No one else sees with his or her eyes. Of course,
these are basic hermeneutical questions;[60] the issues involved and the proposed
answers are legion, and we cannot hope to survey them here. But narrativity helps
us address these questions in relation to historiography: How can we articulate
the effect of horizon on historiography without radically relativizing historical
method and its results? Can we describe where or how the 'dialogue' takes place
in historiography?

---

59. Wright, *The New Testament and the People of God*, pp. 43-44.
60. Where, by 'hermeneutics' is meant, not rules for interpretation of texts, but more generally,
the understanding of understanding.

The microhistorians have an appreciation for the role of narrative in historiography that helps us begin to see how narrativity is relevant for hermeneutics. We have seen that microhistory focuses on history on the minute scale. It values the particular, the individual and the anomalous in an effort to balance out a focus on the social with its structures, generalizations and law-like regularities. The latter sometimes threaten to absorb the individual and the unique, offering oversimplifications of what is actually a very complex and fluid reality. Seeing the life of a single, ordinary person, or possibly the life of a small community (which would not ordinarily be considered significant politically, socially, or culturally) as historically significant is the hallmark of microhistory, in a belief that reality is too complex to be exhausted by easy generalizations.[61] Narrative factors into this approach to history specifically as a *means of expression* that qualifies objectivity in historical knowledge. Microhistory sees the complexities of historical reality as calling for fluid conceptualizations and modest assertions on the part of the historian. A large part of this complexity is the relation between large-scale normative social systems and the freedom of the actions of individual agents.[62] Narrative description helps demonstrate the relation between these in that it describes the individual and the anomalous, which cannot be represented properly by generalization and quantitative formalization. The fluidity that characterizes the social, with its shifting interrelationships and constantly adapting configurations, is best captured in the non-discursive descriptions of the narrative mode. Narrativity also shows historical knowledge to be the mediated knowledge that it is: inferred from often fragmentary evidence, by way of hypotheses and arguments. The microhistorians suggest that narrative does this by explicitly describing the research process, making the researcher's point of view an intrinsic part of the historical account. In this way 'The reader is involved in a sort of dialogue and participates in the whole process of constructing the historical argument.'[63]

This explication of narrativity as a means of expression contrasts somewhat with narrativity as a quality of experience which we have seen in Carr. The microhistorians are immediately concerned with the use of narrative for 'writing up' history, though it is not the case that they see narrative as merely an ancillary tool in the service of more properly analytical means of acquiring historical knowledge.

---

61. See the description and critique by Iggers, *Historiography in the Twentieth Century*, pp. 109ff.; also Levi, 'On Microhistory', p. 110. Two classic microhistorical works include Levi, *Inheriting Power: The Story of an Exorcist* (trans. Lydia G. Cochrane; Chicago: University of Chicago Press, 1988); and Carlo Ginzburg, *The Cheese and the Worms: The Cosmos of a Sixteenth-Century Miller* (trans. John Tedeschi and Anne C. Tedeschi; Baltimore: The Johns Hopkins University Press, 1980).

62. This relation is of course an ongoing issue in the social sciences, with 'hermeneutic' approaches emphasizing the individual, while nomological or 'positivist' approaches emphasize the primacy of determinative social structures.

63. Levi, 'On Microhistory', p. 106; see also the discussion of Carlo Ginzburg, who says that, as the study of humans as such, history involves a kind of unformalizable knowledge that infers from clues (which he says is the point of Peirce's abductive reasoning), 'Clues: Roots of an Evidential Paradigm', in *Clues, Myths and the Historical Method* (trans. John Tedeschi and Anne C. Tedeschi; Baltimore: The Johns Hopkins University Press, 1989), p. 106 and *passim*.

The microhistorians are probably not as concerned to work out a rationale for narrativity as is Carr, but they clearly see narrative as significant in that it is the only adequate means of dealing with the complexity and fluidity of the particular and its relation to the general. For the microhistorians this fluidity translates into a substantial qualification of the presumed objectivity of the historian's knowledge. Since social reality is constantly shifting and adapting vis-à-vis individual experience, the past as social will be a constantly moving target for the historian. The historian's knowledge of such a target will necessarily be a modest approximation; anything like a firm, empiricist grip on history is therefore elusive. Narrative reflects both the fluid nature of the historical object and the tentative nature of the historian's knowledge of the object. Something like this seems to be what the microhistorians have in mind when they say that narrativity shows historical knowledge to be 'mediated' by describing the research process and making the researcher's point of view intrinsic to the historical account. In their narratives, historians include a description of their own acquisition of knowledge of the historical object and thereby invite the reader into the knowing process with them. So narrative expression is necessary for dealing adequately with the historical object and for accommodating the nature of the historian's knowledge of the object.

Along with this, one might also say that, more generally, narrative is necessary for dealing with the distinctly human.[64] My observations on narrativity as concerned with human intentionality are relevant here,[65] and lead us back to Carr's narrative realism. Carr makes his contribution to the philosophy of history in distinction from the analytic approach, which deals directly with questions of epistemology. Instead, we have seen, Carr treats narrative in terms of its role in our lived experience. As individuals and as communities, we experience and act out of a narrative intelligibility. This narrativity of experience suggests for Carr that 'we have a connection to the historical past, as ordinary persons, prior to and independently of adopting the historical-cognitive interest.'[66] Phenomenologically speaking, this is a *pre-thematic* awareness of the past which functions as the background for

---

64. Hubert Dreyfus's comments are relevant, on the possibility of observation in the human sciences ('Holism and the Human Sciences'). In a discussion on the implications of holism for the sciences, Dreyfus distinguishes between a theoretical and a practical holism. In the former, a theoretical/conceptual background is the context in which all data are seen. Hypothesis and data form a circle in which we move to verify a theory. In practical holism, shared practices form the background, and cannot be formalized into a theory. All observation takes place within these two wholes. In the natural sciences, the practical whole, which is the procedures and techniques of observation and investigation, need not be referred to as part of an observation. But the practical whole must be an integral part of the observation proper to the human sciences. The latter cannot leave out the social skills that make the isolation of features or attributes of human behaviour possible. '[I]f the human sciences claim to study human activities, then the human sciences, unlike the natural sciences, must take account of those human activities which make possible their own disciplines', p. 240. We might take from this that historiography must take account of the nature of human activities that make its investigation of human history possible.

65. See above, pp. 169, 174ff.

66. Carr, *Time, Narrative and History*, p. 3.

our present experience. In all this, Carr is getting at the roots in ordinary experience of our doing history. Narrative historical accounts arise out of the very nature of historical experience, as an extension of it.[67] Inasmuch as we live presently by means of narrativity, our narration of the past is an outgrowth of our present narrative experience. This is seen most clearly as historians write of the recent past of their own group or society, where they live in the milieu of an already-existing narrative and write out of that story. But it is also true of the histories historians write of the distant past, or of groups of which historians are not a part.[68] It is the historians' own narrative-historical experience that is the very possibility of their doing history. Or, their own human experience is the fundamental possibility of their ability to observe and write about human activities of the past.

Lonergan conceived the field of historical investigation along similar lines.[69] He said that the field of history is characterized by conscious and intentional human actions that are meaningful. Meaning is partly constitutive of human action, and the historical field is the field of meaningful speech and action.[70] Also, in a manner that anticipated Carr's narrative categories, Lonergan noted that the 'psychological present', which seems to be similar to Carr's phenomenology of temporal experience, is constituted by the group's memories of the past and anticipations of the future. In view of the fact that history is about meaningful action, and historical experience is constituted by group memories and anticipations, the human being is a historical being; and being historical means that we 'live off our past'. We are at least partly constituted by our history, or, as Carr would say, by our narrativity. This constituting history Lonergan referred to as 'existential history': 'the living tradition which formed us and thereby brought us to the point where we began forming ourselves.'[71] This existential history is fragmentary and partial, and from it a rudimentary history may be drawn, but beyond this one moves to critical history by a process of objectification. But the existential history, one's narrative experience, is the starting point for any historical enquiry, the context within which history is undertaken.

Narrative experience is not only the context, but also the very possibility for our doing history. Our narrativity is thus not simply something to be bracketed, some-

---

67. Carr, *Time, Narrative and History*, p. 169.

68. Carr, *Time, Narrative and History*, p. 174.

69. Andrew Beards has attempted to show how Lonergan's cognitional theory can serve as a direct support for a kind of narrative realism. He reasons that Lonergan's account of cognitional structure is of a structure that unfolds over time, 'and of which one will present a narrative account if one raises and answers the question "What am I doing when I come to know?" It is an instance of a "narrative" aspect of reality', *Objectivity and Historical Understanding* (Aldershot: Avebury, 1997), p. 142. Beards prefers such a case for narrativity inhering in experience, over the case made by David Carr, because Carr relies on Husserl, and Beards says Husserl did not make a case for the objectivity of knowledge. As we have seen, Carr is not presenting an epistemology of narrativity but a phenomenology; but he clearly is making a case for a 'realist' understanding of narrative in human experience, and such would be amenable to elaboration of narrative as an object of historical knowledge.

70. Lonergan, *Method*, p. 178.

71. Lonergan, *Method*, p. 182.

thing that our method is designed to hold back, lest it intrude on our ability to observe and to understand the historical object. Without the personal resources residing in our narrativity, we would not have the capacity to grasp the historical object in its narrative intelligibility. Out of our narrativity we interact with and lay hold of the narrativity of the human past. An awareness of this narrative milieu in which historical investigation moves allows us to make the narrative medium of our living an integral part of the historical investigation. The sense we make of our present experience is the basis on which we discover the sense-making narratives of the actions of historical agents. All this is fundamentally true to Crossan's hermeneutic awareness of the interactive nature of our knowledge. It is also, and even more so, true to the vision of Ben Meyer, for whom objectivity is contingent upon authentic subjectivity; true knowledge depends on the operation of subjective resources. In the field of history, our knowledge of the past depends upon the narrativity we share with the past.

Appendix 1

THE CRITERIA OF AUTHENTICITY: CRITICISMS AND NEW DIRECTIONS

In the 200-year history of Jesus studies, there has been no lack of discussion of how historical investigation into Jesus should proceed. It would be reasonable to expect such lengthy discussion to result in methodological advancement, or least some consensus on significant issues. A measure of agreement can in fact be shown to be the case, in particular areas. Variety remains, however, in other more substantial areas. We can observe both agreements and disagreements in method; here we will be focusing particularly on those tools that have been the most frequent objects of discussion, the criteria of authenticity. Consideration of the proper role of these criteria points up significant distinctions in method in Jesus studies today. There have arisen certain trends in the formulation of the criteria and in suggestions for their revision. These observations lead us to consider important alternative conceptions of the overall role of the criteria in historical investigation.

We will begin with a survey of some exemplary traditional formulations of the criteria along with general descriptions of how they should operate in investigation of Jesus.[1] We will then note criticisms of the criteria and modifications of them from within the traditional conceptions of their role, followed by criticisms which point in a new direction, what I have called in this study a methodological 'holism'.

1. *The Traditional Formulation of the Criteria*

As they are traditionally formulated, the criteria of authenticity are tests applied to individual traditions in the primary sources on Jesus (both canonical and non-canonical), to determine what of them is actual data on the historical Jesus. Applied to the sayings, the criteria are meant to determine what we can attribute to the speech of the Jesus of history. Applied to narrative material, the criteria are supposed to reveal what is likely to have been an actual occurrence in Jesus' life and career.

In a 1987 paper, Dennis Polkow catalogued 25 separate criteria, compiled from five authors spanning sixteen years.[2] I use this survey as our starting point for exam-

---

1. A recent and thorough survey of the criteria can be found in Stanley E. Porter, *The Criteria for Authenticity in Historical-Jesus Research: Previous Discussion and New Proposals* (JSNTSup, 191; Sheffield: Sheffield Academic Press, 2000).

2. Dennis Polkow, 'Method and Criteria for Historical Jesus Research', *SBL 1987 Seminar*

ining the criteria because it presents an effective distillation of what most scholars would consider all the possible criteria available: as we shall see below, what counts as a criterion is a matter of some debate, and spreading our tent widely in the beginning will allow us to narrow the discussion as we progress. Polkow eliminates four of the criteria as invalid, and combines the others to come up with a total of eight separate criteria, which he orders hierarchically in the following scheme:

1. *Preliminary Criteria*

    a.   *Discounting Redaction* – This involves determining the final redaction of the evangelist, to distinguish it from all earlier material with which the evangelist was working. This material is identified and discounted as inauthentic.

    b.   *Discounting Tradition* – The point of this criterion 'is to basically locate specific tendencies in the transmission of material in the gospels as we now have them and then apply these back into the pre-gospel stages'.[3] The purpose is to identify what is the middle layer of tradition, between the redaction level and the earliest level; this middle layer is bracketed and discounted.

2. *Primary Criteria*

    a.   *Dissimilarity* – What is dissimilar both from tendencies in Jesus' Jewish environment and from the theology of the early church has a claim to authenticity. Polkow notes that this criterion 'is the real basis for the entire "new quest" of the historical Jesus'.[4] He says it was first pioneered by Bultmann, but was a peripheral issue for him. It was put into common usage by the post-Bultmannians, Käsemann and Conzelmann.

    b.   *Coherence* – Material that coheres with other readily accepted Jesus material is authentic.

    c.   *Multiple Attestation* – Polkow says this is the oldest and most obvious of the criteria. It includes attestation of a tradition in multiple independent sources (e.g., Mark, Q, M, L, etc.) as well as in multiple forms (e.g., parable, aphorism, miracle story, etc.).

3. *Secondary Criteria* – These criteria are valid only on material that has passed successfully through one or more of the primary criteria.

    a.   *Palestinian Context* – What reflects the Palestinian milieu of Jesus' time has a claim to authenticity.

Papers (ed. Kent H. Richards; Atlanta: Scholars Press, 1987), pp. 336-56. The five authors are W.O. Walker (1969), N.J. McEleney (1972), R.H. Stein (1980), J. Breech (1980) and M.E. Boring (1985). For fuller bibliography on the criteria, see William Telford, 'Major Trends and Interpretive Issues', pp. 66-67.

  3.   Polkow, 'Method and Criteria', p. 344.

  4.   Polkow, 'Method and Criteria', p. 347.

b. *Style* – That which conforms to various aspects of Jesus' style from what is known to be authentic material also has a claim to authenticity.

c. *Scholarly Consensus* – This amounts to a 'head count' of which material is accepted by which scholars, for whatever reason. It serves a collaborative purpose when all other criteria have been applied.

The inventory provided by Polkow is useful in two ways: (1) in its content, it represents a list of the most widely recognized and utilized criteria; and (2) in its arrangement, it illustrates the role the criteria have played in relation to tradition criticism. Polkow's 'preliminary criteria' are actually just this, principles of tradition criticism that have typically been used in conjunction with the criteria. Tradition criticism, here understood, involves determining as far as possible the history of the oral transmission of an isolated saying or narrative, for the recovery of its earliest detectable form. Polkow describes this method as dealing with the units of tradition like peeling an onion, dealing with outermost layers first and working inward. The outermost layer is redactional material, contributed by the evangelist; the middle layer is traditional material, acquired through the process of oral transmission; and the innermost layer is what may be authentic material on Jesus, insofar as this is historically possible to determine. Once this innermost layer is identified, only this material is then subject to the primary and secondary criteria, to determine what is data on Jesus.

This formulation of the criteria is what John Dominic Crossan has called the 'classic methodological model' for Jesus research: *transmission* followed by *verification*. First, determine the stratigraphic location of a given unit of tradition within the transmission of tradition; second, verification: what cannot be seen to derive from identifiable redactional levels may still derive from some unidentifiable moment in the tradition and not from Jesus. Authentic Jesus material is verified in the earliest stratum by application of the criteria of authenticity.[5] Norman Perrin's description of this classic model is its classic formulation, and one of the best-known sources for linking the criteria, particularly the criterion of dissimilarity, with the placing of the 'burden of proof' upon the one who would claim authenticity for a tradition, due to the theological nature of the synoptic tradition.[6] In these issues Perrin was of course in concert with the New Quest.[7]

2. *Internal Criticisms of the Criteria*

So the traditional conception of the role of the criteria sees them as tests to be applied to the earliest detected stratum or form of an individual unit of tradition, to determine whether the unit can be considered to originate with Jesus. The foremost of these criteria has been, as pointed out by Polkow, that of dissimilarity, ever since

---

5. John Dominic Crossan, 'Divine Immediacy and Human Immediacy', p. 123.
6. See Perrin, *Rediscovering the Teaching of Jesus*, pp. 38-39.
7. See James Robinson, *A New Quest of the Historical Jesus*, p. 38; R.H. Fuller, *A Critical Introduction to the New Testament* (London: Gerald Duckworth, 1966), pp. 94-98.

it was made programmatic for Jesus studies in the New Quest. The traditional formulation of the criteria did not, however, remain unchallenged for long. Criticisms
of them were early, from various perspectives and with varying results. A few of
the more significant suggestions for modification, which still operate mostly within
the original tradition-critical conception of their application, will be considered
here.

In a 1972 article, D.G.A. Calvert expressed some dissatisfaction with the use of
form criticism in Jesus studies, and with the criteria of authenticity that form
criticism had produced.[8] He offered a reexamination of the criteria, in which he
cast them in groups negative and positive. The negative criteria are those which
purportedly can be used to demonstrate that a particular piece of tradition is not
authentic. Inauthentic material includes that which: (1) accords with the teaching
of the early church; (2) accords with the teaching of contemporary Judaism; (3)
presupposes a situation unthinkable at the time of Jesus; (4) contradicts material
known to be authentic; or (5) can be shown through comparison with parallel material to be a development of that other material. The positive criteria demonstrate
that a tradition is authentic. Demonstrably authentic material includes that which:
(1) is positively distinctive from Jewish thought; (2) is positively distinctive from
the thought of the post-Easter church; (3) contains elements that could not be from
the church; (4) exhibits linguistic Aramaisms and reflects the Palestinian environment; (5) is found in more than one tradition or form; and (6) is characteristic of
the teaching of Jesus known to be authentic.

One may note that some of the criteria cast by Calvert as negative are simply
negative restatements of the positive criteria, e.g., positively, a saying is authentic
if it is distinctive from Jewish thought, while negatively, a saying is not authentic if
it accords with the contemporary teaching of Judaism. Calvert himself acknowledges some 'overlap' between the positive and negative criteria,[9] but his final
reason for the negative/positive distinction is clear in his conclusion that *only the
positive criteria should be employed*. He sees no value in ruling out inauthentic
material by means of the negative criteria prior to application of the positive tests,
which he notes has been the common approach. He says that form criticism has
tended to dominate in the determination of criteria, and Calvert recommends a new
approach which draws on form criticism, but also uses the resources of source and
redaction criticism. Source criticism has shown the value of the fifth positive
criterion (multiple attestation), form criticism that of the first two (combined into
one criterion of 'distinctiveness'), and redaction criticism is useful as a criterion
that resembles what Polkow later called 'discounting redaction'.

What we see in Calvert would become a common criticism of the criteria as they
are traditionally formulated: their value as positive support for historicity can be

---

8.   D.G.A. Calvert, 'An Examination of the Criteria for Distinguishing the Authentic Words of
Jesus', *New Testament Studies* 18 (1972), pp. 209-19. Note the use of the term 'form criticism' for
what some would call 'tradition criticism'. Though there is a technical difference between these
terms, their overlap causes them to be used practically interchangeably in the literature, at least
when it comes to discussion of their relation to the criteria of authenticity.

9.   Calvert, 'An Examination', p. 211.

maintained, but whether they can legitimately demonstrate that a tradition is not authentic is a different matter. Even Polkow, in his traditional casting of the various criteria, has observed that, once the preliminary tradition-critical methods have been applied, the primary and secondary criteria could be used only positively, to demonstrate historicity, not negatively, to deny it.[10] I would point out, however, that his criticism holds specifically for the critics within the original conception of how the criteria are to function: as tests to be applied to individual and isolated bits of tradition, in order to determine their authenticity, thereby contributing to the pool of historical data on Jesus.

Another major modification of the criteria has concerned the criterion of dissimilarity. Perhaps because it has been widely acknowledged as the most significant criterion, and the most assured in its potential results, it has also been subject to the most scrutiny. Crossan's use of the criterion throughout his career illustrates in microcosm the course that the criterion has taken. In his 1973 work *In Parables*, Crossan commenced his contribution to the historical and literary analysis of Jesus' parables. In this work he outlined a five-step methodology for the New Quest of the historical Jesus, which he employed to determine what of the parable material of the Gospels can be attributed to the Jesus of history.[11] There is clearly reflected in this method what Crossan later called the 'classic methodological model' for Jesus research: the history of transmission of a piece of tradition is reconstructed, to determine its earliest form. To this form are applied the criteria of authenticity, in this case dissimilarity, to determine the tradition's historicity. Throughout his parables research in the 1970s, Crossan continued the quest for recovery of the authentic words of Jesus, using such a method.[12]

In the late 1980s Crossan offered a revision of the criterion of dissimilarity, in the form of his *criterion of adequacy* which he suggested as a new 'first principle' in historical Jesus studies.[13] '[T]hat is original which best explains the multiplicity engendered in the tradition.'[14] With this Crossan posed a serious challenge to the criterion of dissimilarity, which had dominated among the criteria. He is, however, like Calvert, still operating with the criteria as they have been traditionally conceived. As I have shown in my analysis of Crossan, the criteria are tests applied to isolated traditions to determine historicity; and they still function within a tradition-critical context. In the above article, after proposing his new first principle Crossan undertakes a transmissional analysis of the aphoristic cluster of sayings in Mt. 5.39b-42 = Lk. 6.29-30 = *Gos. Thom.* 95 ('turn the other cheek'), followed by a linking of the authentic form of the sayings with the historical Jesus by application of his new criterion. Crossan's criticisms of the criterion of dissimilarity remain securely within the traditional context.

10. Polkow, 'Method and Criteria', pp. 351-52. Note also Marcus Borg, 'What Did Jesus Really Say?' *Bible Review* 5 (1989), pp. 18-25.

11. See above, pp. 19-20.

12. This in spite of ever-extensive forays into the literary-critical domain of structuralism and deconstruction, which he (somewhat inconsistently) applied to the recovered historical form of the parables. See Chapter 1.

13. See above, p. 47.

14. Crossan, 'Divine Immediacy', p. 125.

In a recent monograph, Gerd Theissen and Dagmar Winter have mounted a rigorous and cogent criticism of the criterion of dissimilarity.[15] They identify it, along with the criterion of coherence, as the only true criteria of *authenticity* that have been proposed. They divide all other criteria into two groups: those that establish the value of sources, and those that look for distinctive features of Jesus' speech. The former category can be seen to be parallel with Polkow's preliminary, tradition-critical criteria; these establish the relative age, interdependence and provenance of sources, with a view to discounting redactional and transmissional elements in the tradition. The 'distinctive features' category, roughly parallel to Polkow's secondary criteria, utilizes such criteria as the linguistic ones developed by Jeremias. Theissen and Winter list several examples of such criteria, whose significance for Jesus research has been both over- and underestimated. The criteria in these two categories are applied to traditions apart from the actual application of authenticity criteria proper. The source-value arguments belong to discussion prior to true authenticity criteria, in a way similar to the application of transmissional analysis, while the evidences of distinctive features presuppose those criteria. The latter establish the distinctive features of Jesus' preaching vis-à-vis all other traditions only with the prior help of the criterion of dissimilarity. But both of these criteria (source value and distinctive features) together decide whether the authenticity or the inauthenticity of a Jesus tradition is to be proven: they determine whether the burden of proof will be on the one who claims authenticity or the one who claims inauthenticity. But they themselves are not sufficient proofs of either. Proof is born by the other criteria, dissimilarity and coherence. The authors point out that the criterion of dissimilarity, however, has been a problem in the latest developments of Jesus research.[16]

The authors demonstrate that, though the criterion of dissimilarity became programmatic in the period of the New Quest, it has in fact been latent in Jesus research since the early nineteenth century; different phases of Jesus research simply cast the criterion differently depending on contemporary interests in Jesus. For the liberal lives of Jesus, his dissimilarity with the later church was the important point. For the New Quest, dissimilarity with the Jewish context maintained central importance. But all formulations of the criterion overlook the possible continuity of Jesus with both his Jewish environment and early Christianity. The criterion also fails to take into account the limitations of our knowledge both of early Christianity and first-century Judaism; and in view of the plurality within both early Christianity and Judaism, the claims to difference or differentiation lose their particularity. In point of fact, 'every piece of Jesus tradition would fit within the manifold spectrum of Judaism and early Christianity.'[17] The question would become rather, against

---

15. Theissen and Winter, *Die Kriterienfrage in der Jesusforschung*.

16. Theissen and Winter, *Die Kriterienfrage in der Jesusforschung*, pp. 18-19.

17. Theissen and Winter, *Die Kriterienfrage in der Jesusforschung*, pp. 6-7. This echoes Crossan's observation of plurality within ancient Christianity and Judaism. The authors identify Crossan as one who renounces the criterion of dissimilarity in favour of a combined criterion of stratification and multiple attestation. They say his method has an undeniable intellectual charm; its clarity and methodological consequence are attractive. But ultimately his method is only useful for establishing the relative age of traditions, not their authenticity.

which form of early Christianity is Jesus to be seen? How did the various pictures of Jesus develop? And where do they meet? These questions call for a new identification of criteria.

Alternatively, the authors propose a criterion of double *plausibility*. It is not possible to maintain the criterion of double dissimilarity in its traditional form. The historian cannot be concerned with 'differentiation' only. The historian must be interested in locating Jesus in relation to his context and resulting effects, whether continuity or discontinuity is established. Both are important for a methodologically comprehensible reconstruction of the historical Jesus. That is historical in the tradition which can be plausibly explained in terms of Jesus' Palestinian Jewish context, and in terms of the historical impact that he had upon his followers which resulted in the early church. As far as these authors are concerned, 'Only the transformation of research strategy by theological demands (grounded in the hero- and genius-cults of the nineteenth century and in the kerygma-theological reduction of the historical Jesus to a bare 'that' in the twentieth) can...cancel out the connection between historical method and the embedding of Jesus in a relationship with Jewish origins and Christian effects.'[18]

A final criticism of the criterion of dissimilarity that deserves mention is that of Craig Evans.[19] His evaluation is one that has become standard: the criterion is inadequate because it only identifies what is unique to Jesus, and the quest is for what is distinctive, not necessarily what is unique.[20] After reviewing possible criteria,[21] Evans proposes a criterion that tweaks the criterion of dissimilarity and combines several of the other criteria as well: 'Material that reflects the social, political and theological context of Jesus' time, but does not reflect the interests of the church in ways that are inconsistent with those of Jesus, has a reasonable claim to authenticity. This is especially so, if the material enjoys early and widespread attestation.'[22] This criterion fulfils the condition that 'an appropriate criterion should call for coherence with conditions that prevailed in Jesus' time, which, by definition, will often mean dissimilarity to a greater or lesser extent to the conditions that prevailed in the early church'.[23]

Evans acknowledges that his new criterion presupposes several of the older criteria; this is most clearly the case in the fact that authentic tradition should not be 'inconsistent with [the interests] of Jesus'. Those interests would have to be established by other criteria; so the second half of Evan's criterion is something like the criterion of coherence, or perhaps a criterion of 'lack of conflict'. I would

---

18. Theissen and Winter, *Die Kriterienfrage in der Jesusforschung*, p. xi.

19. Craig Evans, 'Authenticity Criteria in Life of Jesus Research', *Christian Scholar's Review* 19 (1989), pp. 6-31.

20. Evans, 'Authenticity Criteria', p. 25.

21. Evans's list includes ten criteria: multiple attestation, multiple forms, Semitic features and Palestinian background, proleptic (futurist) eschatology, dissimilarity, least distinctive (similar to the criterion in text-criticism), tradition contrary to editorial tendency, prophetic criticism, contradiction (of known authentic traditions or of the Palestinian environment) and consistency (coherence).

22. Evans, 'Authenticity Criteria', pp. 26-27.

23. Evans, 'Authenticity Criteria', p. 26.

note, however, that Evans's two examples of application of his criterion (to the parable of the wicked tenants and the parable of the prodigal son) seem most concerned to demonstrate dissimilarity from the early church, in response to the observation frequently made that these particular parables reflect specific church concerns and are therefore not from Jesus.[24] So in effect, Evans's modification of dissimilarity amounts to dropping the requirement of dissimilarity from Judaism and keeping that of dissimilarity from the church.

Apart from the matter of whether there is genuine novelty in Evans's new criterion, I would point out his general posture on the criteria, reflecting his overall understanding of how the criteria are to function in Jesus studies. In this we see that Evans falls mostly within the traditional conception of the criteria. He grants to them the status of independent tools that can determine the historicity of individual traditions: they provide a measure of 'objective control over the task of assessing the individual components that make up the gospels'.[25] Such objective control is meant to be a check against a haphazard selection of material based upon a preconceived picture of what the Jesus of history was or was not like.

The dangers of the kind of subjectivity described by Evans are real. So too is the need for some form of 'objectivity' in an area of public discourse such as historical enquiry into a figure like Jesus. It will not do simply to have a tacit preconception of Jesus in control of the historical enterprise. It is for this reason that matters of historical method need the fullest explication. What we now turn to consider is whether the criteria of authenticity as they have been traditionally conceived and formulated are up to the task they have been assigned. The authors we have surveyed in this section have offered necessary modifications of the criteria, especially the criterion of dissimilarity,[26] while remaining within the tradition of enquiry that uses the criteria in the context of tradition criticism and/or as tools capable of scrutinizing individual traditions for their likely status as historical data on Jesus.[27] But the status of the criteria as the most effective means of control over historical

---

24. See a similar argument in Evans, 'Reconstructing Jesus' Teaching: Prospects and Proposals', in Bruce Chilton and Craig A. Evans (eds.), *Jesus in Context: Temple, Purity, and Restoration* (Arbeiten zur Geschichte des Antiken Judentums und des Urchristentums, XXXIX; Leiden: E.J. Brill, 1997), pp. 145-76.

25. Evans, 'Authenticity Criteria', p. 24.

26. For a dissenting voice on dissimilarity, see David Mealand, 'The Dissimilarity Test', *Scottish Journal of Theology* 31 (1978), pp. 41-50. Mealand sees the criterion of double dissimilarity as valuable for isolating sayings and deeds of Jesus which would help account for the transition from Judaism to Christianity. It assumes that Jesus was, to some degree, the middle term between Judaism and early Christianity, and seeks to understand the way this was so by seeing what of his message can function as a distinct middle term. It is this function of Jesus as the middle term that justifies our looking for what is 'dissimilar' in his message, vis-à-vis both Judaism and Christianity. Mealand believes this answers the objection that the dissimilarity criterion gives us not what is characteristic of Jesus, but only what is unique.

27. The recent monograph by Porter gives a thorough survey of the course of development of the criteria, along with suggestions for new linguistic criteria that take account of the possibility of a Greek-speaking milieu for Jesus. But Porter's overall conception of the criteria remains within the traditional one as described here.

enquiry has been seriously challenged in some quarters. We will next consider some of those challenges.

3. *Criticisms in New Directions*

In two articles written in the early 1970s, Morna Hooker offered critique that has come to be much-cited in reviews of method in Jesus studies.[28] Her comments were incisive in two areas: (1) their evaluation of the criteria of dissimilarity and coherence, and (2) their general observation of the limitations of tradition criticism. Hooker's insights represent the beginning of new directions in the use of the traditional tools, directions that began to manifest themselves at a very early stage in the application of the criteria and their tradition-critical milieu.

Hooker criticizes 'traditio-historical' method, which she says is characterized by the criteria of dissimilarity and coherence. She cites Bultmann, Käsemann, Conzelmann, Perrin and Fuller as advocates of the method. Her listing of faulty logic in the criteria has been borrowed frequently enough that most of its arguments have become standard; many of the authors in the previous section echo her observations. For this reason her list bears repeating:

1. dissimilarity gives us what is *unique* to Jesus, but not necessarily what is *characteristic* of him
2. dissimilarity assumes considerable knowledge of both early Christianity and Judaism against which to compare Jesus, and such knowledge is today not assured
3. dissimilarity begs the question it is supposed to address. 'We begin our examination of the Gospel material with a tool which denies the possibility of overlapping [between Jesus and the church], and which insists on Jesus' uniqueness. Such a tool is bound to produce a picture in keeping with its assumption – and that is precisely what we get… The method dictates its own conclusions'[29]
4. the determination of what is 'dissimilar' is subjective. Such a criterion is also at odds with criteria such as Aramaic substratum and the general notion that an authentic saying should be 'at home' in first-century Judaism
5. the determination of what is 'coherent' is also subjective
6. errors made in the application of dissimilarity will be magnified in the application of coherence[30]
7. the criteria are, in practice, often inconsistently applied

28. Morna Hooker, 'Christology and Methodology', *New Testament Studies* 17 (1971), pp. 480-87; 'On Using the Wrong Tool', *Theology* 75 (1972), pp. 570-81.

29. Hooker, 'Christology and Methodology', p. 482.

30. The 'critically assured minimum' of material supposedly produced by the criterion of dissimilarity is, in the traditional formulation, to be expanded by addition of further material that may not pass that criterion but coheres with that core material. But if the application of dissimilarity results in an erroneous core, then the addition of material coherent with that core will magnify the error.

In view of these objections to the criteria, how is one to proceed in historical enquiry into Jesus? At this stage, Hooker appreciates form criticism, but insists that it is not 'a key to unlock all mysteries'.[31] She is not optimistic about tradition criticism's ability to reconstruct the process of development of the tradition. Concerning the criteria themselves, rather than separating the Gospel material into rigid divisions of 'authentic' or 'non-authentic', Hooker recommends grading traditions on a scale based on several criteria, with more relative weight given to some traditions than to others. This is because 'All the material comes to us at the hands of the believing community, and probably it all bears its mark to a lesser or greater extent; to confine our picture of Jesus to material which passes all our tests for genuineness is too restricting.'[32] The criteria used to determine relative probability will include dissimilarity and multiple attestation (both used positively only), Aramaisms, parable form and paradox and irony.

If she previously saw some value in form criticism, Hooker later abandoned that optimism. In the latter of the two articles we are considering, Hooker insists plainly at the outset that 'the tools which are used in an attempt to uncover the authentic teaching of Jesus cannot do what is required of them.'[33] As opposed to her earlier view, she now wonders whether form criticism is of any use at all in historical Jesus studies. Form criticism seems to be a legitimate *literary* tool, to the degree that it identifies and distinguishes, e.g., what is a miracle story, an apophthegm, etc., but Hooker finds this use uninteresting. The second stage of form criticism is more interesting, that of determining the *Sitz im Leben*, the way the material was used by the community when it was put into writing. The circularity of this tool, however, makes it imprecise: we do not have independent knowledge of the communities behind the traditions, so our knowledge of such must be based upon what is found in the traditions themselves; but our knowledge of the community is what is used to make the traditions intelligible as traditions of those communities. Without some independent knowledge of the community setting, great imaginative (creative) ability on the part of the historian is involved.

Hooker says that the form critic gets 'carried away' at the stage where he attempts to describe the traditions' function within the community. This is where he attempts to deduce what earlier forms of the tradition may have looked like. To do this, 'laws' of transmission have to be established, by looking at tendencies in the written traditions and reading those tendencies back into the oral period. Hooker comments on the dangers of this method: one has to assume that principles of written tradition also apply to oral, and such 'laws' are inadequate generalizations that often do not fit specific historical circumstances.[34]

Once a *Sitz im Leben* is established, the form critic too often equates it with the *origin* of the material. That is, the situation that contributed to the material's written form is assumed to be the *creator* of that material. Form is thereby confused with content. Form criticism tells us nothing about the material itself and its reli-

31. Hooker, 'Christology and Methodology', p. 485.
32. Hooker, 'Christology and Methodology', p. 486.
33. Hooker, 'On Using the Wrong Tool', *Theology* 75 (1972), p. 570.
34. Hooker, 'On Using the Wrong Tool', p. 572.

ability, except where it can demonstrate, through comparison with parallel tradition, that material elements have been added or changed.[35]

Above all, Hooker criticizes the certainty that the 'radical' critic thinks he possesses in the use of his tools, including form- and tradition criticism and the criteria of authenticity. All attempts to get behind the Gospel portraits of Jesus are speculative. Hooker repeats her observation from the previous article, that all one can hope for in Jesus studies is relative certainty, that sayings are more or less probably authentic.

> For in the end, the answers which the New Testament scholar gives are not the result of applying objective tests and using precision tools; they are very largely the result of his own presuppositions and prejudices... Every scholar likes to produce assured results. To say, as I am doing, that there are none, and can be none, may seem like a counsel of despair. But assured results are dangerous things. Too many hypotheses have been regarded as proved, and have become accepted dogmas. Of course one must have working hypotheses; but it should never be forgotten that these are only hypotheses, and that they must constantly be re-examined. Perhaps every New Testament scholar should have before him on his desk, as he writes, as a constant reminder of the dangers of dogmatism, the words of R.H. Lightfoot: 'We do not know.'[36]

The concerns conveyed here are, so far, new among the scholars we have been considering. The criteria of authenticity, though not abandoned completely, are so closely scrutinized, and the form- and tradition-critical context from which they arose so roundly discounted, that the criteria have taken an unprecedentedly modest role. For Hooker, this modesty is a function of the modest nature of historical knowledge in general: due to the speculative nature of the type of reconstruction attempted in Jesus studies, the criteria and their tradition-critical home should be appropriately deflated. The assured results they were thought to be able to produce are not to be had in the historical study of Jesus.

Hooker's discernment of the weaknesses of the criteria and of tradition criticism were in their time penetrating; but it remained for others to elaborate on the nature of historical enquiry that made the traditional formulation of the criteria not only too optimistic, but in specific ways also methodologically illegitimate. Questions began to be asked about the role of the hypothesis in doing history, how data should be handled, and what the Gospel context has to do with the historical meaning of individual pieces of tradition.

A brief monograph by R.S. Barbour in 1972 anticipates many of the observations on method in Jesus studies that would arise over the next two decades.[37] On the heels of the New Quest, Barbour proposed a two-part examination of its practice of tradition criticism. In the first part he discussed technical aspects of the method, including the criteria of authenticity; the second part was devoted to a discussion of the relationship between the Jesus of history and the Christ of the

---

35. Hooker, 'On Using the Wrong Tool', p. 573.

36. Hooker, 'On Using the Wrong Tool', p. 581.

37. R.S. Barbour, *Traditio-Historical Criticism of the Gospels* (Studies in Creative Criticism, 4; London: SPCK, 1972).

kerygma, on mostly epistemological grounds. This latter part was clearly directed at the particular theological issues driving the New Quest (seeking continuity between the historical Jesus and the kerygma); but the first part deals with methodological issues that bear directly on our study.

Barbour divided the criteria of authenticity into two broad categories: formal criteria and material criteria. The former have to do with the form of a given tradition, the latter with its contents. Formal criteria include multiple attestation, Aramaisms or other Palestinian-milieu-indications, poetic form and parallelism with the logia Jesu, and perhaps others. These criteria have limited usefulness by themselves.[38] The material criteria were Barbour's main concern. He noted the criterion of dissimilarity as formulated by Ernst Käsemann and R.H. Fuller, and reviewed what we have come to see are some common objections to it. I would note briefly that in the context of one of these objections (that Jesus' dissimilarity from the early church is difficult to determine because we know little about the church with which to compare Jesus) Barbour made the important observation that we too easily assume that our knowledge of the early church is direct, but our knowledge of Jesus is indirect, mediated through the 'multi-colored spectacles' of the early church. Barbour pointed out that in fact, *no* historical knowledge is direct or unmediated; for this reason 'we must cease speaking as if, in passing from the early Church back to the figure of Jesus, we are moving from a known to an unknown; rather we are moving from one partially known to another partially known.'[39] These comments anticipate what we have observed in the epistemological foundations for critical history expounded by Ben Meyer; the latter espoused a critical realism that emphasizes the mediated nature of all knowledge, including that of history. We have seen that such an epistemology has considerable ramifications for the application of the criteria.[40]

So Barbour critiqued the criteria of dissimilarity and coherence with many of what have become common objections (most of them we encountered in Hooker's list). To these objections Barbour added further observations on the way the materials of the Gospel tradition are to be handled in the application of the criteria. He insisted that a method which takes individual sayings or pericopae in isolation and applies criteria of authenticity to each in turn is bound to distort the resulting historical picture. '[Individual pericopae cannot] be handled one by one and dropped into the appropriate boxes, as the use of criteria like that of dissimilarity almost inevitably tends to suggest. If an individual saying or *perikope* has to be handled in that way, so be it; but the provisional result always has to be integrated into an overall hypothesis, and such hypotheses are almost certain to soften the sharp edges of distinction produced by the methods under discussion.'[41] These comments may be taken to reflect the type of modesty regarding historical results that is advocated by Hooker, the conviction that the type of historical certainty that form criticism is supposed to produce cannot be had by those tools. Barbour's

38. This category is similar to what Polkow later called 'secondary criteria'.
39. Barbour, *Traditio-Historical Criticism*, p. 7.
40. See Chapters 4 and 5.
41. Barbour, *Traditio-Historical Criticism*, p. 18.

comments above, on the 'indirect' nature of all historical knowledge would be of a piece with that understanding. Barbour was also delving further, however, into the relation between a historical hypothesis and the scrutiny of individual historical data. Not only does the isolation of individual pieces of tradition for the application of criteria of authenticity end up distorting the historical picture, but there is also serious doubt, says Barbour, about whether the identification of a 'critically assured minimum' of genuine material is the first step in the historical process, which is precisely how the traditional application of the criteria conceives the task: apply the criteria to individual traditions, to determine what is data on Jesus; then suggest a hypothesis to explain the resulting data. According to Barbour, there is no way around the arduous process of formulating historical hypotheses and testing them by all available means.[42] Newly formulated hypotheses are at work even while authentic data are being detected, and will in part determine what the 'critically assured minimum' of material is; in turn, the techniques for isolating that material will affect the formulation of hypotheses. The use of the criterion of dissimilarity, for example, is not merely a heuristic method, 'but is in itself the adoption of an hypothesis about the historical Jesus and his relation to the early tradition'.[43] In this Barbour was pointing out that the choice of criteria amounts to the adoption of certain hypotheses about the historical Jesus and his relation to early Christianity. But application of those criteria also affects the further formulation of hypotheses. Barbour sees what we may call a type of hermeneutic circle at work here, understanding of the whole (hypothesis) from its parts (application of the criteria), and the parts in light of the whole.

Barbour's conclusion on the criteria of authenticity: they may produce a critically assured *minimum* of material, but they cannot be said to produce an adequate historical *core*.[44] His conclusions on the relation of the criteria to the formulation of hypotheses:

> There is no way of avoiding the elaboration of hypotheses which must seek to cover as much of the evidence as possible, and in this process the factors leading to such elaboration and development as took place in the early tradition must be described and tested as rigorously as any others. Of course the elaboration of overall hypotheses and the isolation of a core of genuine material are not mutually exclusive activities; but the laying of stress on one or the other may indicate deeper differences of approach to the whole business of research into Christian beginnings.[45]

What we see in Barbour's formulation back in 1972 is a turning point in the understanding of the role of the criteria of authenticity. Besides the sceptical posture toward tradition-critical results met with in Hooker, Barbour asks questions regarding the legitimacy of application of the criteria to discrete units of tradition, in isolation from some larger whole that would give those units fuller meaning.

42. Barbour, *Traditio-Historical Criticism*, p. 18.
43. Barbour, *Traditio-Historical Criticism*, p. 19.
44. Barbour, *Traditio-Historical Criticism*, p. 26.
45. Barbour, *Traditio-Historical Criticism*, p. 26.

The larger whole that Barbour has in mind is the overall hypothesis that will inter-act with the way these units are scrutinized, 'softening the sharp edges of distinc-tion' that the criteria produce. We will see that other scholars, in various ways, join in this concern for the larger picture that the traditional formulation of the criteria seems not to take seriously.

E.P. Sanders's historical approach to Jesus in *Jesus and Judaism* stands out because he deliberately avoids the starting place of most studies of Jesus up to his time: scrutiny of the individual sayings. Instead he begins with a core of 'virtually indisputable facts' about Jesus.[46] He avoids beginning with the sayings for two reasons: (1) studies which begin with the sayings have often assumed Jesus was primarily a teacher; this assumption, says Sanders, does not account for the known facts; and (2) determining the authenticity of the sayings is problematic; even if this is determined, the sayings still must be placed within a broader context if they are to shed historical light on Jesus. This latter point reflects a certain 'holistic' concern in Sanders, to locate isolated sayings in a broader historical context. Sanders is critical of the supposed certainty of form-critical results, but he is not opposed to the application of criteria to individual sayings.[47] Yet he makes the point that, even if such criteria are used, the sayings would have to be set in a broader context than a summary of their contents if they are to address historical questions about Jesus. We can see in Sanders's earlier work a similar concern for seeing parts in relation to their function in a whole. His stated method in *Paul and Palestinian Judaism* is to focus on the comparison of the whole 'pattern of relig-ion' in Paul with the 'pattern of religion' in contemporary Judaism, as opposed to comparing only reduced essences or individual motifs of each.[48]

I would note that, though Sanders shows an appreciation for dealing with larger historical contexts, the type of context he has in mind is that provided by his list of 'virtually indisputable facts'. Sanders is in fact not opposed to using criteria to test individual sayings,[49] but sees such tests as, not necessarily illegitimately applied,

---

46. Sanders's list of the 'indisputable facts' has become well known in Jesus studies: Jesus was baptized by John the Baptist; Jesus was a Galilean who preached and healed; he called disciples and spoke of there being twelve; he confined his activity to Israel; he engaged in a controversy about the temple; he was crucified outside Jerusalem by the Roman authorities; after his death Jesus' followers continued as an identifiable movement; at least some Jews persecuted at least parts of the new movement…and it appears that this persecution endured at least to the time near the end of Paul's career, *Jesus and Judaism* (Philadelphia: Fortress Press, 1985), p. 11. See also Mark Allan Powell's comparison of this list with a list Sanders gives later in *The Historical Figure of Jesus* (1993); Powell, *Jesus as a Figure in History*, p. 117. In the later list Sanders drops a few of the earlier facts, and adds new ones.

47. He even confesses a general scepticism about the authenticity of the Gospel traditions, *Jesus and Judaism*, p. 16.

48. He even mentions structuralism in anthropology and literary criticism, much in vogue at the time and concerned to make sense of parts in relation to wholes. *Paul and Palestinian Judaism* (Philadelphia: Fortress Press, 1977), p. 17 n. 8.

49. See the section on 'Research into the Life and Teaching of Jesus' in his introductory text to the Gospels (E.P. Sanders and Margaret Davies, *Studying the Synoptic Gospels* [Philadelphia: Trinity Press International, 1989], pp. 301-344). He notes that seeking historically sound material in the Gospels goes against their grain because they were written as propaganda. His methodo-

but simply incomplete. Individual traditions need to be set in a larger context, and for Sanders that context needs to be more *secure* and *historically assured* than the criteria of authenticity and the methods of tradition criticism can be. He sees his list of facts providing the most secure bedrock for historical investigation.[50] So Sanders's scepticism of form-critical results and his concern for a larger context in which to see individual traditions is shared by some of our other authors, but he retains what some would call a historically 'positivistic' approach that does not fully appreciate the nature of historical knowledge or the relation of hypotheses to criteria and discrete data.

Two other authors that are critical of criteria of authenticity as applied to isolated traditions are Alan Winton and Anthony Harvey. The former, in his work on Jesus' proverbs, is highly critical of the use of criteria in any context. After a critique of dissimilarity and coherence, Winton concludes that historical study of Jesus cannot proceed with what are thought to be sure criteria of authenticity. Rather, historical work would have to be carried out in the context of broad principles concerning the activity of Jesus and the impact of his life as seen from other evidence. We can see these principles to be something like the hypotheses that Barbour says will inevitably interact with examination of data on a smaller scale. Winton acknowledges that the kind of principles he proposes would be blunt tools, yielding competing reconstructions, but this would be preferable to the false certainty that results from invalid criteria of authenticity.[51]

From a different perspective, Anthony Harvey defends the need to consider the Gospel narratives as wholes in historical investigation. He notes that the Gospels present accounts of Jesus that are 'original and consistent' and give much information which 'all points in the same direction and allows [one] to infer a character of consistency in integrity'. For this reason, Harvey says, 'Attention has moved away from establishing the truth or falsity of any particular report about Jesus, and is now directed more towards the impression made by the narrative as a whole.'[52] Harvey's own method in fact consists of a combination of authenticity criteria and evidence drawn from non-canonical sources to illuminate the 'historical constraints' that constituted the parameters within which Jesus would have necessarily worked. But even Harvey's criteria involve consideration of the consistency of the broad outlines of the overall portrait of Jesus emerging from the entire Gospel tradition, determined largely through multiple attestation, in combination with a form of the criterion of dissimilarity.

So we see that the criteria of authenticity have been evaluated and found wanting, in one way or another. One scholar calls for the abandoning the criteria as

logical presentation there consists of review of various tests of historicity, beginning with something like redaction criticism (that is historical which goes strongly 'against the grain' of a given Gospel presentation), and including the criteria of uniqueness, multiple attestation and 'views common to friend and foe'.

50. Sanders, *Jesus and Judaism*, p. 10.

51. Alan Winton, *The Proverbs of Jesus*, p. 122.

52. Harvey, *Jesus and the Constraints of History* (Philadelphia: Westminster Press, 1982), pp. 4, 5.

useless for the purpose for which they were designed. Most would insist that a form of the criteria can be retained, in some context. The consistent theme that we have observed here is the need to pursue historical enquiry in a broader context than is provided by the traditional formulation of the criteria, in which individual traditions are examined for their historical value. This theme leads us in the direction of what I am calling a 'holistic' historical method. This method appreciates that individual data are only understood within the context of some larger whole. The criteria of authenticity are traditionally applied to discrete data to determine their authenticity as data on Jesus, but these scholars represent those who recognize that individual traditions must be seen in some sense-making context. They cannot simply be handled, evaluated and interpreted as self-contained units. I am presenting the two subjects of my larger study partly as exemplars of contrasting ways of handling historical data and applying criteria to them. Crossan represents the traditional formulation and application of the criteria, while Meyer takes up the holistic programme that we have observed here and gives it specific epistemological and hermeneutical underpinning in the work of Bernard Lonergan.

4. *Conclusion*

The criteria of authenticity as classically formulated in the New Quest were characterized by two interrelated features: (1) an association with tradition criticism, in their application to the earliest recoverable stratum of the reconstructed transmission of the tradition; and (2) application to individual pieces of tradition in order to determine what of them is historical data on Jesus. Apart from attempts to reformulate the criteria, particularly the criterion of dissimilarity, we have seen that criticisms of them range from scepticism about the certainty of their results to comprehensive re-examination of the conception of historiography and even epistemology that gave rise to them. The latter forms of opposition should prove to be the most formidable for the criteria because they are not in any sense arguments against them from within their own conceptions of history. My examination of Meyer in this monograph reveals his basic reconception of the tasks exigent to historical Jesus studies, grounded in a consideration of the nature of historical knowledge and historical criticism.

The issues raised by Meyer and his 'holistic' predecessors are beginning to permeate the literature. The criteria, and the historical rationale behind them, are being rethought from different perspectives. Most would not suggest that the criteria be jettisoned altogether, though there are some scholars who have no use for them. Sean Freyne would fall in that category. Based on a literary-critical, reader-oriented appreciation of the narrative context of the Gospels, he criticizes form and redaction criticism which 'have for the most part approached the gospels as stratified layers of tradition that can, through the use of proper criteria, be stripped off and dated after the manner of an archaeological dig, until eventually bed-rock Jesus tradition is arrived at'.[53] But such an approach is hindered by inadequate dating

---

53. Sean Freyne, *Jesus, Galilee and the Gospels*, p. 12.

criteria, especially the criterion of dissimilarity. This approach is also biased against the editorial seams, which were significant for and carefully composed by the author. 'Foremost among these narratorial markers are the geographical and other topographical references in the text, and, on the assumption of a far greater degree of conscious verisimilitude than is currently regarded as likely, these passages become significant pointers for testing our hypothesis about historical value of some, at least, of the realistic features of our gospel narratives.'[54]

As true as these critiques of form and redaction criticism are, that all criteria of historicity are therefore illegitimate does not necessarily follow. I would note that there are certain general historiographic principles that the criteria may reflect, such as the comparisons that are a part of all critical history. It may be possible to reconceive and reformulate the criteria with such principles in mind,[55] along with the epistemological and literary observations that are presently impinging on historical and biblical studies. That reformulation to a greater or lesser degree has been taking place for some time should be evident from this survey.

54. Freyne, *Jesus, Galilee and the Gospels*, p. 13.
55. See above, pp. 184-85.

Appendix 2

VARIETIES OF CRITICAL REALISM

We would do well to clarify some issues surrounding the use of a 'critical realist' epistemology. The notion, or at least the term, is gaining some ascendancy in New Testament studies, due largely to the important contributions of N.T. Wright.[1] But with that ascendancy comes potential for confusion, for not all who use the term mean the same thing by it, and as a result not all users agree on its significance for New Testament and historical studies. Its major proponent has called the term 'slippery',[2] attestation enough that caution is called for as we try to find our footing.

1. *Three Forms of Critical Realism*

1. *Early Critical Realism*
Critical realism (CR), as an epistemological tag, has a history. There can be identified at least three separate schools of thought that have adopted the label. The earliest of these was the CR of the early twentieth century, advocated by, among others, R.W. Sellars, A.O. Lovejoy and George Santayana.[3] In 1920 they along with others collaborated on a collection of essays which captures both the similarities and the differences among the early critical realists.[4] This CR was a reaction to the neo-realism of the late nineteenth century, which was in its turn a reaction to idealism, of both the critical Kantian kind and the absolute Hegelian kind. CR saw in neo-realism an untenable and naive identification of the object of knowledge with the starting point of knowledge, with the 'given' of our experience with which we have to work in achieving knowledge.[5] Such an identification, at the very least, cannot answer the problem of perceptual error, and was sometimes equated with a naive perceptual realism, with all its attendant problems.[6]

---

1.   Especially in *The New Testament and the People of God*, pp. 32ff.
2.   N.T. Wright, 'In Grateful Dialogue', p. 245.
3.   See the brief descriptions of this movement in Lewis W. Beck, 'Critical Realism', in Ted Honderich (ed.), *The Oxford Companion to Philosophy* (New York: Oxford University Press, 1995), p. 171; C.F. Delany, 'Critical Realism', in Robert Audi (ed.), *The Cambridge Dictionary of Philosophy* (Cambridge: Cambridge University Press, 1995), pp. 194-95.
4.   Durant Drake, Arthur Lovejoy, *et al.*, *Essays in Critical Realism* (London: Macmillan, 1920; reprint, 1921).
5.   R.W. Sellars, 'Knowledge and Its Categories', in *Essays in Critical Realism*, p. 189.
6.   Naive realism as a theory of perception holds that objects retain all their qualities apart from perception, including qualities such as colour or temperature, which are commonly con-

Against the identification of the object of knowledge with what is experientially 'given' for us, these critical realists insisted rather that what is given is to be distinguished from the object itself. Between the object and the knower there exists some type of mediator, which serves as the given for our knowledge. Various mediators were proposed, but a common candidate was character-complexes, which are the essences of the real objects we experience, and which are grasped in intuition.[7] To this was sometimes added the notion of an idea that gives content to the object of perception.[8] Any such mediator between knower and known is what makes realism *critical*. But this critical position would seem to resemble a representational theory of perception and thus be susceptible to the criticisms lodged against idealism or phenomenalism. The critical realists respond that their position is in fact *realist* because one's knowledge is not only of the mediator, but of the actual existent. How this is so is described differently by different critical realists: some posit a sort of logical (though not ontological) identification of the existent with the character complex, others an instinctive belief in the existent which is pragmatically justifiable.[9] But all agree that knowledge is of real objects (against idealism), by means of the mediation of perceptual givens that are distinct from the objects (against naive realism).

1.2. Critical Realism in the Philosophy of Science

From this early form of CR we turn to a recent version, proposed by Ian Barbour[10] and other philosophers of science and religion such as Arthur Peacocke[11] and

sidered secondary qualities and dependent upon perception. See Durant Drake, 'The Approach to Critical Realism', in *Essays in Critical Realism* (London: Macmillan, 1920; reprint, 1921), pp. 15ff. Jonathan Dancy's discussion of various versions of realism and theories of perception is especially clear and helpful, in *An Introduction to Contemporary Epistemology* (Oxford: Basil Blackwell, 1985), chs. 10 and 11.

7.   'Our data – the character-complexes "given" in conscious experience – are simply character-complexes, essences, logical entities, which are irresistibly taken to be the characters of the existents perceived, or otherwise known', Drake, 'The Approach', p. 5. Also Sellars, 'Knowledge and Its Categories', p. 189; Drake, 'The Approach', p. 20.

8.   Sellars, 'Knowledge and Its Categories', p. 190.

9.   Regarding the former, Sellers says that the existent is not inferred from the character-complex, but is rather affirmed 'through the very pressure and suggestion of our experience', 'Knowledge and Its Categories', p. 195. The given character-complex is the content of perception and is intuited, while the existent is the object of perception, and is affirmed, 'Knowledge and Its Categories', p. 196. Drake says that the given character-complexes 'are irresistibly taken to be the characters of the existents perceived', 'The Approach to Critical Realism', p. 5. Our instinctive belief in the existence of the physical world is pragmatically justifiable in that we instinctively feel that the appearances that are character-complexes are of real objects, and this instinct *works*. That is, one who denies anything beyond appearances can *describe* the appearances, but cannot explain them. 'The peculiar nature and sequence of our data remain unintelligible to the subjectivist, surds in his doctrine. Whereas, if there is a whole world of existents, the characteristics and relations of our data become marvelously intelligible…Everything is *as if* realism were true; and the *as if* is so strong that we may consider our instinctive and actually inescapable belief justified', p. 6.

10.   Ian Barbour, *Myths, Models and Paradigms: A Comparative Study in Science and Religion* (New York: Harper & Row, 1974).

11.   Arthur Peacocke, *Intimations of Reality: Critical Realism in Science and Religion* (The

Wentzel van Huyssteen.[12] Though there are some broad similarities with the earlier CR (inasmuch as most proposals for something called 'critical realism' share certain general concerns, as we will discuss below), these authors in fact seem to be working independently of the former. Among Barbour and company there is no explicit reference to R.W. Sellars, Lovejoy, *et al.* and certainly no theoretical indebtedness. This may be largely attributed to the context within which both groups work, which determines where their theoretical interests lie. The later critical realists work principally in the philosophy of science, and are particularly concerned with the intelligibility and validity of theological statements in light of the nature of science; science and theology are thought to be two complementary rather than contradictory ways of speaking about reality. These critical realists see their work as a development beyond the logical positivism that dominated the philosophy of science for much of the twentieth century,[13] incorporating, but avoiding the excesses of, the insights in the philosophy of knowledge that had become prominent in philosophy of science since Thomas Kuhn.[14] The early critical realists, on the other hand, were philosophers focusing on the general philosophical problems of epistemology and theories of perception, dealing in classic post-Kantian categories. The specific methodological concerns of a post-positivist science were not in their purview, so the particular issues of the general nature of knowledge and perception with which they were occupied are in some respects outside the pale of the later critical realists.

Mendenhall Lectures 1983; Notre Dame, IN: University of Notre Dame Press, 1984); *Theology for a Scientific Age* (Theology and the Sciences; Minneapolis: Fortress Press, enlarged edn,1993), esp. 11-19.

    12. Wentzel van Huyssteen, *Essays in Postfoundationalist Theology* (Grand Rapids: Eerdmans, 1997); also *The Realism of the Text: A Perspective on Biblical Authority* (Pretoria, South Africa: University of Pretoria, 1987); *The Shaping of Rationality* (Grand Rapids: Eerdmans, 1999); and *Theology and the Justification of Faith: Constructing Theories in Systematic Theology* (trans. H.F. Snijders; Grand Rapids: Eerdmans, 1989).

    13. Logical positivism considers meaning in language to be a matter of the means of its empirical verification, with the result that the only meaningful language is that which can be empirically verified. The classic statement of this position is found in the work of A.J. Ayer, *Language, Truth and Logic* (London: Victor Gollancz, 2nd edn, 1946).

    14. In his work *The Structure of Scientific Revolutions*, Kuhn demonstrates that scientific observation and knowledge of 'normal science' takes place within a 'paradigm' or conceptual context; only in such a context do observations and theories have their sense. A paradigm is the intelligible context of all explanation and as such is not subject to explanation. Paradigms are socially constructed within and perpetuated by the scientific community, and are not subject to change based upon application of scientific method, because all method has its applicability and usefulness only *within* the paradigm. Rather, paradigms change by means of 'revolution', or disruption in the old paradigm in light of observational anomalies for which the paradigm cannot account. A new paradigm is offered as a way of incorporating the anomalies, and is not simply an expansion of the old paradigm but a shift to a wholly new way of viewing the data. The possible excess of this view, which the CR of Barbour *et al.* attempts to counter, is the instrumentalist conclusion that, because knowledge is paradigm-dependent or socially contextualized, the conclusions of science are *merely* social constructs like any other cultural product, useful fictions for dealing with the world but not purporting to be about real objects. See Peacocke, *Intimations*, p. 20.

Typical of the later CR is its expression by Peacocke. CR in science is offered over against naive realism on the one hand and the 'strong program' in the sociology of knowledge on the other. According to naive realism, descriptions of scientific concepts and mechanisms are 'literal descriptions of the world, reproductions of objective reality' and thought to be such for pragmatic reasons, because science makes real progress and the conclusions of science 'work'. Science discovers 'the hidden mechanisms of the world of nature and shows us what is *actually* there'.[15] But it is not clear *how* many scientific terms refer, for example, 'mass', 'energy', 'black holes', or 'antimatter', or what their relation is to empirical observation. The 'received view' of the structure of scientific theories was dominant from the 1920s to the 1970s, based on naive realism, a universal scientific language and the correspondence theory of truth.[16] This view was called into question in the 1970s, following the observations of Kuhn. Socially contextualized views of scientific theory became dominant. The eventual 'strong program' in the sociology of knowledge regarded the terms, theories and conclusions of science as social constructs, to be understood in strictly instrumentalist terms. In response, various scientific realisms have been proposed, all of which emphasize the role of reason in formulation of and selection between scientific theories, and distance themselves from naive realism by qualifying scientific knowledge as 'conjectural', 'skeptical and qualified' or 'critical'.[17] Peacocke presents CR as emphasizing the role of *model* and *metaphor* in scientific knowledge, along with an experimental and social understanding of reference in language.[18] Scientific knowledge and theory take place via models that approximate reality and give rise to speaking *metaphorically*: models are never *literal* representations of reality. There is always a certain inadequacy attached to models, leaving room for multiple models or approximations of the same reality and for development of a theory to predict and accommodate new observations.[19] Since scientific understanding is by way of model and metaphor, it would seem that actual specific referents for scientific terms would be lacking and the terms themselves would be vague. Peacocke suggests a social theory of reference, by which 'reference may be fixed without being restricted by the straightjacket of a definition and have the virtue of separating reference from *un*revisable description and grounding it instead in the experience of a continuous linguistic community'.[20]

15. Peacocke, *Intimations*, p. 15. A similar description is found in Barbour, *Myths*, p. 11.

16. Peacocke, *Intimations*, p. 16.

17. Peacocke, *Intimations*, p. 29.

18. Peacocke, *Intimations*, p. 34. See also Barbour, *Myths*, pp. 6, 7; and an early statement of van Huyssteen, *Realism of the Text*, p. 24.

19. Peacocke, *Intimations*, p. 31.

20. Peacocke, *Intimations*, p. 33. We could understand Peacocke's social theory of reference to be a species of what is usually termed a causal theory of reference. On this theory, terms refer to objects not by virtue of the sense (intension; concept or meaning) of the terms, but by some means of causation. Such causation could be a chain historically linking present use of a term with an occasion in the past when the referent was fixed; or the causal link could be between, not historical referent and current use, but between referent and the current body of knowledge. In any case, reference is thought to be fixed not by the definition of the term, but by some social or theoretical context. See the discussion in A.C. Grayling, *Philosophical Logic*, pp. 195-202. Barbour speci-

1.3. *Roy Bhaskar*

A third form of CR is to be found in the work of Roy Bhaskar and those following him.[21] Like the second version this CR has been formulated in relative isolation from the others.[22] (For ease of reference, I will call the second version CR_2 and Bhaskar's CR_3, making the earliest form of Sellars and company CR_1.) Also like CR_2, CR_3 has its point of departure in the methodology and nature of knowledge of the natural sciences; but Bhaskar's concern for broader application is not in the area of theology, but rather in the human sciences. 'Critical realism' as a label for Bhaskar's philosophy did not originate with him, but arose as an elision of his terms 'transcendental realism' and 'critical naturalism' among his interpreters.[23] The first term Bhaskar expounded in the context of the natural sciences, the second in the human sciences.

Bhaskar offers transcendental realism (TR) in science as a reaction against positivism, and also against other anti-positivist reactions that recognize the sociology of knowledge but at the cost of abandoning realism (e.g., Kuhn, according to Bhaskar). TR holds that the domain of the real is distinct from and greater than the domain of the empirical or the actual.[24] Put another way, ontology cannot be reduced to epistemology.[25] The distinction of the real from the experiential would be a feature Bhaskar would have in common with other versions of CR. But the domain of the actual is what sets Bhaskar apart. Bhaskar's TR is concerned to posit

---

fically appropriates Kuhn's notion of paradigm, though with the qualification that paradigms are subject to paradigm-independent criteria of assessment. See Barbour, *Myths*, p. 10.

21. Bhaskar's major critical realist works include *A Realist Theory of Science* (New York: Verso, 2nd edn, 1997); *The Possibility of Naturalism: A Philosophical Critique of the Contemporary Human Sciences* (Atlantic Highlands, NJ: Humanities Press, 1979); *Scientific Realism and Human Emancipation* (New York: Verso, 1986); and *Dialectic: The Pulse of Freedom* (New York: Verso, 1993). Secondary introductory texts include Andrew Collier, *Critical Realism: An Introduction to Roy Bhaskar's Philosophy* (New York: Verso, 1994); and the anthology of Margaret Archer, *et al.* (eds.), *Critical Realism: Essential Readings* (New York: Routledge, 1998). The latter contains an introduction by Bhaskar, outlining his version of CR, pp. ix-xxiv.

22. One advocate of Bhaskar's CR displays this isolation well, when in an encyclopedia article he defines CR as 'a movement in philosophy and the human sciences starting from Roy Bhaskar's writings'. The article goes on to explicate Bhaskar's work, without mention of either of the versions of CR we have outlined above, both of which appeared before Bhaskar (around 1920 and 1974; Bhaskar's first critical realist exposition appeared around 1975). Andrew Collier, 'Critical Realism', in Edward Craig (ed.), *Routledge Encyclopedia of Philosophy*, 2 (London: Routledge, 1998), p. 720. Bhaskar himself describes CR as 'a movement in philosophy and the human sciences and cognate practices most closely associated with…the work of Roy Bhaskar', in the introduction to Archer, *Critical Realism*, p. ix.

23. Archer, p. ix.

24. The empirical is of course the experiential domain. The *actual* is Bhaskar's term for the domain of events understood in terms of their causal connections, the connections of cause-and-effect between events. Bhaskar sees a deeper level of reality, underlying the events themselves, which is necessary to account for the events. The explanation 'event A caused event B' is not sufficient. See Collier, *Critical Realism*, p. 7.

25. Archer, p. xi.

as real the 'deeper levels' of reality underlying the causes and effects described in natural science. Like Barbour, Bhaskar recognizes the role of models in scientific explanation and description. But Bhaskar sees these models as often identifying newly discovered deeper levels of reality. The general laws and regularities of scientific observation are real things, given ontic reference by Bhaskar. They are seen as the real underlying mechanisms or powers producing empirical regularities. Theoretical entities or processes that are offered to explain observed phenomena, themselves come to be established as real, and in turn serve as the phenomena for formulation of new theoretical entities and the discovery of ever-deeper layers of reality. This results in the stratification of reality which is mirrored in a 'depth realism' or vertical realism in science.[26] 'Science could now be seen as a continuing and reiterated process of movement from manifest phenomena, through creative modeling and experimentation or other empirical controls, to the identification of their generative causes, which now become the phenomena to be explained. The stratification of nature imposes a certain dynamic logic to scientific discovery, in which progressively deeper knowledge of natural *necessity a posteriori* is uncovered.'[27] Not only is there stratification within the methods and observations of a single science, but also between the sciences.[28] The latter is the recognition of emergent mechanisms, those which are grounded in others but cannot be reduced to them or deduced from them. This leads to consideration of the human or social sciences. The social sciences treat levels of reality that, while grounded in the objects of the natural sciences, are emergent from them, existing in their own right and not reducible to the objects of natural science.

It is in the area of the social sciences that Bhaskar formulated his critical naturalism. CN seeks to overcome a traditional dualism in the social sciences, seen in the split between its positivist and hermeneuticist understandings. The former, roughly, see the social sciences as operating analogously to the natural sciences, seeking to account for phenomena in the arena of human behaviour by observing regularities that can be formulated in terms of laws and generalizations; the generalizations are reified as social objects, seen as having a life of their own external to and coercing the behaviour of social agents. The hermeneutic understanding, by contrast, denies that the social sciences are like the natural sciences, and seeks to preserve the integrity of intentional human behaviour, seeing social objects as constituted by that behaviour rather than existing independently of it. Bhaskar says that both positions incorrectly assume a positivist account of natural science, which denies a depth ontology and the stratification of reality and the sciences. Bhaskar offers instead a critical naturalism for the social sciences, which recognizes the latter as *emergent*

---

26. Bhaskar also posits a 'horizontal realism', which holds that observable laws continue to 'exist' and be in effect outside their observation under experimental conditions or their instantiation or actualization in any particular instance. The application in the social sciences will be apparent below.

27. Archer, *Critical Realism*, p. xi.

28. Archer, *Critical Realism*, p. xiii.

from the natural sciences and stresses a reciprocal relation between the intentional actions of the individual and the social object, as distinct and real strata: the society is a pre-existing and necessary condition for intentional agency, but the society exists and persists only in virtue of that agency. '[S]ociety is both the condition and outcome of human agency and human agency both reproduces and transforms society.'[29]

So we see that CR_3 is founded on a 'depth realism' in the sciences, with specific application in the social sciences. It emphasizes the reality of underlying powers, tendencies or generative mechanisms that account for observed phenomena, and which can in principle serve as phenomena themselves, for discovery of powers and mechanisms on ever deeper levels of reality. We can understand CR_3 as sharing the concern of CR_2, to counter possible tendencies in the sociology of knowledge to regard science's theories as merely social constructs or useful fictions. We can also see similar concerns to understand scientific understanding as taking place by the use of models. But the similarities seem to stop there. CR_3 posits a stratification of reality that has only superficial parallel in CR_2.[30] Some proponents of CR_2 would even regard a realism with regard to science's generalities as an untenable reification, a form of naive realism.[31]

What, if anything, might these three distinct versions of CR have in common? All three versions are offered in reaction to what they regard as epistemological extremes: for CR_1 and CR_2, the extremes of naive realism and a form of non-realism (either idealism or instrumentalism), for CR_3 the extremes of logical positivism and instrumentalism. But CR_3 conceives of one of these extremes, and reacts against it, in a way that sets it apart from CR_1 and CR_2. CR_3 reacts against positivism, but in a way that wants to be even more 'realist'. It insists on the *reality* of what positivism does not: scientific generalizations as descriptions of *real things*, 'deeper' powers or mechanisms that underlie observed phenomena. I noted above that CR_2 considers this orientation naively realistic; it seems that, in this respect, CR_3 is more 'realist' than 'critical'.[32] Based on this difference, I would bracket the unique concerns of CR_3 from further consideration of general critical realist issues.

29. Archer, *Critical Realism*, p. xvi.

30. Peacocke does speak of a hierarchy of order in the natural world, mirrored by a hierarchy of systems in sciences, e.g., physics, chemistry, biology, psychology, sociology, in which higher systems are not reducible to the terms of explanation of the lower systems. At the highest level in the hierarchy of complexity stands theology (*Intimations*, pp. 34ff., 51). It does not seem to be the case, however, that Peacocke and other proponents of CR_2 would want to commit to the 'depth realism' that is behind Bhaskar's notion of stratification. See below, n. 31.

31. According to Peacocke, naive realism believes that scientific concepts and mechanisms are 'literal descriptions of the world, reproductions of objective reality', and that science discovers 'the hidden mechanisms of the world of nature and shows us what is *actually* there', Peacocke, *Intimations*, p. 15. But this view is problematic because it does not recognize that many scientific terms and theories do not have clear referents, and does not take seriously enough what is valid in observations on the sociology of knowledge (e.g., Kuhn) and the metaphorical nature of scientific language.

32. That, in the service of ultimate conclusions for the social sciences, especially the concern to

So we are left with CR_1 and CR_2, and the fact that they share a basic concern to avoid epistemological extremes. It seems that this concern is the most likely candidate for any commonality between them; we noted above that the two have distinct differences, such that their remedies for this basic concern share little. Both present their version of CR as a *via media* between the extremes of naive realism, which does not take account of how knowledge is 'critical', and idealism or instrumentalism, which do not take seriously the claim that knowledge is of objects that exist prior to and independently of knowledge. As *via media*, they also intend to borrow from the strengths of both extremes and thereby offer a *realism* that is *critical*. CR_1 sees the critical component as consisting of some form of mediator, between the knower and the known. CR_2 sees the critical component as the role played by models in science, which give rise to speaking of the real only metaphorically and in a social context.[33]

2. *Critical Realism in Jesus Studies*

With these distinctions in mind we now consider CR in New Testament and historical Jesus studies. I noted above that Ben Meyer is to be credited with introducing the terminology to the biblical studies field, but it was left to N.T. Wright to give it wider currency. It seems that the situation created by this currency is not completely happy. With these new applications we can make even further distinctions among varieties of CR: Meyer and Wright both have their versions, adding to the inventory. While these additions make some important advances, as epistemological positions they are formulated in such a way that they suffer from the same isolation that we have seen among other forms of CR: they define themselves without specific reference to other versions of CR. Now this isolation is not necessarily problematic as long as the position being defined is clear enough in itself, but it becomes a problem when several of the various forms of CR become simply equated with one another in common usage. It appears that this has come to be the case in New Testament studies. The result is a lack of clear understanding about what is being claimed epistemologically by any given version of CR, and this lack of clarity results in some obscurity regarding the nature of CR's implications for New Testament and historical studies. Since such implications are the

---

preserve both intentional human agency and real social structures. I can agree with the concerns in the latter area, but it may be possible to provide for them without having to posit a reification of scientific theories or models. Recall also that the label 'critical realism' for Bhaskar simply results from the elision of 'transcendental realism' with 'critical naturalism'. For Bhaskar, the point is not so much that realism ought to be 'critical' (i.e., not naive) as that it ought to be 'transcendental' (i.e., penetrating to deeper levels of reality). It is specifically *naturalism* that ought to be critical, in the sense that the social sciences recognize the role of human agency along with observations on generalizable social phenomena.

33. The *models* of CR_2 could possibly be expressed as examples of the *mediators* of CR_1, but it is not clear whether the necessarily *metaphorical* nature of the models would fit with the nature of mediators as character-complexes, intuited essences, or content-constituting ideas.

whole point of introducing an epistemological position into an applied field, the need for clarity is paramount. The alternative may be to run the risk of 'critical realism' having such a surplus of meanings that it becomes practically meaningless and thus useless as an epistemological position with specific implications for historical Jesus studies.

2.1. *N.T. Wright*

The way Wright presents his CR (henceforth CR_W) illustrates some of the current problems. He defines his version thus:

> Over against both [positivism and phenomenalism], I propose a form of *critical realism*. This is a way of describing the process of 'knowing' that acknowledges the *reality of the thing known, as something other than the knower* (hence 'realism'), while also fully acknowledging that the only access we have to this reality lies along the spiralling path of *appropriate dialogue or conversation between the knower and the thing known* (hence 'critical'). This path leads to critical reflection on the products of our enquiry into 'reality', so that our assertions about 'reality' acknowledge their own provisionality. Knowledge, in other words, although in principle concerning realities independent of the knower, is never itself independent of the knower.[34]

CR_W as an epistemology recognizes a reciprocal relation between the knower and the known in the process of knowing, resulting in the provisionality of all knowledge. A major feature of this reciprocity for CR_W is the worldview context within which knowledge takes place, and the narratives by which worldview is articulated.

> This critical-realist theory of knowledge and verification, then, acknowledges the essentially 'storied' nature of human knowing, thinking and living, within the larger model of worldviews and their component parts. It acknowledges that all knowledge of realities external to oneself takes place within the framework of a worldview, of which stories form an essential part. And it sets up as hypotheses various stories about the world in general or bits of it in particular and tests them by seeing what sort of 'fit' they have with the stories already in place.[35]

CR_W, then, affirms knowledge as 'realist' in that knowledge is about objects external to the knower, and as 'critical' in that knowledge is dialogical, provisional, and always formed in the context of worldview.

What is significant about CR_W, aside from the features of worldview and narrative,[36] is the way that it is presented as a sort of general epistemological sentiment in reaction to epistemological extremes. Of course, the reaction to extremes is not unique to Wright; I have pointed it out as a feature of both CR_1 and CR_2. But Wright reacts in a way that makes it difficult to have a clear picture of what he

---

34. Wright, *New Testament*, p. 35.
35. Wright, *New Testament*, p. 45.
36. I would not want to minimize these features; they are important contributions to CR and are discussed in my Chapter 8, where I find a place for them, especially in historiography, that differs somewhat from Wright's use.

offers as a true epistemological alternative, aside from his observations on narrative and worldview. The epistemological extremes are presented as strawpersons, and CR_W is offered in such a way that almost anyone who utilizes historical method in New Testament studies would claim to be a 'critical realist'.[37] Few in today's epistemological climate would deny that knowledge is ultimately fallible and provisional, or that there is a certain reciprocity between the knower and the known object.[38] Wright has given us a CR that broadly expresses a dissatisfaction with naive realism and phenomenalism, but offers little in the way of a specific alternative. If an epistemology is going to be introduced that is to have a genuine impact on New Testament studies and historiography, it will need to do more than reflect a general attitude of epistemic modesty.[39]

Part of the difficulty is Wright's somewhat monolithic treatment of other versions of CR. He treats CR as though it is a singular epistemological position, but with varied application in different fields.[40] As the preceding comparison shows, there may be the broadest of similarities among the varieties of CR, for example, in their reaction against epistemological extremes; but the varieties certainly cannot be easily identified with one another, and in some cases may be irreconcilable. If Wright were to describe a specific version of CR to which he were indebted, we could locate his position more clearly. He in fact cites several different advocates

---

37. This would of course exclude those interpreters of a post-structuralist, deconstructionist, or a certain 'postmodernist' orientation, who maintain that we must dispense with any form of 'realism'. I would note that, even among historians in general, we find the posture reflected in CR_W. Appleby, Hunt and Jacob advocate what they call 'practical realism' in contrast to naive realism and the relativism of post-structuralism. Practical realism acknowledges that the relation of language to reality is not simple correspondence, but that language develops in interaction with real objects. For the historian, this means that historical representation only dimly responds to the past, but the historian must still aim for accuracy and completeness; historical work is approximate and revisable, but still reaches out to the past to give a reasonably true description of it. See Appleby, Hunt and Jacob, *Telling the Truth about History,* pp. 248-50.

38. Note especially the response of Crossan, whom I have singled out in this study as representing the hermeneutic and epistemological position that something like CR is supposedly undermining. But Crossan has responded to Wright's epistemological observations with the insistence that he is indeed sensitive to the issues Wright has raised, and claims that his method in fact reflects it. Crossan claims that his understanding of historical method is not positivist but 'interactive'. See my Chapter 3; also Crossan, 'What Victory? What God?', pp. 345-58; and *The Birth of Christianity,* pp. 42-45.

39. Such an understanding of CR seems to be operative in its use by Kevin Vanhoozer, *Is There a Meaning in This Text? The Bible, the Reader and the Morality of Literary Knowledge* (Grand Rapids: Zondervan, 1998), pp. 301-302. Vanhoozer sees CR as promoting interpretive fallibilism and recognizing the existence of interpretive frameworks.

40. Wright, *New Testament,* p. 32 n. 4. He is followed in this treatment by his interpreter Robert Byron Stewart, who describes CR as originating with R.W. Sellars in the early twentieth century, and later 'revived' by Roy Bhaskar, with application in theology and/or biblical studies by van Huyssteen, Barbour, Meyer and others. See Robert Byron Stewart, 'The Impact of Contemporary Hermeneutics on Historical Jesus Research', pp. 149ff. Stewart goes on to describe Wright's CR as 'necessarily broad' (p. 152 n.9).

of forms of CR that he says are in harmony with his position, but seems to treat them as all of a piece.[41] In fact they can only be classified together at the expense of a clarity that would make a genuine methodological difference. Wright appears to be most conscious of the work of Ben Meyer,[42] presumably because up to that time Meyer had been the greatest proponent of CR for New Testament studies. It may be that Wright has borrowed the label 'critical realism' from Meyer, but curiously, Wright does not mention Lonergan or any of the specifics of Lonergan's cognitional theory, which is the very heart of Meyer's CR. What began with Lonergan as a deliberate and specific cognitional theory has become in Wright an epistemological posture that is somewhat diffuse and diluted.[43]

2.2. *Lonergan and Critical Realism*
Perhaps it remains for me to show that all the distinctions I have been drawing among varieties of CR and the protests I have raised over lack of clarity are anything more than hair-splitting and philosophical pedantry. It would appear that, since the use of CR in New Testament studies is due mostly to Meyer's introduction of the term, and since Meyer's presentation of CR is essentially that of Lonergan, and since current use of CR in New Testament studies has gone beyond what we encounter in Lonergan's work, I would do well to measure the other versions of

41. For example, Wright cites, without expounding upon, T.F. Torrance and Andrew Louth. Torrance is most similar to CR_2, in viewing the methods of science and theology as similar and complementary ways of talking about reality; for Torrance this similarity is due to the presence of theoretical contexts (similar to Kuhnian paradigms, though Torrance does not cite Kuhn here) within which observation takes place. In a note, he comments on the inseparability of empirical and theoretical components in knowledge as a 'deeply but critically *realist* position'. See his *Time, Space and Resurrection* (Grand Rapids: Eerdmans, 1976), p. 6 n. 9. Louth, on the other hand, is critical of Torrance's suggestion of methodological similarity between science and theology, and instead maintains a methodological split between the sciences and the humanities, following Gadamer, with theology most like the humanities and unlike the sciences. See his *Discerning the Mystery: An Essay on the Nature of Theology* (Oxford: Clarendon Press, 1983), especially Chapter Three. There may in fact be similarities between Torrance and Louth, in their recognition of the legitimacy of theological method and talk vis-à-vis science, but there is enough distinction to question the propriety of a single epistemological label for both.

42. Wright, *New Testament*, p. 32 nn. 3, 4.

43. Alister McGrath goes some way toward locating CR_W in relation to other forms of CR, but seems to have in mind only CR_2 as a basis for comparison. He cites Barbour, van Huyssteen, and Alston as advocates of a relevant theological realism (and Alisdair MacIntyre, George Lindbeck and Stanley Hauerwas as stressing community in a way similar to Wright, though it is questionable whether any of those three would commit themselves to any form of realism). See McGrath, 'Reality, Symbol and History', in *Jesus and the Restoration of Israel*, pp. 163-64. Elsewhere, McGrath says CR is characterized by belief in (1) the existence of a mind-independent reality; (2) the intelligibility of reality; (3) the lack of neat distinction between theoretical and observational terms; and (4) the role of the interpretive community. See *The Foundations of Dialogue in Science and Religion* (Malden, MA: Blackwell, 1998), pp. 154-64. All this fits well with CR_2, but, as we will see, doesn't quite cover the CR of Meyer and Lonergan.

CR against Lonergan, to see if the latter can serve as a guide and corrective at this point, to help prevent CR from becoming so diluted as to be nondescriptive and methodologically impotent.

Lonergan first began using the term 'critical realism' in his work in the early 1960s, soon after the publication of his magnum opus, *Insight*.[44] But in fact his use of the term throughout his career is fairly infrequent. He reserves it for those places where he specifically compares his cognitional theory to epistemological extremes, usually naive realism and idealism,[45] or to a more sophisticated form of the former, such as empiricism.[46] His use of the term in this respect is similar to the other versions of CR, all of which share the concern to avoid extremes, as we have seen. But Lonergan presents his alternative in a way that sets him apart. Lonergan sees both extremes as based upon the same error, the error of 'picture thinking'. Both naive realism and idealism understand knowing to be like taking a look at an object, receiving it by means of vision. For the naive realist the vision is ocular vision, or else the other senses receiving the real object; for the idealist the vision is mental, an intuition, receiving not the real object but the appearance of the object, or phenomena. In both *Insight* and later work Lonergan urges that knowledge is more than a matter of looking or 'receiving' either a real or an apparent object.

At the beginning of *Insight* he presents the problems created by failure to break with a 'duality' in knowing, the duality between two presumed types of knowing: empirical and rational. He denies that the solution to the duality is a way between these; the solution is rather the recognition that neither of these in itself constitutes a distinct kind of knowing. The two are actually two moments in *one process of knowing*, the moments of experience and understanding.[47] After *Insight*, he notes the problem of 'picture thinking' that underlies both naive realism and idealism.[48] The problem as expressed here is that one moment in the knowing process (the empirical, 'seeing') is commonly taken to be an independent type of knowing, and serves as the paradigm for knowledge in general.

In neither the early *Insight* formulation (the duality of knowing) nor the later formulation ('seeing' as a paradigm for knowing) does Lonergan see his realism as a way *between* extremes, and it is in this that Lonergan is set apart from other versions of CR. In the *Insight* formulation, a realism between materialism and

---

44. Some of the earliest references are found in Lonergan, *Collection*. The papers in *Collection* were written between the publication of *Insight* (1957) and *Method in Theology* (1972). Note that Lonergan's use of 'CR' antedates all other versions we have surveyed, except CR_1, but none of those later versions references Lonergan.

45. 'Cognitional Structure' in *Collection*, p. 217; '*Existenz* and *Aggiornamento*', in *Collection*, p. 225; 'The Dehellenization of Dogma', in *A Second Collection*, p. 30; 'The Origins of Christian Realism' in *A Second Collection*, p. 239; *Method*, p. 264.

46. 'The Origins of Christian Realism', in *A Second Collection*, p. 239; *Method*, p. 239; 'Unity and Plurality: The Coherence of Christian Truth' in *A Third Collection*, p. 240.

47. Lonergan, *Insight*, p. 22.

48. See Lonergan, 'Cognitional Structure', p. 218; 'The Subject' in *A Second Collection*, pp. 76-79.

idealism would maintain an untenable split between two supposed types of knowing, and fail to recognize both as *inseparable parts of one knowing process*. In the later formulation, a critical realism between naive realism and idealism would fail to break with picture thinking that characterizes both. Lonergan's CR is not in any sense a *via media* between extremes, as are CR_1 and CR_2, but is rather off the axis, as it were, upon which naive realism and idealism are the poles, the axis of picture thinking.

In light of Lonergan's basic concern to be done with a duality in knowing and with picture thinking, it does not seem that CR_1 would be reconcilable with Lonergan's vision, for CR_1 continues to see knowledge as a matter of intuition of character-complexes, essences, or ideas immediately apprehended. Its realism is critical by virtue of a mediator, but the mediator itself serves as an object of perception, a given that is received by the knower's intuiting or mentally 'taking a look' at it. CR_2, on the other hand, may be of use in Lonergan's overall scheme, as an account of knowledge in one area, namely science. But the models by which science knows its objects, according to CR_2, must be properly conceived. Such models may be seen as part of the apparatus of understanding and judgement that Lonergan says is a spontaneous and necessary part of any form of knowledge (not just the scientific).[49] But if models are understood simply as mediators that are the givens of knowledge, objects of knowledge which are immediately known by looking, then Lonergan would not acknowledge them as distinct features of the knowing process; such models would be similar to the intuited mediators of CR_1. CR_2 offers us an understanding of knowledge in science that may be useful, but in itself does not go far enough to rival Lonergan's cognitional theory.

What of CR_W? It stacks up similarly to CR_2. If Wright could avoid the temptation to a duality of knowing, and cast his concern for the reciprocity between knower and known and the roles of narrative and worldview, in such a way that the latter are not understood as mediators of knowledge, to be immediately apprehended, but as tools in the operation of understanding and judgement, and if he consistently presents knowledge as always a matter of understanding and judgement in combination with experience, then CR_W could make a significant contribution to the CR of Meyer and Lonergan that Wright has taken as his point of departure. But as it stands, CR_W seems to be more of a disposition or predilection than a formidable epistemology. Once again, what is required of an epistemology, for it to contribute to genuine methodological advances in an applied area such as New Testament and historical Jesus studies, is enough specificity to make the methodological options clear. Lonergan's cognitional theory provides that specificity.

2.3. *Ben Meyer*

If Wright has taken CR and, to an extent, obscured it, we can in fact locate some roots of this tendency in Meyer himself. We have noted a distinction between

---

49. The recognition of the social location of knowledge in CR_2 also has affinities with Lonergan, in his notion of 'horizons' within which knowledge takes place, to be discussed below.

Meyer's use of CR, and Lonergan's use of CR which is fairly infrequent. Whereas Lonergan's use is limited to contexts where he compares his theory with naive realism and idealism, Meyer uses CR as a broad designation for Lonergan's theory.[50] We could attribute this difference to the fact that Meyer's overriding interest in the appropriation of Lonergan is specifically in the area of New Testament hermeneutics; Meyer is attempting to forge an alternative to both a naive realist understanding of reading, which sees textual meaning as already completely constituted on the page and passively registered by the reader, and a reader-response orientation that sees meaning as entirely a matter of the reader's creative contribution. Meyer intends to show that CR provides a way between these hermeneutical extremes: 'Every act of successful reading illustrates the middle position, corresponding...to the critical-realist view of insight.'[51] Interpretation of the New Testament, as of any text, recognizes the reader's contribution to construal of meaning ('critical') but also acknowledges that the reader 'takes his marching orders' for that construal from the text itself ('realist'). On this understanding, a CR hermeneutic is a sort of *via media*, combining the realism of one extreme with the critical component of the other.

These hermeneutical concerns most likely account for Meyer's use of 'CR' as a designation for Lonergan's overall theory. As I will show below, this critical realist hermeneutic is probably the best application of Lonergan's theory in the area of New Testament hermeneutics; this is one application where Lonergan's theory, itself no epistemological *via media*, does indeed result in a sort of hermeneutical *via media*. But it may also be the case that Meyer's occupation with this area as his point of departure for reading Lonergan causes Meyer sometimes to lapse into the errors that Lonergan was most concerned to avoid in his cognitional theory. In *Reality and Illusion* Meyer shows his hermeneutic orientation when he presents Lonergan's cognitional theory by using the act of reading as a paradigm of the act of knowing. Just as reading is neither a passive registering of meaning already fully contained on the page, nor an active creation of meaning by the reader, but rather a way between these, so knowing is neither a passive reception of objects nor a solipsistic creation of them, but a way between these extremes. But this presentation gets Meyer into trouble. Although Lonergan's theory may legitimately be applied to hermeneutics such that a sort of *via media* results, to carry this *via media* over into a general description of Lonergan is problematic, and Meyer tends to do this. At times Meyer seems to lapse into the duality of knowing that Lonergan warned against, the idea that sense knowledge is indeed a distinct kind of knowledge over

---

50. I should note that, among interpreters of Lonergan, Meyer is not alone in this tendency. See for example Joseph M. Vertin, *Critical Realism: Cognitional Approach and Ontological Achievement According to Bernard Lonergan* (Washington, DC: Theological Publications, 1970); Webb, *Philosophers of Consciousness*, p. 8; Margaret M. Welch, 'A Critical Realist Assessment of the Moral Realism Debate: Objectivity as Authentic Subjectivity and the Epistemology of Bernard Lonergan' (PhD dissertation, Loyola University of Chicago, 1998).

51. Meyer, *Reality and Illusion*, p. 3.

against an active understanding.[52] Meyer correctly introduces the acts of insight and judgement as 'the two main intellectual acts that constitute fully human knowing'.[53] But he presents these acts as coming *after* a sense-knowledge and after the wonder that supervenes on sense-knowledge.[54] He contrasts understanding or insight (the second level of cognition) with experience (the first level) by noting that, whereas insight is incomplete and purely hypothetical, needing completion in judgement (the third level), experience is a sense-knowledge that 'has a kind of *per se* infallibility'.[55] Experience is in a sense passive because the senses merely register their objects, and so it has a kind of intrinsic integrity and completeness.[56] Meyer seems to be casting experience as a distinct kind of knowledge, a knowledge provided by the senses, over against the knowledge that comes from understanding and judgement.[57] This resembles the duality in knowing that Lonergan was concerned to counter. For Lonergan, the senses do not provide a distinct form of knowledge, viz., the empirical, in contrast to the rational knowledge of understanding. Experience and understanding are inseparable parts of the one process of knowing. Immediately operative upon the data of experience is the exercise of understanding and judgement, such that knowledge is from first to last, in all its forms and applications, an understanding and judging activity. Now it is certainly the case that, as an informed interpreter of Lonergan, Meyer appreciates Lonergan's objections to the 'picture thinking' that underlies both naive realism and idealism.[58] But Meyer's applications of Lonergan in hermeneutics may tend to cause him to understand Lonergan as a *via media* that continues to operate with a duality of knowing. As I have shown, the *via media* conception fits comfortably

52.   Earlier, in *Critical Realism*, Meyer had in fact explicitly stated that there exists 'a duality in our knowledge: elementary knowing, which is prior to questions, and fully human knowing, which follows on questions, includes the quest of answers, and culminates in the ascertainment that such-and-such answers are exact', pp. 85ff. He cites Lonergan's discussion (*Insight*, pp. 277-78) of these two types of knowing in support. But he fails to consider that the distinct 'elementary knowing' that Lonergan describes he also attributes only to non-human animals (to kittens, in his example). In humans the two types of knowing are linked together, for the human 'at once is an animal, intelligent, and reasonable' (p. 278). Lonergan seems here to be making a heuristic distinction between 'types of knowing', while insisting that the two are not truly distinguishable in the human cognitional activity that results in knowledge.

53.   Meyer, *Reality and Illusion*, p. 1.

54.   Meyer, *Reality and Illusion*, p. 5.

55.   Lonergan mentions a per se infallibility (i.e., infallibility 'as a rule' rather than absolutely) that Aristotle and Aquinas noted in the operations of sense and intelligence. See *Insight*, pp. 431-32. But Lonergan does not make an easy association of this infallibility with his level of 'experience'.

56.   Meyer, *Reality and Illusion*, p. 24.

57.   This in fact seems to be the case also in Meyer's presentation of CR in 'The Challenges of Text and Reader', pp. 5-7. Contrast this with Lonergan's description of experience in *Insight*: '[Experience's] defining characteristic is the fact that it is presupposed and complemented by the level of intelligence, that it supplies, as it were, the raw materials on which intelligence operates, that, in a word, it is empirical, given indeed but merely given, open to understanding and formulation but *by itself not understood and ineffable*', *Insight*, p. 298 (emphasis added).

58.   Meyer, *Reality and Illusion*, p. 64; *Critical Realism*, p. 198.

with other versions of CR, but distorts some of Lonergan's basic concerns. In New Testament studies, Meyer's tendencies toward this duality may have set CR on the road to ambiguity, to be furthered by Wright.[59]

59. Another point may help to clarify Lonergan's cognitional theory as an alternative to various critical realisms. We can see other CR's as making realism 'critical' by suggesting that, while knowledge is of real, mind-independent objects, this knowledge is not direct, but mediated. The way this mediation is conceived by these CR's amounts to a form of indirect realism: real objects are known mediately, by the intervention of mediators, which themselves are known immediately. (As we have seen, this is most pronounced in CR_1, which approaches the issue in the standard categories of theories of perception; but CR_2, though concerned not specifically with theories of perception but with the nature of scientific knowledge, also offers something like an indirect realism when it suggests that the objects of scientific knowledge are not known directly but through the mediation of models and the metaphorical talk to which the models give rise.) For the various CR's, one could say that knowledge is indirect or mediated, and the mediators are themselves understood as *objects* of some type. Now Lonergan shares with this perspective the notion that knowledge is mediated, but for Lonergan, the mediator is not in any wise an object, but is rather an *activity*, the activity of the cognitional operations of experience, understanding and judgement. For Lonergan, real objects are not immediately known, but neither is there a mediator or tertium quid with which the knower has some immediate epistemic contact, because the mediator is not an *object* to be known, but an *activity* by means of which the real object is apprehended. Seeing the real object as mediated by an activity and not another, intervening object avoids the difficulties of representationalism to which indirect realism is susceptible, particularly the charge of scepticism and the tendency toward phenomenalism. It answers the concern for how one could be truly 'realist', how one could know that one's knowledge is of a real object, if one's immediate contact is only with a mediator. In Lonergan's theory, knowledge is of the real because the only *object* to be known is the real object, and not a mediatorial object. A form of CR that is strikingly similar to this notion of a mediating activity, and in fact antedates Lonergan's cognitional theory (and possibly even CR_1; see Hicks, *Critical Realism*, p. v), is that of British philosopher G. Dawes Hicks. Hicks's CR is concerned to present all knowledge as essentially an act of judgement, and denies that knowledge comes by means of a mediating object, phenomenon or mental construct. Hicks describes the activity of 'discrimination' that takes place upon the data of sense, an activity that in the mature mind is informed by one's past discriminatory experiences. There is a strong similarity here to Lonergan's notion of insight, which is completed in judgement. See G. Dawes Hicks, 'From Idealism to Realism', *Contemporary British Philosophy: Personal Statements*, 2nd series (ed. J.H. Muirhead; New York: Macmillan, 1925); and *Critical Realism: Studies in the Philosophy of Mind and Nature* (London: Macmillan, 1938).

BIBLIOGRAPHY

Allison, Dale, *Jesus of Nazareth: Millenarian Prophet* (Minneapolis: Fortress Press, 1998).
—'The Secularizing of the Historical Jesus', *Perspectives in Religious Studies* 27 (2000), pp. 135-51.
Appleby, Joyce, Lynn Hunt and Margaret Jacob, *Telling the Truth About History* (New York: W.W. Norton, 1994).
Archer, Margaret, *et al.* (eds.), *Critical Realism: Essential Readings* (New York: Routledge, 1998).
Arnal, William E., and Michel Desjardins (eds.), *Whose Historical Jesus?* (Studies in Christianity and Judaism, 7; Waterloo, ON: Wilfrid Laurier University Press, 1997).
Ayer, A.J., *Language, Truth and Logic* (London: Victor Gollancz, 2nd edn, 1946).
Banks, R.J., 'Setting "The Quest for the Historical Jesus" in a Broader Framework', in R.T. France and David Wenham (eds.), *Studies of History and Tradition in the Four Gospels* (Gospel Perspectives, 2; Sheffield: JSOT Press, 1981).
Barbour, Ian, *Myths, Models and Paradigms: A Comparative Study in Science and Religion* (New York: Harper & Row, 1974).
Barbour, R.S., *Traditio-Historical Criticism of the Gospels* (Studies in Creative Criticism, 4; London: SPCK, 1972).
Barzun, Jacques, *From Dawn to Decadence: Five Hundred Years of Western Cultural Life* (New York: Harper Collins, 2000).
Batdorf, Irvin, 'Interpreting Jesus Since Bultmann: Selected Paradigms and Their Hermeneutical Matrix', in Kent H. Richards (ed.), *Society of Biblical Literature 1984 Seminar Papers* (Chico, CA: Scholars Press, 1984), pp. 187-215.
Beards, Andrew, *Objectivity and Historical Understanding* (Aldershot, England: Avebury, 1997).
Beck, Lewis W., 'Critical Realism', in Ted Honderich (ed.), *The Oxford Companion to Philosophy* (New York: Oxford University Press, 1995), p. 171.
Bhaskar, Roy, *Dialectic: The Pulse of Freedom* (New York: Verso, 1993).
—*The Possibility of Naturalism: A Philosophical Critique of the Contemporary Human Sciences* (Atlantic Highlands, NJ: Humanities Press, 1979).
—*A Realist Theory of Science* (New York: Verso, 2nd edn, 1997).
—*Scientific Realism and Human Emancipation* (New York: Verso, 1986).
Bloch, Marc, *The Historian's Craft* (trans. Peter Putnam; New York: Alfred A. Knopf, 1953).
Borg, Marcus, *Jesus in Contemporary Scholarship* (Valley Forge, PA: Trinity Press International, 1994).
—'What Did Jesus Really Say?', *Bible Review* 5 (1989), pp. 18-25.
Borg, Marcus, and N.T. Wright. *The Meaning of Jesus: Two Visions* (San Francisco: HarperSanFrancisco, 1999).
Boring, Eugene, 'The Historical-Critical Method's "Criteria of Authenticity": The Beatitudes in Q and Thomas as a Test Case', *Semeia* 44 (1988), pp. 9-44.

Boyd, Gregory A., *Cynic Sage or Son of God? Recovering the Real Jesus in an Age of Revisionist Replies* (Wheaton, IL: Victor Books, 1995).

Brown, Colin, 'Historical Jesus, Quest of', in Joel Green, Scott McKnight and I. Howard Marshall (eds.), *Dictionary of Jesus and the Gospels* (Downers Grove, IL: InterVarsity Press, 1992), pp. 326-41.

—*Jesus in European Protestant Thought: 1778–1860* (Grand Rapids: Baker Book House, 1985).

—*Miracles and the Critical Mind* (Grand Rapids: Eerdmans, 1984).

Brown, Frank Burch, and Elizabeth Struthers Malbon, 'Parabling as a *Via Negativa*: A Critical Review of the Work of John Dominic Crossan', *Journal of Religion* 64 (1984), pp. 533-39.

Bultmann, Rudolf, *History of the Synoptic Tradition* (trans. John Marsh; Oxford: Basil Blackwell, rev. edn, 1963).

—*Jesus and the Word* (trans. Louise Pettibone Smith and Erminie Huntress Lantero; New York: Charles Scribner's Sons, 1934).

—*The Presence of Eternity: History and Eschatology* (The Gifford Lectures 1955; New York: Harper & Brothers, 1957).

Burke, Peter (ed.), *New Perspectives on Historical Writing* (Cambridge: Polity Press, 1991).

Cadbury, Henry J., *The Peril of Modernizing Jesus* (New York: Macmillan, 1937).

Calvert, D.G.A., 'An Examination of the Criteria for Distinguishing the Authentic Words of Jesus', *New Testament Studies* 18 (1971–72), pp. 209-219.

Carlson, Jeffrey, and Robert A. Ludwig, *Jesus and Faith: A Conversation on the Work of John Dominic Crossan* (Maryknoll, NY: Orbis Books, 1994).

Carr, David, 'Narrative and the Real World: An Argument for Continuity', *History and Theory* 25 (1986), pp. 117-31.

—*Time, Narrative and History* (Bloomington, IN: Indiana University Press, 1986).

Charlesworth, James H., 'Intertextuality: Isaiah 40.3 and the Serek he-Yahad', in Craig A. Evans and Shemaryahu Talmon (eds.), *The Quest for Context and Meaning: Studies in Biblical Intertextuality in Honor of James A. Sanders* (Leiden: E.J. Brill, 1997), pp. 197-224.

—Charlesworth, James H. (ed.), *Jesus' Jewishness: Exploring the Place of Jesus in Early Judaism* (Shared Ground among Jews and Christians: A Series of Explorations, Vol. 2.; New York: Crossroad, 1996).

—*Jesus within Judaism: New Light from Exciting Archeological Discoveries* (New York: Doubleday, 1988).

Charlesworth, James H., and Walter P. Weaver (eds.), *Images of Jesus Today* (Faith and Scholarship Colloquies, 3; Valley Forge, PA: Trinity Press International, 1994).

Childs, Hal, *The Myth of the Historical Jesus and the Evolution of Consciousness* (SBLDS, 179; Atlanta: Society of Biblical Literature, 2000).

Chilton, Bruce, 'Assessing Progress in the Third Quest', in Bruce Chilton and Craig Evans (eds.), *Authenticating the Words of Jesus* (New Testament Tools and Studies, 28.1; Leiden: E.J. Brill, 1999), pp. 15-25.

Chilton, Bruce, and Craig A. Evans (eds.), *Authenticating the Activities of Jesus* (New Testament Tools and Studies, 28/2; Leiden: E.J. Brill, 1999).

—*Authenticating the Words of Jesus* (New Testament Tools and Studies, 28.1; Leiden: E.J. Brill, 1999).

—*Studying the Historical Jesus: Evaluations of the State of Current Research* (Leiden: E.J. Brill, 1994).

—*Jesus in Context: Temple, Purity and Restoration* (New York: Brill, 1997).

Collier, Andrew, 'Critical Realism', in Edward Craig (ed.), *Routledge Encyclopedia of Phi-
    losophy*, 2 (London: Routledge, 1998), pp. 720-22.
—*Critical Realism: An Introduction to Roy Bhaskar's Philosophy* (New York: Verso, 1994).
Collingwood, R.G., *An Autobiography* (New York: Oxford University Press, 1939).
—*The Idea of History* (New York: Oxford University Press, 1946. Reprint, 1956).
Copan, Paul (ed.), *Will the Real Jesus Please Stand Up? A Debate Between William Lane
    Craig and John Dominic Crossan* (Grand Rapids: Baker Book House, 1998).
Crossan, John Dominic, *The Birth of Christianity: Discovering What Happened in the Years
    Immediately after the Execution of Jesus* (San Francisco: HarperSanFrancisco, 1998).
—*Cliffs of Fall: Paradox and Polyvalence in the Parables of Jesus* (New York: Seabury,
    1980).
—*The Cross that Spoke: The Origins of the Passion Narrative* (San Francisco: Harper & Row,
    1988).
—*The Dark Interval: Towards a Theology of Story* (Niles, IL: Argus Communications, 1975).
—'Difference and Divinity', *Semeia* 23 (1982), pp. 29-40.
—'Divine Immediacy and Human Immediacy: Towards a New First Principle in Historical
    Jesus Research', *Semeia* 41 (1988), pp. 121-39.
—*Finding Is the First Act: Trove Folktales and Jesus' Treasure Parable* (Philadelphia: For-
    tress Press, 1979).
—*Four Other Gospels: Shadows on the Contours of the Canon* (Minneapolis: Winston Press,
    1985).
—*A Fragile Craft: The Work of Amos Niven Wilder* (Chico, CA: Scholars Press, 1981).
—*The Gospel of Eternal Life: Reflections on the Theology of St. John* (Milwaukee: Bruce
    Publishing, 1967).
—'The Historical Jesus: An Interview with John Dominic Crossan', *Christian Century* 108
    (December 18-25, 1991), pp. 1200-1204.
—'Historical Jesus as Risen Lord', in *The Jesus Controversy: Perspectives in Conflict* (Har-
    risburg, PA: Trinity Press International, 1999), pp. 1-47.
—*The Historical Jesus: Life of a Mediterranean Jewish Peasant* (San Francisco: Harper-
    SanFrancisco, 1991).
—*In Fragments: The Aphorisms of Jesus* (San Francisco: Harper & Row, 1983).
—*In Parables: the Challenge of the Historical Jesus* (New York: Harper & Row, 1973).
—*Jesus: A Revolutionary Biography* (San Francisco: HarperSanFrancisco, 1994).
—*A Long Way from Tipperary* (San Francisco: HarperSanFrancisco, 2000).
—'Materials and Methods in Historical Jesus Research', *Foundations and Facets Forum* 4.4
    (1988), pp. 3-24.
—*Raid on the Articulate: Comic Eschatology in Jesus and Borges* (New York: Harper &
    Row, 1976).
—'Responses and Reflections', in Jeffrey Carlson and Robert A. Ludwig (eds.), *Jesus and
    Faith: A Conversation on the Work of John Dominic Crossan* (Maryknoll, NY: Orbis
    Books, 1994), pp. 142-64.
—*Sayings Parallels: A Workbook for the Jesus Tradition* (Philadelphia: Fortress Press, 1986).
—'What Victory? What God? A Review Debate with N.T. Wright on *Jesus and the Victory of
    God*', *Scottish Journal of Theology* 50 (1997), pp. 345-58.
—*Who Killed Jesus? Exposing the Roots of Anti-Semitism in the Gospel Story of the Death of
    Jesus* (San Francisco: HarperSanFrancisco, 1995).
Crossan, John Dominic and Jonathan L. Reed, *Excavating Jesus: Beneath the Stones, Behind
    the Texts* (San Francisco: HarperSanFrancisco, 2001).

Crossan, John Dominic, and Richard G. Watts, *Who Is Jesus? Answers to Your Questions about the Historical Jesus* (Louisville, KY: Westminster/John Knox Press, 1999).

Crowe, Frederick E., SJ, *Lonergan* (Collegeville, MN: Liturgical Press, 1992).

Dancy, Jonathan. *An Introduction to Contemporary Epistemology* (Oxford: Basil Blackwell, 1985).

Delany, C.F., 'Critical Realism', in Robert Audi (ed.), *The Cambridge Dictionary of Philosophy* (Cambridge: Cambridge University Press, 1995), pp. 194-95.

den Heyer, C.J., *Jesus Matters: 150 Years of Research* (Valley Forge, PA: Trinity Press International, 1997).

Douglas, Mary, *The Idea of Purity and Danger: An Analysis of Concepts of Pollution and Taboo* (London: Routledge & Kegan Paul, 1966).

Downing, Gerald, 'Towards a Fully Systematic Scepticism: In the Service of Faith', *Theology* 89 (1986), pp. 355-61.

Drake, Durant, 'The Approach to Critical Realism', in *Essays in Critical Realism: A Co-operative Study of the Problem of Knowledge* (London: Macmillan, 1920. Reprint, 1921), pp. 3-32.

Drake, Durant, Arther Lovejoy, *et al.*, *Essays in Critical Realism: A Co-operative Study of the Problem of Knowledge* (London: Macmillan, 1920. Reprint, 1921).

Dray, William, *On History and Philosophers of History* (Leiden: E.J. Brill, 1989).

Dreyfus, Hubert L., 'Holism and hermeneutics', in R. Hollinger (ed.), *Hermeneutics and Praxis* (Notre Dame, IN: University of Notre Dame Press, 1985), pp. 227-47.

Dungan, David Laird, *A History of the Synoptic Problem: The Canon, the Text, the Composition, and the Interpretation of the Gospels* (New York: Doubleday, 1999).

Dunn, J.D.G., 'Can the Third Quest Hope to Succeed?', in Bruce Chilton and Craig Evans (eds.), *Authenticating the Activities of Jesus* (New Testament Tools and Studies, 28.2; Leiden: E.J. Brill, 1999), pp. 31-48.

—'Jesus in Oral Memory: The Initial Stages of the Jesus Tradition', in *Society of Biblical Literature 2000 Seminar Papers*, 39 (Atlanta: Society of Biblical Literature, 2000), pp. 287-326.

—Review of *The Aims of Jesus*, by Ben F. Meyer. *Scottish Journal of Theology* 34 (1981), pp. 474-76.

Evans, Craig A., 'Authenticity Criteria in Life of Jesus Research', *Christian Scholar's Review* 19 (1989), pp. 6-31.

—*Jesus* (Grand Rapids: Baker Book House, 1992).

—*Jesus and His Contemporaries: Comparative Studies* (Arbeiten zur Geshcichte des Antiken Judentums und Des Urchristentums, 25; Leiden: E.J. Brill, 1995).

—'Reconstructing Jesus' Teaching: Prospects and Proposals', in *Jesus in Context: Temple, Purity, and Restoration* (Arbeiten zur Geschichte des Antiken Judentums und des Urchristentums, XXXIX; Leiden: E.J. Brill, 1997), pp. 145-76.

—*Life of Jesus Research: An Annotated Bibliography* (Leiden: E.J. Brill, 1990).

—*Life of Jesus Research: An Annotated Bibliography* (Leiden: E.J. Brill, 1996).

Evans, Craig A., and Shemaryahu Talmon (eds.), *The Quest for Context and Meaning: Studies in Honor of James A. Sanders* (Leiden: E.J. Brill, 1997).

Farmer, William R., 'Reflections upon "The Historical Perimeters for Understanding the Aims of Jesus"', in Bruce Chilton and Craig A. Evans (eds.), *Authenticating the Activities of Jesus* (New Testament Tools and Studies, 28.2; Leiden: E.J. Brill, 1999), pp. 59-81.

Fisher, David H., 'The Pleasures of Allegory', *Anglican Theological Review* 66 (1984), pp. 298-307.

Fowl, Stephen, 'Reconstructing and Deconstructing the Quest of the Historical Jesus', *Scottish Journal of Theology* 42 (1989), pp. 319-33.

—'The Role of Authorial Intention in the Theological Interpretation of Scripture', in Joel B. Green and Max Turner (eds.), *Between Two Horizons: Spanning New Testament Studies and Systematic Theology* (Grand Rapids: Eerdmans, 2000), pp. 71-87.

Fredriksen, Paula, *Jesus of Nazareth: King of the Jews* (New York: Random House, 1999).

Frei, Hans W., *The Eclipse of Biblical Narrative: A Study in Eighteenth and Nineteenth Century Hermeneutics* (New Haven, CN: Yale University Press, 1974).

—*The Identity of Jesus Christ: The Hermeneutical Basis of Dogmatic Theology* (Philadelphia: Fortress Press, 1975).

Freyne, Sean, 'Galilean Questions to Crossan's Mediterrean Jesus', in William E. Arnal and Michel Desjardins (eds.), *Whose Historical Jesus?* (Studies in Christianity and Judaism, 7; Waterloo, ON: Wilfrid Laurier University Press, 1997), pp. 63-91.

—*Galilee, Jesus and the Gospels* (Philadelphia: Fortress Press, 1988).

Fuller, R.H., *A Critical Introduction to the New Testament* (London: Gerald Duckworth, 1966).

Funk, Robert, *Honest to Jesus: Jesus for a New Millennium* (San Francisco: HarperSanFrancisco, 1996).

—*The Poetics of Biblical Narrative* (Sonoma, CA: Polebridge Press, 1988).

Gadamer, Hans-Georg, *Truth and Method* (trans. Joel Weinsheimer and Donald G. Marshall; New York: Continuum, 2nd rev. edn, 1997).

Gerhardsson, Birger, *Memory and Manuscript: Oral Tradition and Written Transmission in Rabbinic Judaism and Early Christianity* (Grand Rapids: Eerdmans, rev. edn, 1998).

Ginzburg, Carlo, *The Cheese and the Worms: The Cosmos of a Sixteenth-Century Miller* (trans. John Tedeschi and Anne C. Tedeschi; Baltimore: The Johns Hopkins University Press, 1980).

—*Clues, Myths and the Historical Method* (trans. John Tedeschi and Anne C. Tedeschi; Baltimore: The Johns Hopkins University Press, 1989).

—'Microhistory: Two or Three Things That I Know about It' (trans. John Tedeschi and Anne C. Tedeschi; *Critical Inquiry* 20 [1993], pp. 10-35).

Gnilka, Joachim, *Jesus of Nazareth* (trans. Siegfried S. Schatzmann; Peabody, MA: Hendrickson, 1997).

Gottschalk, Louis, *Understanding History: A Primer of Historical Method* (New York: Alfred A. Knopf, 1951).

Grayling, A.C., *An Introduction to Philosophical Logic* (Oxford: Basil Blackwell, 3rd edn, 1997).

Gundry, Robert H., 'Reconstructing Jesus', *Christianity Today* (27 April 1998), pp. 76-79.

Hagner, Don, 'An Analysis of Recent "Historical Jesus" Research', in *Religious Diversity in the Greco-Roman World: A Survey of Recent Scholarship* (The Biblical Seminar, 79; Sheffield: Sheffield Academic Press, 2001).

Harvey, A.E., *Jesus and the Constraints of History* (Philadelphia: Westminster Press, 1982).

Harvey, Van A., *The Historian and the Believer: The Morality of Historical Knowledge and Christian Belief* (Urbana and Chicago: University of Illinois Press, 1996).

Hempel, Carl G., 'Explanation in Science and History', in R. Colodny (ed.), *Frontiers of Science and Philosophy* (Pittsburgh: University of Pittsburgh Press, 1962).

—'The Function of General Laws in History', *The Journal of Philosophy* 39 (1942), pp. 35-48.

Hens-Piazza, Gina, *The New Historicism* (Minneapolis: Fortress Press, 2002).

Herzog, William R., III, *Jesus, Justice and the Reign of God: A Ministry of Liberation* (Louisville, KY: Westminster/John Knox Press, 2000).

Hicks, G. Dawes, *Critical Realism: Studies in the Philosophy of Mind and Nature* (London: Macmillan, 1938).

—'From Idealism to Realism', in J.H. Muirhead (ed.), *Contemporary British Philosophy: Personal Statements* (New York: Macmillan, 2nd edn, 1925), pp. 107-28.

Hogan, John P., *Collingwood and Theological Hermeneutics* (College Theology Society Studies in Religion, 3; Lanham, MD: University Press of America, 1988).

Hooker, M.D., 'Christology and Methodology', *New Testament Studies* 17 (1970–71), pp. 480-87.

—'On Using the Wrong Tool', *Theology* 75 (1972), pp. 570-81.

Horsley, R., *Jesus and the Spiral of Violence* (Minneapolis: Fortress Press, 1993).

—*Sociology and the Jesus Movement* (New York: Crossroad, 1989).

Iggers, Georg G., *Historiography in the Twentieth Century: From Scientific Objectivity to the Postmodern Challenge* (Hanover, NH: Wesleyan University Press, 1997).

Jenkins, Keith, *On 'What Is History?' From Carr and Elton to Rorty and White* (New York: Routledge, 1995).

Johnson, Luke Timothy, 'A Historiographical Response to Wright's Jesus', in Carey C. Newman (ed.), *Jesus and the Restoration of Israel: A Critical Assessment of N.T. Wright's* Jesus and the Victory of God (Downers Grove, IL: InterVarsity Press, 1999), pp. 206-24

—*The Real Jesus: The Misguided Quest for the Historical Jesus and the Truth of the Traditional Gospels* (San Francisco: HarperSanFransicso, 1996).

Jonsson, Ulf, *Foundations for Knowing God: Bernard Lonergan's Foundations for Knowledge of God and the Challenge from Antifoundationalism* (European University Studies, Series XXII: Theology. vol. 664. New York: Peter Lang, 1999).

Käsemann, Ernst, *Essays on New Testament Themes* (Studies in Biblical Theology, 41; trans. W.J. Montague; London: SCM Press, 1964).

Keck, Leander, 'The Second Coming of the Liberal Jesus?', *Christian Century* (24 August 1994), pp. 784-87.

—*Who Is Jesus? History in Perfect Tense* (Colombia, SC: University of South Carolina Press, 2001).

Kee, Howard Clark, 'A Century of Quests for a Culturally Compatible Jesus', *Theology Today* 52 (1995), pp. 17-28.

Kelber, Werner, 'Jesus and Tradition: Words in Time, Words in Space', *Semeia* 65 (1994), pp. 139-67.

—*The Oral and Written Gospel: The Hermeneutics of Speaking and Writing in the Synoptic Tradition, Mark, Paul, and Q* (Philadelphia: Fortress Press, 1983).

—'The Quest for the Historical Jesus', in *The Jesus Controversy: Perspectives in Conflict* (Harrisburg, PA: Trinity Press International, 1999), pp. 75-115.

Kuhn, Thomas S., 'Logic of Discovery or Psychology of Research?', in Imre Lakatos and Alan Musgrave (eds.), *Criticism and the Growth of Knowledge* (Cambridge: Cambridge University Press, 1970), pp. 1-23.

—*The Structure of Scientific Revolutions* (Chicago: University of Chicago Press, 2nd edn, 1970).

Kümmel, W.G., 'Jesusforschung seit 1981', *Theologische Rundschau* 53 (1988), pp. 229-49.

Langlois, C.V., and C. Seignobos, *Introduction to the Study of History* (trans. G.G. Berry; New York: Henry Holt and Co., 1898).

Leavy, John P., 'Four Protocols: Derrida, His Deconstruction', *Semeia* 23 (1982), pp. 43-57.
Levi, Giovanni, *Inheriting Power: The Story of an Exorcist* (trans. Lydia G. Cochrane; Chicago: University of Chicago Press, 1988).
—'On Microhistory', in Peter Burke (ed.), *New Perspectives on Historical Writing* (Cambridge: Polity Press, 1991), pp. 93-113.
Lonergan, Bernard J.F., *Insight: A Study of Human Understanding* (ed. Frederick E. Crowe and Robert M. Doran; Collected Works of Bernard Lonergan, 3; Toronto: University of Toronto Press, 1997).
—*Collection* (ed. Frederick E. Crowe and Robert M. Doran; Collected Works of Bernard Lonergan, 4; Toronto: University of Toronto Press, 2nd edn, 1988).
—*Method in Theology* (London: Darton, Longman and Todd, 1973).
—*Philosophical and Theological Papers, 1958–1964* (ed. Robert C. Croken, Frederick E. Crowe and Robert M. Doran; Toronto: University of Toronto Press, 1996).
—*A Second Collection: Papers of Bernard J.F. Lonergan, S.J.* (ed. William F.J. Ryan and Bernard J. Tyrell; Philadelphia: Westminster Press, 1975. Reprint, Toronto: University of Toronto Press, 1996).
—*A Third Collection: Papers of Bernard J.F. Lonergan, S.J.* (ed. Frederick E. Crowe; New York: Paulist Press, 1985).
Louth, Andrew, *Discerning the Mystery: An Essay on the Nature of Theology*. (Oxford: Clarendon Press, 1983).
Malina, Bruce, and Richard L. Rohrbaugh, *Social-Science Commentary on the Synoptic Gospels* (Minneapolis: Fortress Press, 1992).
Marsh, Clive. 'Quests of the Historical Jesus in New Historicist Perspective', *Biblical Interpretation* 5 (1997), pp. 403-437.
Marshall, I. Howard, Review of *The Aims of Jesus*, by Ben F. Meyer, *Journal for the Study of the New Testament* 7 (1980), pp. 67-69.
McEvenue, Sean E., and Ben Meyer, (eds.), *Lonergan's Hermeneutics: Its Development and Application* (Washington: Catholic University of America Press, 1990).
McGrath, Alister, *The Foundations of Dialogue in Science and Religion* (Malden, MA: Blackwell, 1998).
—'Reality, Symbol and History', in Carey C. Newman (ed.), *Jesus and the Restoration of Israel: A Critical Assessment of N.T. Wright's* Jesus and the Victory of God (Downers Grove, IL: InterVarsity Press, 1999).
Mealand, David L., 'The Dissimilarity Test', *Scottish Journal of Theology* 31 (1978), pp. 41-50.
Meier, John P., *A Marginal Jew: Rethinking the Historical Jesus*. I. *The Roots of the Problem and the Person* (New York: Doubleday, 1991).
Merkley, Paul, 'New Quests for Old: One Historian's Observations on a Bad Bargain', *Canadian Journal of Theology* 16 (1970), pp. 203-218.
Meyer, Ben F., *The Aims of Jesus* (London: SCM Press, 1979).
—'The Challenges of Text and Reader to the Historical-Critical Method', in Wim Beuslen, Sean Freyne and Anton Weiler (eds.), *The Bible and Its Readers* (Concilium; London: SCM Press, 1991), pp. 3-12.
—*Christus Faber: The Master-Builder and the House of God* (Princeton Theological Monograph Series, 29; Allison Park, PA: Pickwick, 1992).
—*The Church in Three Tenses* (Garden City, NY: Doubleday, 1971).
—*Critical Realism and the New Testament* (Princeton Theological Monograph Series, 17; Allison Park, PA: Pickwick Publications, 1989).

—*The Early Christians: Their World Mission and Self-Discovery* (Wilmington, DE: Michael Glazier, 1986).

—'Historical Understanding and *Jesus and the Gospel*: A Review Article', *The Second Century* 5 (1986), pp. 165-71.

—'In Tune with a World that Is Good: Variations on the Theme of Authenticity', *Toronto Journal of Theology* 6 (1990), pp. 3-14.

—'Jesus and the Remnant of Israel', *Journal of Biblical Literature* 84 (1965), pp. 123-30.

—*The Man for Others* (Faith and Life. New York: Bruce Publishing Co., 1970).

—*Reality and Illusion in New Testament Scholarship: A Primer in Critical Realist Hermeneutics* (Collegeville, MN: Michael Glazier, 1994).

—'The Relevance of "Horizon" ', *The Downside Review* 112.1 (1994).

—'Review of *The Five Gospels*', *Interpretation* 48 (1994), pp. 405-407.

Meyer, Ben, David J. Hawkin and Tom Robinson (eds.), *Self-Definition and Self-Discovery in Early Christianity: A Study in Changing Horizons* (Studies in the Bible and Early Christianity, 26; Lewiston, NY: The Edwin Mellen Press, 1990).

Meyer, Ben F., and E.P. Sanders, *Self-Definition in the Greco-Roman World* (London: SCM Press, 1982).

Meynell, Hugo, *An Introduction to the Philosophy of Bernard Lonergan* (New York: Barnes and Noble, 1976).

Mitton, C.L., Review of *The Aims of Jesus*, by Ben F. Meyer, *The Expository Times* 90 (1979), pp. 346-47.

Moore, Stephen D. *Literary Criticism and the Gospels: The Theoretical Challenge* (New Haven: Yale University Press, 1989).

—*Poststructuralism and the New Testament: Derrida and Foucault at the Foot of the Cross* (Minneapolis: Fortress Press, 1994).

Moore, Stephen, and Susan Lochrie Graham, 'The Quest of the New Historicist Jesus', *Biblical Interpretation* 5 (1997), pp. 438-64.

Munslow, Alun, *Deconstructing History* (New York: Routledge, 1997).

Nash, Ronald H., *Christian Faith and Historical Understanding* (Grand Rapids: Zondervan, 1984).

Newman, Carey C. (ed.), *Jesus and the Restoration of Israel: A Critical Assessment of N.T. Wright's* Jesus and the Victory of God (Downers Grove, IL: InterVarsity Press, 1999).

Neill, Stephen, and Tom Wright, *The Interpretation of the New Testament* (New York: Oxford University Press, 1988).

Novick, Peter, *That Noble Dream: The 'Objectivity Question' and the American Historical Profession* (Cambridge: Cambridge University Press, 1988).

Peacocke, Arthur, *Intimations of Reality: Critical Realism in Science and Religion* (The Mendenhall Lectures 1983; Notre Dame, IN: University of Notre Dame Press, 1984).

—*Theology for a Scientific Age* (Theology and the Sciences; Minneapolis: Fortress Press, enlarged edn, 1993).

Peirce, C.S., 'Abduction and Induction', in J. Buchler (ed.), *Philosophical Writings of Peirce* (New York: Dover, 1955), pp. 150-56.

Perrin, Norman, *Rediscovering the Teaching of Jesus* (New York: Harper & Row, 1967).

Polkow, Dennis, 'Method and Criteria for Historical Jesus Research', *Society of Biblical Literature 1987 Seminar Papers* (ed. K.H. Richards; Atlanta: Scholars Press, 1987).

Porter, Stanley E., *The Criteria of Authenticity in Historical-Jesus Research: Previous Discussions and New Proposals* (JSNT Supplement Series, 191; Sheffield: Sheffield Academic Press, 2000).

Powell, Mark Allan, *Jesus as a Figure in History: How Modern Historians View the Man from Galilee* (Louisville, KY: Westminster/John Knox Press, 1998).

Reumann, John, Review of *The Aims of Jesus*, by Ben F. Meyer, *Journal of Biblical Literature* 100 (1981), pp. 296-300.

Richardson, Alan, *History Sacred and Profane* (London: SCM Press, 1964).

Ricoeur, Paul, 'The Narrative Function', in *Hermeneutics and the Human Sciences: Essays on Language, Action and Interpretation* (ed and trans. John B. Thompson; Cambridge: Cambridge University Press, 1981).

—*Time and Narrative* (3 vols.; trans. Kathleen Blamey and David Pellauer; Chicago: University of Chigago Press, 1984–88).

Roberts, Geoffrey (ed.), *The History and Narrative Reader* (New York: Routledge, 2001).

Robinson, J.M., *A New Quest of the Historical Jesus* (Studies in Biblical Theology, 25; London: SCM Press, 1959).

Sanders, E.P., *Jesus and Judaism* (Philadelphia: Fortress Press, 1985).

—*The Historical Figure of Jesus* (New York: Penguin Press, 1993).

—*Paul and Palestinian Judaism: A Comparison of Pattterns of Religion* (Minneapolis: Fortress Press, 1977).

Sanders, E.P., and Margaret Davies. *Studying the Synoptic Gospels* (Philadelphia: Trinity Press International, 1989).

Saussure, Ferdinand de, *Course in General Linguistics* (ed. Charles Bally and Albert Sechehaye; trans. Wade Baskin; New York: Philosophical Library, 1959).

Schröter, Jens, 'The Historical Jesus and the Sayings Tradition: Comments on Current Research', *Neotestamentica* 30 (1996), pp. 151-68.

Schweitzer, Albert, *The Psychiatric Study of Jesus* (trans. Charles Rhind Joy; Boston: Beacon Press, 1948).

—*The Quest of the Historical Jesus: A Critical Study of Its Progress from Reimarus to Wrede* (Baltimore: The Johns Hopkins University Press, 1998).

Scott, Bernard Brandon, 'to impose is not / To Discover: Methodology in John Dominic Crossan's *The Historical Jesus*', in Jeffrey Carlson and Robert A. Ludwig (eds.), *Jesus and Faith: A Conversation on the Work of John Dominic Crossan* (Maryknoll, NY: Orbis Books, 1994), pp. 22-30

Sellars, R.W., 'Knowledge and Its Categories', in *Essays in Critical Realism: A Co-operative Study of the Problem of Knowledge* (London: MacMillan and Co., 1920. Reprint, 1921).

Stanford, Michael, *A Companion to the Study of History* (Oxford: Basil Blackwell, 1994).

Stegemann, Wolfgang, Bruce J. Malina and Gerd Theissen (eds.), *The Social Setting of Jesus and the Gospels* (Minneapolis: Fortress Press, 2001).

Stone, Lawrence, 'The Revival of Narrative: Reflections on a New Old History', *Past and Present* 85 (1979), pp. 3-24.

Stuhlmacher, Peter, *Historical Criticism and Theological Interpretation of Scripture: Toward a Hermeneutics of Consent* (trans. Roy Harrisville; Philadelphia: Fortress Press, 1977).

Tatum, W. Barnes, *In Quest of Jesus: A Guidebook* (Atlanta: John Knox Press, 1982).

Telford, William, 'Major Trends and Interpretive Issues in the Study of Jesus', in Bruce Chilton and Craig Evans (eds.), *Studying the Historical Jesus: Evaluations of the State of Current Research* (Leiden: E.J. Brill, 1994), pp. 33-74.

Theissen, Gerd, 'Historical Scepticism and the Criteria of Jesus Research', *Scottish Journal of Theology* 49 (1996), pp. 147-76.

—*Sociology of Early Palestinian Christianity* (trans. John Bowden; Philadelphia: Fortress Press, 1978).

Theissen, Gerd, and Annette Merz, *The Historical Jesus: A Comprehensive Guide* (trans. John Bowden; Minneapolis: Fortress Press, 1998).

Theissen, Gerd and Dagmar Winter, *Die Kriterienfrage in der Jesusforschung: Vom Differenzkriterium zum Plausibilitätskriterium* (Göttingen: Vandenhoeck & Ruprecht, 1997).

Tolbert, Mary Ann, 'Polyvalence and the Parables: A Consideration of J.D. Crossan's *Cliffs of Fall*', *SBL 1980 Seminar Papers* (ed. Paul J. Achtemeier; Chico, CA: Scholars Press, 1980).

Torrance, T.F., *Time, Space and Resurrection* (Grand Rapids: Eerdmans, 1976).

Tracy, David, *The Achievement of Bernard Lonergan* (New York: Herder & Herder, 1970).

Troeltsch, Ernst, 'Über historische und dogmatische Methode in der Theologie', in *Gesammelte Schriften II: Zur religiösen Lage, Religionsphilosophie und Ethik* (Tübingen: J.C.B. Mohr [Paul Siebeck], 1922).

Tuckett, Christopher M., 'The Historical Jesus, Crossan and Methodology', in *Text und Geschichte: Facetten theologischen Arbeitens aus dem Freundes- und Schülerkreis*, ed. Stefan Maser and Egbert Schlarb, 257-79; Marburger Theologische Studien 50, ed. Hans Grass and Werner Georg Kümmel; Marburg: N.G. Elwert , 1999).

van Beeck, Franz Josef, SJ, 'The Quest of the Historical Jesus: Origins, Achievement, and the Specter of Diminishing Returns', in Jeffrey Carlson and Robert A. Ludwig (eds.), *Jesus and Faith: A Conversation on the Work of John Dominic Crossan* (Maryknoll, NY: Orbis Books, 1994), pp. 83-99

Vanhoozer, Kevin, *Is There a Meaning in This Text? The Bible, the Reader, and the Morality of Literary Knowledge* (Grand Rapids: Zondervan, 1998).

van Huyssteen, Wentzel, *Essays in Postfoundationalist Theology* (Grand Rapids: Eerdmans, 1997).

—*The Realism of the Text: A Perspective on Biblical Authority* (Pretoria, South Africa: University of Pretoria, 1987).

—*The Shaping of Rationality* (Grand Rapids: Eerdmans, 1999).

—*Theology and the Justification of Faith* (trans. H.F. Snijders; Grand Rapids: Eerdmans, 1989).

Vermes, Geza, *The Religion of Jesus the Jew* (Minneapolis: Fortress Press, 1993).

Vertin, Joseph M, *Critical Realism: Cognitional Approach and Ontological Achievement According to Bernard Lonergan* (Washington, DC: Theological Publications, 1970).

Wachterhauser, Brice R. (ed.), *Hermeneutics and Modern Philosophy* (New York: State University of New York Press, 1986).

Walsh, W.H., *An Introduction to Philosophy of History* (London: Hutchinson & Co., rev. edn, 1958).

Wansbrough, Henry (ed.), *Jesus and the Oral Gospel Tradition* (JSNTSup, 64; Sheffield: Sheffield Academic Press, 1991).

Weaver, Walter P., *The Historical Jesus in the Twentieth Century, 1900–1950* (Harrisburg, PA: Trinity Press International, 1999).

Webb, Eugene, *Philosophers of Consciousness: Polanyi, Lonergan, Voegelin, Ricoeur, Girard, Kierkegaard* (Seattle: University of Washington Press, 1988).

White, Hayden, *The Content of the Form: Narrative Discourse and Historical Representation* (Baltimore: The Johns Hopkins University Press, 1987).

—*Metahistory: The Historical Imagination in Nineteenth-Century Europe* (Baltimore: The Johns Hopkins University Press, 1973).

—*Tropics of Discourse: Essays in Cultural Criticism* (Cambridge: Cambridge University Press, 1991).

Wimsatt, William K., Jr, and Monroe Beardsley, 'The Intentional Fallacy', in *The Verbal Icon: Studies in the Meaning of Poetry* (Lexington, KY: University of Kentucky Press, 1954), pp. 3-18.

Winton, A.P., *The Proverbs of Jesus: Issues of History and Rhetoric* (JSNTSup, 35; Sheffield: Sheffield Academic Press, 1990).

Wilson, Norman J. *History in Crisis? Recent Directions in Historiography* (Upper Saddle River, NJ: Prentice Hall, 1999).

Wink, Walter, 'Neither Passivity Nor Violence: Jesus' Third Way', in *Society of Biblical Literature 1988 Seminar Papers*, 27 (Atlanta: Scholars Press, 1988), pp. 210-24.

Witherington, III, Ben, *The Jesus Quest: The Third Search for the Jew of Nazareth* (Downers Grove, IL: InterVarsity Press, 1995).

Wittgenstein, Ludwig, *Philosophical Investigations*. (trans. G.E.M. Anscombe; Englewood Cliffs, NJ: Prentice Hall, 3rd edn, 1958).

Wright, N.T., 'Doing Justice to Jesus: A Response to J.D. Crossan: "What Victory? What God?"', *Scottish Journal of Theology* 50 (1997), pp. 359-79.

—'In Grateful Dialogue: A Response', in Carey C. Newman (ed.), *Jesus and the Restoration of Israel: A Critical Assessment of N.T. Wright's* Jesus and the Victory of God (Downers Grove, IL: InterVarsity, 1999).

—*Jesus and the Victory of God* (Christian Origins and the Question of God, 2; Minneapolis: Fortress Press, 1996).

—'Jesus: Quest for the Historical', in David Noel Freedman (ed.), *Anchor Bible Dictionary* (New York: Doubleday, 1992), pp. 796-802.

—*The New Testament and the People of God* (Christian Origins and the Question of God, 1; Minneapolis: Fortress Press, 1992).

Zammito, John, 'Are We Being Theoretical Yet? The New Historicism, the New Philosophy of History, and "Practicing Historians"', *Journal of Modern History* 65 (1993), pp. 783-814.

UNPUBLISHED SOURCES

Brant, Jo-Ann, Goshen, IN, to the author, Glendale, CA, 22 August 2001.

Martens, John, St Paul, MN, to the author, Glendale, CA, 22 August 2001.

Martin, Brice, Arthur, ON, to the author, Glendale, CA, 21 August 2001.

Meyer, B.F., Curriculum Vitae, 1975, obtained from the Lonergan Research Institute, Regis College, Toronto, ON.

Robertson, John, Hamilton, ON, to the author, Glendale, CA, 30 August 2001.

Robertson, John, Hamilton, ON, to the author, Glendale, CA, 5 September 2001.

Rollmann, Hans, St John's, Newfoundland, to the author, Glendale, CA, 22 August 2001.

Stevens, Galdstone Hudson, III, 'Towards a Theological Assessment of the Third Quest of the Historical Jesus' (PhD dissertation, Marquette University, 1997).

Stewart, Robert Byron, 'The Impact of Contemporary Hermeneutics on Historical Jesus Research: An Analysis of John Dominic Crossan and Nicholas Thomas Wright' (PhD. dissertation, Southwestern Baptist Theological Seminary, 2000).

Welch, Margaret M., 'A Critical Realist Assessment of the Moral Realism Debate: Objectivity as Authentic Subjectivity and the Epistemology of Bernard Lonergan' (PhD dissertation, Loyola University of Chicago, 1998).

INDEX

INDEX OF REFERENCES

BIBLE

Old Testament

Exodus
20.22–23.33   32

Deuteronomy
21.18-21   140-41

Ruth
32

2 Samuel
7.12-14   134 n.20

Ecclesiastes
32

Isaiah
43.3f.   134
52.13–53.12   134

New Testament
Matthew
5.3ff.   133
5.39-41   32
5.39-42   197
10.29   132
11.16-19   139
13.44   34
13.45-46   23

15.24   140
16.16   134
19.10   140
22.1-14   26
23.26-27   141

Mark
2.16   140
6.7-13   53
7.19   141
8.27-30   134
8.29   134
8.31-33   134
9.40   45
10.10   140
10.38   134
10.45   134
11.15-18   73

Luke
32
197
7.27   140
9.20   134
12.50   134

John
73

Acts
11.19   140
13.1-3   140

1 Corinthians
7.10ff.   140

Galatians
3.28   56

Other Ancient Sources
Gospel of Peter
44

Gospel of Thomas
26, 44,
48, 50, 73
8   23
14.2   53
22.1-2   51
64   53
95   197

Secret Mark
44

INDEX OF AUTHORS

Allison, D. 3-5, 58, 157-58, 159, 160, 161-62, 163, 164, 165

Barbour, I. 211, 212, 215
Barbour, R.S. 203-206
Barthes, R. 29
Batdorf, I. 179 n. 41
Baur, F.C. 102
Beardslee, W.A. 35
Beardsley, M. 95
Bhaskar, R. 214-17
Bloch, M. 61-62
Borg, M. 69, 70
Brown, F. 27, 41
Bultmann, R. 3, 4, 6, 44, 98, 103, 125-26, 144, 194, 201

Cadbury, H. 108
Calvert, D.G.A. 196, 197
Carr, D. 171-75, 180, 189, 190-91
Charlesworth, J.H. 109, 110 n. 33
Childs, H. 2, 170 n. 9
Chilton, B. 13, 165-67, 177, 183
Collingwood, R.G. 12, 13, 65, 71, 110-12, 114-15, 116-17, 118, 122-24, 149, 160, 162

Dalman, G. 116
Derrida, J. 32-33, 35, 37
Dodd, C.H. 22, 135
Dray, W. 174 n. 28
Dreyfus, H. 157 n. 14, 190 n. 64
Dunn, J.D.G. 63-64, 159-60, 161, 164

Evans, C. 199-200

Farmer, W. 13, 109
Fowl, S. 109

Fredriksen, P. 70, 163
Frei, H. 170 n. 11
Freyne, S. 109, 146, 178, 182, 208-209
Fuller, R.H. 201, 204
Funk, R. 10, 156, 170 n. 11

Gadamer, H-G. 12, 88 n. 33, 99-101, 126-27
Ginzburg, C. 174
Gödel, K. 38
Gottschalk, L. 69

Harnack, A. von 11
Harvey, A. 207
Harvey, V.A. 163 n. 37
Heidegger, M. 22, 24, 35, 36, 87, 98
Heisenberg, W. 19
Herzog, W. 158-59
Hicks, G.D. 225 n. 59
Holtzmann, H.J. 102
Hooker, M. 201-203, 204, 205
Horsley, R. 58, 112
Husserl, E. 171

Jaspers, K. 87
Jeremias, J. 22, 116, 135, 140, 198
Johnson, L.T. 180, 181-82

Käsemann, E. 24, 194, 201, 204
Kelber, W. 63, 64
Kierkegaard, S. 87
Kuhn, T. 157, 212, 213, 214

Langlois, C.V. 69
Lévi-Strauss, C. 23, 25
Lightfoot, R.H. 203
Lonergan, B. 11, 12, 14, 80-93, 99-100, 104-106, 113-14, 115, 117, 121,

124, 125, 128-29, 137-38, 143, 150,
160, 164-65, 191, 208, 220-25
Lovejoy, A.O. 210, 212

Malbon, E.S. 27, 41
Malina, B. 58
Merleau-Ponty, M. 171

Newman, J.H. 87, 100
Nietzsche, F. 35, 87

Peacocke, A. 211, 213
Peirce, C.S. 166 n. 44, 189 n. 63
Perrin, N. 5, 35, 47, 69, 70, 195, 201
Polkow, D. 193-95, 196, 197, 198

Rad, G. von 22
Ranke, L. von 19, 168
Reimarus, S. 3, 102
Ricoeur, P. 35, 37, 178
Robinson, J.M. 5, 25 n. 23, 108

Sanders, E.P. 13, 70, 109, 163, 206-207
Santayana, G. 210
de Saussure, F. 25-26
Schopenhauer, A. 87
Schweitzer, A. 3, 6, 22
Scott, B.B. 18
Seignobos, C. 69

Sellars, R.W. 210, 212, 214
Stone, L. 169
Strauss, D.F. 102-103
Stuhlmacher, P. 101

Theissen, G. 58, 109, 198-99
Troeltsch, E. 103
Tuckett, C. 59, 73
Tyrell, G. 11

van Huyssteen, W. 212
Via, D. 35

Wachterhauser. B.R. 155
Walsh, W.H. 163 n. 36
Weaver, W. 4
Weiss, J. 3
Weiffenbach, W. 135
White, H. 169-70
Whitehead, A.N. 35
Wimsatt, W.K. 95
Winter, D. 109, 198-99
Winton, A. 109, 207
Wittgenstein, L. 147 n. 55
Wrede, W. 3, 6, 103
Wright, N.T. 6-7, 13, 60, 76, 155-56,
158, 160, 162, 164, 175, 179-81,
182, 188, 210, 217, 218-20, 222,
225